DATE DUE

Ill 12 '1896	

Karakoram Highway
the high road to China

a travel survival kit

John King

Karakoram Highway: the high road to China – a travel survival kit

2nd edition

Published by
    Lonely Planet Publications
    Head Office: PO Box 617, Hawthorn, Vic 3122, Australia
    Branches: PO Box 2001A, Berkeley, CA 94702, USA
                12 Barley Mow Passage, Chiswick, London W4 4PH, UK

Printed by
    Colorcraft Ltd, Hong Kong

Photographs by
    John King (JK)
    Richard I' Anson (RI' A)
    Paul Jones (PJ)
    Julia Wilkinson (JW)

    Front cover: Women crossing suspension bridge, Gojal, Northern Areas, Pakistan (JK)
    Back cover: Gilgit River at sunrise (JW)

First Published
    August 1989

This Edition
    May 1993

Although the authors and publisher have tried to make the information as accurate as possible, they accept no responsibility for any loss, injury or inconvenience sustained by any person using this book.

National Library of Australia Cataloguing in Publication Data

King, John (John S.).
    Karakoram Highway: the high road to China.

    2nd ed.
    Includes index.
    ISBN 0 86442 165 6.

    1. Karakoram Range Region – Guidebooks. 2. Karakoram Highway (Pakistan) – Guidebooks.
    I. Title. (Series: Lonely Planet travel survival kit).

915.46

John King

John King grew up in the USA, destined for the academic life (in past incarnations he was a university physics teacher and an environmental consultant), but in a rash moment in 1984 he headed off to China to have a look around. Since then he has eked out a living as a travel writer, encouraged by his wife, Julia, who is also one. Together they split their time at 'home' between south-west England and remoter parts of Hong Kong. John has spent eight months as a traveller in Pakistan and thirteen months as an English teacher and traveller in China. He is also co-author of LP's *USSR* and *Pakistan* and has helped update *West Asia on a shoestring*.

Dedication

In 1989 an ageing Fokker Friendship plane en route from Gilgit to Islamabad disappeared without a trace around Nanga Parbat, and Gilgit lost one of its most extraordinary citizens. This edition of *The Karakoram Highway – a travel survival kit* is dedicated to the memory of Ghulam Mohammad Baig – bookseller and trader, historian and 'cultural consultant', writer and raconteur – whose Mohammad Book Stall was (and still is) a required stop for all serious Northern Areas travellers, trekkers and book-junkies.

Acknowledgements

New in this edition are chapter notes for cyclists; for help with these, grateful thanks to Dieter & Irene Kerschbaumer (Switzerland). For the excellent Geology section (and for suffering my layperson's reinterpretations) I'm indebted to Dr Peter J Treloar of Kingston University, Surrey, and Dr Michael Searle of the University of Leicester (UK). Thanks to Kurt Gruessing (Austria) for Uyghur language help and much else, and to Pakistan veteran Ray Wallace (USA) for tips and trekking information.

Many others helped with this edition with information, advice and hospitality. Certain tourism officials rose above the call of duty; special thanks are due to Mr Ashab Naqvi (Deputy Managing Director, Pakistan Tourism Development Corporation, Islamabad).

Thanks also to Arshad Mahmud (PTDC Naran) and Sadaqat Ali (Tourism Development Corporation of the Punjab, Murree).

For an update on Aga Khan Rural Support Programme work in the Northern Areas I am grateful to Ms Shahida Jaffery, Public Relations Officer, AKRSP, Gilgit. Lok Virsa, the National Institute of Folk & Traditional Heritage, generously allowed me free run of their library in Islamabad.

For limitless patience and the answers to 10,000 questions, my warmest thanks to Raja Latif Anwar and Ali Anwar of Chalt. Thanks to Mohammed Shuaib Khan and Fazl-i-Akbar of Alai for first-class Pathan hospitality. Others along the highway who gave help and advice for this edition are John Hu and Mokimjian (Kashgar), Izatullah Baig (Passu), Abdul Bari, Mohammed Jaffar and Mohammed Rahbar (Gulmit), Iftikhar Hussain (Ganesh) and Ikram Beg (Gilgit).

Nature photographer Daniel Aubort (Switzerland) told me about KKH fauna. Geographer Thomas Hoffman (Germany) offered insights on life in the Astore Valley. Hydrologist Jonathan Rubery (UK) shared Passu hiking tips. Cheers to itinerant cartographer John Callanan (UK) for his elegant regional and town maps.

Other travellers and Lonely Planet correspondents who made valuable contributions to this edition are Edward John Hasbrouck (USA), Gaby & Norbert Holtschmidt (Germany), another John King (UK), Chris Koh (USA), Ron Levy (Australia), Carl Lipo (USA), Mark Madsen (USA), Maurus Masetig (Austria), Gabriel M Rebeiz (USA), Barry Robinson (UK), M D Ross (UK), James Salmon (UK) and John Teitler (USA).

Finally, love and thanks to Julia Wilkinson for putting up with me and frequently making do without me.

From the Publisher

This 2nd edition of *Karakoram Highway: the high road to China – a travel survival kit* was edited by Jeff Williams of LP's Melbourne office. Sue Mitra proofed the final product.

The updated maps were redrawn by Paul Clifton and Peter Flavelle. The cover design, layout and illustrations were completed by Paul. Vicki Beale assisted with the layout.

Thanks also to Eric Kettunen of LP's USA office for timely research help, Dan Levin for prompt computer support, and Sharon Wertheim for her comprehensive index.

A Warning & a Request

Tourism is growing along the KKH. Hotels and restaurants are sprouting in Kashgar, Sust, Hunza and Gilgit; prices are climbing; jeep roads are being pushed into remote valleys. If you find the book isn't quite right any more, don't get mad; instead, write to Lonely Planet and help us make the next edition better.

Your letters will be used to help update future editions and, where possible, important changes will be included as a Stop Press section in reprints.

We greatly appreciate all information that is sent to us by travellers. Back at Lonely Planet we employ a hard-working readers' letters team to sort through the many letters we receive. The best letters will be rewarded with a free copy of the next edition or another Lonely Planet guide that you prefer. We give away lots of books, but, unfortunately, not every letter/postcard receives one.

Contents

Map Legend

BOUNDARIES

—·—·—·—	........International Boundary
—··—··—	................Internal Boundary
++++++++++	....National Park or Reserve
——————	........................The Equator
....	.........................The Tropics

SYMBOLS

◉	NATIONAL	..........................National Capital
●	PROVINCIAL	........Provincial or State Capital
●	Major	...............................Major Town
●	Minor	...............................Minor Town
■		............................Places to Stay
▼		..............................Places to Eat
✉		..................................Post Office
✈		....Airport
i		....................Tourist Information
⊖		............Bus Station or Terminal
66		............Highway Route Number
☪ ✝ ⛪ ✝		...... Mosque, Church, Cathedral
∴		..........................Temple or Ruin
✚		....Hospital
❋		......................................Lookout
⛺		.... Camping Area
⊓		..............................Picnic Area
⌂		............................Hut or Chalet
▲		..........................Mountain or Hill
⊢⊣		..........................Railway Station
═		...............................Road Bridge
++++		..........................Railway Bridge
⇒ ⇐		..............................Road Tunnel
→) (←		..........................Railway Tunnel
⌇⌇		....................Escarpment or Cliff
⌣		....Pass
⌐⌐⌐⌐		.............Ancient or Historic Wall

ROUTES

——————	.......Major Road or Highway
- - - - - - -	.... Unsealed Major Road
————	.... Sealed Road
- - - - - - -	..... Unsealed Road or Track
═══	...........................City Street
++++++++++	.................................Railway
●━━◉━━●	.... Subway
------	.....................Walking Track
- - - - - - -	.... Ferry Route
++++++++++	.... Cable Car or Chair Lift

HYDROGRAPHIC FEATURES

	.....................River or Creek
	..............Intermittent Stream
	........Lake, Intermittent Lake
	...........................Coast Line
	....Spring
	.... Waterfall
	.... Swamp
	.... Salt Lake or Reef
	...................................Glacier

OTHER FEATURES

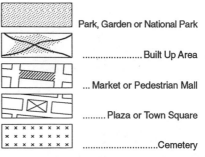

Park, Garden or National Park

.... Built Up Area

... Market or Pedestrian Mall

.... Plaza or Town Square

...........................Cemetery

Note: not all symbols displayed above appear in this book

Introduction

Between the central Asian desert and the plains of Pakistan is a geographical vortex that is rich with history, natural beauty and cultural diversity. In this 'collision zone' of the Indian and Asian continents, the Pamir, Kunlun, Hindu Kush, Karakoram and Great Himalaya ranges are knotted together and China, Tajikistan, Afghanistan, Pakistan and India all come within 250 km of each other.

In the 1960s and 1970s, Pakistan and China jointly cut a road across these mountains, following a branch of the ancient network of trade routes called the Silk Road. In 1986 their mutual border was opened to travellers, completing an Asian 'high road' loop taking in Pakistan, China, Tibet, Nepal and north India.

The Karakoram Highway (KKH) connects the Silk Road oasis of Kashgar with Rawalpindi and Islamabad, Pakistan's capital, via the 4730-metre Khunjerab Pass, the semi-mythical Hunza Valley and the trading post of Gilgit. Despite half a dozen languages, the region crossed by the highway has an identity of its own, defined by religion (almost everyone is Muslim), commerce (from the Silk Road era to present-day Kashgar-Gilgit barter trade), a demanding environment and a sense of alienation from greater China or Pakistan.

Within reach of the KKH is some of the most mind-bending mountain scenery anywhere and, in the Karakoram, the highest concentration of lofty peaks and long

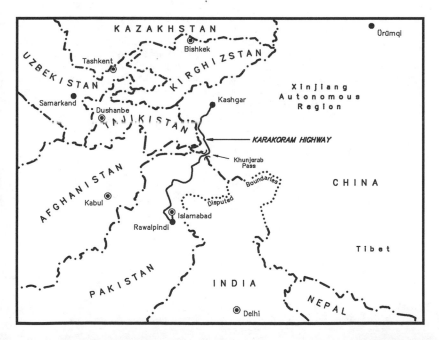

9

glaciers in the world, some virtually at the edge of the road. As the 20th-century scholar-traveller John Staley has written: 'This is terrain in which even birds in flight are seen against a background of mountains.'

The region is also dense with history and artefacts, from the campaigns of Alexander the Great to the 19th-century rivalry between the British and Russian empires. It was through here that Buddhism first reached China and Tibet. In a sense, history is still alive in the camel caravans of Xinjiang and the tribal traditions of Indus Kohistan. Some of that history is disappearing before our eyes, in part because of the KKH itself.

Travel is cheap; going overland from one end to the other can cost as little as US$35. Theoretically you could make the 1300-km trip in 48 hours, but you might go crazy trying to do it in less than two or three weeks. Tourist development is accelerating but still mercifully modest outside Gilgit. And – at least for men and mixed couples – the Islamic tradition of hospitality can make visiting northern Pakistan a pleasure.

One thing KKH travel doesn't have is predictability. You may experience first-hand the fickleness of the Karakoram: steep and loose to begin with, shattered by KKH construction, always trying to bury the road. Rockfalls, floods and mud introduce unplanned delays. This is a frustrating place to be on a fixed schedule.

In Pakistan the highway can sometimes feel like a tunnel of ragged roadside bazaars, slapped together to take advantage of the money coming through, and not at all typical of what may lie half a km away. The best of the KKH is usually off the road.

This book describes what you can find within one or two days' village-hopping from the highway. It goes from north to south because that direction prolongs the good weather in the best travelling season, September-October.

Note to Visitors

Many Westerners have exaggerated fears of Islamic fundamentalism. In fact the Muslim peoples along the KKH are likely to offer you only unfeigned hospitality. What *can* cause ill-will, however, are insults to Islamic sensibilities, in particular about dress. Clothes revealing the shape of the body or significant flesh beyond face, hands and feet, especially on women, are offensive to most Pakistanis. On the KKH, only in Islamabad will you find some acceptance of Western dress or Western attitudes.

The other urge likely to anger Pakistanis is photographing women without permission, even in liberal-minded communities like the Ismailis. The Muslims of Xinjiang are less vocal about these matters.

KIRGHIZSTAN

Kashgar

Karakoram Highway

0   50   100 km

Kongur
7719

Muztagh Ata
7546

TAJIKISTAN

Tashkurghan

CHINA

Xinjiang
Autonomous
Region

AFGHANISTAN

Pirali

Khunjerab Pass

HUNZA   Sust

NAGAR

Baltit

CHITRAL

Rakaposhi
7790

Northern
Areas

Gilgit

BALTISTAN

North-West
Frontier
Province

Skardu

Dasu   Chilas

Nanga Parbat
8126

SWAT

Naran

Besham

Saidu Sharif

Disputed   Boundary

Mansehra

Abbottabad

Leh

Srinagar

Indian-held
Kashmir

Taxila

Islamabad

Rawalpindi

Azad Jammu & Kashmir

INDIA

Punjab

Facts about the Region

THE KARAKORAM HIGHWAY

Following a warming of China-Pakistan relations in the 1960s the two countries embarked on one of the biggest engineering projects since the Pyramids: a two-lane, 1300-km road through some of the highest mountains in the world, from Kashgar in China to Havelian in Pakistan. Much of this Karakoram Highway (KKH) would be in terrain which until then had barely allowed a donkey track. It took 20 years to finish.

The workforce in Pakistan at any one time was about 15,000 Pakistanis and between 9000 and 20,000 Chinese, working separately. Landslides, savage summer and winter conditions and accidents claimed 400 to 500 lives on the Pakistani side of the border, one for every 1½ km of road-way (though some claim the Chinese took away many more dead than they admitted). The highest toll was in Indus Kohistan.

All the 100 or so bridges from the Khunjerab Pass to Thakot were built by the Chinese. The face-saving official assertion that Pakistanis did the rest ignores an almost total Chinese effort in Gojal and the Khunjerab. Some old-timers blame Chinese blasting techniques, even in the Indus Valley, for much of the road's continuing instability.

Few statistics are available about work on the Chinese side. Ghez River canyon road-cuts and bridges were only completed in 1988, and paving in 1989. Crews were a mixture of soldiers, convicts and well-paid volunteers with nothing but picks and shovels, hauling dirt on shoulder-poles, sun-burned and half-crazy.

Maintenance is a huge, endless job. The mountains continually try to reclaim the road, assisted by earthquakes, encroaching glaciers and the Karakoram's typical crumbling slopes, and by the KKH itself: blasting so shattered the mountainsides that they are still settling. Rockfalls, mud and floods are routine, and travel is inherently unpredictable.

Why a Road?

The KKH is a great travel opportunity, but what's it for? At such a cost in lives and displaced production – especially for the Chinese at the height of the Cultural Revolution – it was obviously more than a joust with nature.

KKH Distances

Signs, maps, officials and drivers all tell you different numbers, each with the utmost certainty. The following distances in km are probably accurate to within about 5%.

	Kash	Tash	Khun	Sust	Kari	Gilg	Chil	Besh	Abbt	Rwpi
Kashgar		290	420	505	595	700	835	1040	1190	1300
Tashkurghan	290		130	215	305	410	545	750	900	1010
Khunjerab	420	130		85	175	280	415	620	770	880
Sust	505	215	85		90	195	330	535	685	795
Karimabad	595	305	175	90		105	240	445	595	705
Gilgit	700	410	280	195	105		135	340	490	600
Chilas	835	545	415	330	240	135		205	355	465
Besham	1040	750	620	535	445	340	205		150	260
Abbottabad	1190	900	770	685	595	490	355	150		110
Rawalpindi	1300	1010	880	795	705	600	456	260	110	

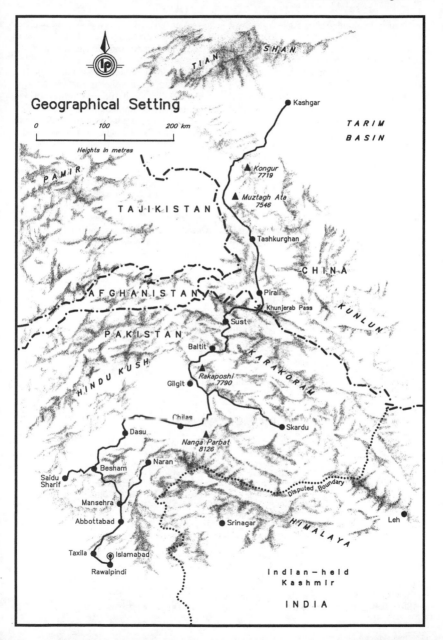

Geographical Setting

The original Indus Valley Road from Swat to Gilgit was the Northern Areas' first-ever all-weather connection to the outside world. The Pakistan government may have hoped development would bind Kohistan and the north closer to the rest of the country.

The Karakoram crossing gives both countries a back door for mutual aid, but the road seems too fragile to be a strategic asset. Cross-border trade is minimal. Mostly, the KKH looks like a symbol, a geopolitical announcement in the face of ties between India and Russia.

Cross-Border Trade

Caravans are once again crossing between Gilgit and Kashgar, but now diesel lorries have replaced yaks and camels. From Pakistan, the government-sponsored Northern Areas Traders Cooperative (NATC) sends up to two or three caravans a year bearing cigarettes, dried fruit, medicinal herbs, razor blades, woollens and bright nylon cloth ('Moonlight', all the rage with Kashgar women). From China, the Kashgar office of the Ministry of Foreign Trade sends farm tools, bicycles, quilts, cotton cloth, crockery, tea, electrical equipment – and silk.

All the government-sponsored business is barter trade. The NATC did about US$4 million worth in 1991. Pakistani freelancers, their rickety trucks loaded two storeys high, accounted for further trade, though they have been hit by high Pakistani import duties and unfavourable exchange rates.

HISTORY

Although it straddles some of the highest mountains in the world, the KKH region is held together by several historical currents.

Historical Summary, KKH Region

2300-1700 BC	Harappa or Indus Valley Civilisation
1500-1000 BC	Aryan invasions; birth of Hinduism
563-483 BC	Life of Buddha
560-330 BC	Persian Achaemenian Dynasty
336-323 BC	Hellenic Empire of Alexander the Great
321-185 BC	Mauryan Empire; patronage of Buddhism under Ashoka
206 BC-220 AD	Chinese Han Dynasty; growth of Silk Road
70 AD-240 AD	Kushan Empire; spread of Buddhism on Silk Road
399-414	Fa-Hsien's journey from China to India
570-632	Life of Mohammed, founder of Islam & Arab Empire
618-907	Chinese Tang Dynasty; Silk Road flourishes
629-633	Hsuan Tsang's journey from China to India
711	Arab naval expedition to the mouth of the Indus
714?	Arab expeditions visit Tarim Basin & Indus Valley
752	Tang Dynasty displaced from Tarim Basin by Turks
870-1001	Hindu Shahi Dynasty; Hindu resurgence in Indus Valley
977-1186	Ghaznavid Dynasty in Afghanistan & north-west India
999-1211	Qarakhan Dynasty, Tarim Basin; appearance of Islam
1206-1227	Campaigns of Genghis Khan; start of Mongol Empire
1369-1405	Campaigns of Timur (Tamerlane)
1526	Babar takes Delhi; founding of Moghul Empire
1600	Charter granted to British East India Company
1755	Tarim Basin falls to Qing (Manchu) Dynasty
1757	Battle of Plassey (Bengal); beginning of Moghul decline
1799	Ranjit Singh founds Sikh Empire from Lahore
1838-1842	First Anglo-Afghan War
1846	First Anglo-Sikh War; creation of Kashmir state
1849	Second Anglo-Sikh War
1857-1858	Great Mutiny (Sepoy Rebellion); British Raj begins

These are the Silk Road and the spread of Buddhism; the arrival of Islam; imperial struggles, particularly the 'Great Game' between Britain and Russia; and of course the highway itself.

On the other hand, the mountains have so hindered communication and movement that local histories are quite distinct. Each chapter, therefore, also has its own historical introduction.

Early History
Over 4000 years ago a rich farming and trading culture flourished in the Indus Valley as far north as Gandhara (the historical name for the Peshawar Valley), but collapsed under an influx of central Asian tribes which historians call Indo-Aryans, starting about 1700 BC. Under the Indo-Aryans and the later Persian Achaemenian Dynasty, Hinduism was born in the south. After defeating the Achaemenians in 330 BC, Alexander of Macedonia (Alexander the Great) crossed the Hindu Kush, resting in the spring of 326 BC at Taxila, capital of Gandhara, just before a mutiny of his troops ended his expansion.

This short visit resonates in the legends of northern Pakistan. Some tribes claim descent from Alexander or his stay-behind generals. Some people of the Northern Areas do have arrestingly Mediterranean features. Anthropologists are doubtful, though the visitors may well have enlivened local gene pools.

Silk Road & the Flowering of Buddhism
Allied with Alexander's successors a local king, Chandragupta, founded India's first empire, the Mauryan Dynasty, which at its peak covered most of the subcontinent. The most famous Mauryan king was

1862-1875	Muslim rebellions in China
1877, 1889	British Agency at Gilgit opened, re-opened
1884	Xinjiang Province created under Qing Dynasty
1878-1880	Second Anglo-Afghan War
1882, 1890	Russia, then Britain, open Kashgar consulates
1897, 1907	Anglo-Russian agreements on Pamir boundaries
10 October 1911	Chinese Revolution; end of Chinese dynasties
7 November 1917	Russian Bolshevik Revolution
1931-1934	Muslim uprisings in Xinjiang
March 1940	Muslim League demands separate Pakistan
14 August 1947	Partition; independence of Pakistan & India
1 November 1947	Gilgit Uprising
1947-1948	India-Pakistan War; UN cease-fire January 1949
1 October 1949	Founding of People's Republic of China
7 October 1958	Martial law in Pakistan under General Ayub Khan
1960	Pakistan starts 'Indus Valley Road', Swat-Gilgit
1964	China and Pakistan talks on 'Friendship Highway'
September 1965	India-Pakistan War
March 1969	Martial law in Pakistan under General Yahya Khan
December 1971	India-Pakistan War; secession of Bangladesh
1974	Bhutto ends autonomy of Northern Areas princely states
5 July 1977	Martial law under General Zia ul-Haq
4 April 1979	Bhutto hanged
December 1979	Karakoram Highway finished
August 1982	Khunjerab Pass opens to official traffic & trade
30 December 1985	Zia lifts martial law
1 May 1986	Khunjerab Pass opens to tourism
17 August 1988	Zia dies in air crash
1 December 1988	Benazir Bhutto becomes prime minister
6 August 1990	Bhutto dismissed
6 November 1990	Nawaz Sharif becomes prime minister
25 December 1991	USSR formally dissolves into constituent republics

Ashoka (272 to 235 BC), a patron of the new philosophy of Buddhism, who developed Taxila as a centre for religious study.

After Ashoka's death, Hindu backlash and invasions by Bactrian Greeks, central Asian Scythians (or Sakas), and Persian Parthians dragged Gandhara through 250 years of chaos.

Meanwhile, in China the Han Dynasty was pushing its frontiers west and south over a growing network of trade routes that later came to be called the Silk Road. From the early Han capital of Chang'an (now Xian), a line of oases skirted north and south around the Takla Makan Desert to Kashgar. From there, tracks ran west across the Pamir and Turkestan (central Asia) to Persia (Iran), Iraq and the Mediterranean, and south across the Karakoram to Kashmir. Caravans went west with porcelain, silk, tea, spices and seeds of peach, orange and other trees, and brought back wool, gold, ivory, jewels and European delicacies such as figs and walnuts – as well as new ideas.

Bandits from Mongolia, Tibet and the little Karakoram state of Hunza made these expeditions dangerous, often impossible, and Han emperors spent vast resources policing the road. Most powerful was the nomadic Mongolian alliance known as Xiong-nu (ancestors of the Huns who later terrified India and Europe).

Among the tribes driven south by the Han and the Xiong-nu, the Yüeh-chih or Kushans made the most of it and, by the 1st century AD, controlled an empire spanning Kashgar, most of the Karakoram, the Hindu Kush and northern India. Under the Kushan Dynasty, finally centred in Gandhara, Buddhism experienced an artistic and intellectual flowering and spread up the Indus into central Asia, China and Tibet. The Silk Road became as much a cultural artery as a commercial one.

In Gandhara, Buddhism found expression in an extraordinary fusion of Indian and Greek artistic styles. In monasteries across the Tarim Basin, wealthy merchants and pilgrims commissioned works in another fusion of styles – Chinese and Indian – which reached its height during the Tang Dynasty from the 7th to 9th centuries.

The Kushans had fallen to the Persian Sassanians by the end of the 3rd century, and Taxila was destroyed by the Hephthalites (or White Huns) in the 5th century. But pilgrims continued to travel overland to Gandhara and India, providing the only detailed accounts of the Karakoram at that time. The most well-known is the Chinese monk Fa-Hsien who, on a 15-year journey across Turkestan and the Karakoram to India, found Buddhism still dominant in early 5th-century Gandhara. Hsuan Tsang, another monk-traveller in the 7th century, found it fading, carried on by monks who no longer understood their own scriptures.

Nourished by Kushan patronage and fertile soil along the Silk Road, Buddhism left an extraordinary record in western China and northern Pakistan, from the cave frescoes of Dunhuang (Gansu) and Bezeklik

Stucco head of Buddha, Taxila

(near Turfan in Xinjiang) to the petroglyphs at Ganesh and Chilas, the bas-relief Buddha-figures near Gilgit and Skardu, and the fabulous trove of sculpture at Taxila.

After the 8th century, a Hindu revival under the Shahi Dynasty probably pushed Hinduism as far north as Gilgit.

Advent of Islam & Decline of the Silk Road

An Arab navy reached the coast of what is now Pakistan in 711 and Arab armies from Persia visited Kashgar and Gilgit at about the same time, but it wasn't until the 11th century that Islam began to establish itself in this region.

Muslim Turkic raiders from Afghanistan, led by the warlord Mahmud of Ghazni, battered the Indus Valley in the early 11th century. Ultimately, the Persian-influenced Ghaznavid Empire spanned Afghanistan and the north-west of the subcontinent, destroying the Hindu kingdoms of the Indus Valley and paving the way for a series of Turkic-Afghan sultanates that ruled from Delhi from the 13th to 15th centuries. Conversion to Islam was widespread, for pragmatic as well as spiritual reasons.

In Turkestan the Silk Road was fading along with the Tang Dynasty. The Tarim Basin fell to the Turks in the 8th century and then to a series of Turkic and Mongol kingdoms, among them the Qarakhan in the 11th and 12th centuries. The earliest appearance of Islam in Turkestan was under the Qarakhan.

In the early 13th century, the Mongol armies of Jenghiz Khan had subdued central Asia and began raiding south into the subcontinent. With the largest contiguous land empire in history cleared by the Mongols of bandits and boundaries, the Silk Road enjoyed a last burst of activity into the 14th century. Europeans, forced to take note of Asian power, also took an interest in Asia itself; Marco Polo made his epic journeys during this time. The subsequent eclipse of the Silk Road has been variously attributed to the arrival of Islam, the collapse of the Mongols and the drying up of oasis streams.

Of the Muslim invaders from central Asia the cruelest was Timur (or Tamerlane), a Turkic or Mongol warlord from the western Pamir, who at the end of the 14th century savaged most of the Islamic cultural centres of Asia – including Kashgar and Delhi – in the name of 'purification'. Paradoxically, his capital city of Samarkand was one of the most splendid and cultured in Asia, full of his spoils.

The final nail in the Silk Road's coffin was the discovery in 1498 of a sea route from Europe around Africa to India by the Portuguese navigator Vasco da Gama. By this time the entire region now spanned by the KKH was Muslim, but it was in total disarray, fractured by quarrelling remnants of the Mongol Empire in the north, petty chieftains in the mountains and Timur's successors and Pathan (Pashtun) tribes in the south. A traveller wouldn't have stood a chance on any long-distance roads.

In 1526, Zahiruddin Babur, ruler of Kabul, displaced King of Ferghana and Samarkand and descendant of both Timur and Jenghiz Khan, marched into Delhi to found a line of Persian-speaking Turkic Muslim emperors of India known as the Moghuls (a corruption of 'Mongol', local parlance for anybody from Central Asia). For six generations, often harassed by Pathans west of the Indus, they presided over a 'Golden Age' of Islamic art, architecture, literature and music, across what is now Pakistan and north India.

Britain, Russia & the 'Great Game'

In 1600 Queen Elizabeth granted monopoly trading rights in Asia to a small merchant group, the East India Company. Starting with one-off expeditions to the Bay of Bengal for cotton and spices, within 50 years they had established a permanent presence on the subcontinent, trading under Moghul grants, gaining territory and influence by cunning and keeping it by force, gradually edging out French, Dutch and Portuguese competition.

The defeat of a Moghul viceroy in 1757 at the Battle of Plassey in Bengal demonstrated the strength of 'the Company' at the expense of the Moghuls, and trade began to give way to plain old imperialism. A century later, a mutiny in the Bengal Army set off a two-year rebellion against the British. After it was put down, the crown in 1858 took control of Company territory, bringing the Moghul Empire to a formal end. The 'Raj' (Britain's Indian Empire) by then covered most of present-day India, through alliance or direct control. (The East India Company later distinguished itself by introducing opium to China, in exchange for tea.)

Meanwhile, in Turkestan, a Manchu army marched into Kashgar in 1755 and the Tarim Basin fell within China's Qing Dynasty for a century. A series of Muslim rebellions in the 1860s temporarily weakened its grip but in 1878 Qing authority was tightened and a formal province, Xinjiang ('New Dominions'), was created.

Westward, Russian expansionism triggered the Crimean War in 1853. Within 15 years Russia was to take for itself an area the size of Europe between the Caspian Sea and the Pamir, and start eyeing Xinjiang and Afghanistan.

The British, anxious about this (and ever eager to trade) set out to pacify their insecure north-west frontier. In 1839 they installed a hand-picked ruler of Afghanistan, which resulted in an uprising, a death-march from Kabul by the British garrison and a vengeful 'First Afghan War'. By the end of it, Britain's puppet was murdered and his predecessor was back on the throne. This failure to either control or befriend the headstrong Afghans was repeated in an equally ill-fated 1878 invasion.

Pathans from west of the Indus, in the course of tormenting the Moghuls, had in 1799 given control of Lahore to an aggressive 19-year-old Sikh chief named Ranjit Singh. Over the next three decades he carved out his own little military state across the Punjab, the Kashmir Valley, Ladakh, Baltistan, Gilgit, Hazara and the Peshawar Valley, and pushed the Pathans right back to the Khyber Pass.

A treaty barring expansion into 'Company' India was violated by his successors and in 1846 the British fought the first of two short, bloody wars with the Sikhs and annexed Kashmir, Ladakh, Baltistan and Gilgit. Renaming it 'the State of Jammu and Kashmir' they sold it for £750,000 to a sycophantic Hindu prince named Gulab Singh, declared him the first Maharajah of Kashmir and thereby created a friendly buffer state on the Russian flank. A second Sikh War brought an end to the Sikh state, and Britain took the Punjab and the Peshawar Valley.

With a grip now on the 'Northern Areas' Britain began a kind of cat-and-mouse game with Russia across the vaguely mapped Pamir and Hindu Kush. Agents posing as scholars, explorers, merchants, even Muslim preachers, crisscrossed the mountains, mapping them, spying on each other, courting local rulers, staking subtle claims like dogs in a vacant lot. The British called it the 'Great Game', and the Russians, the 'Tournament of Shadows'.

In 1882, Russia established a consulate in Kashgar. A British Agency at Gilgit, opened briefly in 1877, was urgently reopened after the Mir (ruler) of Hunza entertained a party of Russians at Baltit in 1888. Britain set up its own Kashgar office in 1890.

In advanced stages of the Game the British tried to persuade reluctant Afghan and Chinese authorities to assert a common border in the Pamir, sealing Russia's southward moves.

In 1890, Francis Younghusband (later to head a British incursion into Tibet) was sent to do some politicking with Chinese officials in Kashgar. On his way back through the Pamir he found the range full of Russian troops, and was told to get out or face arrest.

This electrified the British, who raised hell with the Russian government and invaded Hunza the following year; at the same time Russian troops skirmished in north-east Afghanistan. After a burst of diplomatic manoeuvring, Anglo-Russian boundary agreements in 1897 and 1907 gave Russia most of the Pamir and established the Wakhan Corridor, the awkward tongue of Afghan territory that stretches across to meet Xinjiang.

The Pamir settlement merely shifted the

focus of the Great Game toward Kashgar, where the two powers went on conniving over Turkestan. But in the chaos following the Chinese Revolution of 1911 the British were no match for Russian economic and political influence in western Xinjiang, despite Russian absence from Kashgar for almost a decade after the 1917 Bolshevik Revolution.

Autonomous Xinjiang, Muslim Pakistan

On both sides of the Karakoram the idea of a separate state had a strong appeal to Muslims living under non-Muslim rule. In 1865 Yaqub Beg, an officer from Tashkent, had briefly established an independent Turkestan. Muslims rose up in Xinjiang in the 1930s; in Khotan a short-lived Turkestan Republic was again declared.

Soon after the 1949 founding of the Peoples' Republic of China, Xinjiang was made an 'Autonomous Region', a formality that failed to calm things down. Unrest has continued, including riots in Kashgar in the 1970s, an armed uprising in 1981 that may have left hundreds dead, and another in 1990 in which scores of Muslim protesters were said to have been killed by government troops.

As pressure for Indian independence grew after WW I, Muslim-Hindu disagreement over how to achieve it was echoed in communal violence in the 1920s and 1930s. The idea of a Muslim state was first proposed by the philosopher-poet Alama Mohammed Iqbal in 1930, and adopted in 1940 as a platform of the All-India Muslim League.

In the end, Britain was forced to grant separate independence to a Muslim-majority Pakistan and a Hindu-majority India. Following the public announcement of the borders between the two countries a few days after the formal Partition date of 14 August 1947, Muslims fled westward and Hindus and Sikhs eastward, some six million in each direction, probably the biggest mass population transfer in history. In riots and hideous massacres on both sides, somewhere between 200,000 and a million people were killed.

As 14 August came and went, Maharajah Hari Singh delayed his decision on whether Kashmir should accede to India or Pakistan, hoping to remain free of both. At the end of October a band of Pathan tribesmen invaded Kashmir, having been told the Maharajah was about to join India. This he promptly did. India flew troops into Kashmir and Pakistan moved in its own, and the two countries went to war. The Kashmiri governor was arrested at Gilgit and Muslim militiamen and soldiers there demanded to join Pakistan. A United Nations cease-fire in January 1949 gave each country a piece of Kashmir to administer, a temporary arrangement that after 40 years is looking fairly permanent.

India and Pakistan again fought over Kashmir in 1965 and 1971. The latter war was followed by the secession of East Pakistan, which became Bangladesh. At the end of 1989 the Indian army moved heavily into Kashmir to suppress a growing Muslim independence movement, and 1990 saw another war scare. Kashmiri nationalists tried in 1992 to march across the line of control from the Pakistan side but were stopped by Pakistani bullets.

The Karakoram Highway

China, following its invasion of Tibet in 1950, occupied parts of Ladakh, Baltistan and the upper Shimshal Valley in the mid-1950s. All traffic across the border with China stopped. While the China-India border in Ladakh is still in dispute today, a thaw in China-Pakistan relations in 1964 under General Ayub Khan led to a border agreement, China's return of 2000 sq km of territory and talk of a 'Friendship Highway' linking the two countries across the Pamir and the Karakoram, via Hunza and Gilgit. (According to an apocryphal story around Gilgit, General Ayub had politely declined a similar offer by Soviet Premier Bulganin to build a road through Ishkoman.)

The Pakistan army had already started a road of its own in 1960, the 400-km 'Indus Valley Road' between Swat and Gilgit. In 1966 a China-Pakistan decision expanded it to a Havelian-to-the-border two-lane paved road, with Pakistanis working north from the Indus and the Chinese working south from the Khunjerab as well as to Kashgar on their own side.

In 1968 the Indus Valley Road and a link to Havelian were finished, and joined by a bridge at Thakot. Between then and 1973, Chinese crews cut a road over the Khunjerab Pass to Gulmit, and in 1974 returned at Pakistan's request to help south of Gulmit. Chinese workers left in December 1979 and the KKH was declared complete (in Pakistan) in 1980.

In August 1982, the highway was formally inaugurated, the Northern Areas were opened to tourism (as far as Passu) and the Khunjerab Pass opened to official traffic and cross-border trade. On 1 May 1986 the Khunjerab and the entire road to Kashgar were opened to tourism. The Chinese finally finished paving the road on their side in 1989.

GEOGRAPHY

The KKH threads its way through a 'knot' of four great mountain ranges: the Pamir, the Karakoram, the Hindu Kush and the Himalaya, all of them part of the vast collision zone between the Asian continent and the Indian subcontinent. Here the ground rises higher, over a greater area, than anywhere else on the planet.

The Pamir is a range of rounded, 5000 to 7000-metre mountains stretching 800 km across the former Soviet republic of Tajikistan. With very broad, flat valleys nearly as high as the lower peaks, the Pamir might be better described as a plateau. The valleys are treeless, grassy (*pamir* roughly means 'pasture' in local dialects), and often swampy with meandering rivers. The KKH crosses the eastern limb of the Pamir, called the Taghdumbash or Sarikol Pamir.

The Karakoram arches for 500 km along the border between China and Pakistan-held Kashmir, parallel to the Himalaya and cleanly separated from it by the trough of the upper Indus River. To a geographer the Karakoram reaches west to the Ishkoman Valley (beyond which it becomes the Hindu

Kush) and south-east into Ladakh in Indian-held Kashmir. It's characterised by closely-packed, steep, jagged high peaks and deep gorges; immense glaciers (the longest outside the sub-polar regions); and lush high valleys. The world's second highest mountain, K2 or Mt Godwin-Austen, is in Baltistan.

The 'Great Karakoram' is the range's high backbone, grouped in clusters called *muztagh* (Uyghur for 'ice mountain') from which the biggest glaciers descend. In northern Hunza is the Batura Muztagh, source of the Batura, Passu and Ultar glaciers; south-east is the Hispar Muztagh from which Nagar's glaciers flow; in Baltistan is the mighty Baltoro Muztagh, home of K2. This crest-zone is broken at only one point, by the Hunza River (accompanied by the KKH) in southern Gojal.

South of Gilgit the Indus River divides the Himalaya from the Hindu Kush, which extends over 800 km into central Afghanistan. The western anchor of the Himalaya is 8126-metre Nanga Parbat. Under the force of the collision that gave birth to the Himalaya, Nanga Parbat continues to rise at almost seven mm per year.

Statistics

The highest peaks near the KKH (approximate heights in metres, all in the Karakoram except as noted) are: Nanga Parbat (Himalaya, 8126), Rakaposhi (7790), Batura Peak (7785), Mt Kongur (Pamir, 7719), un-named (at the head of the Passu Glacier, 7611), Muztagh Ata (Pamir, 7546), Malubiting (7450), Haramosh (7400) and Ultar Peak (7388). In the Northern Areas alone there are about three dozen peaks over 7000 metres.

The Karakoram has four glaciers over 50 km long: Batura, Hispar, Baltoro and Biafo. The Batura comes right down to the KKH at Passu.

GEOLOGY

A trip along the Karakoram Highway reveals one of the world's greatest geological exhibits. The mountain chain comprised of the Himalaya, Karakoram and Hindu Kush ranges was born 50 million years ago in a stupendous collision between India and Asia, a collision that is still going on today. The highway climbs right over the 'wreckage'.

According to the theory of plate tectonics, the earth's crust is made up of continent-sized slabs of rock (plates), afloat on a more fluid layer (mantle). As a result of currents and upwellings from below, the plates move around, bump into each other, break up and reform, all in ultra-slow motion.

About 130 million years ago, when dinosaurs still roamed the earth, the 'Indian Plate' broke away from a primordial super-continent that geologists call Gondwanaland (the ancestor of Africa, Australia and Antarctica) and drifted north toward another landmass called Laurasia, the 'Asian Plate'. Between the converging continents lay a wide,

shallow sea called Tethys, and off the shore of Laurasia was a chain of volcanic islands, similar to present-day Indonesia or Japan.

In the collision that followed, the Indian Plate buried its leading edge under the Asian Plate, lifting it up. Both plates compressed and piled up against each other. Trapped in the middle, the small oceanic plate supporting the offshore island chain was flipped very nearly on end, and the Sea of Tethys was swallowed up.

Continents are not easily slowed down. India continues to plough northward (at about five cm per year), and the mountains are still rising, in some cases faster than erosion can wear them down. Frequent earthquakes across the region reveal the strains underneath.

From the Khunjerab Pass to Islamabad, the Karakoram Highway crosses the entire

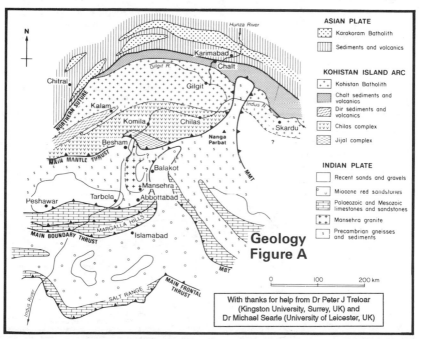

Geological map of northern Pakistan, showing the major rock units and thrust zones in the three 'plates' crossed by the KKH

collision zone – the Asian Plate, the remnants of the offshore volcanic islands, and the Indian Plate. The evidence of this on-going encounter is easy to see, both on the grand scale – in the size and sequence of the mountains – and up close, in the colours and patterns of road-side rocks and minerals.

The Asian Plate

From Khunjerab to Chalt (in the lower Hunza Valley) the road crosses old Laurasia, its former southern shore now heaved up into the Karakoram Range itself.

The geology from Khunjerab to Passu is dominated by dark and light-coloured metamorphic shale and limestone, seen prominently in the saw-tooth peaks around Passu. ('Metamorphic' refers to rocks reformed from older ones deep in the earth's crust under high temperatures and pressures.) From Passu to Karimabad, the high spine of the Karakoram is composed mostly of 50-million to 100-million-year-old granite (the Karakoram Batholith in the diagrams), part

of a vast body extending eastward for 2500 km along the India-Asia boundary, to Lhasa and beyond.

In the Hunza Valley itself is a variety of metamorphic rocks, with large red garnets very common. White marble bands are conspicuous around Karimabad. The famous ruby mines of Hunza are in the hills north of the river, between Karimabad and Hasanabad (although the 'rubies' offered to you by the urchins of Baltit are probably garnets).

The edge of the Asian Plate (called the Northern Suture or NS on the diagrams) is exposed near Chalt, in a multicoloured jumble of sedimentary rocks, volcanic material, talc and greenish serpentine. Southward, the road crosses onto the eroded remains of the small oceanic plate that was pinned between India and Asia.

The Kohistan Complex

In the course of the continental collision, the plate bearing the old volcanic island chain

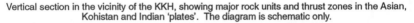

Vertical section in the vicinity of the KKH, showing major rock units and thrust zones in the Asian, Kohistan and Indian 'plates'. The diagram is schematic only.

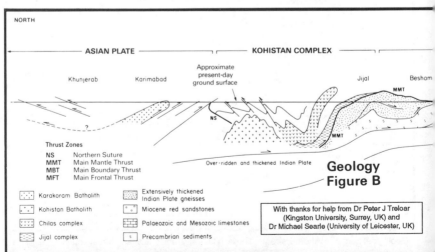

Geology Figure B

Thrust Zones
NS   Northern Suture
MMT   Main Mantle Thrust
MBT   Main Boundary Thrust
MFT   Main Frontal Thrust

Over-ridden and thickened Indian Plate

Karakoram Batholith
Kohistan Batholith
Chilas complex
Jijal complex
Extensively thickened Indian Plate gneisses
Miocene red sandstones
Palaeozoic and Mesozoic limestones
Precambrian sediments

With thanks for help from Dr Peter J Treloar (Kingston University, Surrey, UK) and Dr Michael Searle (University of Leicester, UK)

was effectively up-ended, with the shallower ocean sediments and volcanic materials tilted to the north, and its very deep parts exposed in the south. Consequently, the northern part of this so-called Kohistan Complex, from Chalt to Raikot Bridge (east of Chilas), is a mass of sedimentary and volcanic rocks. Dark patches are remnants of ocean-floor crust upon which the island chain was built. The area around Gilgit and the confluence of the Gilgit and Indus rivers was invaded at a later stage by granites from a deep molten reservoir (the Kohistan Batholith in the diagram). At the confluence especially, hundreds of small intrusive granite sheets cross-cut one another.

By contrast, the southern part of this unit reveals rocks formed under conditions of extreme heat and pressure deep in the earth, ie beneath the old oceanic plate. Examples include the black-banded pinkish rocks seen just east of Chilas (the Chilas Complex on the diagrams), and garnet-rich outcrops between Pattan and Jijal that include some dark-red, nearly pure garnetites (Jijal Complex). Just west of the Shangla Pass, on the Besham-Swat road, are outcrops of the rare rock blueschist, which laboratory studies indicate can form only at depths of at least 25 km.

At Jijal the KKH crosses the boundary from the volcanic island complex to the Indian Plate. The green rocks at Jijal belong to Kohistan, and the contorted white and grey gneisses, 100 metres south, belong to the Indian Plate.

The Indian Plate

As it drove into and under Asia, the top of the Indian Plate was compressed and bull-dozed back, most severely along the leading edge. Under the resulting compression the crust became fractured and sliced. Along certain fronts or 'thrusts', individual slices, some up to 10 km thick, slid southwards and upwards over originally higher rocks. The effect was to throw up great piles of material, some still visible as hill or mountain ranges.

The direct contact between Kohistan and the Indian Plate (called the Main Mantle Thrust or MMT in the diagrams) is not marked by a distinct chain of hills but does pass through the rugged terrain from Babusar Pass via Besham into the Swat Valley. The emerald deposits at Mingora, in Swat, are within this zone.

To the south, major thrusts are associated with escarpments (mountain fronts), eg the steep terrain between Abbottabad and Havelian (the Panjal Thrust in the diagram), the Margalla and Murree hills along Islamabad's northern side (the Main Boundary Thrust or MBT in the diagrams) and the Salt Range, 100 to 150 km south of Islamabad (the Main Frontal Thrust or MFT in the diagrams).

The severest compression, right at the northern edge of the plate, tended to push up the oldest and deepest material, subsequently exposed by erosion. Thus, as you go southward the exposed surface gets younger. Material from deep in the plate's crust, where temperatures are high and rock is slightly plastic, tended to fold and deform, and the geology south as far as Mansehra is dominated by contorted and streaky metamorphic rocks from the plate's Precambrian 'basement' (more than 600 million years

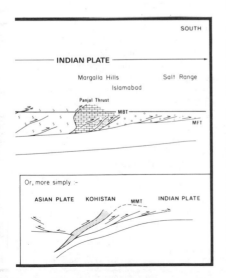

old). Precambrian slate outcrops are visible along the road between Mansehra and Abbottabad.

From here, south through the Taxila Valley to the Margalla Pass, the road crosses 600 million to 160 million-year-old Palaeozoic and Mesozoic limestones. At the road-cut through the Margalla Pass, the thrusting of these limestone strata, southward up and over younger rock, is well-exposed. South of Margalla, red rock outcrops indicate Miocene-age (about 20 million years old) sandstones, originally eroded from the embryonic Himalaya chain.

Nanga Parbat

An unmistakable feature of the region is massive Nanga Parbat, 8126 metres high and rising by seven mm every year, faster than almost any other part of the Himalaya chain. Here are the sharpest elevation differences found anywhere on earth: 6½ vertical km from the summit into the adjacent Indus gorge, and the mountain's sheer, unbroken 4000-metre south wall (the Rupal Face).

Nanga Parbat sits atop a mass of ancient Indian-Plate rocks, sticking oddly northward into the volcanic-island material of the Kohistan Complex. Its unusual position and growth are still matters of active research; explanations involve the dynamics of the entire Himalayan system.

At the Liachar Valley, about four km upstream from the Raikot Bridge over the Indus (between Gilgit and Chilas), across from the KKH, you can see the grey Precambrian granite of the Indian Plate, hundreds of millions of years old, pushed over on top of river sediments less than 100,000 years old. This reversal is part of the continuing disruption as Nanga Parbat rises.

This geological instability, coupled with an earthquake, caused a colossal landslide near Liachar in 1841, which dammed up the Indus and created a lake stretching nearly to Gilgit. The remnants of the slide can be seen in a steep-sided, two-km-long ridge on the river's east bank, below Liachar. When the dam broke, the wall of water thundering down the canyon and out onto the plains of the Punjab washed away scores of towns and villages and drowned thousands of people, including an entire Sikh army battalion camped at Attock.

At another side valley just above Raikot Bridge, the boundary between the Kohistan Complex and the Indian Plate is visible. Across the river from the highway, a 100-metre stretch of jeep track passes from grey Indian-Plate granite, southward through a layer of brown garnet-bearing schists that formed a sedimentary cover to the granite, and into the greenish rocks of Kohistan.

Other Evidence of Geological Activity

Insistent reminders of the strains of mountain-building are the earthquakes that constantly jar the Karakoram.

The worst in recent times struck near the Indus River village of Pattan, north of Besham, in December 1974. Pattan and many smaller villages virtually disappeared under collapsing hillsides. Between 5000 and 8000 people died, and tens of thousands were injured. Pattan has been entirely rebuilt with government and international relief money but, like many towns along the KKH, it continues to be at the mercy of its tormented surroundings.

In the same year, earthquakes probably triggered a mud and rock slide out of the Shishkat Valley in Gojal (Upper Hunza) that dammed the Hunza River. The resulting lake, extending to well above Passu, lasted so long before the river cut its way through again, that the once deep and fertile valley filled with silt and gravel, and is now a shallow, flat-bottomed wasteland. A section of the KKH, including a major bridge, was permanently buried, and had to be re-routed and rebuilt.

A happier consequence of geological activity is the high frequency of hot springs in the area. Relatively recent 'faults' or fractures permit easy upward movement of underground water that has been in contact with hot rock deep in the crust.

CLIMATE

The hottest months all along the KKH are

June, July and August; the coldest are January and February. The wettest months are during the monsoon, mid-July to mid-September, with steady rain and high humidity as far north as Kohistan and the Kaghan Valley and random summer storms as far north as Hunza. The same regions are also drizzly through the winter and early spring.

The driest months generally are June and September through November in Pakistan, and anytime in Xinjiang. From Kashgar to Gilgit, winter is long and cold (often well below freezing), and snow is common in the mountains. Snow usually closes the Khunjerab Pass from November through April. For more about when to go, see the Facts for the Visitor chapter.

FLORA

One of the delights of the Karakoram is its unexpectedly lush, glacier-watered pastures, hidden in high valleys. The few alpine trees there are mainly dwarf juniper.

Lower down are pine, spruce, juniper, deodar (Indian cedar), birch and willow – plus violets, poppies, columbine, forget-me-nots, mallow, geranium and other wildflowers in spring. Domestic crops include wheat and maize; orchards of apricots, peaches, apples, mulberries and other fruit, as well as walnuts; and poplars for fodder, firewood, timber and erosion control.

Parts of the lower Hindu Kush and Himalaya are heavily forested, especially where the monsoon reaches. The forests of Hazara include oak, chestnut and eucalyptus, plus acacia and other plantations for fodder and erosion control.

FAUNA
Kashgar to Pirali

Birds sighted at East Lake in Kashgar include kingfishers, terns, bitterns, gulls, plovers, grouse, hoopoe, wagtail, sparrows, crows and buzzards. Geese, gulls, terns, sandpipers, crows, falcons and hawks were observed at Kara Kul lake. Rabbits and marmots were also seen at Kara Kul lake.

The High Karakoram

Wildlife is rich at these elevations, though many species have been hunted almost to extinction – snow leopard, Himalayan ibex and markhor (wild goats that figure in the region's oldest legends), wild sheep including the big-horn Marco Polo sheep, musk deer and black bear. Other residents are urial, Himalayan marmot, brown bear, wolf, marten, ermine and lynx. In the air are hawks, falcons, vultures, eagles and at least four varieties of pheasant (two of them, the ram chakor and trapogan, are nearly extinct).

Snow leopard

The main domesticated animals are yaks and a cow-yak hybrid called a dzu.

Pakistan's Khunjerab National Park, along the border with China, was established largely to protect the threatened Marco Polo sheep. On the Xinjiang side is the Tashkurghan Nature Reserve.

Temperate Mountain Forests
Wild animals in the forests of Pakistan include Himalayan black bear, brown bear, wild cats, wild boar, jackals, foxes, hares, monkeys, porcupines, small rodents and reptiles, bats and common birds like kites, crows and magpies. Some cattle are kept, and goats and sheep are driven into higher valleys in summer.

RURAL DEVELOPMENT
Most people living near the KKH are subsistence farmers or herders. For their maize, wheat, barley, rice, fruit and (in Xinjiang) cotton, farmers depend heavily on irrigation, from wells and isolated streams around Kashgar or channelled glacial melt-water in the Northern Areas. Plots are tiny and harvests are meagre (though yields per hectare are well above those in the rest of Pakistan). Herders, especially in Kohistan and the Northern Areas, make long migrations to pastures only accessible in summer. Little except fruit is exported from the Northern Areas, where annual per capita income is estimated to be about US$150.

Into this setting the KKH has brought government grants, down-country developers, tourists and a kind of wealth, but it has also tended to unravel old traditions, social structures and community self-reliance. A social redevelopment effort initially funded by the private Aga Khan Foundation has had interesting results in the Northern Areas.

The Aga Khan Foundation
This foundation was started by the Aga Khan, spiritual head of Ismaili Muslims, to provide capital for health, education and rural development projects in certain low-income areas of Asia and Africa. Ismailis actually make up only a fraction of its current beneficiaries, although it's obvious in northern Pakistan that the Ismaili community has provided the enthusiasm and energy necessary to get many AKF-funded programmes off the ground.

The main recipients of AKF (and now other) money in northern Pakistan are the Aga Khan Rural Support Programme, the Community Basic Services Programme, Aga Khan Educational Services and Aga Khan Health Services.

Aga Khan Rural Support Programme
When General Yahya Khan ended the semi-autonomy of Hunza, Nagar and other princely states in 1969 (and especially after Prime Minister Z A Bhutto withdrew subsidies in 1974), the local rulers' traditional power to initiate collective works also ended.

The central government's own public-works projects tended to be vast in scale and run from Islamabad. At the same time population growth was exceeding the capacity of the land under cultivation and forcing people into the towns for work. Village productivity and collective confidence seemed to be fading away.

The AKRSP was formed in 1982 to encourage a home-grown solution in the form of self-sustaining, co-operative village organisations that could carry out their own development projects. It offered starter loans, technical resources and management advice to any village that would form its own decision-making body (Village Organisation or VO), name its projects and commit itself to acquiring the necessary skills and saving its own money. AKRSP's role was to act as a catalyst only until the projects were self-managing.

The effects have been quite dramatic. As of mid-1991, over 90% of all rural households in Hunza, Nagar and the Gilgit River basin were in villages with VOs (over 70% counting Chitral and Baltistan as well). All had self-help projects underway or completed, and most had several further projects, undertaken with their own funds. The work covers both Ismaili and non-Ismaili villages.

Early projects tended to be irrigation

schemes and link roads; AKRSP signs sprouted weekly by the highway, announcing new works. Some impressive ones close to the KKH are a 400-metre irrigation tunnel above Sust; a 45-km road being pioneered up the Shimshal Valley; an irrigation channel from the Batura Glacier at Passu; and the Karimabad-Aliabad link road. Later projects have included other infrastructure development, flood control, afforestation, seed improvement, pest control, livestock management, commercial development and marketing. About a third of these villages have also started separate women's organisations, with their own projects.

Nowadays, significant AKRSP money also comes from private organisations such as Oxfam in the UK and the Konrad Adenauer Foundation in Germany, from EC, Dutch, Canadian, US and British overseas aid agencies, and even from the Pakistan government.

You can go and look at the projects, but local VO staff and AKRSP staff in Gilgit are spread too thinly to meet casual visitors. One way to learn more about the programme is the video presentation, *The First Harvest*, which is said to be available for viewing by arrangement at the Gilgit Serena Lodge. Those with a serious professional interest should write ahead to the General Manager (☎ (0572) 2480; fax 2779), AKRSP, PO Box 506, Babar Rd, Gilgit,. The Aga Khan Foundation is at 7 Rue Versonnex, PO Box 435, 1211 Geneva 6, Switzerland.

Other Programmes Aga Khan Health Services operates a network of local centres whose main emphasis is maternity and child health. AKHS also run an expanding primary health-care programme for villages and rural areas (roughly hand-in-hand with AKRSP programmes), including general health education and basic medical training.

Aga Khan Educational Services operates several hundred schools in northern Pakistan (two prominent ones are the huge Girls' Academy on the west side of Karimabad and a school in Sher Qila in Punial). Most are for girls, and provide the main access to

education for women in the Northern Areas. Both AKES and local government-run schools are involved in an AKF-funded teacher development scheme.

The Community Basic Services programme is a joint effort by UNICEF and the Pakistan government, with the participation of Canadian agencies, to improve rural drinking water, sanitation and other facilities.

Local Bodies & Rural Development (LB&RD) is the Pakistan government's lower-profile, low-budget equivalent of AKRSP, though it has apparently been helping to fund local public-works projects for longer.

RELIGION

Although the Indus Valley saw the birth of Hinduism and an early flowering of Buddhism, both traditions were swept aside by Islam. With the exception of small Christian and Hindu communities in Pakistan and scattered Buddhists in western China, nearly everyone from Turkestan to the Arabian Sea is Muslim, and a good deal of the flavour of KKH travel stems from this fact.

Islam – History & Schisms

In 612 AD, the Prophet Mohammed, then a wealthy Arab of Mecca, began preaching a new religious philosophy, Islam, based on revelations from Allah (Islam's name for God). Islam incorporated elements of Judaism, Christianity and other faiths (eg heaven and hell, a creation story much like the Garden of Eden, myths like Noah's Ark) and treated their prophets simply as forerunners of the Prophet Mohammed. These revelations were eventually to be compiled into Islam's holy book, the Koran (or Qoran).

In 622, Mohammed and his followers were forced to flee to Medina (the Islamic calendar counts its years from this flight or *Hejira*). There he built a political base and an army, taking Mecca in 630 and eventually overrunning Arabia. By the end of his life Mohammed ruled a rapidly growing religious and secular dynasty. The militant faith meshed nicely with a latent Arab nationalism, and within a century the empire reached from Spain to central Asia.

Succession disputes after the Prophet's death soon split the community. When the fourth caliph (ruler), the Prophet's son-in-law Ali, was assassinated in 661 his followers and descendants became the founders of the Shia (or Shi'ite) sect. Others accepted as caliph the governor of Syria, a brother-in-law of the Prophet, and this line has become the modern-day orthodox Sunni (or Sunnite) sect. In 680 a chance for reconciliation was

Detail of Islamic script on mosque tiles (PJ)

lost when Ali's surviving son Hussain and most of his male relatives were killed at Karbala in Iraq by Sunni partisans. Today over 90% of Muslims world-wide are Sunni.

Among Shia doctrines is that of the *Imam* or infallible leader who continues to unfold the true meaning of the Koran and provides guidance in daily affairs. Most Shias recognise an hereditary line of 12 Imams ending in the 9th century (though *imam* is still used, loosely, by modern Shias). These Shias are known as Ithnashari ('Twelvers'). This book refers to them simply as Shias.

An 8th-century split among Shias gave rise to the Ismaili or Maulai sect, who disagreed on which son of the sixth Imam should succeed him. For Ismaili Shias the line of Imams continues into the present. Ismailis today number several million in pockets of Pakistan, India, East Africa, Iran and Syria, and their present leader, Prince Karim Aga Khan, is considered to be Imam No 49. Doctrines are more esoteric and practices less regimented than those of Ithnashari Shias or Sunnis. The style of prayer is a personal matter (eg there is no prostration), the mosque is replaced by a community hall called a *jamat khana* and women are less secluded.

Islam along the KKH

Although an Arab expedition reached Kashgar in the 8th century, the earliest conversions to Islam in the Tarim Basin were by rulers of the Qarakhan Dynasty in the 12th century. Today most non-Chinese there are Sunni Muslims.

Almost simultaneously with the 8th-century central Asia explorations an Arab naval force arrived at the mouth of the Indus, but likewise left little religious imprint. In the following centuries many conversions were accomplished by Sufi missionaries wandering across central and south Asia.

Conversions to Sunnism under duress followed raids from Afghanistan by Mahmud of Ghazni in the 11th century, and later work by Pathan missionaries. Today, people as far north on the KKH as Chilas are all Sunnis, and more fervently so than their Kashgar counterparts.

Sufi preachers brought Shia doctrines to the northern mountains in the 12th to 16th centuries – Ithnashari from Persia and Ismaili from Afghanistan and central Asia. By the 13th century most people of the Gilgit River basin were Ismaili, while Nagar and the Bagrot and Haramosh valleys were Shia. Hunza and Gojal, Shia at first, adopted Ismailism in the mid-1800s. Even today a few old carved Shia mosques can be seen there, a sharp contrast to the spanking green-and-white jamat khanas.

Gilgit is the only KKH town with sizeable proportions of all three sects, and it's always a bit on edge. In past years during the Shias' gripping Ashura processions, Shias and Sunnis have exchanged taunts, even gunshots. Ismailis and Shias are anxious about puritanical Wahhabi Sunni missionaries. Sunnis and Shias are ambivalent about Aga Khan-funded development work, even in their own villages.

In 1988, at the end of Ramadan, gun battles erupted between Shias and Sunnis around Gilgit, leaving at least 100 dead; despite efforts at reconciliation there were more killings in 1989 and 1991. Some Gilgitis see an orchestrated anti-Shia campaign by zealots from outside the area.

Perhaps hardest for Muslims along the KKH are the internal tensions between their traditions and the libertarian popular culture imported by southern Pakistanis and by foreign tourists.

Practice

Islam translates loosely from Arabic as 'the peace that comes from total surrender to God'. God's will is articulated in the Koran. In addition to the creeds set out there, Muslims express their surrender in the form of daily prayers, alms-giving, fasting and pilgrimage to Mecca. In its fullest sense Islam is an entire way of life, with guidelines for doing nearly everything. Among prohibitions honoured by the devout are those against eating pork and drinking alcohol.

In addition to mid-day congregations on the Friday day of rest, devout Muslims pray five times each day, in a mosque if possible (though women may not enter mosques). Sunnis pray at prescribed times: before sunrise, just after high noon, late afternoon, just after sunset and before retiring. For Shias there are three fixed times – before sunrise and twice in the evening – the other two being at one's discretion. Prayers are preceded if possible by washing, at least of hands, face and feet.

Just before fixed prayers a *muezzin* calls the Sunni and Shia faithful, traditionally from a minaret, nowadays often through a loudspeaker. The Arabic *azan* or call to prayer translates roughly as, 'God is most great. There is no God but Allah. Mohammed is God's messenger. Come to prayer, come to security. God is most great.'

Islam has no ordained priesthood but *maulvis* or *maulanas* (commonly called *mullahs*) are rather like priests, trained in theology, respected as interpreters of scripture, and very influential in rural areas. Many educated people in Pakistan despise them, not out of scorn for Islam but because some mullahs are corrupt and distort teachings for their own ends.

When visiting a mosque, always take your shoes off at the door, and make sure your feet or socks are clean. Often at larger mosques there is an attendant to look after your shoes, who may expect a small tip, say Rs 5.

It is polite to refer to the Prophet Mohammed as such, rather than by his name alone.

Sufism

The original Sufis were just purists, seeking knowledge of God through direct personal experience, unhappy with the worldliness of the early caliphates. There never was a single Sufi movement, but numerous branches. For many of them music, dance or poetry about the search for God were routes to trance and revelation. This is the mystical side of Islam, just like similar traditions in other faiths.

Sufis were singularly successful as missionaries, perhaps because of their tolerance of other creeds. It was largely the Sufis, not Arab or other armies, who took Islam into central Asia and the subcontinent. In some ways southern Pakistan is Sufism's 'home' now, abounding with colourful shrines to Sufi holy men or *pirs*.

Ramadan

Ramadan (also called Ramazan in Pakistan) is the Muslim month of fasting, a sort of ritual cleansing of body and mind, with eating, drinking (even water) and smoking forbidden from sunrise to sunset. The devout take meals in the evening and just before sunrise; muezzin calls signal the end of each day's fasting. Ismailis don't take part.

Children, pregnant women, very old and/or ill people, travellers and non-Muslims are exempt, though they are expected not to eat or drink in front of those who are fasting. Food and drink are hard to find during daylight hours, offices keep odd hours, tempers are short and very little serious business gets done. On the KKH, the best places for non-Muslims to find food are tourist hotels, bus stands, Ismaili neighbourhoods in Gilgit, or anywhere in Gojal or Hunza (but not Nagar).

Oddly enough, Pakistanis are said to eat *more* during Ramadan than at other times, putting away bigger-than-normal meals during the night. Food prices actually go up then. The approximate dates for Ramadan are 12 February to 15 March (1994), 1 February to 4 March (1995), and 22 January to 22 February (1996).

Facts for the Visitor

VISAS & EMBASSIES

You can't live with bureaucrats and you can't live without them. In Islamabad they're fond of implying that only they are keeping your plans from collapsing. In remote Pakistan they're unnervingly off-hand. In China they're wildly unpredictable. There are many stories of hassles, mostly on arrival or departure. The moral in all of them is: keep your papers in order.

(1) Get a visa *before* you arrive at the border; you can't enter China without one, and obtaining a Pakistan visa in advance avoids a stressful paper-chase in Islamabad.

(2) Don't let anything expire, even by one day; it's just an excuse for impromptu 'regulations' and 'fees' you can't verify.

(3) Treat your entry-exit form, China customs declaration, Pakistan registration papers and foreign exchange receipts with reverence.

(4) If you're staying more than 30 days in Pakistan, register with the police.

Important-looking cards and documents with seals, stamps, logos and plastic laminations may also come in handy. Smile through your clenched teeth as they shuffle, staple, stamp and sign.

Some embassies in Western countries accept visa applications by post. In addition to fee, passport and passport-size photos you may need to show an onward or return ticket or a receipt for one. This might be deflected by saying you're leaving over the Khunjerab Pass, but then they might want to see a wad of travellers' cheques. Advance hotel bookings are not required.

Some travel agents will get visas for you, and there are specialist visa agencies – eg Visa Services (☎ (202) 387-0300), 1519 Connecticut Ave NW, Washington, DC 20036, USA, and Worldwide Visas (☎ (071) 379 0419; fax 497 2590), 9 Adelaide St, London WC2 4HZ, UK.

China Visa

Everyone needs a visa to enter China, and you cannot get one at the border. Tourists only get single-entry visas. Usual durations are one and three months, from the date of *issue*. Some travellers say one-month visas are easier to get, and a one-month extension can be obtained in China. With the visa you can visit any open city or region, and while in China you can get travel permits for some restricted areas.

Abbreviations
People talk in initials along the KKH. Following are the most common abbreviations you'll hear.

AKRSP Aga Khan Rural Support Programme
AKES Aga Khan Educational Services
AKHS Aga Khan Health Services
CAAC Civil Aviation Administration of China (or Air China)
CBS Community Basic Services Programme
CITS China International Travel Service
CTS China Travel Service
C&W NWFP Communication & Works Department
GTS Government Transport Service
GPO General Post Office
IYHA International Youth Hostel Association

NAPWD Northern Areas Public Works Department
Natco Northern Areas Transportation Company
NWFP North-West Frontier Province
PCO Public Call Office
PIA Pakistan International Airlines
PRC People's Republic of China
PTDC Pakistan Tourism Development Corporation
PTL Pakistan Tours Ltd
PYHA Pakistan Youth Hostels Association
TDCP Tourist Development Corporation of the Punjab

You must identify an itinerary and entry/exit points in your application, but nobody will hold you to it when you get there. Avoid listing too many big tourist cities (Beijing, Shanghai, Xian, Guilin) in big tourist months (May, August, September, October) and don't list Tibet. Don't give your occupation as writer or journalist. Fees depend on your nationality.

One traveller crossing from Xinjiang to Alma Ata in Kazakhstan was asked by Chinese border officials for the endorsement on his China visa allowing him to exit there. He didn't have one but persuaded them to issue one on the spot. If you're thinking of arriving or leaving via a former Soviet republic, you might avoid a major headache by getting written permission on your China visa to do so.

Where to Get It Visas can be obtained through the People's Republic of China embassy or consulate in your country. The Chinese Embassy in Islamabad gives a one-month visa in four working days; see Getting Foreign Visas in Pakistan, in this section.

It's easy to get a three-month visa in Hong Kong. It's cheapest (HK$90) and quickest (one working day) directly from the Visa Office of the PRC Ministry of Foreign Affairs (☎ 835-3657, 835-3660), 5th floor, lower block, China Resources Building, 26 Harbour Rd, Wanchai. They're open 9 am to noon and 2 to 5 pm Monday to Friday, plus Saturday mornings.

Travel agencies charge more to do it. Four in Hong Kong geared to independent travellers are in the Tsimshatsui area of Kowloon – Time Travel (☎ 723-9993), 16th Floor, Block A, Chungking Mansions, 40 Nathan Rd; Shoestring Travel, 4th Floor, Block A, Alpha House, 27 Peking Rd; Hong Kong Student Travel (☎ 723-2306), 10th Floor, Star House, by Star Ferry; and Phoenix Travel (☎ 725-3898), 6th Floor, Milton Mansion, 96 Nathan Rd at Granville Rd (☎ 722-7378).

Visa Extensions Rules vary from year to year. You can get at least one one-month extension at the Foreign Affairs section of any Public Security Bureau office, for Y25 FEC. In Kashgar, this office (called the Border & Administrative Office for Foreigners & Visitors) is on Shengli Lu.

Travel Permits Besides the open areas you can visit with just a visa, there are others you can go to by applying at a Public Security Bureau office for an Alien's Travel Permit *(Waiguoren Lüxingzhen)*. An example in the Kashgar area is Kara Kul lake. Permits for this can be obtained at Kashgar or Tashkurghan (see the Kashgar & Tashkurghan chapter). Each permit is Y5 FEC, though at Kashgar you may also have to pay for a certificate from CITS.

Bicycles can be ridden in and around open Chinese cities with only a visa, but in theory you need a special permit to ride *between* them. A few cyclists have ridden the Kashgar-to-Khunjerab Pass road unhindered, but most have been hassled by police and told to pack their bikes on top of the next bus. An Alien's Travel Permit for Kara Kul may satisfy some officials. For more on cycling see the Getting Around and Kashgar & Tashkurghan chapters.

Embassies & Consulates of the People's Republic of China
Australia
  Embassy of the PRC, 247 Federal Highway, Watson, Canberra, ACT 2602, Australia (☎ (06) 241 2448)
Canada
  Embassy of the PRC, PO Box 8935, 515 St Patrick St, Ottawa, Ontario K1N 5H3 (☎ (613) 234 2706)
  Consulate, 240 St George St, Toronto, Ontario M5R 2P4 (☎ (416) 964 7260)
  Consulate, 3380 Granville St, Vancouver, BC V6H 3K3 (☎ (604) 736 3910)
Hong Kong
  Visa Office, PRC Ministry of Foreign Affairs, China Resources Building, 26 Harbour Rd, Wanchai (☎ 827-4163)
India
  Embassy of the PRC, 50-D Shantipath, Chanakyapuri, New Delhi 110021 (☎ 600328)
New Zealand
  Embassy of the PRC, 2-6 Glenmore St, Kelburn, Wellington 5 (☎ 72 1382)

Left: Men chat on the KKH, Hunza (JK)
Right: Besham Bazaar, Indus Kohistan (JK)
Bottom: Leaving the Sunday Market, Kashgar (RI'A)

Top: Tajik children, Tashkurghan (JK)
Middle, Left & Right: Men of Kashgar (RI'A)
Middle, Centre: Goatherd of Thalpan Village, Chilas (JK)
Bottom: Children of Farphu Village, Bagrot Valley (JK)

Pakistan
> Embassy of the PRC, Diplomatic Enclave, Islamabad (☎ 821114, visa office)

Russia
> Embassy of the PRC, Leninskie Gory, ulitsa Druzhby 6, Moscow

UK
> Embassy of the PRC, 31 Portland Place, London W1N 3AH (☎ (071) 636 1835, 636 9375)
> Consulate, 49 Denison Rd, Rusholme, Manchester MI4 5RX (☎ (061) 224 7478)

USA
> Embassy of the PRC, 2300 Connecticut Ave NW, Washington, DC 20008 (☎ (202) 328-2517)
> Consulate, 104 South Michigan Ave, Suite 1200, Chicago, IL 60603 (☎ (312) 346-0287)
> Consulate, 3417 Montrose Blvd, Houston, TX 77006 (☎ (713) 524-4311)
> Consulate, 502 Shatto Place, Suite 300, Los Angeles, CA 90020 (☎ (213) 380-2507)
> Consulate, 520 12th Ave, New York, NY 10036 (☎ (212) 330-7409)
> Consulate, 1450 Laguna St, San Francisco, CA 94115 (☎ (415) 563-4857)

Pakistan Visa

Everyone from European and English-speaking countries needs a visa to enter Pakistan. With a tourist visa you can enter up to six months from the date of *issue*, and stay for up to three months from the date of *entry*. The visa lets you go almost anywhere except sensitive border areas and remote or high-elevation places where you'd need a trekking or mountaineering permit.

Travellers arriving without a visa may get a Landing Permit (transit visa) good for 72 hours, at no charge – but policies on this change as fast as the weather. Coming from China, that barely gives you time to get to Islamabad and extend it. Immigration officials at Sust can be a bit arbitrary with these.

If you decide while in Pakistan to go up to Kashgar and back, you can get your single-entry visa changed to double-entry at the same Visa Section Office in Islamabad where visas are extended (see Visa Extension or Replacement in this section) and probably for the same fee.

Where to Get It You can apply at any embassy or consulate of Pakistan. From the one in your own country you're more likely to get the full three months (thus avoiding the misery of extending it in Islamabad), and you may have multiple-entry options too. Visas from some consular offices – eg Hong Kong (and reportedly Beijing) – are only valid for three months and good for a one-month stay.

Foreigners' Registration Your visa is just permission to *enter* Pakistan. When you arrive you get permission to stay, and after that permission to leave! This keeps many civil servants employed.

On arrival immigration gives you an entry stamp, and usually a paper called Form C, Temporary Certificate of Registration. If you're staying for 30 days or less on a tourist visa, you just give Form C back when you leave, in exchange for an exit stamp.

If you stay more than 30 days you become a 'resident', and before the 30 days are up you're supposed to register. Most large towns have a foreigners' registration office, usually part of the police office. Bring two passport-size photos and Form C and they give you a Certificate of Registration and a Residential Permit. There is no fee. You turn these in to the foreigners' registration or police office at the last town where you stay the night, and in exchange for an Exit Permit which you show to immigration on departure.

Some officials will tell you to just give the Certificate of Registration and Residential Permit directly to immigration on departure, and another traveller was told British citizens need not register at all because their visa fees are so high! *Don't believe any of it*; failure to go by the rules leaves you open to trouble.

On my first trip I entered at Sust, got no Form C and did nothing. At Karachi Airport two months later I had to write a letter on the spot, saying there'd been a big mistake and could I please be allowed to go. On another trip I took the advice of the Gilgit police and handed immigration my registration and residence papers instead of an Exit Permit. Bags already checked and boarding pass in hand, I was very nearly turned out onto the streets of Karachi at 1 am. You may have similar problems at other departure points.

Travellers coming from China may not get Form C at Sust, but somebody may want to see it later, so ask for one. On the KKH you can easily register at Gilgit, Abbottabad, Rawalpindi or Islamabad.

Some sensitive regions of Pakistan, eg border areas in Azad Jammu & Kashmir and the North-West Frontier Province, have additional registration requirements.

Visa Extension or Replacement Islamabad is the only place to extend your visa or Landing Permit, or deal with an expired visa or lost papers (although if you're somewhere else and time's running out the police might write a letter giving you a few extra days to get to Islamabad or the border). Allow a whole day for the paper chase.

First, try to get a letter from your embassy, or the Ministry of Tourism in Jinnah Market, asking that your stay be extended or papers replaced, and specifying how long you want to stay. (For lost papers you might have to detour after this to the Ministry of the Interior, Block R of the Secretariat.)

Second, go to the Visa Section office of the Directorate of Immigration & Passports, on Khayaban-i-Suhrawardy in Aabpara, above the National Bank. With letters, fee and photocopies of the front pages of your passport, you get a form saying your visa has been granted, extended or replaced. They're open 8.30 am to 2.30 pm in summer, 9 am to 2 pm in winter. At the time of writing this was free for US citizens, Rs 35 for Australians and New Zealanders, Rs 880 for British and Rs 1000 for Canadians. If you dislike handing that much cash to a bureaucrat you can pay National Bank downstairs and they'll give you a voucher for the visa office.

Third, go to the Foreigners' Registration office in the city (Islamabad or Rawalpindi) where your hotel is. With two passport-size photos, the Visa Section's form and the Temporary Certificate of Registration (Form C) you got when you entered Pakistan, they'll give you a Certificate of Registration and a Residence Permit.

Embassies & Consulates of Pakistan

Afghanistan
> Embassy of Pakistan, Shar-e-nau, Kabul (☎ 21374).
> Consulate, Herat Rd, Kandahar (☎ 2452)

Australia & New Zealand
> Pakistan High Commission, 59 Franklin St, PO Box 198, Manuka, Canberra, ACT 2603, Australia (☎ (06) 290 1676).
> Consulate, 500 George St, 11th floor, Sydney, NSW 2000 (☎ (02) 267 7250)

Canada
> Pakistan High Commission, 151 Slater St, Suite 608, Ottawa K1P 5H3 (☎ (613) 238-7881).
> Consulate, 3421 Peel St, Montreal, Quebec H3A 1W7 (☎ (514) 845-2297).
> Consulate, 4881 Yonge St, Suite 810, Willowdale, Toronto, Ontario M2N 5X3 (☎ (416) 250-1255)

China
> Embassy of Pakistan, 1 Dongzhimenwai Dajie, Sanlitun Compound, Beijing (☎ (01) 532-2504). There is no Pakistan consulate in Kashgar

Hong Kong
> Consulate of Pakistan, Suite 3806, China Resources Building, 26 Harbour Rd, Wanchai (☎ 827- 0681)

India
> Pakistan High Commission, 2/50-G Shantipath, Chanakyapuri, New Delhi (☎ 600604)

Iran
> Embassy of Pakistan, Kheyabun-e Doktor Fatemi, 1 Kheyabun-e Shahid Sarhang Ahmad E'temad Zade (☎ 934 331/2). There are also consulates at Zahedan and Mashhad

UK
> Pakistan High Commission, 35 Lowndes Square, London SW1X 9JN (☎ (071) 235 2044)
> Consulate, 45 Cheapside, Bradford BD1 4HP (☎ (0274) 721921)
> There are also Vice Consulates at Birmingham, Glasgow and Manchester

USA
> Embassy of Pakistan, 2315 Massachusetts Ave NW, Washington, DC 20008 (☎ (202) 939-6200), for Washington area only
> Consulate, 12 East 65th St, New York, NY 10021 (☎ (212) 879-5800)

Getting Foreign Visas in Pakistan

You can get foreign visas from embassies in Islamabad, and very occasionally from consulates in other Pakistani cities. Some applicants need a letter from their own embassy; NZ passport holders should get this from the British High Commission.

India A three-month, single-entry visa can be obtained from the visa office in Islamabad (☎ 814371/5, ext 240) at the back of the Indian Embassy, open from 9.30 to 11 am and closed Friday. British and Australian nationals need a letter from their embassy. When Pakistan-India tension is high they drag their feet; at the time of writing they were saying 'minimum 10 days' to get one, though travellers said up to a month. The fee was Rs 1250 for everybody. You need two passport-size photos.

China A one-month, single-entry Chinese visa takes three or four working days. The embassy's visa office is open from 9 am to noon, except Fridays and major Chinese holidays. Fees at the time of writing were Rs 250 for US passport holders, Rs 300 NZ, Rs 550 Australia, Rs 800 UK and Rs 1000 Canada. Bring two passport-size photos. British (at least) reportedly also need a letter from their embassy, who charge Rs 200 for it.

Iran Transit visas are valid for two weeks, and tourist visas for a month; both can be extended inside Iran. Bring up to three passport-size photos. An invitation (approved by the Ministry of Foreign Affairs in Tehran) from sponsors in Iran is a big help. You'll probably also need a letter from your own embassy. A reply from Tehran is possible in two weeks, but may take three months or more. Costs vary according to your nationality and the type of visa, from nothing for Australians to a lot for Britons. Modest dress will give a good first impression and may help your prospects.

Afghanistan At the time of writing the old communist government had fallen, but nobody was yet issuing tourist visas! But business and press visas were being issued straightforwardly within a few days after reference to Kabul.

Crossing the Khunjerab Pass
The Khunjerab Pass is formally open to travellers from 1 May to 30 November, but it may open later or close sooner on account of weather. This is only decided at the last possible moment. The only people who know when this will be are senior immigration or transportation officials near the border, and only within a week or so of the date. In the past it has tended to open on time and close early, around the middle of November.

It stays open year round for traders, officials and postal service. Pakistan immigration officials at Sust say off the record that they'd let you in or out at any time, but Chinese officials almost certainly wouldn't. There is no longer any such thing as a special permit to cross the Khunjerab Pass.

CUSTOMS & IMMIGRATION
Following are normal entry and exit formalities. For more on KKH border-posts, see the Khunjerab Pass chapter.

China
Arrival At immigration, fill out a health form and an entry-exit card; passports are inspected and stamped. China won't issue transit visas on the spot. At customs, fill out a form declaring money, cameras, radios and so on; you get a copy, which you must present on departure. Baggage inspection is usually cursory for foreigners but they like to see your high-tech stuff.

Departure At customs you turn in the declaration you filled out when you entered, and they may want to see listed items again.

You're not allowed to take out antiquities; purchase receipts can save arguments. At immigration, turn in the entry- exit card you got when you arrived (if you don't have one you may have to pay Y1 for another), and get an exit stamp.

If you're taking the bus from Kashgar to Pakistan, anything you don't carry on board will be customs-inspected at Kashgar and locked on the top of the bus, inaccessible for the whole journey. Carry-ons are inspected at Pirali; be sure to carry with you anything you declared when you entered China, such as electronic gear.

Pakistan

Arrival At immigration, fill out a health form and an entry-exit card. They give you an entry stamp and (at most ports of entry) a Temporary Certificate of Registration (Form C). If you don't have a visa they may give you a landing permit free of charge, good for 72 hours, which you must extend in Islamabad.

At customs they ask if you're bringing in liquor (you're not supposed to). Unless you're here to hunt, you can't bring in firearms. There are no other significant restrictions. If before entering you swapped other currencies for large amounts of Pakistani rupees, keep them out of sight.

Departure Baggage inspection is usually cursory for foreigners unless you have obvious items like furniture, in which case you may be asked for sales receipts and bank encashment receipts. You'll need an export permit for carpets (see the following). You may not export antiquities; if in doubt about something, ask a museum curator or top-end hotel shopkeeper who deals in it. Airport security staff may confiscate batteries from cameras, walkmans, etc, so put these in your checked baggage.

At immigration you present your entry-exit card, turn in your Form C (or if you stayed more than 30 days, your Exit Permit; see Visas & Embassies in this chapter) and get an exit stamp.

Export Permits An export permit is necessary to *post* out any purchase whose declared value is over Rs 500. You also need one to *carry* out carpets; carpet dealers may help you with this. Getting one on your own is a headache, though PTDC or your hotel-wallah might smooth the way. To the export office in Islamabad or other big city you must bring purchase receipt, encashment receipts to at least the value of the purchase, an explanatory letter from you to the Controller (Import & Export), plus photocopies of these and of the front pages of your passport.

MONEY
Chinese Money

The formal unit of Chinese money is the *yuan* (Y), divided into 10 *jiao* or 100 *fen*. But when talking prices in Chinese, yuan is called *kuai (koi* in Uyghur), jiao is called *mao (mo* in Uyghur) and fen is still *fen* (pronounced 'fun').

There are two parallel currencies: *renminbi* (RMB) or people's money, and Foreign Exchange Certificates (FEC) or tourist money *(wai hui*, 'wye-hway' in Chinese). FEC is meant to be the basis for a separate visitors' economy, but the distinction has faded and the system is a black-marketeer's dream.

RMB comes in paper notes down to 1 fen (5 fen is a green boat, 2 fen a blue aeroplane, 1 fen a yellow truck) and aluminium coins for 5, 2 and 1 fen. FEC comes in notes only, down to 1 jiao.

In Kashgar, CITS, CAAC, hotels and the bus station demand FEC. Restaurants and other non-tourist places may accept RMB. It's not illegal for you to have RMB, only to get it on the black market. You often get RMB change when you tender FEC (a loss of purchasing power, and a good reason to avoid carrying large-denomination FEC notes).

Pakistani Money

The unit of Pakistani money is the *rupee* (R), divided into 100 *paisa*. Paper notes come in denominations down to one rupee and there are one-rupee and half-rupee coins (and a few 25 and 10 paisa coins). Try to avoid change in very worn or tattered notes as these may be refused later by others.

Foreign Exchange

In China you must go to the Bank of China; there's a branch in Kashgar. In Pakistan you can exchange at half a dozen domestic banks, the most competent being National Bank of Pakistan. In Rawalpindi and Islamabad you can also go to top-end hotels and to some foreign banks including Grindlays, Bank of America, Citibank and American Express.

US dollar cash and travellers' cheques are

by far the easiest to cash, followed by British pounds. The bank at Sust accepts only US dollars. In Kashgar and the Northern Areas, cash dollars are very welcome and can be exchanged unofficially when nothing else can (usually at elevated rates), making them good emergency money. Some banks accept other Western currencies.

Pakistani banks in remoter places may refuse to accept travellers' cheques early in the day, until someone can be roused to telex the main office for that day's rates, but cash is rarely a problem. American Express cheques can, if lost, be replaced at their offices in Islamabad, Rawalpindi, Lahore and Karachi.

Reconversion When you leave China you can change FEC (but usually not RMB) back to hard currency, though you're supposed to show exchange receipts. With receipts you can also reconvert FEC at the Bank of China in Hong Kong.

Unspent rupees can be reconverted by some Pakistani branch banks, including all those at customs and immigration posts. Old regulations say you can't sell back more than Rs 500 but I've never had trouble with much more, up to the total value of my encashment receipts.

Reconvert before immigration as there's no bank on the other side. Save some rupees for international departure tax (Rs 480 on economy tickets bought in Pakistan, Rs 200 on those bought elsewhere).

Exchange Rates
Approximate exchange rates at the time of writing were as follows (Chinese rates are the same everywhere, Pakistani rates aren't):

US$1	= Y5.7 FEC	= Rs 26
UK£1	= Y8.2 FEC	= Rs 37
A$1	= Y3.8 FEC	= Rs 17
C$1	= Y4.5 FEC	= Rs 21

Save your encashment (exchange) receipts in China to avoid a scene at customs. In Pakistan you might need them to reconvert your rupees;

they also come in handy for air ticket purchases, export permits, etc. To be of any use they must have the amounts in both currencies, the exchange rate, an official signature and the bank's stamp.

You can't officially trade yuan in Pakistan or rupees in China. At the China-Pakistan border you're normally given US dollars which you change again on the other side.

The Black Market
In China, because FEC gives access to foreign goods and currency, local people will trade X yuan of your FEC for more than X yuan of their RMB, despite some risk of punishment. In Kashgar it's a Uyghur business, and they trade US and Hong Kong dollars too. For tips on avoiding rip-offs, see Kashgar – Information. Kashgar rates at the time of writing were nearly 1-to-1 and hardly worth the bother.

In Pakistan some shopkeepers will buy US dollars at slightly elevated rates, but it hardly deserves to be called a black market.

Credit Cards & Money from Home
Credit cards aren't widely accepted for purchases except at top-end hotels and shops in Rawalpindi and Islamabad, but you can get cash with a major card at Western banks in Rawalpindi and Islamabad and at Bank of China in Kashgar and Ürümqi. They usually need a day, charge a fee for an international telex to verify the card, and may have upper limits on how much you can get. American Express readily accepts their own cards for cash or travellers' cheques; cardholders can also cash personal cheques.

Failing that, banks suggest a telex or telegraphic transfer of funds from your home bank, which takes about a week – though it's simpler to have someone post a bank draft by express registered mail to you at a reliable address, eg your embassy.

Costs
With modest self-control you can spend three weeks on the KKH for US$10 to US$15 a day. This includes a total ground transport cost (Kashgar to Rawalpindi) of as

little as US$35, daily per-person accommodation (double rooms) of US$3 to US$5 and about US$4 each for food. This means staying in lower-cost hotels, eating local food and travelling by bus.

You can of course do better by staying in dorms or a tent, self-catering, and hitch-hiking. Rooms and food are cheaper in the north, dearer toward Rawalpindi. Bargaining is appropriate in bazaars and sometimes works in bottom-end Pakistani hotels.

Overland travel between Kashgar and Hong Kong adds at least US$180 plus accommodation and food; or by air, about US$400. An overnight train journey with sleeping berth between Rawalpindi and Karachi adds about US$15; by air it's about US$85 (or US$65 by 'Night-Coach'). See the Getting There & Away chapter for more on links to/from Kashgar and Islamabad.

At the time of writing, inflation was high in China so prices in this book will go out of date quickly, though not so quickly for Pakistan.

Tipping

If you're flush enough to tip, you'll find it expected (around 10%) in top-end hotels and restaurants, appreciated in mid-range places in Rawalpindi, Abbottabad and Gilgit, and possibly returned in rural areas where it runs counter to the Islamic obligation to be hospitable.

Baksheesh is a way of life in Pakistan. It doesn't just mean a hand-out or bribe, but any gratuity for services rendered. Lower-echelon staff who depart even minutely from normal routine – opening a closed gate, getting a bigwig's signature, fixing a broken tap – may expect something for it, and a bit here and there goes a long way when it's deserved.

Resist the temptation to see those who ask for it as beggars. It's part of the Islamic code that better-off people give part of their income to the less well-off. Pakistan has relatively few 'career' beggars.

WHEN TO GO

Assuming you like sunshine and moderate temperatures, the best time to travel the KKH is September-October, and a south-bound journey will stretch out the good weather. Mountain cold and lowland heat are both quite bearable at this time. Mountain roads are in decent condition. Fresh vegetables and fruit are still plentiful. Since most tourists have gone home, hotels may lower their rates. The next-best time is May-June, and a north-bound trip will prolong the pleasure.

Summer is ferociously hot and dry in Kashgar, pleasantly warm and occasionally stormy in Gojal and Hunza, very hot and rainy from Kohistan south. From Kashgar to Gilgit, winter is long and cold (often well below freezing), with snow common in the mountains. Kashgar can be unpleasant from mid-October, when wet cold sets in, to mid-November, when winter officially arrives and the heat is turned on. The Khunjerab Pass is formally open to travellers from 1 May to 30 November; it tends to open on time but close early, around mid-November, because of snow. See the Facts about the Region chapter for more about the climate.

Another consideration is that the KKH from Gilgit south can be difficult during Ramadan, the Muslim month of day-time fasting. People are irritable and food can be hard to find until sunset except in Ismaili areas (north of Gilgit) or at tourist hotels – though one traveller reported a strong atmosphere of camaraderie (shared suffering?) at this time. The dates change each year; see Holidays & Festivals in the Facts for the Visitor chapter.

WHAT TO BRING

Of course, bring as little as you can. You can pick up many items in Kashgar, Gilgit or Rawalpindi. It's cheap to have clothes and sleeping sheets made in Pakistani bazaars; you can even get your Western clothes copied. You can usually find toilet paper, candles, matches, batteries (but not as good as those from home), laundry soap, toothbrushes, old-style razor blades, shampoo, aspirin and instant coffee.

For putting it all in, an internal-frame or soft pack is most manageable on buses; a 'convertible' (with a handle, and a flap to hide the straps) looks respectable when you want to.

Clothing

For the range of KKH conditions and the potential for cold-weather exertion, many light layers work better than a few heavy ones. On the China-Pakistan bus you'll need your warmest clothing in any season. Rain can strike in Pakistan at any time but especially July and August.

Clothing has powerful social overtones in Islamic countries, and nowhere have more Westerners offended more Asians without knowing it than in this matter. To a devout Muslim, clothes that reveal flesh (other than face, hands and feet) or the shape of the body look ridiculous on men, and scandalous on women. Shorts and halter-tops are especially offensive. For women visitors this is not only an elementary courtesy but may also reduce hostility or harassment.

This doesn't mean you have to wear a choir-robe – just long, loose, non-revealing shirts, trousers or skirts (which are in any case the most comfortable in summer). For women a light scarf over the hair is also appropriate when visiting homes. The local baggy trousers and long shirt (shalwar qamiz) are very comfortable and can be made cheaply in the bazaar. In big cities conservative Western dress is common.

Shoes

Light walking shoes are adequate for all but long or snowy treks. You could get away with gym shoes except at monsoon time. Sandals are a relief in warm, dry weather.

Camping Gear

For one-off trips you can find tents, pads and cooking equipment in Gilgit and Skardu. Sleeping bags are hard to find. You can find basic food for camping but you might want to bring some favourite dried foods like soup mixes, etc. Serious trekkers will have their own detailed equipment list.

Gifts

Some portable but well-received gifts are postcards and flower and vegetable seeds from home, and family photos.

Miscellaneous

Besides the usual take-alongs, good KKH ideas are eating utensils, water bottle, sunglasses, sunscreen, lip salve, sun-hat, a light day-pack, pen-knife, thermal long-johns, shower flip-flops and a compass. A torch is welcome in places with dodgy or nonexistent electricity. A universal sink plug is very handy: Islamic custom favours washing in running water so lower-end hotels rarely have plugs. Hotels tend not to give you towels, either. Other ideas are a length of cord as a washing-line, stuff-sacks or plastic bags, and a small sewing kit.

Seasoned travellers will already have a secure passport-and-money pouch. Half a dozen passport-size photos will save you trouble in case of paperwork, though it's possible to get them en route. Photocopies of the first few pages of your passport will ease the headaches if you lose it.

Women should buy tampons before coming to Pakistan, though you can find them in up-market shopping areas of Islamabad. Chinese department stores, including those in Kashgar, have sanitary towels.

For a suggested medical kit see Health on page 51. For photography pre-requisites see Film & Photography on pages 49-50.

TOURIST OFFICES
China International Travel Service

CITS (Lüxingshe in Chinese) is the government travel bureau that handles non-Chinese group tourists. CITS has some 200 offices within China, but they're generally less than thrilled about helping budget travellers who've come on their own. They'll book hotels, transport, tours and tickets, but at high group rates and usually with a service charge.

CITS in Kashgar rents jeeps, and their package trips are the only convenient or legal way to get to some remote areas. The Uyghur staff there are friendly sources of local information.

Head Office
  6 East Chang'an Ave, Beijing (☎ 512-1122)
Ürümqi
  72 Heping North Rd (☎ 27467)
Kashgar
  Chini Bagh Hotel
Hong Kong
  Main Office, 6th floor, Tower II, South Seas Centre, 75 Mody Rd, Tsimshatsui, Kowloon (☎ 732-5888)
  Central Branch, Room 1018, Swire House, 11 Chater Rd, Central (☎ 810-4282)
USA
  Suite 465, 60 East 42nd St, New York, NY 10165 (☎ (212) 867-0271)

China Travel Service
CTS originally looked after Chinese 'compatriots' from Hong Kong, Macau and overseas with cheaper hotels, lower fares, etc. Now they're after the non-Chinese market too. Standards are more modest than at CITS but fees are lower and you're more likely to get cheap bookings. In Hong Kong, CTS is the clear choice over CITS for individual travellers. They have perhaps 350 offices inside China, but the nearest one to the KKH is in Ürümqi.

Head Office
  8 Dongjiaominxiang, Beijing (☎ 512-9933)
Ürümqi
  51 Xinhua South Rd (☎ 28833)
Australia
  757-759 George St, Ground floor, Sydney, NSW 2000 (☎ (02) 211 2633)
Canada
  556 West Broadway, Vancouver, BC V5Z 1E9 (☎ (604) 872-8787)
Hong Kong
  Foreign Passenger Dept, 78 Connaught Rd, Central (☎ 853-3533)
  Central Branch, 77 Queen's Rd, Central (☎ 525-2284)
  Kowloon Branch, 27 Nathan Rd, Tsimshatsui (☎ 721- 1331)
UK
  24 Cambridge Circus, London WC2H 8HD (☎ (071) 836 9911)

USA
  Main Office, 212 Sutter St, 2nd floor, San Francisco, CA 94108 (☎ (415) 398-6627)
  Los Angeles Branch, 223-E Garvey Ave, Suite 138, Monterey Park, CA 91754 (☎ (818) 288-8222)

China National Tourism Office
CNTO is purely promotional but can refer you to local travel agents who co-operate with CITS or CTS.

Australia
  55 Clarence St, 11th floor, Sydney, NSW 2000 (☎ (02) 29 4057)
USA
  New York office, 60 East 42nd St, Suite 3126, New York, NY 10165 (☎ (212) 867-0271)
  Los Angeles Office, 333 West Broadway, Suite 201, Glendale, CA 91204 (☎ (818) 545-7505)
UK
  4 Glentworth St, London NW1 (☎ (071) 935 9427/9)

Xinjiang Tourist Corporation
This regional tourism office offers some interesting group-tour packages in the Kashgar region.

Ürümqi Office
  32 Xinhua South Rd (☎ & fax 78691; telex 79027 XJTC CN)

China Mountaineering Association
The Xinjiang branch of the CMA can arrange trekking and other group sports trips in the Kashgar region, and the Kashgar branch can also give on-the-spot help with guides, transport and equipment. For addresses see Trekking & Other Sports in this chapter.

Pakistan Tourism Development Corporation
PTDC is the promotional arm of the Tourism Division, Pakistan Ministry of Culture, Sports & Tourism. They run a string of up-market motels and maintain Tourist Information Centres in several towns, with brochures, advice and sometimes jeeps to hire. Some regional centres are managed by surprisingly intelligent and helpful people. PTDC's group-tour affiliate is Pakistan Tours Ltd (PTL).

Head Office
    No 2, St 61, F-7/4, Islamabad (☎ 828814)
PTL
    Flashman's Hotel, The Mall, Rawalpindi
    (☎ 564811, 565449)

Tourist information centres near the KKH include:

Abbottabad
    Club Annexe, Jinnah Rd (☎ 4946)
Balakot
    PTDC Motel (☎ 8)
Besham
    PTDC Motel (☎ 92)
Gilgit
    Chinar Inn, Babar Rd (☎ 2562)
Islamabad
    Tourism Division, 13-T/U College Rd, F-7/2
    (☎ 816932); 52 Nazimuddin Rd, F-7/4
    (☎ 816815)
Naran
    PTDC Motel
Rawalpindi
    Flashman's Hotel, The Mall (☎ 581480)
Saidu Sharif
    Swat Serena Hotel (☎ 5007)
Skardu
    K2 Motel (☎ 104)
Taxila
    PTDC Motel, Museum Rd (☎ 2344)

Overseas PTDC offices include:

Canada
    Suite 202, 2678 West Broadway, Vancouver,
    British Columbia V6K 2G3 (☎ (604) 732-4686)
UK
    Suite 433, 52-54 High Holborn, London WC1V
    6RL (☎ (071) 242 3131)

Tourism Development Corporation of the Punjab

This provincial tourism office has a few brochures and maps of the Punjab, and runs comfortable buses between Rawalpindi, Lahore and Murree. In Murree they're much more helpful than PTDC.

Lahore
    4-A Lawrence Rd (☎ 869216)
Murree
    Cart Rd (☎ 2729); The Mall (☎ 2730)
Rawalpindi
    44 Mall Plaza, corner of The Mall and Kashmir
    Rd (☎ 564824)

TREKKING & OTHER SPORTS
Trekking in China

The Xinjiang Mountaineering Association, a branch of the China Mountaineering Association, used to concern itself only with expeditions but now handles trekking and other group sports (eg white-water boating, mountain biking, camel and horse safaris) as well. They, and the Kashgar branch, can also help with the hiring of guides, transport or equipment, with a few days' notice.

Chinese Mountaineering Association
    c/o All-China Sports Federation, Tiyu Guan Rd,
    Beijing
Xinjiang Mountaineering Association
    1 Renmin Lu, Ürümqi 830002 (☎ (0991)
    227882, 217776; fax 218365; telex 79064
    CXMA CN), attention Mr Jing Ying Jie
Kashgar Mountaineering Association
    8 Tiyu Lu (off Jiefang Nan Lu), Kashgar 844000
    (☎ 22957; telex 79123 KSBTH CN), attention
    Mr Arslan Yusup

Trekking in Pakistan
Regulations For trekking, the Pakistan Ministry of Culture, Sports & Tourism has designated open, restricted and closed zones. Treks in open zones are well removed from sensitive areas. They need no permits and get no official support; routes and arrangements, and guides if you want them, are up to you.

Restricted zones include sensitive areas and anything above 6000 metres. Travel there requires more planning and is expensive and full of red tape; you need a Ministry permit and a government-approved guide or liaison officer. Permit conditions include per-head fees; a detailed application; official requirements for insurance, wages, equipment, food and transport for guides and porters; and meetings with tourism officials in Islamabad before and after the trek.

An easy (but not cheap) way to obtain a permit is through a trekking agency. Getting a permit on your own involves minimal fees but lots of time; figure on a minimum of two months.

A booklet setting out regulations, permit procedures, recommended agencies and a more or less current list of 'approved' treks is *Trekking Rules and Regulations*, available from Mr Zafarullah Siddiqui, Deputy Chief for Operations, Tourism Division (☎ 82 0856), College Rd, Sector F-7/2, Islamabad (if you're calling by, this is in the central area of Jinnah Market).

At present, the Ministry has a coordination officer based in Skardu with the authority to arrange services and issue permits for treks in Baltistan only, given two to three months' lead time. Contact Mr Aqil (☎ 946) Coordination Officer, Ministry of Tourism, K2 Motel, Skardu, Northern Areas (except for two months in winter when he is at House 551, Street 53, Sector G-9/1, Islamabad).

Where to Go Along the KKH, open trekking zones are in *certain* parts of Shimshal and the Batura Muztagh (the crest zone in Hunza-Gojal); Hopar, Hispar, the north side of Rakaposhi and Chalt-Chaprot (Nagar); Naltar, Ishkoman, Yasin, Bagrot and Haramosh (Gilgit area); across the Shandur Pass into Swat and Chitral; the Skardu area; Nanga Parbat; and the Kaghan Valley.

The short trips noted in the regional chapters are all in open zones. The popular big treks are described in detail in LP's *Pakistan – a travel survival kit*, and listed in the Tourism Division's booklet and in brochures from PTDC. A first-rate source of information (as well as anecdotes) on trekking in Pakistan is the late Hugh Swift's *Trekking in Pakistan and India* (Hodder & Stoughton, 1990).

Equipment It's best to bring your own. Trekking equipment is not manufactured in Pakistan, and the most you can hire or buy are the bits left behind by expeditions. Guides, agencies and a few shops in Gilgit and Skardu may have tents, sleeping pads, stoves and mountaineering gear. Sleeping bags are scarce.

Guides, Porters & Other Help For short trips in open zones you probably won't need any help, though a local shepherd with a little English, or a student home for the holidays, might be content with Rs 150 to Rs 250 a day

for trail finding and possibly some carrying and cooking.

A week-long open-zone trek for two people carrying their own packs, sharing one porter, using public transport to/from trailheads, buying their food locally and cooking it themselves could cost as little as US$10 (about Rs 250) per person per day. But hiring help can be a tricky business. Reasonable daily wages (including food) at the time of writing were Rs 300 to Rs 400 for an experienced guide, Rs 150 to Rs 200 per porter, and about Rs 200 for a cook.

Agencies in Gilgit and Skardu have English-speaking guides with enough experience and reliability for modest treks, though they won't necessarily be from the area. Local agencies typically charge US$40 to US$80 (Rs 1000 to Rs 2000) per person per day for trailhead transport, food, equipment rental, porters and/or guides, and any permits. Group travel organised by an overseas company is about US$100 to US$150 per person per day (excluding the cost of getting to/from Pakistan).

Trekking Alone Some people who've trekked alone don't recommend it. Villagers in remote areas can be suspicious of solo foreigners and may be tempted to take advantage of them. You may be driven mad by children demanding sweets, pens or money; some may even throw stones if you refuse.

Other Sports
Some agencies noted here offer packages for fishing trips, yak or pony treks, jeep safaris or bicycle trips. A few can provide support for white-water boating. River stretches open for rafting or kayaking include the Hunza from Aliabad to Gilgit, the Indus from Jaglot to Thakot, the Swat from Bahrain to Saidu Sharif and the Kunhar (Kaghan Valley) from Naran to Kaghan.

Trekking & Tour Agencies in Pakistan
The Adventure Foundation was started to promote special-skills training and Outward-Bound-style adventures for young

Pakistanis. Though not a tour agency, they will now arrange small-group mountaineering, trekking, white-water boating, winter skiing and even hot-air ballooning trips for anyone able to contact them well in advance (say six months). They are at No 1 Gulistan Colony, College Rd, Abbottabad (☎ (05921) 5526).

The following reputable agencies can help you with your own plans or sell you packages for KKH trips, general or special-interest tours, and treks. The largest ones, Adventure Pakistan and Sitara, work mostly as ground agents for overseas companies and may be reluctant to deal with small groups. Also listed are some reliable private guides.

Adventure Centre (☎ (0572) 2409; telex BEGSONS PK), Shahrah-i-Quaid-i-Azam, PO Box 516, Gilgit

Adventure Pakistan (Travel Walji's Ltd) (☎ (051) 812151, 823963; fax 823109; telex 5769 or 5836 WALJI PK), 10 Khayaban-i-Suhrawardy, PO Box 1088, Islamabad

Adventure Tours Pakistan (☎ (051) 852505), House 447, Street 51, G-9/1, PO Box 1780, Islamabad

Adventure Travel (☎ (051) 819727), 15 Wali Centre, 86 South Blue Area, Islamabad

Ali, Qurban, Mountain Guide, PO Box 519, Gilgit

Baig, Hunar, Mountain Guide, Village Passu, Gojal Hunza, Gilgit

Bashir, Mohammad, Mountain Guide, c/o Alim Shopkeeper, Shinkiari, District Mansehra

Concordia Trekking Services (☎ (0575) 3440, 2707; cable KESAR), PO Box 626, Skardu

Himalaya Nature Tours (☎ (0572) 2946), Chinar Bagh Link Rd, Gilgit

Hindukush Trails (☎ (0533) 581 or 781), Mountain Inn, Chitral

Hussain, Iftikhar, Mountain Guide, Ganesh, Hunza

Indus Guides (☎ (042) 304190), 7-E Egerton Rd, Lahore

Karakoram Tours (☎ (051) 829120), 1 Baltoro House, Street 19, F-7/2, Islamabad

Nazir Sabir Expeditions (☎ (051) 853672; telex 5811 NAIBA PK), PO Box 1442, Islamabad

Pakistan Express (☎ (0521) 74631), 21I, The Mall, Peshawar

Pakistan Tours Ltd (an affiliate of PTDC) (☎ (051) 564811, 565449), Flashman's Hotel, The Mall, Rawalpindi

Pamir Tours (☎ (0572) 3939; fax 2525), JSR Plaza, PO Box 545, Gilgit

Panorama Travels & Tours (☎ (051) 815266, 817424; fax 822313), 8 Safdar Mansion, Blue Area, PO Box 1064, Islamabad

Sitara Travel Consultants (☎ (051) 564750, 566272; fax 568105), 163-A Bank Rd, PO Box 63, Rawalpindi

Trans-Pakistan Adventure Services (☎ (051) 819579; fax 822313; telex 5945), PO Box 2103, 8 Muzaffar Chambers, Unit 82, West Blue Area, Islamabad

Overseas Trekking & Tour Agencies

Following are some of the bigger overseas agents with packages for multi-week KKH trips, general and special-interest tours and treks in China or Pakistan.

Encounter Overland (☎ (071) 370 6845; fax 244 9737), 267 Old Brompton Rd, London SW5 9JA, UK. Truck/bus safaris

Exodus Expeditions (☎ (081) 675 5550; fax 673 0779), 9 Weir Rd, London SW12 0LT, UK

Explore Worldwide (☎ (0252) 344161; fax 343170), 1 Frederick St, Aldershot, Hants GU11 1LQ, UK

Hann Overland (☎ (0883) 744705; fax 744706), 2 Ivy Mill Lane, Godstone, Surrey RH9 8NH, UK. Truck/bus safaris

InnerAsia Expeditions (☎ (415) 922-0448; fax 346-5535), 2627 Lombard St, San Francisco, CA 94123, USA

Karakoram Experience (☎ (07687) 73966, 72267; fax 74693), 32 Lake Rd, Keswick, Cumbria CA12 5DQ, UK. Specialists in Karakoram treks

Mountain Travel (☎ (415) 527-8100; fax 525-7710), 6420 Fairmount Ave, El Cerrito, CA 94530, USA

Wilderness Travel (☎ (415) 548-0420; fax 548-0347), 801 Allston Way, Berkeley, CA 94710, USA

World Expeditions (☎ (0753) 581808, fax 581809), 101c Slough Rd, Datchet, Berkshire SL3 9AQ, UK

BUSINESS HOURS

In Pakistan nearly everything official is closed on Friday, the Muslim day of rest, and often for a half-day on Thursday or Saturday. In Xinjiang the Chinese-imposed day of rest is Sunday; a few offices may take a half-day off on Saturday. Business hours are variable and are listed under individual towns.

HOLIDAYS & FESTIVALS
National Holidays

Banks, businesses and government offices are closed in China or Pakistan.

1 January (China)
New Year's Day
Late January-Early March (China)
Spring Festival or Chinese New Year. For the Chinese this is the biggest holiday of the year, their only three-day break. It's calculated on the Chinese lunar calendar so dates change from year to year. The Chinese embassy in Islamabad is also closed.
23 March (Pakistan)
Pakistan Day, celebrating the 1940 demand by the All-India Muslim League for an independent Muslim state (or the 1956 proclamation of Pakistan as a republic).
1 May (China & Pakistan)
International Labour Day
1 July (Pakistan)
Bank holiday; government offices and businesses remain open.
14 August (Pakistan)
Independence Day, the anniversary of the founding of Pakistan with the Partition of India in 1947. The real Northern Areas celebrations, however, are on 1 November.
6 September (Pakistan)
Defence of Pakistan Day, commemorating the India-Pakistan War of 1965.
11 September (Pakistan)
Anniversary of the death of Mohammed Ali Jinnah, regarded as the founder of Pakistan.
1 October (China)
National Day, celebrating the founding of the People's Republic of China in 1949; in Xinjiang, just a day or two off work.
9 November (Pakistan)
Iqbal Day, honouring the poet Mohammed Iqbal, who in 1930 first proposed the idea of a Muslim Pakistan.
25 December (Pakistan)
Birthday of Mohammed Ali Jinnah, founder of Pakistan.
31 December (Pakistan)
Bank holiday; government offices and businesses remain open.

Muslim Holy Days

The Islamic calendar is lunar. It's shorter than the Western solar calendar, beginning 10 to 11 days earlier in each solar year. Modern astronomy notwithstanding, religious officials have formal authority to declare the beginning of each lunar month, based on sightings of the moon's first crescent. Future holy days can be estimated, but are in doubt by a few days until the start of that month, so dates given here are only approximate.

These holy days are observed in Pakistan, and in a low-key way in Xinjiang; those marked with a (*) are also public holidays in Pakistan. They normally run from sunset to the next sunset. As a result of differences in official moon sightings, they may be celebrated on different days by Sunnis and Shias, which has led to sectarian tension in the past.

* 12 February to 15 March (1994), 1 February to 4 March (1995), 22 January to 22 Feb (1996)
Ramadan, the month of sunrise-to-sunset fasting (see Religion in the Facts about the Region chapter for more information).
* 15 March (1994), 4 March (1995), 22 Feb (1996)
Eid-ul-Fitr (also *Chhoti Eid* or Small Eid in Pakistan, *Ruza Eid* in Xinjiang), two or three days of celebrations at the end of Ramadan. This may be the closest thing to Christmas in the Islamic world, with family visits, gifts, banquets, bonuses at work, donations to the poor. You'd be pretty happy too, if you'd just finished fasting for a month.
* 2 June (1993), 22 May (1994), 11 May (1995), 30 April (1996)
Eid-ul-Azha (also *Bari Eid* or Big Eid in Pakistan, *Kurban* in Xinjiang), the Feast of Sacrifice. Those who can afford it buy and slaughter an animal, sharing the meat with relatives and with the poor. For the rich it's one-upmanship time. In Xinjiang, Uyghur men may gather to dance the *sama* to hypnotic drumbeats. This is also the season for *hajj* (pilgrimage to Mecca).
* 1 July (1993), 20 June (1994), 9 June (1995), 29 May (1996)
Ashura, 10th day of the month of Muharram. Shias begin 40 days of mourning the death of Hussain at Karbala. In trance-like processions, led by a riderless white horse, men and boys pound their chests and chant the names of those killed at Karbala; some practise *zuljinnah*, flailing their backs with blade-tipped chains. It's an awesome and bloody spectacle, not for the squeamish. Sunnis mourn Hussain's death in less dramatic ways. In the Northern Areas, Sunni-Shia tension is high. Police may keep foreigners away from the procession in Gilgit, and visitors are not welcome in the Shia villages of Nagar.
* 10 Aug (1993), 30 July (1994), 19 July (1995), 8 July (1996)
Chhelum, 40 days after Ashura, sometimes with similar but smaller processions.
* 31 August (1993), 20 August (1994), 10 August (1995), 29 July (1996)
Eid-Milad-un-Nabi, the Prophet's birthday.

Seasonal Celebrations

These are associated with planting, harvesting, annual migrations or local traditions. The most visible ones are noted here; others are listed in the local chapters.

Late February-Early March

First (Wheat) Ploughing or Sowing. Called *Taghun* in Gojal and *Bo Pho* in Hunza and Nagar, this is now only celebrated privately by a few farmers in the Northern Areas, usually with food and prayers in the field. Some plough in November-December and celebrate then.

21 March

Nauroz ('New Days'), a spring festival and a Shia celebration of the succession of the Prophet's son-in-law Ali. Polo matches may be held in Gilgit; in smaller Northern Areas villages there is visiting, sometimes music and dancing.

Late June-Early July

First (Wheat) Harvest. This is called *Chinir* in Gojal and *Ginani* or *Ganoni* in Hunza and Nagar, and is similar to First Sowing.

Other Festivals

April

Polo matches are common in Gilgit

July or early August

Polo on the Shandur Pass, between Gilgit and Chitral: a four-day jamboree with dynamite polo, folk dancing and high-jinks. Dates are set only a month or so ahead, though the Ministry of Tourism wants to fix it at the end of June and tart it up for tour groups.

1 November

Northern Areas Independence Day or *Jashan-i-Gilgit* ('Gilgit Festival'), commemorating the 1947 uprising against the Maharajah of Kashmir after he decided to join India. The major event is a week-long polo tournament in Gilgit, starting on the 1st.

Weekly Holidays

The Muslim day of rest is Friday; banks, businesses and government offices throughout the KKH region are closed, and Thursday or Saturday is often a half-day as well.

POST & TELECOMMUNICATIONS

Post

Receiving Mail International service is slow but fairly dependable for letters to Kashgar, Gilgit, Rawalpindi and Islamabad, and to smaller towns if the address is well known.

Parcels – especially books or magazines – are less likely to make it.

Big-town GPOs will hold letters at poste restante for months, and the Kashgar GPO has even returned unclaimed mail. Kashgar charges Y1 per letter picked up. American Express card and travellers' cheque holders can have letters (but not registered ones, nor parcels) held for up to a month at American Express offices in Islamabad or Rawalpindi. In China where family names come first – and even in Pakistan – check under your given name too.

Sending Mail International service is good for letters and parcels from Kashgar, Gilgit, Rawalpindi and Islamabad. They're usually happy to frank letters on the spot, eliminating the risk of stamp theft.

Except for printed matter, outgoing parcels generally must be sewn into cloth bags in both countries – a tedious job, though it probably helps them survive the trip. All require customs declaration forms and an inspection, so leave the bag open when you take it in, and finish the job there. Getting an

overseas parcel on its way can take up to half a day at the post office.

Avoid posting out any purchase with a declared value of over Rs 500 from Pakistan, as you'll need an export permit, which is a headache to get (see Customs & Immigration in this chapter).

Services & Rates – China You can buy stamps with RMB. Overseas airmail letters up to 10 grams are Y2 (except Y0.55 to Hong Kong). Airmail postcards are Y1.60 and aerogrammes are Y1.90. Parcels under one kg can go at lower 'small packet' rates, up to Y23.90 for ½ kg to one kg by surface mail, plus Y0.50 per 10 grams for airmail. Rates for parcels over one kg depend on the country of destination. Registration is Y3 extra.

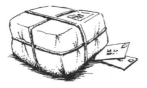

Services & Rates – Pakistan Overseas airmail letters up to 10 grams are Rs 6 to Europe, and Rs 7 to North America, Australia and New Zealand; airmail postcards are Rs 4 and Rs 4.50, and aerogrammes are Rs 5. The cheapest parcels are printed matter by surface mail, from about Rs 15 for up to one kg to a limit of Rs 55 for five kg; these must be left unsealed and marked 'book post'. Other parcels are more expensive, eg Rs 200 to Rs 330 for five kg by surface mail. Registration is an extra Rs 6 – a good idea for letters and parcels.

Telephone

Domestic and international calls can be made from government-run telephone exchanges, from top-end hotels in Kashgar, Gilgit, Abbottabad, Rawalpindi and Islamabad and, in Pakistan, from PCOs (public call offices, many privately run). The exchanges, usually open 24 hours a day, are quickest; your biggest problem may be the man in the next booth screaming his lungs out down a domestic line.

Most large towns in both countries now have direct dialling – even Kashgar and Hunza were expected to have it soon – so international calls can be direct-dialled *in*, though not out. In any case, late-night outward connections can be surprisingly quick. A three-minute overseas station call from China is about Y60, from Pakistan about Rs 150 to Rs 230. Hotels may charge considerably more.

Dialling codes along the KKH include 0572 Gilgit, 0575 Skardu, 0598 Mansehra, 05921 Abbottabad, 0593 Murree and 051 Islamabad-Rawalpindi.

Telegraph, Telex & Fax

Domestic and international telegrams, telexes and sometimes faxes can be sent from most telephone exchanges and some top-end hotels. The cheapest quick message is a telegram, with overseas rates of around Y4 a word from China, Rs 2 to Rs 3 a word from Pakistan. Telex is also a bargain from Pakistan. A one-page overseas fax costs about the same as a three-minute call.

TIME

All China officially runs on Beijing time, but Kashgar, 3500 km away, runs on (unofficial) 'Xinjiang time', two hours earlier. Visitors have to keep track of both. A single timezone covers all of Pakistan.

This would be easy enough except that in summer China (along with the USA, Canada, Britain, Australia and New Zealand) sets its clocks ahead one hour, but Pakistan doesn't. Thus China and Pakistan are four hours apart from mid-May to mid-September, and three for the rest of the year.

When it's noon in Pakistan, it's

11 pm (midnight) the previous day in San Francisco
2 am (3 am) in New York and Toronto
7 am (8 am) in London
12.30 pm in Delhi
1 pm (2 pm) in Kashgar (unofficial)
3 pm (4 pm) in Beijing
6 pm (5 pm) in Sydney

Figures (except Sydney and Wellington) are for northern-hemisphere winter; those in parentheses are for northern-hemisphere summer. Each country switches to summer time on its own schedule, so in early spring and early autumn expect other one-hour differences to come and go.

ELECTRICITY

Electricity in both countries is 220 volt, 50 cycle AC; some hotels have 110-volt shaver outlets. On the KKH, lower Hunza, Nagar and most tributary valleys aren't yet 'electrified' except by generators; most other regions have hydroelectric ('hydel') stations in their side canyons. Gilgit's power supply is the flakiest.

WEIGHTS & MEASURES

Officially both countries are metric but some traditional units persist locally. Old Chinese units include the *chi* ($\frac{1}{3}$ metre), *li* ($\frac{1}{2}$ km), *jin* ($\frac{1}{2}$ kg) and *liang* ($\frac{1}{10}$ jin or 50 grams).

Imperial units linger in Pakistan. Short distances are often quoted in furlongs; one furlong is $\frac{1}{8}$ mile or about 200 metres. Pakistanis habitually confuse miles and km, no matter how confident they sound. Cloth merchants and tailors still use yards. Some traditional Pakistani weights still in use are the *tola* (about 11.7 grams) and *seer* (0.933 kg).

BOOKS & MAPS

If you can't find these at home, many are available as reprints in Pakistan bookshops.

Guidebooks

Other Lonely Planet guidebooks with information on the Northern Areas and western Xinjiang are *Pakistan – a travel survival kit* and *China – a travel survival kit*.

Ali, Haqiqat, *Trekker's Guide to Hunza*. Introduction to Hunza and Gojal treks by a Passu guide, with Burushaski and Wakhi glossaries and good advice on cultural awareness. Experienced mountaineers say some route descriptions may be unreliable.

Shaw, Isobel, *Pakistan Handbook*. A good guide by an ex-expatriate who obviously loves the place, rich in detail and background on historical sites, though aimed at travellers who can afford to hire cars, and short on tips for the budget-minded.

Swift, Hugh, *Trekking in Pakistan and India*. The best resource on trekking in the Hindu Kush, Karakoram and Himalaya – a detailed, sensible, affectionate book by the late king of Himalayan walkers. It includes a medical appendix and glossaries of Chitrali, Burushaski, Wakhi, Balti and Urdu phrases.

Travel

Danziger, Nick, *Danziger's Travels*. An incredible modern-day overland odyssey through Turkey, Iran, Afghanistan, Pakistan, China and Tibet – without much regard for visas, immigration posts, civil wars and the like.

Fa-Hsien, *A Record of Buddhistic Kingdoms* (paperback reprint by Lok Virsa, Islamabad). The Buddhist monk's own dry account of his 5th-century pilgrimage through Xinjiang and the Karakoram, down the Indus to Gandhara and on to India. Excellent and more lively descriptions of this and the later journey of another pilgrim, Hsuan Tsang, are in *The Great Chinese Travelers*, edited by Jeannette Mirsky.

Jamie, Kathleen, *The Golden Peak: Travels in Northern Pakistan*. A finely written, insightful, occasionally drifting book about the Northern Areas, by a poet with an eye for the ironies of life for women, Muslims and travellers. The innocence of the first-time visitor has not been edited out. Included are glimpses of private lives that male visitors will never see. It could use a bit of background for those who haven't been there.

Knight, E F, *Where Three Empires Meet* (recent Pakistani hardback reprint). Travels of a Victorian journalist in Kashmir, Ladakh and the Northern Areas, including a thrilling but lopsidedly colonial version of the 1891 invasion of Hunza.

Murphy, Dervla, *Full Tilt*. The first quest of the legendary eccentric Irish traveller: a solo bicycle journey from Ireland to India, including Pakistan. Hair-raising adventures recounted in a matter-of-fact, almost deadpan, tone.

Murphy, Dervla, *Where the Indus is Young*. The redoubtable Irishwoman's account of a winter in Baltistan, travelling on foot and horseback with her six-year-old daughter.

Schomberg, Colonel R C F, *Between the Oxus & the Indus* (hardback 1935, also Pakistani paperback reprint). Chronicles of 19th-century Gilgit and Hunza by an acidic British officer who found the landscapes nobler than the people.

Stein, Sir Aurel, *On Alexander's Track to the Indus* (hardback 1929). Stein, a Hungarian-English archaeologist famous for his ravaging of central Asian sites between 1900 and the 1940s, was the first Westerner into parts of Indus Kohistan. He also retraced the routes of earlier travellers including Alexander the Great and the monk Fa-Hsien.

History & Culture

Fairley, Jean, *The Lion River: The Indus* (hardback). A detailed and elegant book about the Indus River and the people along it, from Tibet to the Arabian Sea.

Keay, John, *When Men & Mountains Meet* (hardback). Gripping and often hilarious stories of the Europeans who first penetrated the western Himalaya in the early 1800s.

Keay, John, *The Gilgit Game* (hardback). A very readable account of the explorers and oddballs who played in the 'Great Game', the imperial rivalry between Britain and Russia across the Pamirs, Hindu Kush and Karakoram in the late 1800s.

Staley, John, *Words For My Brother* (hardback). The culture, politics, religious traditions and recent history of pre-Karakoram-Highway Chitral, Kohistan, Gilgit and Hunza. Staley and his wife studied and travelled here in the 1960s. This scholarly but affectionate book is my favourite on the Northern Areas.

Waller, Derek, *The Pundits* (hardback). An account of the heroic but unsung journeys of Indian scholars and soothsayers trained by the British to be undercover surveyors and spies across the Hindu Kush and Karakoram during the Great Game.

Younghusband, Sir Francis, *The Heart of a Continent* (hardback). The adventures in Kashgar and the Karakoram of one of Britain's foremost players in the Great Game.

Petroglyphs

Dani, Dr Ahmad Hasan, *Human Records on Karakorum Highway*. A paperback guide to rock inscriptions along the KKH from the Khunjerab Pass to Mansehra, by a Pakistani researcher who has translated many of them; available in Pakistani bookshops.

Jettmar, Dr Karl, *Rockcarvings & Inscriptions in the Northern Areas of Pakistan*. By a German colleague of Dani, it's stuffy but illuminating; available in Pakistani bookshops.

Fiction

Kipling, Rudyard, *Kim*. The master storyteller's classic epic of the Raj during the Great Game.

Geology & Geography

Mason, Kenneth, *Abode of Snow* (hardback). Mason was a well-known Himalayan explorer. Chapter 3 introduces the geography of the Karakoram.

Miller, Keith, ed, *Proceedings of the International Karakorum Project* (hardback). Staggering detail on the Karakoram's geology and geography and their overlap with disciplines as diverse as architecture and cultural anthropology; based on an expedition in 1980 and later studies.

Miller, Russell, *Continents in Collision* (hardback). An illustrated laymen's introduction to plate tectonics and the birth of the Himalaya.

Islam

Guillaume, Alfred, *Islam*. Dry as dust but dense with information on history, doctrine and practice.

Health

Schroeder, Dirk, *Staying Healthy in Asia, Africa, & Latin America*. The perfect take-along medical handbook – small and easy to use, covering prevention, basic first-aid, and advice on just about anything you might catch. If you can't find it write to Moon Publications, 722 Wall St, Chico, CA 95928 USA.

Maps

Contour Maps Best is the US Army Map Service (AMS) U-502 series at 1:250,000 (2½ km per cm). There's apparently a new two-colour edition, though some sources have only black & white copies. Last revised in 1962, they show most villages but not the KKH and many other roads. Along the KKH, only Pakistan sheets seem to be available: NI 43-1 (Churrai, covers northern Indus Kohistan), NI 43-2 (Gilgit), NI 43-3 (Mundik, covers Skardu), NJ 43-14 (Baltit, covers Hunza and Gojal) and NJ 43-15 (Shimshal, covers the Khunjerab area).

The Swiss Foundation for Alpine Research has a two-sheet 1:250,000 trekking map of the Karakoram. An excellent three-sheet Karakoram set at 1:200,000 is published by Leomann Maps. Most gorgeous of all are finely detailed three-colour maps at 1:50,000 of the north slopes of Rakaposhi (Minapin) and Nanga Parbat by Deutscher Alpenverein (DAV).

The coloured ONC aeronautical chart series at 1:1,000,000 includes two maps of the KKH, ONC G-6 and ONC G-7, but precision is low and many place names are obsolete. The Survey of Pakistan has coloured topographic maps at 1:1,000,000 (10 km per cm) and 1:500,000. Overseas shops report difficulty in getting these but you may find them in Pakistani bookshops.

Ordering Good mail-order sources include:

Edward Stanford Ltd, 12-14 Long Acre, Covent Garden, London WC2E 9LP, UK, (☎ (071) 836 1321).

Geo Buch Verlag, Rosenthal 6, D-8000 Munchen 2, Germany

ILH GeoCenter, Schockenriedstrasse 40a, Postfach 80 08 30, D-7000 Stuttgart 80, Germany.

Libreria Alpina, Via C Coroned-Berti 4, 40137 Bologna, Zona 3705, Italy.

Maplink, 25 East Mason St, Santa Barbara, CA 93101, USA.

Michael Chessler Books, PO Box 2436, Evergreen, CO 80439, USA, (☎ (800) 654-8502, (303) 670-0093).

NOAAA Distribution Branch (N/CG33), National Oceanic & Atmospheric Administration, Riverdale, MD 20737, USA

US Library of Congress, Geography & Map Division, 101 Independence Ave, Washington, DC 20540, USA.

Regional & City Maps PTDC has brochures on the KKH and the Silk Road, Trekking, the Northern Areas, Hunza, the Gilgit Valley, Skardu, Swat, the Kaghan Valley and Taxila, but the tiny maps are of little use for finding your way around. PTDC's tourist map of Rawalpindi and Islamabad, for sale at the Tourist Information Centres in both cities, is good for Islamabad but not much help in Rawalpindi. There's no PTDC map of Gilgit.

The Survey of Pakistan's *Islamabad & Rawalpindi Guide Map* at 1:30,000 (300 metres per cm) is quite detailed, although many street names are out of date. It's available at the London Book Company, the Book Centre or other shops in the capital area.

Other Maps The Capital Development Authority in Islamabad has a good map-brochure, *Trekking in the Margalla Hills*, showing walks and resthouses in the hills behind Islamabad. PTDC might have it, or go to CDA on Khayaban-i-Suhrawardy

(south G-7, west of Aabpara) and ask for the Public Relations office.

Keep an eye out for the beautiful hand-drawn maps of KKH towns by legendary itinerant map-maker John Callanan.

FILM & PHOTOGRAPHY
Customs
A Pakistan customs regulation says you can bring in only one camera and five rolls of film, but tourists routinely bring in much more. Registering your equipment with customs at home is not only proof against paying double duty there, but gives you a paper full of government stamps and serial numbers to wave around if trouble arises.

Restrictions & Etiquette
In China it's forbidden to photograph military sites, factories, airports, railway stations and bridges, and often there are people nearby who'll collar you and take your film. You're not supposed to take pictures from aeroplanes but I've never seen a CAAC hostess swoop down on anybody. The insides of museums and temples are often off-limits. Some older Chinese shy away from cameras but nearly everyone loves having their kids photographed.

Prohibited subjects in Pakistan are military sites, airports, major KKH bridges and, above all, women. To Muslims, especially in rural areas and even among Ismailis, it's an insult to photograph any woman older than a child. If a husband or brother is nearby it's risky as well. Women photographers may get lucky if they've established some rapport. Pakistani men, on the other hand, are irrepressible in front of a camera, and quick to ask you for a print.

Hazards
Heat To avoid magenta-tinted memories of the KKH, keep film away from heat. If you line a stuff-sack with a patch cut from an aluminised mylar 'survival blanket', film will stay cool inside through fierce summer days. Be careful where you buy film; some shops proudly display their film in the window – which cooks it.

Condensation In very cold weather, avoid ruinous moisture on film and inside the camera by putting them in plastic bags *before* going indoors, and leaving them there till they're warm.

Dust Some back roads are a wallow of fine dust that gets into everything. Keep everything bagged up, and carry a squeeze-bulb for blowing dust from inside the camera.

Cold Camera batteries get sluggish in down-jacket weather. Keep the camera inside your coat and keep some spare batteries warm in your pocket.

X-Rays One dose of airport x-rays for inspecting carry-on bags won't harm slow or medium-speed films, but the effects are cumulative and too much will fog your pictures. I don't trust the machines at Chinese airports, and in Hong Kong the x-rays for *checked-in* baggage are notoriously strong. Lead 'film-safe' pouches help but the best solution is hand inspection. Officials hate you for it but in Pakistan and China they'll do it if you persist. Having all your film in one or two clear plastic bags makes it easier.

Equipment
This is a personal matter, but with an SLR camera a mid-range zoom – eg 35-to-135 mm – covers a wide range of situations; a good second lens might be a 28 mm for panoramas and indoors. 'Skylite' filters protect lenses and cut down on high-altitude UV glare.

Film & Processing
Western-brand colour print film (much of it quite fresh) and processing are available in Kashgar, Karimabad, Gilgit, Rawalpindi and Islamabad. In Rawalpindi at the time of writing, a 36-frame roll of Kodak Gold 100 was about Rs 80, developing about Rs 12 a roll, prints Rs 4 each (much less than US and Australia prices). Northward, prices rise and reliability drops. Kashgar department stores have cheap Chinese film and lots of Fujicolor and Konica, though processing there is second-rate and dusty.

Colour slide film (E6 only, eg Fujichrome, Agfachrome, Ektachrome) is available in Pakistan, but it may have to go to Lahore or Karachi for processing. It's about three times as expensive as prints. Kodachrome is scarce and cannot be processed in China or Pakistan. Black & white film is cheap and common in China. It's rare and of doubtful quality in Pakistan, and processing costs more than for colour.

Posting film from anywhere in China or Pakistan is asking for trouble; better to take it home or to a reliable place like Hong Kong for posting or processing.

HEALTH
By far the most frequent health problems Westerners have along the KKH are gut infections – dysentery, giardia and hepatitis-A – but these are mostly avoidable with good sense concerning food and drink. A significant risk anywhere from Gilgit south is malaria, against which you can protect yourself with drugs plus common sense about mosquitoes. Other diseases considered significant in this region – typhoid, polio and tuberculosis – are a matter of immunisation in advance.

Travel Health Information
A thorough, well-organised and portable guide is *Staying Healthy in Asia, Africa, & Latin America*. If you can't find it write to Moon Publications, 722 Wall St, Chico, CA 95928, USA. *Travel with Children* by Maureen Wheeler (Lonely Planet) is full of basic advice on travel health for young people.

Medical Advisory Services for Travellers Abroad (MASTA), a private group connected with the London School of Hygiene & Tropical Medicine, offers detailed 'health briefs' tailored to specific journeys, for UK£5 and up, plus mail-order health supplies. In the UK they're at (071) 631 4408 or (0705) 511420; fax (071) 323 4547. In Australia, call (02) 905 6133; fax (02) 905 1151.

Pre-Departure Preparations

Health Insurance A policy for theft, loss, flight cancellation and medical treatment overseas is a good idea. A clause that pays the cost of an emergency flight out is worth considering.

Check the small print. Some exclude 'dangerous activities' like scuba diving, motorcycling, even trekking. If these are on your agenda, ask about an amendment to permit some of them (at a higher premium). Some policies, rather than paying doctors or hospitals directly, require you to pay first and claim later; if so, bring all the paperwork home.

Medical Kit A small kit for routine problems might include tweezers, scissors, thermometer (mercury thermometers are prohibited by most airlines), aspirin, antiseptic, plasters (band-aids), a few gauze pads and adhesive tape, insect repellent, moleskin (for foot blisters) and something for diarrhoea (kaolin preparation – eg Pepto-Bismol – or Imodium or Lomotil). For severe diarrhoea, especially in children, a rehydration mixture is a good idea. Water-purification tablets or iodine tincture is useful for when there's no boiled or bottled water. Other suggestions are sunscreen, lip salve and foot powder.

If you wear corrective lenses bring a spare pair, and the prescription. If you're prone to motion sickness and plan to travel by bus anywhere, bring your Dramamine!

A broad-spectrum antibiotic like tetracycline or penicillin is useful if you'll be off the beaten track, but be sure you have no allergies to it. For this and any other prescription drug, bring the prescription too, as proof of what it is. If you're required to take a narcotic drug, carry a doctor's letter to this effect. Considering the potential for contamination through dirty needles, some travellers now routinely carry a sterile pack of disposable syringes, available from medical supply shops.

Teeth If you're on a long trip get your teeth checked; Pakistan and remoter China are not good places to visit the dentist!

Immunisations If you arrive from an area infected with cholera or yellow fever, both China and Pakistan may ask for proof of immunisation. There are no other health requirements for tourists. Most Western travellers will have been immunised against measles and polio in childhood but your doctor may recommend boosters. Children of any age should be immunised against tuberculosis.

If you're going through Hong Kong a convenient place for shots is the Port Health Office (☎ 572-2056), Centre Point Building, 2nd floor, 181 Gloucester Rd, Wanchai – across the road from the China visa office.

Tetanus & diptheria: Recommended as general protection. Boosters are needed every 10 years.

Typhoid: Also recommended. Protection lasts for three years. Older people who've had several boosters may not need any more. There is now an oral typhoid vaccine too.

Polio: This is still common in the Third World. Boosters are needed every five years.

Infectious hepatitis (hepatitis-A): Gamma globulin is not a vaccine but a prepared antibody that reduces the chances of infection. It's good for at most six months and later doses may be less effective; some doctors feel its effects are far outweighed by common-sense eating habits. You don't need it if you've had the disease before. There is now a hepatitis-A vaccine, too. Two initial shots two to four weeks apart give a year's protection; a booster six to 12 months later extends that to 10 years.

Anti-Malarials Malaria drugs are pills, not shots, but you should sort them out before you go too; see the following section on malaria.

Basic Rules

Food & Drink What you put in your mouth is the most important thing, but don't get paranoid – after all, eating local food is part of being there. Upset stomach is the most common problem but it's rarely serious.

Play safe and *don't drink the water*; that includes no brushing your teeth in tap water, even in better hotels, and no ice in your drinks (a nice reminder: the Urdu word for ice is *barf*!). Name-brand bottled water or soft drinks are usually OK; so is tea or coffee from fully boiled water.

Choose street food with care. Go for hot, freshly made dishes; avoid salads (usually washed in untreated water); avoid undercooked meat; peel fruit yourself or wash it in water you trust. Even the wonderful dried apricots of Hunza should at least be soaked in hot water because of the way they're handled. Brand-name ice cream from shops is OK but beware of street vendors. In remote areas milk may be unpasteurised, but yoghurt is always hygienic.

A good hepatitis-A defence is to carry your own utensils. Restaurant chopsticks ('hepsticks') may be the worst culprit; if you're stuck with nothing else, soaking them in boiling hot tea will at least reduce the risk. You can buy your own in Chinese department stores.

Wash your hands often – it's easy to contaminate your own food.

Water Purification The best way to purify water is to boil it for 10 minutes. If you can't do that, treat it chemically. Iodine treatment kills bacteria, amoebae and giardia and is safe for short-term use unless you're pregnant or have thyroid problems. It's available in tablet form (eg Potable Aqua or Globaline) or you can buy 2% tincture of iodine from Pakistani or Chinese pharmacies; add two drops per litre or quart of clear water. With either, let treated water stand half an hour before you drink it. Iodine degrades if it's exposed to air so keep it sealed.

Chlorine tablets (eg Puritabs, Steritabs) won't kill amoebae or giardia. Most commercial water filters – charcoal, ceramic or resin – won't stop all pathogens, particularly the hepatitis-A virus. However, combined charcoal and iodine-resin filters will.

Nutrition Eggs, beans, lentils (dhal) and nuts are safe protein sources. Fruit you can peel is always safe and a good vitamin source. Don't forget grains (eg rice) and bread. In remote areas it's not always possible to find these things, so a vitamin-mineral supplement is not a bad idea. Well-cooked food is

safer, but when overcooked it loses much of its value.

Diagnostics You should know how to take temperature and pulse readings. Normal body temperature is 37°C (98.6°F). More than 2°C (4°F) higher is a serious fever. Normal adult pulse rate is 60 to 80 per minute (children 80 to 100, and babies 100 to 140). As a rule pulse increases about 20 beats per minute for each 1°C rise in fever.

Breathing rate is another indicator of illness. Adults and older children breathe about 12 to 20 times a minute (up to 30 for young children, and 40 for babies). People with high fever or serious respiratory illness breathe faster than normal.

Medications Ideally, antibiotics should be taken under medical supervision, and never indiscriminately. Overuse weakens the body's natural immunities and can reduce the drug's future effectiveness. Take the prescribed dose at the prescribed times – and *don't* discontinue it early, even if you feel better. But stop immediately if there is any serious reaction, and don't use it at all if you're not sure it's the right one. Be sure you have no penicillin allergy before taking penicillin or ampicillin.

Give children from eight to 12 years old half the adult dose, and younger children one-third to one-fourth the adult dose.

Hospitals
There are hospitals at Kashgar, Karimabad, Gilgit, Abbottabad, Rawalpindi and Islamabad, and clinics in many smaller towns. The hospitals are OK for routine stool and other tests, but care and standards are not what you are used to at home! For problems beyond the level of first aid – including any problems involving hospitalisation – get down to Islamabad as soon as possible and ask your embassy there for advice.

Sanitation-Related Diseases
Diarrhoea A change of water, food or climate, even jet-lag, can bring on the runs; even drinking silt-laden glacier melt-water

will do it. But a few dashes to the loo with no other symptoms is nothing to worry about. More serious is diarrhoea due to contaminated food or water.

Dehydration is the main danger, particularly in children. Weak black tea with sugar, or soft drinks allowed to go flat and diluted with purified water, are good for replacing fluids. In severe cases a rehydrating solution is necessary to replace minerals and salts. If you didn't bring a commercial mix, add a level teaspoon of salt and eight level teaspoons of sugar to a litre of purified water and sip it slowly all day. An alternative is rice water with some salt. Stick to a bland diet as you recover.

Lomotil or Imodium plugs you up but doesn't cure you. Use it only if absolutely necessary – eg if you *must* travel. Don't use it if you have a fever or are severely dehydrated.

Dysentery The main symptom of this serious illness, caused by contaminated food or water, is severe diarrhoea, often with traces of blood or mucus. There are two forms.

Bacillary or bacterial dysentery shows rapid onset, high fever, headache, vomiting and stomach pains. It generally doesn't last more than a week, but is highly contagious. Amoebic dysentery develops more gradually, has no fever or vomiting but is a more serious illness – it will persist until treated and can recur and do long-term damage. Only a stool test can reliably distinguish the two.

Treat severe cases of bacillary dysentery with tetracycline – adults 250 mg four times a day for seven to 10 days. This should be given to children only if it's essential. Pregnant women should not take it after the fourth month.

Treat amoebic dysentery with metronidazole (brand-name Flagyl, adults 800 mg three times daily for five days) or tinidazole (brand-name Fasigyn, adults 600 to 700 mg three times daily for three to six days); stay away from alcohol while taking these. Avoid

Enterovioform or Mexaform, which can have serious side effects.

Giardia *Giardia lamblia* is a parasite found in contaminated water. Symptoms of infection – cramped or bloated stomach, nausea, watery foul-smelling diarrhoea and frequent gas – may not appear for weeks, and can come and go for weeks or months more.

There is no preventative drug. Treat it with metronidazole (brand-name Flagyl) or tinidazole (brand-name Fasigyn) – adults 600 to 700 mg three times daily for two or three days. Don't take any alcohol while taking these. Avoid Enterovioform and Mexaform, which can have serious side effects.

Hepatitis Hepatitis-A or infectious hepatitis is spread by contaminated food, water or utensils. Minimal symptoms are fatigue, aches and pains, loss of appetite; you may also have a fever, chills, headache and in later stages nausea, vomiting, liver pain (under the rib cage), dark urine, light-coloured faeces and jaundiced skin. The whites of your eyes may turn yellow.

You should seek medical advice, though there isn't much you can do but rest, drink lots of fluids, eat lightly and avoid fatty foods. People who've had hepatitis-A must forego alcohol for six months afterward, since the disease attacks the liver.

Hepatitis-B or serum hepatitis is spread through sexual contact or the use of dirty needles. Avoid injections where you have doubts about sanitation. Symptoms and treatment are much the same as type A. Gamma globulin is only effective against type A, and boiling in water only kills type A.

An unusual strain of hepatitis was epidemic around Kashgar in 1987 and many eating places were shut down for cleaning. It was allegedly under control a year later, but the need for caution is obvious.

Problems of Climate & Geography

Altitude Sickness The low oxygen above about 3000 metres can cause headaches, dizziness, breathlessness, nausea, insomnia and/or low appetite, especially if you're dehydrated or exerting yourself. Even the bus trip from Kashgar up to the Khunjerab Pass can bring it on. Flying straight to a high altitude can make these problems acute. You're less likely to suffer if you take it easy for a few days, drink plenty of water, eat well and avoid alcohol and cigarettes.

The symptoms usually go away after a few days but if they don't the only treatment is to descend – even a few hundred metres can help. Continuing breathlessness, severe headache, nausea, lack of appetite or dry cough – sometimes with frothy pink sputum – are cause for concern. Profound tiredness, confusion, lack of coordination and balance are real danger signs. Acute mountain sickness (AMS) can be fatal.

Sunburn In the desert or at high elevations you can get burnt very fast, even through cloud, and a sunscreen is recommended. Calamine lotion eases the pain of mild sunburn.

Dehydration & Heat Exhaustion You breathe and sweat away body water very fast in the mountains as well as the hot plains around Kashgar. Dark yellow urine and not much of it are signs you're dehydrated, though you may not feel very thirsty. Dehydration and salt deficiency from sweating a lot can bring on lethargy, headaches, giddiness, rapid pulse and possibly muscle cramps. In severe cases, vomiting or diarrhoea deplete fluid and salt levels further. Drink lots of water, salt food generously and take the heat in small doses until you've acclimatised.

Heat Stroke This serious, sometimes fatal, condition is a failure of the body's heat-regulating mechanism caused by long periods in extreme heat. Symptoms are general discomfort, little or no sweating and a dangerously high body temperature (39 to 41°C). When sweating ceases the skin becomes flushed. Severe headaches, poor coordination, sometimes confusion or aggression may also occur, and eventually delirium or convulsions. Hospitalisation is essential but meanwhile get victims out of the sun, remove clothing, cover them with a wet sheet or towel and fan them continuously.

Cold Excess cold is as dangerous as excess heat. Trekkers run a risk of hypothermia, in which the body loses heat faster than it can generate it and the body's core temperature drops. It's surprisingly easy to go from chilly to dangerously cold with a combination of wind, wet clothing (from rain or sweat), fatigue and hunger, even when the air temperature is well above freezing.

Symptoms are exhaustion, lethargy, dizzy spells, numbness (especially in toes and fingers), shivering, muscle cramps, slurred speech, clumsiness, irrational behaviour and violent bursts of energy. You're more likely to recognise it in someone else than in yourself.

To prevent it, dress in easily-donned layers. Silk, wool and some synthetic fibres insulate well even when wet; cotton doesn't. A hat makes a big difference, as much heat is lost through the head. A waterproof outer layer is obviously important. Water and sugary snacks help to generate heat quickly.

To treat it, take shelter and replace wet clothing with dry. Drink hot liquids (not alcohol) and eat high-calorie, easily digestible snacks. In more advanced cases it may be necessary to put the victim in a sleeping bag and get in with them. Don't rub a victim down or put them near a fire. If possible give them a warm (not hot) bath.

Insect-Borne Diseases

Malaria This serious disease is spread by mosquitoes infected with a parasite. There is a risk in Pakistan all year round, anywhere below about 2000 metres (ie well into the mountains). Symptoms, which may not appear for three to six months or even longer, include headaches, fever, chills and sweating which may subside and recur. Untreated malaria is potentially fatal.

It's very important to take anti-malarial drugs. These don't prevent the disease but interfere with the parasite's life-cycle. At the time of writing the recommended regimen along the KKH was chloroquine (common brands Nivaquine, Avloclor or Aralen), 300 mg once a week. If you're going on to the NWFP, Punjab or Sind in Pakistan, you should supplement this with proguanil (brand name Paludrine), 200 mg once a day.

Always take them at the same time of day or day of the week, from two weeks before you get to a malarial area to at least four weeks after you've left it. Women who are pregnant (or plan to be soon after the course of treatment) should consult a doctor since some drugs are not safe.

An improvement on chloroquine is mefloquine, but it's not recommended for stays of more than two or three weeks. Fansidar has dangerous side effects, though it's used as a treatment for known cases. Others with possible side effects are Maloprim and Amodiaquine.

Malarial parasites mutate into drug-resistant forms almost faster than science can come up with new drugs, and information about what's needed and where gets old fast, so see your local health authority for a proper update.

Malarial mosquitoes appear from dusk to dawn. Thus wearing long clothes, using a repellent or burning mosquito coils, and sleeping under a mosquito net will reduce the chances of being bitten in the first place. Mosquitoes may be attracted by perfume or aftershave.

Typhus In Pakistan, typhus is spread by ticks. It begins as a bad cold, followed by a fever, headache, muscle pains and a body rash. There may be a painful sore at the site of the bite and swollen, painful lymph nodes. A strong insect repellent may discourage ticks. Search for them after walking in scrub, pasture or forests but don't just pick them off as that can leave the 'stinger' in place. Vaseline, alcohol or oil (or the touch of a freshly extinguished match) will persuade them to let go.

Bites
Bedbugs especially like dirty mattresses and bedding. They leave itchy bites in neat rows. Calamine lotion may ease the itch. Spots of blood on bedding or on the wall near the bed can be read as a suggestion to find another hotel.

Lice make themselves at home in your hair (head lice), clothing (body lice) or pubic hair (crabs). You catch them by direct contact with infected people or by sharing combs, clothing, etc. Powder or shampoo treatments available in pharmacies will kill them; infected clothing should then be washed in very hot water.

Sexually Transmitted Diseases
Abstinence is the only sure preventative, but use of a condom is very effective. Gonorrhoea and syphilis are the most common; symptoms include sores, blisters or a rash around the genitals and discharge or pain when urinating. Syphilis symptoms eventually disappear but the disease continues and can cause severe problems in later years. Treatment of gonorrhoea or syphilis is by antibiotics.

Infection by the herpes virus is unpleasant but not dangerous. Symptoms include tiny blisters around the genitals or mouth and sometimes fever, aches, fatigue or swollen lymph nodes. Herpes is spread by sexual activity when genital sores are present. There's no cure, though symptoms may be milder after the first appearance.

HIV/AIDS HIV (human immuno-deficiency virus) may develop into AIDS, aquired immune deficiency syndrome. Always practising safe sex using condoms is the most effective preventative; it is impossible to detect the serapositivity (HIV-positive status) of an otherwise healthy-looking person without a blood test.

HIV/AIDS can also be spread through infected blood transfusions; most developing countries cannot afford to screen all blood used for transfusions. It can also be spread by dirty needles, so vaccinations, acupuncture, tattooing and ear or nose piercing can potentially be as dangerous as drug use if the needle is not clean. If you need an injection, it may be a good idea to buy a new syringe from a pharmacy (or bring your own from home) and ask the doctor to use it.

China and Pakistan have reported AIDS cases. Visitors staying in China longer than six months or in Pakistan longer than a year must give proof of a negative HIV test when they apply for a visa.

Women's Health

Poor diet, lowered resistance from the use of antibiotics, even contraceptive pills can pave the way for vaginal infections in hot climates. Keeping the genital area clean, wearing cotton underwear and skirts or loose-fitting trousers will minimise the risk.

Yeast infections, characterised by a rash, itch and discharge, can be treated with a vinegar or lemon juice douche or with yoghurt. Nystatin suppositories are the usual medical prescription.

Trichomonas is a more serious infection with discharge and a burning sensation when urinating. Male sexual partners must also be treated and if a vinegar-water douche is not effective medical attention should be sought. Metronidazole (brand-name Flagyl) is the prescribed drug; do not drink alcohol while taking this.

WOMEN TRAVELLERS

Travel in Pakistan can be hard work for women. Most Muslim men there keep wives and daughters out of sight of other men – in the house, behind the veil, in special sections of buses, and in the 'family' areas of restaurants. To non-Muslims this looks like imprisonment, but to a Muslim it's an act of utmost devotion.

By the same token, most Muslim men also go out of their way to avoid direct contact with women outside their family – in some places (eg the Tribal Areas of the NWFP) for fear of their lives. That is why a foreign woman's questions, for example, are often answered to her male companion; it's not a sign of contempt but of respect, Muslim-style.

But unfortunately, because men are prohibited from what Westerners consider

normal interactions with women outside the family, their views of 'other' women come mostly from the media. Western women travelling on their own may be considered crazy, or vaguely cheap. They're constantly asked, 'Where is your husband?'.

To make matters worse, the sexuality suppressed by traditional culture is inflamed by popular films full of full-hipped women, guns and violence. Younger Pakistani men rarely miss the chance to point out to Western women how sexually frustrated all Pakistani men are. Actual harassment is rare but it does happen, usually away from the public eye – eg a grope in a crowded Suzuki at night.

Standing up for yourself can produce confusion, loss of attention or laughter in others – though refusal to eat in the family section or sit at the front of the bus is usually tolerated. Wearing local-style *shalwar qamiz* – with a light *dupatta* or scarf to cover the hair in conservative company – can make things easier. It's also quite comfortable, and easy and cheap to have made in the bazaar.

Even if you don't opt for local styles, it's very important – for your own stress-level and as a sign of respect – to dress in a way that doesn't inflame the libidos of young men or the indignation of older ones. It would be difficult to overstate the sensitivity of this matter. Clothes that reveal flesh (other than face, hands and feet) or the shape of the body are deeply offensive to practising Muslims. Especially avoid halter-tops and shorts. Stick to long, loose, non-revealing blouses and skirts or trousers.

Women do travel solo in Pakistan without trouble, though they need to know themselves pretty well. Especially in conservative rural areas, it's an unfortunate fact that you're much better off travelling with other women, or with men. There are stories of assaults on women cyclists in northern Indus Kohistan; the region from Chilas to Thakot is a good place to keep an especially modest profile.

Paradoxically, women travellers are more likely to get a look into people's private lives. Even in the most traditional areas women may ask you in, feed you, show you around if there are no men about.

China, even Muslim Xinjiang, tends to be a relief for women in this respect. Chinese men are at least deferential. Uyghurs seem equally uninterested in men and women foreigners, except for their money.

CULTURAL CUES
Hospitality
In Islam, a guest – Muslim or not – has a position of honour not understood in the West. If someone visits you and you don't have much to offer, as a Christian you'd be urged to share what you had; as a Muslim you're urged to give it all away. Traditionally in Hunza, guests are seated higher than the head of the household. In several places I've been the only one eating in a room full of hungry-looking spectators.

In the Northern Areas this is a constant source of pleasure, embarrassment, and temptation. Most people have little to offer *but* their hospitality, and a casual guest could drain a host's resources and never hear a word about it. It's tactful to politely refuse gifts or invitations once or twice before accepting them. Someone who doesn't persist with an offer after you decline once probably can't afford it anyway. Pulling out your own food or offering to pay someone for a kindness may well humiliate them. All you can do is enjoy it, and take yourself courteously out of the picture before you become a burden.

If you're invited to someone's house, consider taking a small gift, like postcards from home or sweets for the kids. Don't be surprised if you aren't thanked for it: gifts are taken more as evidence of God's mercy than of your generosity. You'll probably be showered with snacks; here refusing would be rude – though meat for a vegetarian or a glass of water from an unknown source can be a problem. Try to present your excuses before it's put in front of you; a useful one for drinks is a bad stomach and doctor's orders to drink only hot tea.

In China, at least on the tourist trail, reflex generosity is rare. Uyghurs mainly ignore you in Kashgar. Han Chinese officials, attendants and drivers are generally beastly to everyone.

Clothing
Nowhere is it easier to offend and insult Muslims – and nowhere have more foreigners done so without thinking – than in the matter of dress. To a devout Muslim, clothes that reveal flesh or the shape of the body are roughly equivalent to walking around in your underwear in the West – ridiculous on men and scandalous on women. Shorts and halter-tops are especially offensive. Stick with long, loose, non-revealing garments. One option is the shalwar qamiz worn by both men and women in Pakistan – amazingly comfortable, and cheap off the shelf or made by a tailor.

This sounds preachy but cannot be emphasised enough. It's not a matter of brownie-points for 'dressing native'. Muslims from everywhere, fundamentalist and liberal, beg to know why so many foreigners refuse this simple courtesy.

Eating With Your Left Hand
The left hand is considered unclean, and handling food with it is revolting to most Muslims. It's an acquired skill to break off bits of chapatti with only the right hand and not everybody bothers, but no-one raises food to their mouth with the left hand. (Many Westerners recoil at the thought of eating with *either* hand here, but even the grottiest cafe usually has a wash-stand somewhere.)

Body Language
Between Pakistani men a handshake is as essential to conversation as eye contact in the West. Don't be offended if someone offers you his wrist; he just considers his hand unclean at the moment, eg if he's been eating with it. If you try to shake hands with someone in China, on the other hand, they may act as if you're trying to kiss them.

Never point the sole of your shoe or foot at a Muslim, step over any part of someone's body or walk in front of someone praying to Mecca. The thumbs-up sign looks obscene to at least some Pakistanis.

Public physical contact between men and women – with fellow travellers or with local people – is a 'touchy' matter. Holding hands in public is acceptable only between members of the same sex (and is not a sign of homosexuality). Offering a handshake to a Pakistani of the opposite sex may put them in an awkward position; let them make the first move.

Inquiries
Avoid phrasing questions for yes/no replies, because people will say anything just to avoid saying nothing. For example, ask 'Which bus goes to Gilgit?', not 'Is this the bus to Gilgit?' – and don't believe the answer unless several more people give the same answer!

DANGERS & ANNOYANCES
Sectarian Violence Around Gilgit
The Northern Areas is one of the safest parts of Pakistan. But in 1988 tension between Sunni and Shia Muslims erupted into gunbattles at Jalalabad near the Bagrot Valley, in which over 100 people died. There have been smaller incidents in the Gilgit area since then. Tense times are the holy days at the end of Ramadan and around the Prophet's birthday.

No foreigners have yet been injured, but the KKH has sprouted police checkposts all over the place, where foreigners must troop off the bus and sign the register. Many sign false names just for the fun of it, though these log-books have apparently been used to help embassies find their nationals in emergencies.

Travel in Indus Kohistan & Hazara
There is some night-time highway robbery in Indus Kohistan and Hazara, and vehicles on the KKH after dark between Shatial and Mansehra are commonly collected by police into escorted convoys.

Travel Elsewhere in Pakistan
In recent years a combination of corrupt and/or incompetent law enforcement and a vigorous tribal arms industry has caused violence to mushroom in certain parts of Pakistan. This isn't to say you'll be dodging bullets – you just have to make sensible choices about where to go. Nearly all of the North-West Frontier Province, Punjab, and Azad Jammu & Kashmir are perfectly safe, but be aware of the following hot-spots.

North-West Frontier Province Off the main roads in the Tribal Areas, Pakistani law has no force and the authorities are almost powerless to help you; in any case you'll need a permit to go there. It's easier to wander off the roads into trouble without realising it in upper Swat or Indus Kohistan, where there are no permit requirements.

Sind & Baluchistan Provinces *Foreigners are advised to avoid going anywhere in Sind Province except Karachi.* Banditry is now a major danger in the interior, with bandits *(dacoits)* organised into large, efficient gangs. There is negligible police authority in rural Sind and to some extent in extreme southern Punjab. Buses are routinely robbed, sometimes local trains. Pakistanis and some foreigners have been kidnapped for ransom.

Even in a few non-touristy neighbourhoods of Karachi there's a risk of being caught in the crossfire of political terrorism between Sindhis and Mohajirs (post-Partition immigrants from India).

The interior of Baluchistan is also a good place to skip for now, except for Quetta and the roads linking it to Karachi via the Bolan Pass, and to the Iran border at Kuh-i-Taftan.

Long-distance rail travel in Sind and Baluchistan is still fairly safe, but when possible you should go by air. Don't rely on tourist offices outside these provinces for information about them. And don't rely on provincial authorities to keep you away from danger spots; few places are officially off-limits.

Theft
To people on marginal incomes the dollars and expensive baggage of foreign visitors can be hard to resist. Common sense takes care of most risks. Don't leave valuables in

your hotel room, no matter how secure it looks or how fine a fellow the manager is. Keep your money and passport on your person or in your line of sight at all times.

Kashgar abounds with stories of petty theft and other problems. The bus station especially is a good place to keep an eye on your bags and a hand on your wallet. Chinese hotels generally don't give out room keys, entrusting them instead to attendants; those at the Seman Hotel are not very good about locking doors. Another Kashgar pitfall is getting fleeced by moneychangers and donkey-cart drivers; see the Kashgar & Tashkurghan chapter.

I've heard no stories of theft in Hunza or Gilgit, but a few about the villages around Nanga Parbat and Chilas, and plenty about Darel and Tangir.

ACCOMMODATION
Hotels
Hotels are mostly state-run in China, mostly private in Pakistan, and with the growth of KKH tourism they now come in all cost and comfort ranges.

Prices aren't always fixed in Pakistan. Two very popular areas – the Kaghan Valley and the Galis – get so crowded in summer that they're worth avoiding unless you have a booking or a tent. Hotel prices go wild then; off-season, on the other hand, you can strike some of the best bargains in the country. In the Northern Areas, Westerners may be charged *less* than down-country 'Punjabis'.

Mainstream hotels sometimes have cheap rope-beds on the roof, if you ask. There are some bottom-end places where foreigners aren't welcome because the owner (or the state) doesn't care to adjust to Western demands. In Pakistan some save face by saying they have no 'Form D', the government hotel-register form.

Many 'hotels' in Pakistan are just eating-places – eg the *Rakaposhi View Hotel & Restaurant* in Ghulmet is a food-tent!

Government Resthouses
These include some of the best mid-range

bargains on the KKH. Also called Circuit Houses, Inspection Bungalows or Dak Bungalows, most are two or three-unit guesthouses run by government agencies for staff on business. But they're available to tourists (at higher rates) if no-one else is using them.

The best are in isolated, idyllic locations and each has a *chowkidar* (caretaker) living nearby who can, by arrangement, prepare at-cost meals from whatever's available.

Most of the ones near the KKH are run by the Northern Areas Public Works Department (NAPWD), the North-West Frontier Province Communication & Works Department (C&W) or Forestry Districts. A booking is a good idea, just a chit from a regional office to show the chowkidar – or you can drop by and take your chances. The best resthouses and their booking offices are noted in the regional chapters.

Youth Hostels
The Pakistan Youth Hostels Association (PYHA) (☎ 881501), House 110-B, Gulberg-III, Lahore; or Aabpara, G- 6/4, Islamabad (☎ 824866) runs a dozen hostels in Pakistan, with gender-segregated dormitories, gardens where you can pitch a tent and usually cooking facilities.

A bed is Rs 35 per night in Islamabad or Lahore, Rs 25 elsewhere, and Rs 15 for student-card holders. You must be a member of the International Youth Hostel Association (IYHA) or PYHA. If not, you must join IYHA on arrival at your first hostel, for the equivalent of six days' full charges.

In summer the hostels are very popular with Pakistani students; when they're busy you can only stay three days. Guests pitch in with clean-up, and must be in by mid-evening.

There are hostels in the Kaghan Valley, Abbottabad, the Galis and Taxila. Abbottabad's is far from town, those in the Kaghan Valley are in deplorable shape, and some are only open for a short season. But Islamabad's year-round one is excellent (though not yet fitted for cooking or hot water).

Hostellers can apparently use some government resthouses, possibly at reduced rates; see IYHA literature.

Railway Retiring Rooms

Some big-city railway stations in Pakistan have retiring rooms with beds for Rs 15 to Rs 50 or even more per double, available to holders of air-conditioned or 1st-class sleeper tickets, but you must bring your own bedding. The only one near the KKH now is at Taxila.

Camping

In Xinjiang you can't pitch a tent with any security around larger towns but with a travel permit you can camp at places like Kara Kul and below Muztagh Ata.

In Pakistan, hotels will often let you pitch a tent in their yards or on the roof and use their toilets for a small fee. You can even camp in Islamabad, at the very cheap government-run Tourist Campsite.

Vandalism is not a problem in tent-sites or on most trekking routes but don't leave things loose near villages in the Nanga Parbat and Chilas area, or anywhere in Indus Kohistan.

Booking Ahead

Booking a few days ahead can be useful at government resthouses or hostels but KKH travel is too unpredictable for long-range plans. Most middle and bottom-end hotels don't even take bookings and even an arrangement in writing is apt to get screwed up.

FOOD

Food on the KKH is as varied as its ethnic groups. Eating can be a pleasure in Kashgar, Hunza and Rawalpindi. In Gilgit it's uneven, and in Indus Kohistan you won't go hungry but you may go mad from non-stop curried mutton and chapatti. Local specialities are described in the regional chapters. Remember that Muslims avoid taking food to the mouth with the left hand.

Vegetarians can scrape by in big-town produce markets, Kashgar's Chinese restaurants, Hunza and Gilgit cafes and many upper-echelon places in Rawalpindi-Islamabad. Some hotels will stir up a vegetable entree for you, especially if you bring the ingredients.

In Pakistan Tuesday and Wednesday are 'meatless' days, when mutton and beef are not supposed to be sold or served in public places (the reasons are economic, not religious). Restaurants mostly have chicken then.

In bigger towns the cook may sometimes add a side dish you don't remember ordering. It's partly goodwill but of course you'll have to pay for it! Some travellers report being overcharged when they failed to confirm meal prices in advance, and whether prices were per person or per dish.

In 1987 and 1988 an unusual strain of hepatitis was epidemic in western Xinjiang, and in Pakistan gut infections are common with foreign travellers. See the Health section for hygiene suggestions.

Ramadan

Ramadan is the Muslim month of sunrise-to-sunset fasting. In Xinjiang few seem to take it seriously, and in Gojal and Hunza, Ismailis don't take part. But from Gilgit southward, getting food and drink during the

Melon seller, Swat Valley

day takes some planning. See Religion in the Facts about the Region chapter for more about Ramadan and how to cope with it, and Holidays & Festivals in this chapter for the dates, which change from year to year.

DRINKS
Non-Alcoholic Drinks
In Xinjiang you can get Chinese tea *(cha)* everywhere. In Pakistan, 'milky tea' *(dudh-chai)* is usually equal parts water, leaves, sugar and long-life milk brought to a raging boil – though better places serve a proper 'set', complete with warmed milk. Aside from at five-star hotels, the only coffee is instant. Green tea is called *sabz-chai*. *Khawa* is a sweet and delicious green tea with cardamom or other spices.

Bottled water and soft drinks (including imported brands) are available. Always safe are the little boxes of fruit juice that you punch open with a straw. Tap water is almost never trustworthy (see the Health section for tips on purifying it).

Alcohol
In Kashgar, Chinese beer, wine, brandy and spirits are available in Chinese restaurants and department stores, although Muslim Uyghurs rarely drink (in public).

Pakistan is officially dry but on the KKH non-Muslim foreigners can drink in special lounges at top-end hotels in Rawalpindi and Islamabad. You can get a liquor permit, as long-term residents do (see the Rawalpindi & Islamabad chapter), but elsewhere on the KKH there isn't much liquor to get with it.

In Hunza, some people still brew *mel*, a coarse grape wine, and a powerful mulberry brandy called *arak*. This so-called 'Hunza water' may be offered to you by friends or hustlers.

Getting There & Away

The northern end of the KKH is at Kashgar in China's Xinjiang Autonomous Region. Kashgar is linked by air via the provincial capital, Ürümqi, to major Chinese cities and international points. Overland, it's linked by bus to Ürümqi, from where rail lines run to Chinese cities and to Alma Ata in ex-Soviet Kazakhstan. A warm-weather road also crosses between Kashgar and Bishkek (formerly Frunze) in ex-Soviet Kirghizstan.

The official southern end of the KKH is at Havelian in Pakistan's North-West Frontier Province, but in practice it's at Islamabad, the capital, and its sister-city Rawalpindi. These are within easy reach of international air routes, most via Karachi, and they can be reached by rail and road from southern Pakistan, Iran and India.

Travel Insurance
However you go, it's worth taking out travel insurance. Consider covering yourself for the worst possible case – an accident requiring hospitalisation and a flight home. For an extended trip, insurance may seem an extravagance but if you can't afford it, you can't afford a medical emergency overseas either.

AIR
Flying Cheaply
The airlines' own best fares (usually advance-purchase fares) will give you a point of reference, but they usually aren't the lowest. Various types of discounted tickets can save you a lot and/or increase the scope of your travel at marginal extra cost. Shop around, and start early – some cheap tickets must be purchased months in advance (on the other hand, some bargains appear only at the last minute). Check the travel ads in major newspapers.

Especially in London and some Asian capitals (notably Delhi and Bangkok), you'll find the lowest fares offered by obscure 'bucket shops' taking advantage of last-minute airline discounts and other deals.

Many are honest and solvent, but not all. You're safest if an agency is a member of the International Air Transport Association (IATA) or a national association like the American Society of Travel Agents (ASTA) in the USA, the Association of British Travel Agents (ABTA) in the UK or the Australian Federation of Travel Agents (AFTA) in Australia.

If you're told that incredibly cheap flight is 'fully booked, but we have another costing just a bit more...', try someone else. Don't part with even a deposit until you know the name of the airline (both outward and return), airports of departure and destination and the date and time of the flights, long layovers and any restrictions. If the agent won't give this information, try another agent.

Watch for extra charges, eg surcharges (booking fees should not be necessary as agents get commissions from the airlines). Ask whether all your money will be refunded if the flight is cancelled or changed to a date which is unacceptable to you. Once you have the ticket, ring the airline yourself to confirm that you're actually booked on the flight.

You may decide to pay a little more for the security of a better-known agent. Very convenient are agencies who specialise in finding low fares, like Trailfinders and Campus Travel (UK), Council Travel (USA), Travel CUTS (Canada) and STA (worldwide). Most offer the best deals to students and under-26s but are open to all, and they won't play tricks on you.

Fares to Hong Kong and China are 10% to 20% higher in peak travel season (roughly July-September and December in North America and Europe, December-January in Australia and New Zealand); fares to Pakistan are not very seasonal.

Fares quoted here are approximate low-season, discounted economy fares based on advertised rates at the time of writing. None of them constitutes a recommendation for any airline. Because the KKH can make a shambles of fixed-date travel plans and because onward/return tickets are cheap in Asia, one-way fares are quoted here, though you may save even more if you buy a return ticket.

Reconfirmation
To minimise your chances of being 'bumped' from an onward or return flight due to airline overbooking, reconfirm directly with the airline at least 72 hours before departure – and ask about any adjustments to departure information compared to what's on your ticket.

To/From the USA & Canada
The Los Angeles *Times*, San Francisco *Examiner*, Chicago *Tribune*, New York *Times*, Toronto *Globe & Mail* and Vancouver *Sun* have big weekly travel sections with lots of travel-agent ads.

Council Travel and STA are reliable sources of cheap tickets in the USA. Each has offices all over the country. Council's headquarters are at 205 East 42nd St, New York 10017 (☎ (212) 661-1414 or toll-free (800) 223-7402). STA's main USA offices are at 7204½ Melrose Ave, Los Angeles 90046 (☎ (213) 937-5714) and Suite 805, 17 East 45th St, New York 10017 (☎ (212) 986-9470), or call toll-free (800) 777-0112).

The best bargain-ticket agency in Canada is Travel CUTS, with around 50 offices in all major cities. Their parent office is at 187 College St, Toronto M5T 1P7 (☎ (416) 979-2406).

To/From the UK & Europe
The Saturday *Independent* and Sunday *Times* have good travel sections, including advertisements for scores of bucket shops. Also check out the Travel Classifieds in London's weekly *Time Out* entertainment magazine.

The best known bargain-ticket agencies are Trailfinders (☎ (071) 937 5400) at 42-48 Earl's Court Rd, Kensington, London W8

6EJ; Campus Travel (☎ (071) 730 8111) at 52 Grosvenor Gardens, London SW1W 0AG; and STA (☎ (071) 938 4711) at Priory House, 6 Wrights Lane, London W8 6TA. All three have branches all over London and the UK, and Campus Travel is also in many YHA shops. A good agency for travel arrangements to China is China Travel Service & Information Centre (☎ (071) 388 8838), 3-5 Chalton St, London NW1 1JD.

A reliable European source of bargain tickets is NBBS Travels (☎ 638 1738), Leidsestraat 53, 1017 NV Amsterdam; they have another office at Rokin 38 in Amsterdam (☎ 624 0989). STA has offices in Paris; the main one is at 49 Rue Pierre Charron (☎ 43 59 23 69).

To/From Australia & New Zealand
STA Travel and Flight Centres International are major dealers in cheap airfares, each with dozens of offices. STA's headquarters are at 1st Floor, 224 Faraday St, Carlton, Victoria 3053, Australia (☎ (03) 347 6911), and 10 High St, PO Box 4156, Auckland, New Zealand (☎ (09) 399723). Flight Centre's main offices are at 19 Bourke St, Melbourne, Victoria 3000 (☎ (03) 650 2899) and 82 Elizabeth St, Sydney, NSW 2000 (☎ (02) 235 3522).

To/From Hong Kong
Four reliable Hong Kong travel agencies geared to independent travellers are:

Hong Kong Student Travel, 1021 Star House, Tsimshatsui, Kowloon (☎ 730-3269), or 901 Wing On Central Bldg, 26 Des Voeux Rd, Central (☎ 810-7272), plus half a dozen other branches in the territory

Phoenix Services Agency, Room B, 6th floor, Milton Mansion, 96 Nathan Rd, Tsimshatsui, Kowloon (☎ 722-7378)

Shoestring Travel, 4th Floor, Block A, Alpha House, 27 Peking Rd, Tsimshatsui, Kowloon (☎ 723-2306)

Time Travel, 16th floor, Block A, Chungking Mansions, 40 Nathan Rd, Tsimshatsui, Kowloon (☎ 366-6222, 723- 9993)

The Chinese government-run China Travel Service (CTS) can make relatively cheap hotel and transport bookings for China. Their Foreign Passenger Dept (☎ 853-3533) is at 78 Connaught Rd, Central; their Kowloon Branch (☎ 721-1331) is at 27 Nathan Rd, Tsimshatsui.

If the KKH is Closed!

There are no direct flights between Xinjiang and Pakistan. If snow or landslides have closed the highway, the quickest way around is to fly Beijing-Karachi; Air China (China's national carrier, also known by its old name, CAAC) and PIA (Pakistan International Airlines, Pakistan's national carrier) each have twice-weekly direct flights, and Air France and other carriers also have weekly runs.

TO KASHGAR
Air

A discounted one-way ticket to Hong Kong or Beijing is US$550 to US$600 from New York or Toronto, and US$450 to US$500 from Los Angeles or Vancouver. From London a ticket to Beijing, at about UK£250, is considerably cheaper than to Hong Kong.

Although Air China (CAAC) has direct weekly flights to Ürümqi from Alma Ata (in Kazakhstan) and from Istanbul, the cheapest routes from Europe and North America are via Beijing (Peking) or Shanghai, and the cheapest from Australasia are via Guangzhou (Canton). Ürümqi is about Y1160 from Beijing, with at least one flight a day, Y1500 from Shanghai or Y1575 from Guangzhou, each four times a week. The convenience of quick China visas makes Hong Kong a useful stop, though at least to/from the USA or UK it's cheaper to fly directly into China.

The only way to fly to Kashgar is from Ürümqi with Air China. It's Y540, and goes daily in summer and four times a week in winter. The Chinese call Kashgar *Kashi*.

Bilingual Air China timetables make life easier but they're not to be found in China; try for one at an Air China office back home.

Flying from Hong Kong Several carriers link Hong Kong to Guangzhou, Beijing and Shanghai, but flying across the border is pricey compared to the same distance inside China, and you're also nailed with Hong Kong's HK$150 airport tax. Instead try an overnight boat, morning hoverferry or fast train to Guangzhou and fly from there the same day. You may have to stay the night in Ürümqi.

The lowest airfares into China are on Air China (CAAC, called CNAC in Hong Kong). The cheapest tickets are direct from CNAC (☎ 840-1199), 17 Queens Rd, Central.

Train & Road

To/From Hong Kong & Chinese Cities The marathon land journey from Hong Kong to Kashgar is by train to Ürümqi (4900 km, 4½ days) and by bus from there, parallel to the old Silk Road along the northern edge of the Takla Makan desert (1480 km, three days). Few in their right minds would do this all at once, considering not only comfort but all there is to see en route.

The train from Hong Kong to Guangzhou is about HK$70 or Y50 (local) or HK$250 or Y170 (express). An appealing alternative is an overnight boat up the Pearl River to Guangzhou; there is also a morning hoverferry. From Guangzhou to Ürümqi on a 'hard sleeper' rail berth is about about HK$1250 or Y850, foreigners' price; Beijing-Ürümqi is about Y450.

There are two daily Ürümqi-Kashgar buses: ordinary at about Y60 and deluxe at Y80, running year-round. Buy a ticket from China Youth Travel Service, room 130, Hong Shan Hotel, Ürümqi, or from the long-distance bus station, up to three days in advance. There are also buses to Kashgar from Turfan. Baggage goes on the roof and may be inaccessible for the whole trip, so plan your carry-ons. The bus makes meal-stops but, except for delicious Hami melons, the food is grim.

Top: The Karakoram (RI'A)
Bottom Left: Pakistan-China Border post, Pirali (RI'A)
Bottom Right: Musicians in Muharram procession, Rawalpindi (JK)

Top: Children with typical kohl-coloured eyes, Hunza (JW)
Middle: Army road engineers & friends, Astore Valley (JK)
Bottom: Kirghiz men on the Kashgar to Tashkurghan road (JK)

To/From the Former Soviet Union A year-round overland route crosses to Ürümqi from Alma Ata in Kazakhstan, via the border post at Khorgos. Local buses take one to two days from Alma Ata to Yining on the Chinese side, and two days from Yining to Ürümqi. There is also a bus from Yining via Kuche to Kashgar, taking three days.

Another crossing, open from at least June to September, is the 700-km journey to Kashgar from Bishkek (formerly Frunze) in Kirghizstan via the 3100-metre Torugart Pass (*Tuergata* to the Chinese). So far the only approved way is in a group, by advance arrangement with state tourist organisations – the Ürümqi offices of CITS, Xinjiang Tourism or the Xinjiang Mountaineering Association on the China side, and Intourist on the other side of the border.

A third road, not yet open to tourists, runs to Kashgar from Osh, in the Ferghana Valley in Kirghizstan.

In 1992 a weekly rail service began on a new line between Alma Ata and Ürümqi, opening prospects for long-distance train journeys across Central Asia.

Tight booking policies in the old Soviet republics plus erratic Chinese attitudes about foreigners heading for border regions means you'll have fewer screw-ups coming *into* China from Kazakhstan or Kirghizstan than going the other way.

In crossing from Xinjiang to Alma Ata, one traveller reports that Chinese border officials demanded to see the endorsement on his China visa allowing him to exit there. He didn't have one but talked them into providing one on the spot. This may just have been someone looking for a bribe, but if you're thinking of crossing into or out of a former Soviet republic, you might avoid a major headache by getting written permission on your China visa to do so.

To/From Tibet The road between Kashgar and Lhasa is heavily policed, making that journey very problematic. Foreigners caught there are subject to heavy fines. In the past it was easier leaving Tibet than entering. Transport might include bus, truck, donkey,

yak and one's own feet. Between September and June the cold is severe, and there are stories of Westerners freezing to death in the backs of trucks or by the roadside. For more information see LP's *Tibet – a travel survival kit*.

Cycling

To bring your own bicycle into China you need an import permit, which you can theoretically get on arrival at a Chinese port of entry, in return for a fee and a written promise to take it back out when you leave. However, most ports of entry don't admit bicycles, and it's almost impossible to get a straight answer about which ones do. The China National Tourist Office in London, and some travel agents who ought to know, say only Guangzhou admits them, and even that depends on the customs officer's mood. Yet the chief customs official at Pirali (the Chinese border post on the KKH) says they are admitted there without hassle or fee.

Being allowed to *ride* in China is another matter. Few long-distance roads are open to foreign cyclists. You can ride your own bike around Kashgar but you may not be allowed to ride it to/from the Pakistan border. For more on cycling in China, see LP's *China – a travel survival kit*.

Some travel agents with connections can arrange a bicycle permit in advance. In the UK, China Travel Service & Information Centre (☎ (071) 388 8838) will do it for UK£25, given a week's notice. US companies arranging bike tours in China might be able to help; try Open Road Bicycle Tours (☎ (703) 754-4152), 1601 Summit Drive, Haymarket, VA 22069, or Travent Tours (☎ (800) 325-3009), PO Box 305, Waterbury Center, VT 05677. In Hong Kong, cycle shops who might be able to help include Flying Ball (☎ 381-3661), Wing's (☎ 381-2635) and Prestige (☎ 711-6617).

There's no problem with bringing a bicycle into Pakistan, though you're expected to mention it on your visa application.

Your bike can get to the KKH by air. You can dismantle it and put it in a bag or box, though it's easier just to wheel it to the check-in desk, where it should be treated as baggage (you may have to remove the pedals and turn the handlebars sideways). Check with the airline well ahead of time – preferably before you buy a ticket from them.

Before you leave home, go over the bike with a fine-toothed comb and fill your kit with every imaginable spare. You won't be able to find that crucial widget when your steed breaks down in the back of beyond.

For more on cycling the KKH itself, see the Getting Around chapter, and the Cyclists' Notes in the regional chapters.

TO ISLAMABAD
Air
Only PIA, British Airways and Saudia stop in Islamabad. Most international carriers serve only Karachi. But even if you're bound for Islamabad it's cheaper to go via Karachi, from where there are five to eight flights daily to Islamabad, including a 'Night Coach' flight that's 25% cheaper. Since domestic tickets cost about 30% less if you buy them in Pakistan, it's cheaper still to buy the connecting ticket after you arrive.

A discounted one-way ticket to Karachi is about US$800 from Los Angeles, San Francisco or Vancouver, and US$900 from New York or Toronto. One Lonely Planet correspondent claimed that the cheapest flight to Karachi from the US or Canadian west coast is via Beijing on Air China (CAAC).

A ticket to Karachi from London is UK£160 (compared with UK£300 to Islamabad); from Amsterdam or Frankfurt it's UK£280 (or UK£340 to Islamabad).

Travellers report that Istanbul-Karachi on PIA or THY is about US$300. PIA and newborn Uzbekistan Airlines have launched a weekly Tashkent-Karachi connection. Budget flights from New Zealand and Australia connect with PIA in South-East Asia.

Karachi-Islamabad is Rs 2070, except the night flight (departing Islamabad daily about 11 pm and Karachi about 1 am), which is Rs 1560. You normally pay the Rs 20 domestic departure tax in cash at check-in.

To/From India PIA and Indian Airlines fly Delhi-Karachi, Delhi-Lahore and Bombay-Karachi, each three to five times a week. Lahore-Delhi is cheapest (and most popular, sometimes filling up weeks ahead). From Lahore it's a Rs 450 flight or a Rs 65 bus or train ride to Islamabad.

To/From Iran PIA and Iran Air each have weekly flights between Karachi and Tehran, and PIA flies weekly between Quetta and Mashhad.

Train
You can reach the KKH by train from all over Pakistan. Most trains to the capital area go to Rawalpindi's Saddar Bazaar railway station. A spur of the Rawalpindi-Peshawar line runs to Havelian, the official southern end of the KKH. Pakistan Railways publishes a timetable and fare book, for sale in some booking offices and station book stalls.

Trains are Express, Mail or Passenger, in order of increasing frequency of stops; there are several express trains between major cities every day. Classes are 2nd (hard seats, no compartments), economy (soft seats, no compartments), 1st (soft seats, open compartments) and air-conditioned 1st (closed compartments). Long-distance runs have sleepers in air-conditioned and 1st classes. Air-conditioned and 1st-class seats and sleepers should be booked several days ahead, while 2nd-class tickets are usually sold at most a day before departure.

A student ID card gets you a 50% discount on any ticket, in all classes except air-conditioned. Non-student foreign tourists can get 25% off. To get these discounts, ask the local PTDC office for a letter to the Divisional Superintendent of Railways (at the station), who will then give you a form to show at the ticket window. You must go through this at every town where you buy a ticket.

Bedding is not provided on trains, and many travellers booking sleepers get caught out. Air-con sleeper ticket-holders can theoretically hire bedding, soap, towel and toilet paper from reservations offices at

Rawalpindi, Peshawar, Lahore and some other main centres.

To/From Karachi A berth in a 1st-class sleeper to Rawalpindi (30 hours) is Rs 430, and there are two daily Karachi-Rawalpindi express trains.

To/From Lahore A 1st-class seat is Rs 55 on the two daily Lahore-Rawalpindi express trains. The trip takes six hours.

To/From Peshawar A seat in the daily 2nd-class Peshawar-Rawalpindi 'Railcar' shuttle (four hours) is Rs 30.

To/From Quetta The Abaseen and Quetta expresses take about 30 hours, via Lahore. A 1st-class sleeper is Rs 405.

To/From India Daily express trains link Lahore with Amritsar in India. The crossing at Wagah, east of Lahore (Attari on the India side), is open daily from 9 am to at least 3 pm Pakistan time. This, however, depends on the state of India-Pakistan relations and the level of Sikh separatist activity in the Indian Punjab. Get current local information before heading off to the border. See Visas & Embassies in the Facts for the Visitor chapter, about Indian visas.

To/From Iran There is a weekly train service between Quetta and Zahedan in Iran, via the border post at Taftan (also called Kuh-i-Taftan; Mirjave on the Iran side). The trip takes about 28 hours, departing Zahedan Sunday morning or Quetta Friday noon. A second weekly service goes only between Quetta and the border, taking 22 hours, leaving Taftan Wednesday afternoon or Quetta Tuesday morning. West of Zahedan it's 600 km of dusty bus rides to the next-nearest railhead. See Visas & Embassies in the Facts for the Visitor chapter, about Iranian visas.

Road
Swarms of cheap buses and vans link Rawalpindi with Peshawar and Lahore along the Grand Trunk Road at all hours of the day and night. Bus travel further south into the Punjab is possible by linking shorter trips, eg from Lahore to Multan, though it's not much fun. But further south, travel by road is now extremely dangerous.

Warning on Travel in Southern Pakistan Foreigners are advised to avoid going anywhere in Sind Province except Karachi. The interior of the province is the scene of frequent robberies, kidnappings and murders – of foreigners as well as Pakistanis – by well-organised gangs. There is negligible police authority there and to some extent in extreme southern Punjab. When possible you should travel by air.

The interior of Baluchistan and the Tribal Areas of the NWFP are also outside the control of central government, though the Quetta to Kuh-i-Taftan and Karachi to Quetta (Bolan Pass) roads were secure at the time of writing.

For more on these areas, see Dangers & Annoyances in the Facts for the Visitor chapter.

To/From Lahore The Tourism Development Corporation of the Punjab (TDCP) runs air-conditioned coaches between Rawalpindi and Lahore (five hours) for Rs 85. For the same price a government-funded pilot operation called Intercity Transport Systems runs buses from behind the Shangrila Hotel at Liaquat Chowk. Several operators have hourly vans from Committee Chowk for Rs 65.

To/From Peshawar The same Lahore operators also go hourly to Peshawar from Committee Chowk for Rs 40. GTS and private buses go all day from the Pir Wadhai bus stand for about Rs 25.

To/From India You can cross by road at Wagah, though like the train it's subject to the vagaries of Indo-Pak relations and Indian Sikh terrorism. There are no direct Lahore-Amritsar buses, but plenty to/from the border on both sides. Travellers say Lahore-

Amritsar is quicker by bus (as little as 3½ hours) than by train because of the time it takes to process everybody on the train through customs & immigration.

To/From Iran A dusty, exasperating alternative to the train is the bus from Quetta to the Iranian border at Taftan, with several departures daily, taking longer and costing about the same as a 2nd-class berth on the train. Buses run from there to Zahedan and onward in Iran.

LEAVING PAKISTAN
Buying Airline Tickets
Travel agents are as thick as flies in Rawalpindi, Islamabad and other main cities, though none seem to come up with very big discounts on international flights. Some offer great deals and only later mention their 'commission'. You have a better chance of an honest deal from an IATA member; look for the sticker in the window. A few reliable agencies are listed under Information in the Rawalpindi & Islamabad chapter.

If you buy a ticket in Pakistan, to leave Pakistan on a foreign airline, you can only pay in cash rupees bought with foreign currency. You prove this by furnishing the travel agent or airline office with foreign exchange receipts totalling at least the full airline price (even if you're getting a discount). Without these, no matter how much cash you have, you'd have to exchange a further amount equal to the full price, just for the receipts. If you fly out on PIA you don't need receipts.

Some agents also insist on a form from the bank saying the exchange was specifically for airline tickets; others may accept any receipts less than three months old. You don't get them back. After you've bought your ticket, call the airline yourself and confirm that you're booked on the flight. In the box below telephone numbers for major airline booking offices are listed.

Departure Tax
Tickets for international flights out of Pakistan don't include the departure tax – Rs 200 international departure tax on all economy tickets, *plus* a Rs 280 'foreign travel tax' on those bought inside Pakistan – and even more for business and 1st-class tickets. You must have this on hand in cash rupees at check-in before departure.

MAJOR AIRLINE BOOKING NUMBERS
Listed here are the closest booking offices to Islamabad.

Aeroflot Karachi (☎ (021) 520211)
Air Canada Lahore (☎ (042) 305229)
Air China (CAAC) Karachi (☎ (021) 435570)
Air France Lahore (☎ (042) 214422)
Air Lanka Karachi (☎ (021) 528286)
Alia Royal Jordanian Karachi (☎ (021) 512027)
Alitalia Karachi (☎ (021) 511098)
Biman Karachi (☎ (021) 510069)
British Airways Rawalpindi (☎ (051) 566791, 565413)
Cathay Pacific Karachi (☎ (021) 520683)
Egypt Air Karachi (☎ (021) 513233)
Emirates Karachi (☎ (021) 519611)
Gulf Air Lahore (☎ (042) 302111)
Indian Airlines Lahore (☎ (042) 211249)
JAL Lahore (☎ (042) 304265)
KLM Islamabad (☎ (051) 829685/8)

Korean Air Karachi (☎ (021) 529898)
LOT Karachi (☎ (021) 520589)
Lufthansa Islamabad (☎ (051) 820621)
Northwest Orient Islamabad (☎ (051) 812175)
PIA Rawalpindi (☎ (051) 567011, 568071); Islamabad (☎ (051) 815041)
Philippine Airlines Islamabad (☎ (051) 821567/8)
Royal Nepal Airlines Karachi (☎ (021) 515061)
SAS Karachi (☎ (021) 515897)
Sabena Karachi (☎ (021) 219331)
Saudia Lahore (☎ (042) 305413)
Singapore Airlines Islamabad (☎ (051) 522548)
Swissair Lahore (☎ (042) 62007)
Thai Airways Lahore (☎ (042) 305943)
THY Turkish Airlines Lahore (☎ (042) 303503)

Customs

Though customs checks are spotty for incoming international passengers, they're common for those leaving Pakistan.

TOURS

For those with more money than time, some overseas tour operators offer general, special-interest and 'adventure-travel' group-tour packages in Xinjiang and northern Pakistan, ranging from air-conditioned minibus trips between posh hotels, to truck or jeep safaris, to serious trekking and mountaineering.

Alternatively you can deal directly with local outfits in China and Pakistan. You can save some money this way, though more of the headaches will then be yours. Generally, the smaller the group, the higher the costs.

Refer to Trekking & Other Sports in the Facts for the Visitor chapter for a list of some reputable overseas and local companies. If all you want is short-term transport, guides or other help, it's cheapest and easiest to consult local people after you get there.

The Xinjiang Tourist Corporation offers several group-tour packages taking in the Kashgar region – eg a week from the Khunjerab Pass to Kashgar and back, a week from the Torugart Pass (Kirghizstan border) via Kashgar and Ürümqi to Shanghai, or 10 days from Beijing via Ürümqi, Kashgar and Kara Kul to the Khunjerab Pass. Some China Travel Service (CTS) packages with a 'Silk Road' theme include Ürümqi and Kashgar. Contact addresses are listed under Tourist Information in the Facts for the Visitor chapter.

Getting Around

AIR

PIA (Pakistan International Airlines, the state-run airline) has flights linking Gilgit, Skardu and Islamabad. For the prolonged and stunning views of the western Himalaya and High Karakoram, these flights may be the best airfare bargains in the world. Between Islamabad and Gilgit, 8126-metre Nanga Parbat, 8th highest mountain in the world, is straight out the window (on the right north-bound, left south-bound).

The daily Islamabad-Gilgit (Rs 570) and weekly Gilgit-Skardu (Rs 410) flights are in ageing, prop-driven Fokker Friendships, and the daily Islamabad-Skardu (Rs 680) flights in Boeing 737s. With Gilgit's airstrip due for extension, jets will eventually go there too.

Schedules are the same year-round, though the weather isn't. The flights require near-ideal weather so they're very often cancelled, and all bookings are effectively standby. Winter weather grounds many, but not all, Skardu flights and essentially all those to Gilgit. If the flight is cancelled you're wait-listed for the next one. Booking and confirmation procedures are described under the separate towns.

The flights are very popular; Islamabad-Gilgit especially can get booked up months ahead in summer (though Gilgit-Skardu is rarely full). There are two tourist-priority seats on each Gilgit and Skardu flight, so if PIA says it's full, go to PTDC for a 'special booking' letter to show PIA. The only concessions are for residents of the Northern Areas.

Another air approach to the KKH is by daily Fokker from Islamabad to Saidu Sharif in the Swat Valley, from where it's a few hours by bus to Besham in Indus Kohistan.

Now PIA is about to get some competition. The government is to licence at least one private domestic airline, and at the time of writing an Aga Khan Foundation proposal looked set to be accepted, though no name had been announced. Service would start by 1993, possibly with short-take-off jets serving Gilgit, Skardu and Chitral.

Departure Tax

The Rs 20 domestic air-departure tax is normally figured into the ticket price. If not, you pay cash at check-in.

HIGHWAY TRANSPORT

Although you can take a train up to the southern end of the KKH or a plane into the middle of it, the cheapest and easiest way to get around is on the road itself.

Long-distance buses cover the whole thing, and in Pakistan village-hopping is easy; buses will stop almost anywhere for a passenger. Here's what you can ride and what it's called in the book.

Bus

Cheapest and slowest are the old buses of the Government Transport Service (GTS), running on fixed schedules. In the Northern Areas GTS takes the form of Natco (Northern Areas Transportation Company), with red-and-white coaches linking Rawalpindi, Gilgit, Skardu and the China border.

Then there are private Pakistani buses, rolling works of art: chrome-sequinned vintage Bedfords decorated with poetry, Koranic passages and technicolour landscapes, equipped with tinted windows, musical horns and laminated photos of Ayub Khan, the Aga Khan or the Ayatollah Khomeini.

Chinese buses, all government-run, are marginally maintained, tired old crocks, equipped with bad-tempered drivers.

Van

Natco and private operators in Pakistan run 15-seat Toyota Hi-Ace or 21-seat Toyota Coaster vans ('minibuses') on set regional and long-distance routes. They're faster, more reliable and a bit more expensive than buses; they *can* be more comfortable, though many drivers are maniacs.

Wagon

Old 15-seat Ford wagons are common in Pakistan, privately operated on set regional routes.

Datsun

Private Datsun pickup trucks with seats for 10 to 12 are common regional transport in Kohistan. Natco runs a few 4WD pickups to remote villages.

Suzuki

The most common short-haul transport in northern Pakistan is the converted Suzuki light-duty pickup, holding eight to 10 people.

Jeep

Where mountain roads permit nothing else, 4WD passenger-cargo jeeps and land-cruisers serve remote Pakistani villages. The small ones are said to seat seven but I was once on one with 24 people attached to it. They rarely run to set schedules. Don't let them charge you extra for the privilege of a cab seat.

Local Transport

In Kashgar local transport is by pony-cart, and fares are negotiable. In Pakistani towns it's commonly by fixed-fare Suzuki, and in Rawalpindi there are also motor-rickshaws, taxis and horse-drawn *tongas* (with negotiable fares). In Rawalpindi the Suzukis have conductors, but in smaller towns where they don't, stomp on the floor to signal that you

---

Pakistan Trucks & Buses

Vividly painted transport is a feature of many Asian countries – travellers through Sumatra in Indonesia will remember the buses as much for their paint schemes as for their extreme discomfort, whereas visitors to India often have opportunities to examine the brightly painted wreckage of Indian trucks by the roadside. When it comes to pure over-the-top decoration, however, Pakistan's long-haul trucks are undoubtedly the kings of the Asian highways.

Simply painting the bodywork is only the start of the process of transforming a mundane vehicle into a gaudy work of art. Every available cm of the truck will be decorated in some fashion including badges and motifs plastered across the grille, fringes hanging down beneath the bumpers, geegaws dangling from the mirrors, studs tacked on to the mudflaps, a pyramid succession of mascots stacked on the front like the prow of an ancient sailing galleon, a starburst of reflectors across the back and a vision-obscuring decorative edge applied around the inside of the windscreen. Flickering lights, tassels, streamers, plastic flowers, glass-patterned metal cutouts and other kitschery complete the happy picture.

The custom probably derives from the decorations once applied to camel and mule trains, when charms, prayers and religious requests hopefully kept danger at bay. In modern Pakistan dacoits are undoubtedly as great a danger as ever and accidents are certainly much more likely. Despite the vivid flights of fancy which each truck represents, the decorations follow a fairly fixed pattern. The box-like deck above the truck cabin is usually reserved for prayers to Allah, quotes from the Koran, scenes from Mecca and other religious references.

Much of the rest of the truck will then be filled with scenes of rural arcadia – a city trucker's yearning for the peace of the countryside – or, alternatively, orderly and gracious city scenes – a country boy's dream of big city glamour. Both visions are likely to be a long way from reality. Other curious illustrations can zoom across the natural scenery – there may be ocean liners, birds, butterflies or even strangely Islamic looking versions of F-16 jet fighters. In between, random designs and patterns fill in any remaining space. You can find these mobile art galleries in motion at any time or stationary in the sprawling and filthy truck parking areas on the fringes of large cities. The artists who perform on them can also be seen painting the huge movie posters which are another outlet for modern Pakistani art.

Tony Wheeler

want out. Bicycles can be hired in Kashgar and Gilgit.

Schedules & Concessions

Only Pakistan government buses run on genuinely fixed timetables. Nearly everything else goes only when it's full, so departures can be lengthy affairs. Chinese buses seem to be repeatedly loaded, fuelled and repaired after everyone is on board.

If you ask, and have a student card, Natco gives a 50% student discount between Gilgit and Rawalpindi (except for their once-a-day 'deluxe' service), with a maximum of four discount tickets for each departure. They may not give it unless you book your seat in advance.

It's always worth flashing your student card – sometimes you get a contemptuous glare, but often local buses will give you a discount, but only after your green plastic has been passed around the whole bus to admire.

Hire Your Own

When there's no passenger service, you can often hire your own vehicle and driver. In Pakistan a private hire is called a 'special', and it's a great bargain if you've got enough friends to fill it. A clear advantage of your 'own' vehicle is that you can ask the driver to stop for photos or other impulses – and to drive slowly!

Jeeps can be hired from CITS or the Kashgar Mountaineering Association (Kashgar), PTDC (Gilgit, Kaghan Valley and Rawalpindi) or privately (ask your hotel-wallah). They may be hard to find on short notice in summer. Typical rates for a Land Cruiser at the time of writing were Rs 800 per day plus Rs 6 per km (and an additional Rs 3 per km for returning empty), or fixed totals for common destinations. Kashgar CITS wanted Y160 FEC per day for local trips.

You can often hire a Suzuki or other vehicle right off the street (if you just want a seat, be sure you're not hiring the whole vehicle). A Gilgit agency, Pamir Tours, will rent you a car to drive yourself on paved roads, but you'll need an International Driver's Licence and a very big security deposit. Natco at Sust will rent you a van or even a bus (and driver).

Segregation of Women

On most passenger transport in Pakistan, women and families are seated separately. Western couples are often asked to rearrange themselves or sit apart, not to force Muslim habits on foreigners nor for the women's comfort, but because Muslim men may be acutely uncomfortable sitting next to a strange woman.

CROSS-BORDER BUSES

For many people the whole point of visiting the KKH is the demanding and spectacular trip between Xinjiang and the Northern Areas over the Khunjerab Pass. A bus or van is the normal way to do it, or you can hire your own 4WD or Natco van.

China-to-Pakistan travellers ride buses of the Xinjiang Tourism Authority directly from Kashgar to the Pakistani border post of Sust; the buses return empty as far as the Chinese border post of Pirali. Pakistan-to-China travellers ride Natco from Sust to Pirali, and the Chinese buses from there to Kashgar; Natco returns empty to Sust.

The Kashgar-Sust trip takes two days, with an overnight at Tashkurghan; by jeep it's possible in one long day. From June to September there are usually as many buses as necessary to meet demand; earlier or later in the season there are at least a few per week. The Khunjerab Pass is open to travellers from 1 May to 30 November unless snow closes it sooner.

For information on schedules, fares, bookings and border formalities see the chapters on Kashgar-Tashkurghan and the Khunjerab Pass.

TRAIN

Pakistan's rail system ends where the KKH begins. You can round out your journey with a three-hour, Rs 11 ride in an ancient 2nd-class carriage between Rawalpindi and Havelian (the official southern end of the highway), but that's about all. See the Getting There & Away chapter for more about Pakistani trains, including student and tourist discounts.

CYCLING

The Karakoram Highway is a spectacular trip for cyclists who are super-fit and ready for the unexpected. One that I met called the Pakistan side a dream road; said he, 'where else in the world can you find an incredibly scenic paved road from almost sea level to almost 5000 metres?'

In towns, some cyclists say they found themselves more welcome on a bike than on foot; Pakistanis regard people who walk great distances in the heat as slightly mad.

Things are not so idyllic on the Chinese side, where intercity roads are mostly off-limits to independent foreigners on 'self-propelled transportation'. A few have managed to ride all the way between Kashgar and the Khunjerab Pass, but most are told to stow their bikes on a bus. Some cyclists content themselves with a climb to the Khunjerab Pass on the Pakistan side and a smoking cruise right back down.

Most who have cycled the KKH rate Indus Kohistan (Chilas to Besham) their least favourite part. The people are anarchic and suspicious of outsiders, and men tend to have distorted ideas about Western women. The intervals between decent food and rest are long, and summer weather is scorching. Shatial to Mansehra is subject to some night-time highway robberies. Those considering a visit to other parts of Pakistan should note that the interiors of Sind, Baluchistan and extreme southern Punjab provinces are unsafe for tourists on any form of transport; see Dangers & Annoyances in the Facts for the Visitor chapter.

The Cyclists' Notes (boxed in each chapter) are based on excellent logs by Dieter Kerschbaumer (Switzerland). Good sources of current news are the 'rumour books' at various Northern Areas hotels, in which travellers leave their own advice and warnings; these are noted in each chapter. Not covered in this book are opportunities for off-road mountain bikers, who now go into Pakistan's highlands where once only trekkers went (and are bound by the same permit regulations as trekkers).

See the Getting There & Away chapter for information on getting bikes to the KKH.

Note on Equipment

It's not essential to have a mountain bike if you're staying right on the KKH, which is entirely paved except for the bits torn up by landslides. In spring, however, you may find that winter weather has made hash out of many northern stretches.

Tent and stove are essential in the thinly populated region between Ghez and Sust. But if you're only planning to cycle in Pakistan, it's possible to do without them. The reduced weight will allow you to cycle long enough stretches to always find some sort of shelter and food.

HITCHING

Hitching is possible on well-travelled roads in Xinjiang and northern Pakistan, and safe at least for men. Although some drivers just like the company, others hope for the equivalent of the bus fare. Nobody knows the thumbs-up sign; just wave.

Most lorry drivers in Pakistan are Pathans, who are usually very helpful and friendly. But quite a few Pakistani lorries drive off the road every year, so have a good look at your driver first! Gojal people say some truckers are fond of the Chinese wine that turns up at Sust, and there are plenty of speed-freaks on the long-hauls. The closest thing to a central loading yard in any KKH town is Airport Rd in Gilgit, though Besham has a big repair yard.

A few car drivers have been known to offer a lift and then, on arrival, demand payment.

Kashgar to Tashkurghan

The Tarim Basin is a 1500-km-long depression covering most of southern Xinjiang Autonomous Region in China. It consists almost entirely of a hostile desert called Takla Makan (roughly 'Desert of No Return' in the Uyghur language) with a string of oases round the edge.

Kashgar (Chinese name Kashi or Ka-shih) is one of these oases, at the western end of the desert in a cul-de-sac formed by the Tian Shan Mountains, the Pamirs and the Kunlun Range. 'Kashgaria' is the historical name for the western Tarim Basin. Despite its isolation, this was a hub of the world's most famous overland trade route system – the Silk Road, linking China, India and the Mediterranean – and a crossroads for invading armies, and it has bristled with activity for over 2000 years.

History

Kashgaria's terrain, people, languages and religion have more in common with the adjacent former Soviet republics of Kazakhstan, Kirghizstan and Tajikistan, and even with northern Pakistan, than with China. But over the centuries Imperial China has come again and again to control its frontiers or police the Silk Road. History in the Tarim Basin is mainly about conflicts between the Chinese and the indigenous nomadic tribes.

The Han Dynasty was already here in the 1st century AD, protecting its new trade routes to the West, but the prospering Silk Road oases fell to northern nomadic warrior tribes, Mongols and later Turks. The Emperor's power was not reasserted until the Tang Dynasty, China's golden age in the 7th and 8th centuries. Even then, empires were jostling each other; in the 8th century an Arab expedition reached Kashgar, and a Tang army crossed the Pamirs and occupied Gilgit and Chitral for several years in an attempt to deal with Arab and Tibetan expansion.

Tang control in Kashgaria was ended in 752 by the Turks, and the area was ruled by a succession of tribal kingdoms – Uyghur, Qarakhan and Karakitai, ancestors of present-day Uyghurs – for more than four centuries. It was during the Qarakhan Dynasty in the 11th and 12th centuries that Islam, spreading east from Persia (Iran), first took hold here. Qarakhan tombs are still standing in Kashgar and nearby Artush.

In 1219 Kashgaria fell to the Mongol Empire of Jenghiz Khan. In a realm reaching almost to the Atlantic, few boundaries or local conflicts impeded travel, and for another century the Silk Road flourished. Marco Polo journeyed to China during this time. In the late 1300s a Turkic or Mongol warlord of Samarkand, Timur (called Tamerlane in the West), sacked Kashgar in the course of a rampage across Asia to purge it of Mongol 'impurities'. Until the 1700s Kashgaria was under the control of Timur's descendants or various Mongol tribes.

In 1755 China was back, in the form of a Manchu army, and Kashgar became part of the Qing Dynasty. One of China's favourite tales of tragic love concerns the fourth Qing Emperor, Qian Long. Having put down a revolt led by an Uyghur princess named Xiang Fei, he had her brought to the Forbidden City as a concubine – and promptly fell in love with her. Within two years of arriving in Beijing she committed suicide.

Resentment of Qing rule often boiled over in local revolts. In 1847 Hunza, then an independent Karakoram state, helped Chinese put down a revolt in Yarkand. During the 1860s and 1870s a series of Muslim uprisings erupted across China. In 1865 Yaqub Beg, a military officer from Tashkent in Uzbekistan, seized Kashgaria, proclaimed an independent Turkestan and made diplomatic contacts with Britain and Russia. Within a few years, however, a Qing army had returned, Beg committed suicide and Kashgaria was formally incorporated into China's newly created Xinjiang ('New Dominions') Province.

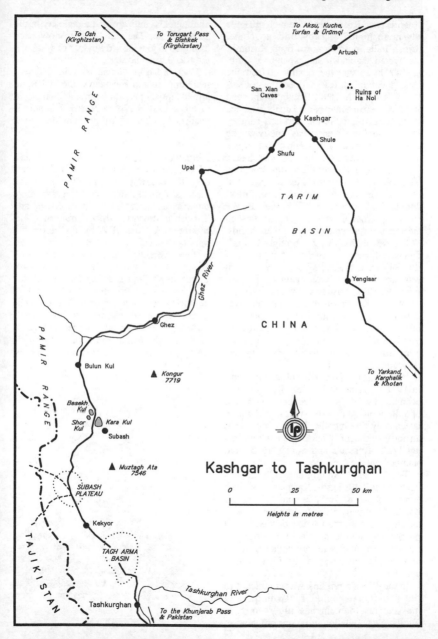

Kashgar to Tashkurghan

0   25   50 km

Heights in metres

British and Russian involvement in Beg's adventure hinted at geopolitics to come. British India, probing north from Kashmir, discovered Tsarist Russia, expanding south. In 1882, by an agreement extracted from the Qing government, Russia opened a consulate in Kashgar. In 1890, Britain established an office there too, and beefed up its presence in the Karakoram. For the next half-century an imperial war of nerves was quietly waged across the Pamirs and Hindu Kush. Spies posed as explorers, scholars and merchants. Kashgar was at the centre of this so-called 'Great Game' (or 'Tournament of Shadows' as the Russians called it) to establish political dominance over eastern Turkestan. In the end Russia took most of the Pamirs, though the Tarim Basin remained in Chinese hands.

The Revolution of 1911 brought China's dynastic history to an end, but the new Republic became a stage for 38 years of civil war, and local warlords again held sway. After the 1917 Bolshevik revolution Russia vacated its Kashgar listening-post, and was not allowed back until 1925. Despite this official absence, Soviet political and economic influence was very strong until Xinjiang fell to the nationalist Chinese (Kuomintang) in 1941.

New Muslim uprisings exploded in Hami in 1931 and Khotan in 1933. Kashgar was occupied by rebels and declared the capital of a 'Republic of Eastern Turkestan' – which lasted only two months. By the mid-1930s an odd coalition of Chinese soldiers, immigrant White Russians and Soviet troops had stamped out these revolts.

The People's Republic of China was declared in 1949, and the Kashgar consulates were shut down. The communists in 1955 declared Xinjiang an autonomous region in an effort to ease the tension between local people and imported Chinese government, but within a few years provincial officials were edging away from the idea of true autonomy.

In the 1960s a rail link was completed to the provincial capital of Ürümqi, and massive resettlement has tilted northern Xinjiang's population in favour of Chinese,

although Uyghurs are still a majority in the Tarim Basin. The rail line has now been extended to join the old Soviet rail system at the Kazakhstan border.

Friction has continued with the Chinese, including riots in Kashgar in the 1970s, an armed uprising by Muslim nationalists in October 1981 that may have left hundreds dead, and further bloody unrest in May 1990.

People

Xinjiang is home to over a dozen of China's 55 official national minorities, and at least six ethnic groups are prominent in the Kashgar region. A walk in the bazaar offers an array of faces from Chinese, Slavic and Turkish to downright Mediterranean – surmounted, incidentally, by an incredible variety of hats.

The overriding majority in the Tarim Basin are the phlegmatic Uyghurs (pronounced WEE-gur), descendants of Turkic nomads who arrived in the 11th and 12th centuries, and now mainly farmers. The Tarim Basin also has some Kazakhs, nomads of Mongol stock, known for their equestrian skill, though most live in northern Xinjiang and the former Soviet republic of Kazakhstan.

Kazakh man

The summer villages and small camel caravans in the Kara Kul region are mostly of Kirghiz, who have retained some nomadic ways. Also here are some Uzbeks. Both are descended from nomadic herders of Turkic ancestry.

Most in evidence near the Pakistan border are the Persian-speaking Tajiks. These mild, rather European-looking people, once renowned as skilled herders, also live in northern Pakistan and eastern Afghanistan (where they are called Wakhi) and in the former Soviet republic of Tajikistan. Most Tajiks in China live in Tashkurghan Tajik Autonomous County, south of Kashgar.

It's a surprise to encounter the occasional Russian here, looking like a visitor from 1950s Eastern Europe. They're descendants of White Russians who fled after the 1917 Soviet revolution. Han Chinese are still a small minority in southern Xinjiang, though dominant in government.

The official language is Mandarin Chinese and each tribe has its own tongue, but Xinjiang's lingua franca is Uyghur (also called Turki). Uyghur is written in both Arabic and Latinised scripts, the latter introduced for a time in an unpopular Chinese attempt to reduce illiteracy.

With the exception of the Chinese and Russians, nearly all are Sunni Muslims, though not as self-consciously devout as those in Pakistan.

Time
A constant problem for visitors is clock time.

Cyclists' Notes, Kashgar-Tashkurghan

The KKH on the China side has km-posts, probably distances from Ürümqi.

The highway between Kashgar and Tashkurghan is within a restricted area, for which independent cyclists apparently need a special permit from Beijing. But an ordinary Alien's Travel Permit for the Kara Kul region appears to satisfy the police at the checkposts at Ghez and Kekyor. Get the permit from the Public Security Bureau at Kashgar or Tashkurghan, but don't tell them you're cycling.

If you're north-bound you may be told at Pirali to pack your bike on top of the bus. Two cyclists shook off Pirali customs officials by saying they were going to spend the night and take the next day's bus – and then rode away. Even if you're not so lucky, you can get off the bus and try for a travel permit at Tashkurghan.

Kashgar to Ghez, 123 km About 40 km from Kashgar is Upal (Chinese Wupaer) with melons, samosas and other snacks. At 86 km from Kashgar is a small cafe with good home-made noodles. After this the road climbs steeply into the Ghez River canyon, where landslides may block the road during rainstorms. The Ghez checkpost has very basic food and accommodation.

Ghez to Kara Kul, about 90 km About 40 km from Ghez you reach the head of the canyon, where you might camp away from the road behind the sand dunes, or continue a few km to the truck stop at Bulun Kul, with basic food and accommodation. Camping by Kara Kul Lake is OK if you have a travel permit. A tourist *yurt* site by the lake has overpriced food and accommodation.

Kara Kul to Tashkurghan, about 80 km The road rises to the Subash Plateau at about 4100 metres. About 40 km from Kara Kul is Kekyor checkpost, where you might find food. A grotty truck stop perches on the steep climb south out of the Tagh Arma Basin. If you're north-bound, get a travel permit from Tashkurghan Public Security, but don't show them your bike or they may put you on a bus. Tashkurghan is about the only place between Kashgar and Sust with food shops.

Tashkurghan to Pirali, 95 km The bumpy road goes slightly downhill, then rises toward the Pirali border checkpost. There is no food or accommodation until Pirali, except possibly at a pinch at the settlement of Dabdar.

All China is supposed to run on Beijing time. Here, 3500 km from Beijing, that is ludicrous, and people work on unofficial 'Xinjiang time', two hours earlier than Beijing time. You must run on both times, always checking which is meant *(Beijing shijian? Xinjiang shijian?)*.

Business Hours

Business hours in Kashgar and Tashkurghan are roughly 10 am to 2.30 pm and 5 to 9 pm in summer, and 10 am to 2 pm and 3.30 to 7.30 pm in winter (Beijing time), Monday through Saturday. Some offices close on Wednesday afternoon. Many locally run shops are open Sunday and closed Monday.

KASHGAR

Some things in Kashgar haven't changed since medieval times. Old town blacksmiths, carpenters and cobblers work by hand. In surrounding fields the loess soil bears wheat, maize, beans, rice, cotton, and fruit in profusion: melons, grapes, figs, pomegranates, peaches and apricots. Id Kah Mosque stands over the town as it has since 1442. Even after two millennia Kashgar is still just a big market town, from the impromptu street-corner negotiations to the perpetual bazaars and the hotel-room deals with Gilgiti traders.

In other ways the past is clearly gone, and not just the jingling camel caravans. Most obvious are the aggressive changes since 1949, symbolised by the huge statue of Mao Zedong. The old town walls have been torn down and factories, schools and even a university have gone up. High-rises are sprouting in the centre. Sleaze, including prostitution, has arrived in the wake of tourism. Kashgar got a rush of Western media culture in September 1992 when the first Paris-Moscow-Beijing car rally thundered through.

The British and Russian consulates, for half a century the nerve centres of the Great Game, were closed in 1949. The British office, known as Chini Bagh (Uyghur for Chinese Garden), was first occupied in 1890 by George Macartney. In 1898 he imported a bride from his native Scotland, and over the next 20 years Catherine Macartney made Chini Bagh an island of gardens and European stateliness.

A 15-minute walk away was the Russian Consulate, never blessed with a Lady Macartney. The imperial rivalry across the Pamirs was matched by personal rivalries across town – for information, Chinese sympathies, even Silk Road antiquities. Both consulates are now reincarnated as tourist hotels.

Kashgar's future may imitate its past. Barter trade across the borders with the old Soviet republics resumed in 1983. China has finished a rail link from Ürümqi to Kazakhstan, and has floated various plans for Special Economic Zones around Kashgar. It's not hard to imagine a new high-tech Silk Road crossing the Tarim Basin one day.

Kashgar is about 1335 metres above sea level. Peak season for tourists (and peak demand for rooms and transport) is late June through September.

Orientation

Kashgar is built around two perpendicular main streets. Official (Chinese) street names are given here. The compass direction is often part of the name; *bei, nan, dong, xi* mean respectively north, south, east, west. The main streets out from the centre are Renmin Dong Lu and Renmin Xi Lu (East and West People's Rd), and Jiefang Bei Lu and Jiefang Nan Lu (North and South Liberation Rd). The perimeter road on the north-west is Shengli Lu (Victory Rd).

For Uyghurs, the heart of town is around Id Kah Mosque and the main bazaar; for Chinese it's probably the Mao statue. For a budget traveller it's the west side, where the middle-range hotels are. The Sunday Market grounds are east of town.

Buses from Pakistan normally go straight to the Chini Bagh Hotel, from where it's a 10-minute walk to the Seman Hotel. If you arrive by air a bus brings you to the Air China (CAAC) booking office on Jiefang Nan Lu, from where you can catch a pony cart to the Seman for Y1 if you bargain.

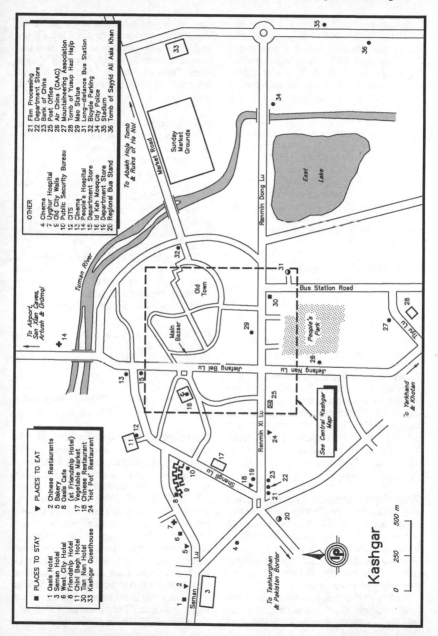

Kashgar

PLACES TO STAY
1 Oasis Hotel
3 Seman Hotel
6 West City Hotel
8 Friendship Hotel
11 Chini Bagh Hotel
30 Tian Nan Hotel
33 Kashgar Guesthouse

▼ PLACES TO EAT
2 Chinese Restaurants
5 Bakery
8 Oasis Cafe
(at Friendship Hotel)
17 Vegetable Market
18 Chinese Restaurant
24 'Hot Pot' Restaurant

OTHER
4 Cinema
7 Uyghur Hospital
9 Old City Walls
10 Public Security Bureau
12 CITS
13 Cinema
14 People's Hospital
15 Department Store
16 Id Kah Mosque
19 Department Store
20 Regional Bus Stand
21 Film Processing
22 Department Store
23 Bank of China
25 Post Office
26 Air China (CAAC)
27 Mountaineering Association
28 Tomb of Yusup Hazi Hajip
29 Mao Statue
31 Long-distance Bus Station
32 Bicycle Parking
34 City Police
35 Stadium
36 Tomb of Seyyid Ali Asla Khan

To Airport,
San Xian Caves,
Artush & Ürümqi

To Abakh Hoja Tomb
& Ruins of Ha Noi

Tuman River

Market Road

Sunday
Market
Grounds

East
Lake

Renmin Dong Lu

Old Town

Main
Bazaar

Bus Station Road

People's
Park

Jiefang Bei Lu

Jiefang Nan Lu

See Central Kashgar Map

Renmin Xi Lu

Shengli Lu

Seman Lu

To Tashkurghan
& Pakistan Border

To Yarkand
& Khotan

0   250   500 m

Information

Tourist Office The FIT (foreign independent travellers) office of China International Travel Service (CITS) is just inside the Chini Bagh Hotel gate. They'll give you a Kashgar map and a rundown of standard tourist sites, and will rent you a jeep for a day trip or a dash to Pakistan.

The Kashgar Mountaineering Association (☎ 22957) is a government liaison office for expeditions and group sports travel (eg trekking, mountain biking, white-water boating). But with a few days' notice they can also help independent tourists – eg with guides, transport, permits, equipment rental (but no sleeping bags) or complete trekking packages to remote areas. They're at 8 Tiyu Lu ('Sports Rd'), off Jiefang Nan Lu beyond CAAC.

Other Tourist Help A genial hustler named John Hu runs an amateur 'service bureau' out of his *John's Cafe* at the Seman Hotel. He can help with bookings and tickets, tours, jeeps, international calls, etc. He also has a good travellers' bulletin board. His lease is perpetually in doubt, so he may have moved by the time you read this.

Banks & Moneychangers You can cash travellers' cheques at the Seman, Chini Bagh and Kashgar Binguan hotels and (if you should find it open) the Bank of China on Renmin Xi Lu. All accept travellers' cheques and cash in most currencies, paying FEC. The bank also buys back FEC, but only gives US dollars. Exchange rates are uniform throughout China.

Black Market Moneychanging in Kashgar is an Uyghur business. Dealers loiter outside the hotels, and you'll be asked to change money – FEC, US dollars and Hong Kong dollars – for RMB until you're sick of it. Most dealers seem to be straight shooters but a few cheat, and the following comments may help you avoid rip-offs.

Trade a round sum, for quick mental calculations. Fold it up in a pocket, to avoid fumbling in an open purse or wallet. Tell them what you have, but don't pull it out (some claim they want to check it for counterfeit). Insist on their money first, and take your time counting it, ignoring their pleas to hurry. Once you're sure it's right, don't let the dealer recount it; hand over your little wad, and split.

Post & Telecommunications The post office is on Renmin Xi Lu. Downstairs are stamp counters; hand your stamped letters over the counter rather than dropping them into what may be the wrong post box. The stamp section is also open during siesta-time and on Sunday. Upstairs at poste restante is a conscientious young man who speaks English well and can help with all international postal matters. There's a Y1 charge for each letter you pick up.

The centre entrance is the telephone & telegraph office, from where you can call and cable overseas. You can also call at competitive rates from John's Cafe, a more pleasant place to spend the hours it sometimes takes.

CAAC The Air China (CAAC) ticket office is on Jiefang Nan Lu near a side entrance to People's Park. This is also the terminus for the airport bus.

Police A city police office is on Renmin Dong Lu, past East Lake.

Travel Permits & Visa Extensions The regional Public Security Bureau (PSB), officially the Border & Administrative Office for Foreigners & Visitors, is on Shengli Lu. One-month visa extensions are Y25 FEC. If you're south-bound and your visa is about to expire, extend it here to avoid potential hassles at the Pirali border post.

Aliens' travel permits *(waiguoren lüxingzhen)*, for areas not freely open to foreigners, are Y5 FEC. Before issuing these, Kashgar PSB may ask for a certificate from CITS (who call it a 'booking form', though apparently you don't have to book anything to get it) – a neat little scam for CITS, who charge at least Y10 for the certificate.

Top: Family in the fields, Xinjiang (RI'A)
Middle Left & Centre: Kashgar Sunday Market (JK & RI'A)
Middle Right: Kirghiz family near Id Kah Mosque, Kashgar (JK)
Bottom: Karakul, between Kashgar and Tashkurghan (JK)

Top: Uyghur men at Id Kah Mosque, Kashgar (JK)
Bottom Left: Shia Muslim Mosque, Altit Village, Hunza (JK)
Bottom Right: Old Mosque, Kashgar (JK)

Hospitals The main Chinese hospital is People's Hospital *(Renmin Yiyuan)* on Jiefang Bei Lu north of the river. There's a hospital of traditional Uyghur medicine on Seman Lu about ½ km east of the Seman Hotel, but travellers say it's filthy.

Film & Photography You can get print film (Fujicolor and Chinese black & white) in bigger department stores. Colour processing is available on Renmin Dong Lu diagonally opposite the Mao statue, and beside the Bank of China. A small camera repair shop is said to be on Jiefang Nan Lu just south of the Renmin Hotel.

Bookshops There is a Xinhua Bookshop on Jiefang Bei Lu, with posters and postcards but few books of interest in English.

Newspapers & Magazines Forget it – even *China Daily* seems to get here only in travellers' rucksacks.

The Sunday Market
Once a week Kashgar's population swells by 100,000, as people stream in to the Sunday Market – surely the most mind-boggling bazaar in Asia, and not to be missed. By sunrise the roads east of town are a single-minded sea of pedestrians, horses, sheep, braying donkeys, bikes and motorcycles, pony carts and push-carts, everyone shouting *boish-boish!* ('coming through!').

In arenas off the road, men 'test-drive' horses or examine the teeth of huge Bactrian camels (you can take one away for about US$200). A wonderful assortment of people sit by their rugs and blankets, clothing and boots, hardware and junk, tapes and boomboxes – and, of course, hats. It's a photographer's dream; bring three times as much film as you expect to use. In fact the whole town turns into a bazaar, with hawkers everywhere.

Getting There & Away The grounds are a 10-minute walk from the Kashgar Guesthouse, but 30 or 40 minutes from the Seman Hotel. You can take a bike and park it in the bike-lot at the corner of the Market Rd and the ring-road. Pony carts are plentiful outside the Seman Hotel on market day. It's best to go fairly early, hiring an entire cart with friends, for Y5 to Y10 for all; less than a full cart means hassles are more likely. Ask for *Yenga Bazaar* (New Market) or *Yekshenba Bazaar* (Sunday Market).

Abakh Hoja Tomb
The best example of Muslim architecture in Kashgar is an elegant mausoleum built in the mid-1600s for the descendants of a Muslim missionary named Muhatum Ajam. With its tiled dome and four minarets, it resembles a brightly coloured, miniature Taj Mahal. There are more than 70 graves, including the small ones of children, beneath the tiled stones in the main chamber. These include Muhatum Ajam's grandson Abakh Hoja, a local Uyghur aristocrat sometimes called the 'patron saint of Kashgar'.

The mausoleum's most celebrated occupant is Abakh Hoja's granddaughter Ikparhan, widow of a Yarkandi prince and better known to Chinese as Xiang Fei (Fragrant Consort). In 1759 she led Uyghurs in an unsuccessful revolt against the Qing Emperor Qian Long, and was then taken off to Beijing as an imperial concubine. There the Emperor fell madly in love with her. Two years later, while Qian Long was out of town, his mother the Empress Dowager – perhaps worried about her son's emotional stability – ordered Xiang Fei to commit suicide. According to legend her body now rests here, and some claim the old sedan chair in the mausoleum is the one that bore her home.

Behind the mausoleum is a vast, run-down Muslim graveyard.

Getting There & Away The tomb is a half-hour bike ride or a two-hour walk north-east of town; a pony-cart round trip from the Seman Hotel is perhaps Y15 to Y20. Avoid arriving at lunchtime, as you may not find anyone to let you in.

Tomb of Yusup Hazi Hajip
A grand mausoleum on Tiyu Lu, off Jiefang

Nan Lu, marks the grave of an 11th-century Sufi preacher who was apparently also the author of a famous Uyghur epic poem.

Tomb of Sayyid Ali Asla Khan

Another historical site is this tomb and small mosque, quite unimpressive considering they mark the grave of a ruler of the 11th century Qarakhan Dynasty. At the end of Renmin Dong Lu, at the roundabout, go about three-quarters of a km south; the tomb is on the right.

Three-Immortals Caves, Ruins of Ha Noi & Mor Pagoda

Twenty km north of Kashgar is one of the area's few traces of the flowering of Buddhism, the Three-Immortals (San Xian) Caves, three grottoes high on a sandstone cliff, in one of which some peeling frescoes can be made out. Unfortunately, the cliff is too sheer to climb, so it's a bit of a disappointment.

At the end of a jarring 35-km drive northeast of town are the ruins of Ha Noi, a Tang Dynasty town built in the 7th century and abandoned in the 12th. Little remains except a great solid pyramid-like structure and the huge Mor Pagoda or stupa.

Getting There & Away You could visit both sites in half a day by jeep, but your driver might miss his lunch and nap, so CITS will only take you to one in the morning and one in the afternoon, for Y195. Your hotel might arrange a better deal.

Id Kah Mosque

The big yellow-tiled mosque is one of the largest in China, with courtyard and gardens that hold 8000 people. From its minarets the *azan*, or call to prayer, is cried through a loud-speaker. It was built in 1442 as a smaller mosque on what was then the outskirts of town. During the Cultural Revolution, China's decade of political anarchy from 1966 to 1976, Id Kah suffered heavy damage, but has since been restored.

It's acceptable for non-Muslims to go in. Local women are rarely seen inside but Western women who go in for a look are usually ignored if they're modestly dressed (arms and legs covered and a scarf on the head). But a woman friend who tried to do *t'ai ch'i* in the courtyard one morning was chased out by a screaming mullah!

In front of the mosque is Id Kah Square, swarming on sunny days with old men in their high boots and long black coats, and women with brown veils over their heads.

There are also more than 90 tiny neighbourhood mosques throughout the city.

Bazaars

East of Id Kah Square, behind the first row of buildings, is the main bazaar, a dusty labyrinth of blacksmiths, farriers, carpenters and jewellers; teashops, bakeries and noodle shops; and vendors of everything, including hats of every description.

On the south side of Id Kah Square is the night market, the best place to sample Uyghur food. There are two covered cloth bazaars, one north of the square and one off Jiefang Bei Lu.

The Old Town

Sprawling across a hill east of the main bazaar is a complex of narrow passages and adobe buildings that seems trapped in a time warp. Off Jiefang Bei Lu are several streets with bright new buildings in traditional Uyghur style. Other old neighbourhoods are north-west and south-west of Id Kah.

City Walls

At the east end of Seman Lu stands a 10-metre-high section of the old wall – actually inner and outer walls, at least 500 years old. Construction around, on and in them makes access impossible, and there's clearly no interest in preserving them.

People's Park

South of the Mao statue is People's Park (*Renmin Gongyuan*), a weedy arboretum with avenues of tall poplars, ponds, a little zoo, and Uyghurs at billiards, chess and *shiang chi* (Chinese chess). Admission is two mao. East of the park, 200 metres down a

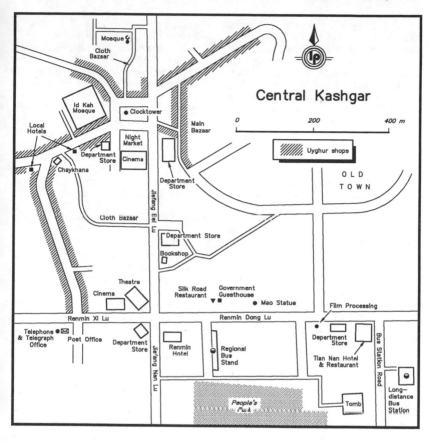

Central Kashgar

back lane, is an old tomb, now quite smashed up and with most of its blue tiles stripped off. According to local people it may have been for an imam (religious leader) in the 19th century.

East Lake

Just outside town along Renmin Dong Lu is a man-made lake lined with willows. It's a popular spot for migratory birds and a good place for a picnic or a peaceful walk among the weeds. In the summer you can rent little boats here.

Pigeon Swap

You may notice flocks of birds wheeling over the city, signalled from house-tops with flags, whistles or hoots. Pigeon-raising is popular here, and on warm evenings there is a quiet pigeon market *(keptey bazari)* in Id Kah Square, where young men buy and sell birds by the light of oil lamps and candles.

Places to Stay

Most of the hotels in Kashgar now insist on FEC from foreigners.

Bottom end The *Chini Bagh, Seman, Tian*

Nan and *Kashgar Guesthouse* have cheap dorm beds. The *Friendship Hotel (Youyi Binguan)*, *West City Hotel* and *Oasis Hotel*, all on Seman Lu, say 'no foreigners' but some staff suggested this was temporary, and you might catch them on a good day; West City Hotel's quads are Y6 a bed. With similar prices and similar attitude are the *Jiaotong Lushe* (Transport Hotel) at the bus station and a small government guesthouse *(zhaodaisuo)* through the second gate west of the Mao statue.

Middle Of the foreigner-friendly mid-range hotels, *Chini Bagh* gets good marks for convenience. It's near the centre and is also the terminus for Pakistan buses. The *Seman* neighbour-hood wins for Western food and travellers' information. The *Tian Nan's* ace is a good Chinese restaurant.

Chini Bagh, favoured by Pakistani traders, is a five-storey tower where the British Consulate's front gate used to be. Signs display Chinese versions of the name like 'Qiniwake'. Rooms are noisy but it's cheerful and well run. Beds are about Y10 in 18-bed dorms, and about Y15 in basic quads with showers. Doubles with TV, bathtub and fan are about Y80. There are Chinese and Uyghur restaurants and a coffee shop. At the back is the original consular house, now tarted up as a banquet hall and deluxe suites.

The Russian Consulate is now the old wing of the *Seman* ('si-MAAN'), also called *Lao Binguan* (Old Hotel). The cheaper old-wing rooms have bad plumbing, falling plaster, broken locks, slack service and/or all-night noise, but most have bathtubs and plenty of hot water. The Chinese have evidently decided to let them fall down by themselves. Beds are Y12 in dorms with communal shower, and about Y20 in doubles, triples and fivers. Doubles in the new building are overpriced at about Y100 and hot water is erratic. The hotel's biggest asset is John's Cafe, with decent food, atmosphere and travellers' help.

The *Tian Nan Hotel* is on Renmin Dong Lu near the long-distance bus station. Beds are about Y10 in dorms, and Y15 in triples

and quads. Doubles are about Y40 and Y50, and a 'suite' is about Y80. Showers are communal. The modern *Renmin Hotel* at the centre says 'no foreigners'.

Travellers report a new hotel, the *Silk Road*, where decent rooms are Y16 per bed.

Top end The group-oriented *Kashgar Guesthouse*, also called *Xin Binguan* (New Hotel), is a spacious, quiet compound east of the centre with Chinese and Uyghur restaurants, a bar and a beer garden. Doubles are Y90 and triples Y65, with bath. Quads with communal shower are Y8 per bed. Its biggest drawback is that it's three km out of town, though you can hire a bike and there are always a few pony carts about.

Places to Eat
At the height of the season Kashgar has some of the best cheap food on the road: Uyghur, Chinese and Western cooking, as well as fresh produce.

In 1987-88 an unusual strain of hepatitis was epidemic in the Tarim Basin and many eateries were shut down. This is now history but it underlines the need for common sense in eating.

Self-Catering This is easy, even for vegetarians. A small vegetable market is on Shengli Lu. In the main bazaar, and near the bus station, are fresh fruit, hard-boiled eggs (dyed red), steamed yams and fat yellow figs sold on leaves. Early in the morning, small bakeries, especially around Chini Bagh and Id Kah Mosque, churn out stout Uyghur nan bread (the flat ones are called ak nan, and the bagels are called gurdah), and women sell yoghurt at hotel gates and in the bazaar for Y1 a bowl.

Department stores may have dried or preserved fruit, biscuits, sweets, peanut butter, bulk honey and nuts. Dried fruit isn't always clean, and it's wise to soak it in water which you are boiling or iodine-treating.

Uyghur Food Best is the smoky night market by Id Kah Square where, urged on by cries of *kasleh-kasleh!* ('welcome!'), you can stuff yourself for about Y5. Try mutton kebabs or shashlik, Kashgar pulau or pilaf (rice, mutton and turnip shavings), meatballs in broth, or delicious deep-fried fish (but get one straight from the pan). You can eat laghman or la-mian (meat, vegetables, chillies and broth over boiled noodles), or somian (noodle bits fried with meat and vegetables). It's no place for a vegetarian, though, and hygiene is variable. There is even ice cream, which is excellent but of questionable cleanliness.

Here and there you'll find chaykhanas (teahouses) full of leather-booted Uyghurs and Uzbeks quaffing tea. One behind Id Kah has a breezy upstairs balcony. But food at these places tends to be grotty.

Various 'Muslim Restaurants' around town also serve cheap, pork-free dishes in dirty conditions.

Chini Bagh and the *Kashgar Guesthouse* have mediocre but clean Uyghur dining halls. If you're lucky enough to be invited into an Uyghur home you may enjoy other delights, eg poshkal, a light rolled-up pancake with savoury filling, like Russian blinys, or a beef and tomato stew called jarkop.

Chinese Food The best food is at the *Tian Nan Restaurant*, behind the hotel of the same name, an obvious favourite of homesick Chinese bureaucrats and their families; fill up for Y10. The restaurant at the *Renmin Hotel* is also said to be good. The tiny, signless *Si Lu Fandian* (Silk Road Restaurant) adjoins the government guesthouse (second gate west of the Mao statue), and back streets have others. Little English is spoken.

Two clean Chinese cafes opposite the Seman Hotel – the *Limin* and *Seman Road* – vie with each other to be warm and friendly, an arresting experience in China. Both have vast menus of oily, spicy dishes, and tea is cheap and plentiful. Fill up for Y10 to Y20. Next door, the *Oasis Restaurant* (not to be confused with the Oasis Cafe) in the hotel of the same name does mainly banquets but the food is good if you find it open.

Several hotels serve decent, meaty set Chinese meals at set times – breakfast about 10 am, lunch 2.30 to 3 pm, and dinner 9 to 9.30 pm (Beijing time). Lunch and dinner are about Y10 at *Chini Bagh* and the *Seman*, and Y20 at *Kashgar Guesthouse*.

A restaurant west of the post office on Renmin Xi Lu, though signposted *Muslim Restaurant*, will on request serve up Mongolian-style hot-pot, or *shui-yan-rou*. In the middle of your table a brass pot with a chimney up the middle and coals underneath keeps broth nearly boiling. You add herbs and salt and dip in rice noodles, cabbage and meat slivers till they cook, and drink the broth afterward. Big mess, great fun – a good group meal.

Western Food Various entrepreneurs have tried to set up Western-style places, only to be thwarted by jealous middle-level apparatchiks. The best at the time of writing are *John's Cafe* at the Seman Hotel and the *Oasis Cafe* at the Friendship Hotel. You didn't come all this way for chips, pizza or chocolate cake, but you can get them here, along with soups, quiche, burgers, apple pie and vegetarian dishes. This isn't the cheapest way to eat in Kashgar but it's a good antidote for burn-out. This is still Asia, however, so don't count on Western-style hygiene. In late evening they turn into pubs.

The *Limin* and *Seman Road* cafes also do chips and other favourites, and almost everybody can stir up an adequate Western breakfast.

Alcohol Local and Beijing beer are available in non-Uyghur restaurants, and department stores carry beer, Chinese wine, brandy and white lightning. A regional favourite is wine from Turfan – red or white, both of them sickly-sweet like sherry.

Entertainment
An old colonnaded theatre at the main intersection features movies and the occasional local variety show (I saw Uyghur music, Kazakh dances, theatre pieces, and even 'Chinese rock'). There are several other cinemas in town too.

Things to Buy

For serious shopping go to the main bazaar or the Sunday Market; Sunday Market prices tend to be lower. The citizens of Kashgar have been selling things for 2000 years, so be prepared to bargain. It helps to listen in on what local people are paying for the same things (a good reason to learn to count in Uyghur).

Leather Boots Not very practical unless you're on horseback, but at Y30 to Y40 they're one of the best deals in China.

Fur Hats The big Russian-looking ones with ear flaps are Y25 and up. But look them over: some ear flaps don't come down, some hats have fleas, and some smell like yak's breath when they're wet.

Musical Instruments Beautiful long-necked stringed instruments run the gamut from junk to collector's items, and include the two-string *tutar* or *dutor*, larger three-string *komuz*, small long-necked *tambur* and the elaborately shaped *ravap* with five strings and a lizard-skin sounding board. The small reed horn is a *surnai*. A *dab* is a type of tambourine.

Rugs There are dealers in the bazaar and some bargains in small shops, but there seem to be more and better ones in Ürümqi. Regionally, the best are said to be in Khotan.

Cradles A common item is garishly painted cradles with a hole to pee through. No, Uyghur babies aren't born toilet-trained; swaddled infants are simply fitted out with little wood or plastic tubes; the one for boys looks like a pipe. These are on sale too, and a source of endless jokes at tourists' expense.

Getting There & Away

According to the PSB, at the time of writing the following towns around the Tarim Basin were open to foreigners: Kashgar, Artush, Shufu, Tashkurghan, Shache (Yarkand), Yecheng (Karghalik), Hetian (Khotan), and three towns on the way to Ürümqi: Aksu,

Kuche and Korla. Kara Kul is a restricted area, for which you need a travel permit, apparently even for a day trip.

Air The only place you can fly to or from is Ürümqi, in a Russian Tu-154 jet, daily in summer and four times a week in winter. It's Y540 FEC and you should try to book it one to 1½ weeks ahead in summer, at the Air China (CAAC) ticket office on Jiefang Nan Lu. There are no discounts.

Bus The terminus for most buses to/from Pakistan is the Chini Bagh Hotel. Other buses use the long-distance bus station (ask local people for *aptoos biket*). Ticket agents usually demand FEC from foreigners, and there are no student discounts.

There have been instances of theft at the bus station, especially in the early-morning crush, sometimes with packs cut open, so keep a close watch on your bags.

Pakistan Direct buses to the Pakistani border post at Sust depart from the Chini Bagh Hotel. At the time of writing, a ticket was Y161 FEC, from the hotel service desk. From June to September they lay on as many buses as needed, so you needn't book very far ahead. Earlier or later in the season there may not be buses on some days. Landslides can cancel departures even in summer.

The first bus leaves about 11.30 am (Beijing time). The 500-km trip takes two days, with an overnight at Tashkurghan. There aren't many food stops, so bringing a day's water and snacks is a good idea. Nights can be cold in any season. Sit on the left side for the overall best views.

To save work at the border, everything that goes on top of the bus (including Pakistani traders' mountainous bundles) is customs-inspected at Chini Bagh and locked up for the entire journey. Only the carry-ons are inspected at Pirali. So carry on whatever you want for the overnight stop, plus whatever you declared to customs on entering China.

The Khunjerab Pass is open to foreign travellers from 1 May to 30 November unless snow closes it sooner. This is only decided at the last possible moment, and the only people who can tell you about this for sure are upper-level immigration or transportation officials, and only within a week or so of the date.

If the buses have stopped for the season but you're desperate to cross the border, Pakistani traders may have space in a truck or chartered bus. You can also hire a jeep from CITS or the Kashgar Mountaineering Association; see Jeeps in this section.

Ürümqi & Turfan The 1480-km trip to Ürümqi takes three days, normally with stops in Aksu and Korla (both open towns). Buses depart from the station every day – usually two or more in summer, so there's no need to plan far ahead. Tickets are about Y60 for an ordinary bus, Y80 for deluxe, and are on sale up to three days ahead.

Separate daily buses go from Kashgar to Turfan (1330 km), and cost a little less. Baggage goes on the roof and may be inaccessible for the whole trip. The bus makes meal stops, but the pickings are slim.

Kara Kul & Tashkurghan See the Kara Kul and Tashkurghan sections of this chapter.

Ex-USSR Border There are checkpoints on the roads toward Kirghizstan and Tajikistan, and unauthorised foreigners are turned back. You can go on a tour, for a price; see Tours in this section. For more on open crossings see To/From the Former Soviet Union in the Getting There & Away chapter.

Lhasa The road to Lhasa (south from Yecheng) is heavily policed and foreigners caught there are subject to fines. See To/From Tibet in the Getting There & Away chapter.

Jeeps Land Cruisers (holding four or five passengers) can be hired from CITS (directly or through your hotel), the Kashgar Mountaineering Association or John at John's Cafe. CITS rates at the time of writing were about Y160 FEC per day for trips within 40 km of Kashgar, or about Y3 per km plus

Y100 per overnight stop for longer journeys. Food and lodging are extra, and the driver pays for his own.

Kashgar-Sust is Y1630 FEC for a one-day (eight to 10-hour) marathon, or about Y100 more to do it in two days. With five passengers this works out to three times the bus price, but more control over stops for food, photos and bodily functions. Sidetrips and/or long waits are a matter for negotiation with the driver. Book ahead, a week or more in peak season.

Hitching Travellers report lifts in trucks to Pirali for about the same cost as the bus, but sometimes the drivers get in trouble for this. From Pirali into Pakistan you'll probably have to wait for an empty seat on a bus.

Tours With as little as a few days' warning, the Kashgar Mountaineering Association might be able to arrange a trek in the Muztagh Ata or Kongur region – for example, a week to Kara Kul, the Ghez River, Subash base camp on Muztagh Ata and summer-village home-stays for about US$100 per person from Kashgar. You'll have better luck with advance arrangements, for which you should write to the Xinjiang office; for the address see Trekking & Other Sports in the Facts for the Visitor chapter.

CITS and the Mountaineering Association can arrange small-group trips to the borders of the former Soviet republics (eg the Torugart Pass into Kirghizstan, three to four hours' drive from Kashgar) but you may have better luck arranging these in advance through their Ürümqi offices. The Xinjiang Tourism Corporation can also make arrangements. See Tourist Information in the Facts for the Visitor chapter for addresses.

Getting Around
To/From the Airport The airport is 12 km from the centre. A Y1 bus and swarms of overpriced vans and underpowered motor-rickshaws meet all incoming flights. The bus goes to the Air China (CAAC) ticket office on Jiefang Nan Lu. A bus also leaves this

office for the airport 2½ hours before each flight departure.

Local Buses There are apparently town buses on the perimeter roads. A local bus stand at the west end of the field opposite the Mao statue, and another west of the bank, are mainly for buses and motor-rickshaws to outlying towns and counties.

Bicycle Rental A bike is the cheapest and most versatile way to get around Kashgar. One-gear clunkers can be hired by the hour or day at many hotels (Seman seems the cheapest, and Kashgar Guesthouse the dearest) and a few bike shops. A deposit is required; don't leave your passport with them instead, as some ask you to do.

Pony Cart This is the most common way to get around the outskirts, though a municipal clean-up campaign is gradually pushing them out of the centre during day-light hours (which is why they may seem to take you the long way round to anywhere). A few drivers are always outside the tourist hotels, eager to take your money. From the Seman, locals pay three or four mao to Id Kah, five to the bus station, and six or seven to the Sunday Market; tourists pay at least twice as much.

If you hire your own, set the price and destination before you go. Ask him *(konch-pul?)* and offer half as much. If he says no, almost certainly someone else will take up your offer (this may not work when you're off to the bus at dawn and he's got the only cart!). Many drivers cheat, especially with a small number of passengers and no locals on board; prices may go up in mid-journey, rides may end early. Being rude or squeezing a driver for a rock-bottom price is a sure way to make this happen. Of course, don't pay till you get there, and have exact change.

ARTUSH

Artush (Chinese *Atu-shih*), an hour's ride north-east of Kashgar, is a Kirghiz market town and the centre of Kyzylsu Kirghiz Autonomous County. It has a large bazaar, heavy on cloth and clothing. It's locally famous for its figs, 'the pride of Artush', which are best in late summer or early autumn. Also here is the tomb of Sultan Sadiq Bughra Khan of the 11th-century Qarakhan Dynasty, reputedly the first local ruler to convert to Islam.

Places to Stay

The official foreigners' hotel is *Kejou Binguan* (who also run the tourist yurts at Kara Kul).

Getting There & Away

Every day a big bus goes from the Kashgar bus station for Y2.50 FEC and numerous smaller ones from People's Hospital *(Renmin Yiyuan)* for about Y2 RMB.

AKSU & KUCHE

These two towns are on the Kashgar-Ürümqi bus route. Aksu, once a major oasis on the branch of the Silk Road passing north of the Takla Makan Desert, is now a boring Chinese regional administrative town, but it has a large Sunday market.

Kuche (or Kuqa) was another oasis, for some time a little kingdom unto itself, and a major Buddhist centre. It has Xinjiang's second-largest mosque (after Kashgar's), an Uyghur old town section, and a Friday market said to rival Kashgar's Sunday market.

Hsuan Tsang, a 7th-century Chinese traveller, wrote about the delicate frescoes at the Buddhist monastery-temples of Kyzyl, 70 km from Kuche, later ransacked (in 1906) by the German archaeologist Albert von le Coq. There's no public transport to Kyzyl, though you might hire a jeep from Kuche for around Y200. You will probably need a travel permit from Kuche PSB.

YARKAND, KARGHALIK & KHOTAN

These towns south-east of Kashgar were stops on the Silk Road branch along the south side of the Takla Makan Desert, and from time to time were also little mini-kingdoms. The craftspeople of Khotan were celebrated throughout Asia for their rugs, silk and carved jade, and to some extent still are. The 4th-century Chinese pilgrim Fa-Hsien described Khotan as a highly developed centre of Buddhism, with no fewer than 14 large monasteries.

At the time of writing, all three towns were open, with *no* travel permit needed, though the trip goes via the still-closed town of Yengisar. But CITS may tell you a permit is needed, in order to charge you for the 'booking form' to show PSB.

In official business or ticket purchases you should refer to these places by their Chinese names – Yarkand is Shache, Karghalik is Yecheng, and Khotan is Hetian.

Places to Stay

Officially permitted hotels are the grotty *Shache Binguan* in Yarkand, the *Dengshan Binguan* in Karghalik and the *Khotan Hotel* (or *Hetian Binguan)* in Khotan.

Getting There & Away

Buses go from Kashgar bus station, five times a day to Yarkand/Shache (200 km from Kashgar, four to five hours by bus, for Y8) and Karghalik/ Yecheng (260 km, Y11), and at least once a day to Khotan/Hetian (520 km, 12 to 15 hours by bus, for Y30).

KASHGAR TO KARA KUL

To the Chinese the road from Kashgar to the Pakistan border is the China-Pakistan Highway (Zhong-Pa Gong Lu, 'China-Pak Big Road'). After 80 km across the flats and a sharp 70-km climb, it runs for 250 km to the border in a high valley through the eastern Pamirs. This is a region of sublime scenery and extremes of weather, a 2000-year-old passage for trade, plunder and religious ideas, and a geopolitical vortex even now. Times given here are for bus travel.

As you leave Kashgar the main attraction, rising straight up from the plain to the west, is the luminous rampart of the Pamirs. About an hour down the road is a food stop at **Upal** village (Chinese say Wupaer). While you're buying your samosas and melons, keep an eye on your bags – some locals have sticky fingers. About three km off the road here is

the small tomb of Mohammad Kashgari, an 11th-century Uyghur scholar famous for writing the first dictionary of the Uyghur language, in Arabic. Most settlements from here on to Kara Kul are Kirghiz.

Two hours from Kashgar you enter the canyon of the Ghez River (in Uyghur, Ghez Darya), with wine-red sandstone walls at its lower end. The scattered adobe houses are the same colour, and during heavy rainstorms the Ghez itself can run red. The white giant to the south is a shoulder of Mt Kongur, at 7719 metres the highest peak near the road until you reach Pakistan's Hunza Valley.

Ghez itself is just a lonely checkpoint. Photographing soldiers or buildings here can result in confiscated film. Upstream the canyon grows steep and lifeless, forbidding even on a sunny day. This is the segment where road construction and frequent landslides made travel to and from Pakistan so problematic in the recent past. The road is cut into sheer walls, or inches across huge tilted boulder fields.

At the top of the canyon, 3½ hours above the Kashgar plain, the landscape changes abruptly. The Ghez, just before dropping into the canyon, seems to lose its way in a huge wet plain ringed with sand dunes. This terrain is typical of the Pamir Range: high, broad, treeless valleys strung between glacier-rounded mountains, with rivers often pooling into shallow lakes.

The word *pamir* refers to pasturage, the valleys' main historical use. Marco Polo came through here seven centuries ago and wrote, 'a lean beast grows fat here in 10 days'.

The corridor from here to the Pakistan border is a pamir valley, the **Sarikol Valley**. The mountains on either side are called the Taghdumbash (or Sarikol, or Chinese) Pamir. Half an hour south, at the foot of Mt Kongur, is the Kirghiz settlement of **Bulun Kul**, 3700 metres above sea level, sometimes a stop for mutton soup, fried vegetables or nan bread at five times the Kashgar price.

An hour south of Bulun Kul is **Kara Kul** (or Karakol Lake) – properly Lesser Kara Kul, as there's a bigger lake of the same name

150 km north-west in Tajikistan – and two small sister lakes across the road, Besekh Kul and Shor Kul.

KARA KUL

Many travellers come to Kashgar hoping to rub shoulders with Kirghiz nomads in the pastures around Kara Kul. (Chinese, Kalakuli Hu). This must be one of the most beautiful places in western China, the deep blue waters (*kara kul* is Uyghur for 'black lake') nestled between two Pamir giants, 7546-metre Muztagh Ata to the south and 7719-metre Mt Kongur to the north-east. Though imposing, Muztagh Ata (Uyghur for 'Father of Ice Mountains') looks deceptively small, possibly because all the available vantage points are themselves over 3300 metres high!

With a tent you could spend days at the lake or on the flanks of Muztagh Ata, and the possibilities for trekking are excellent. But this is a restricted area, for which you need a travel permit from the Public Security Bureau (PSB) – even for a day trip or a day-stop en route to/from Pakistan – and they are thorough about tracking down and fining those who don't have them, even allegedly seizing passports.

To get the travel permit you need to show Kashgar PSB a certificate from CITS (it's also called a 'booking form', though there doesn't seem to be a requirement that you book anything). CITS will charge you at least Y10 for this form, and may be ungracious about it if you don't also book transport with them. At the time of writing you could get a permit from Tashkurghan PSB without a CITS certificate.

There are several Kirghiz summer villages in the area (the nearest, on the lake shore, is Subash), though the PSB presence seems to have made people uneasy about inviting foreigners into their yurts (the cylindrical tent-houses used by Central Asian nomads). You can walk around the lake in half a day; the downstream outflow can be forded at the village nearby. Camping is permitted around the lake if you have a permit; otherwise you

may have to settle for a mock-up yurt in a seedy tour-group site by the lake.

Go between June and September; at other times the villages and the yurt site are usually closed down and you may find only an icy wind and a few marmots. The lake is at 3800 metres and nights are below freezing even in summer; one camper woke to find snow in the middle of August!

Places to Stay

The yurt site is run by Kejou Binguan in Artush (the lake is in Artush District), who seem to make up their rates as they go along, overcharging for everything, eg Y25 or more for a bed, and Y15 for meals. You might be able to bargain them down and pay in RMB. Kashgar CITS will charge you considerably more to arrange a booking there. The obvious way to save money is with your own food and tent.

Getting There & Away

The public bus from Kashgar bus station to Tashkurghan (two or three times a week) will stop at Kara Kul.

Empty seats as far as Kara Kul are also available on the bus to Pakistan on a 'standby' basis, though you may be asked to first show a travel permit. If you plan to continue on from Kara Kul to Pakistan on another day, CITS says you must first return to Kashgar for customs reasons. But travellers have hitched on from Kara Kul to Tashkurghan, talked their way aboard a Pakistan-bound bus and at Pirali sorted out customs matters.

Another option is to hire a van (holds eight), reportedly about Rs 100 per person if you can fill it. Or collect a group and do a trek with the Mountaineering Association; see Kashgar – Getting There & Away – Tours. CITS offers a Kara Kul day trip from Kashgar by 4WD for a staggering Y600 per person in a large group, but it is even more for individuals.

KARA KUL TO TASHKURGHAN

On the high ground west of Muztagh Ata, called the **Subash Plateau**, the highway

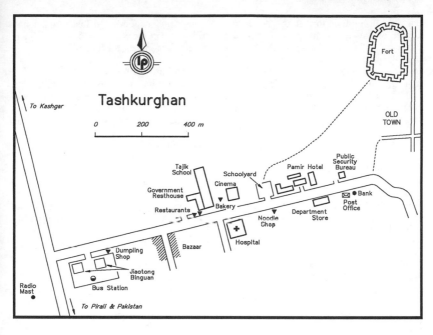

makes its closest approach (about 10 km) to the former USSR; several jeep tracks run from here into Tajikistan. At the turn of the century this area was still in dispute, never having been properly mapped, and this was one of the major issues fuelling the Great Game.

Two to three hours south of Kara Kul is a police checkpoint at **Kekyor**. From there, across the marshy **Tagh Arma Basin**, it's about 1½ hours to Tashkurghan. Settlements from Tagh Arma to Pirali are mainly Tajik.

TASHKURGHAN

In the Uyghur language, *tash kurghan* means stone fortress. The ruins of a huge mud-brick fort still stand on the edge of town, and although this one is estimated to be about 600 years old, local lore says Tashkurghan has been a citadel for over 2300 years. The Greek philosopher-scientist Ptolemy (90 to 168 AD) mentioned Tashkurghan in his *Guide to Geography* as a stop on the road to

China. The Chinese Buddhist pilgrim Hsuan Tsang wrote about its fortress in the 7th century, when it was the furthest frontier outpost of the Tang Dynasty.

Nowadays, this is the administrative centre of the Tashkurghan Tajik Autonomous County, stretching from Muztagh Ata to Pirali, and home to most of China's 20,000 Tajiks. About 5000 of them live in the town. Tashkurghan is about 3600 metres above sea level and 280 km from Kashgar.

Orientation & Information

There's only one main street, one km long, lined with poplars and gated compounds. A small bazaar is on a side street 400 metres down from the western end. A department store, post office and bank are at the other end of the street, but the bank apparently doesn't do foreign exchange.

Fort

The single attraction in Tashkurghan is the

massive, crumbling fort at the north-east corner of town, on the only hill in the Tashkurghan River's flood-plain. Most of its multi-layered walls and battlements are still intact. Development around the fort makes it hard to reach. The easiest way is from the far end of town and up the fort's east side. An alternative route is through the schoolyard west of the Pamir Hotel.

Places to Stay

Tashkurghan is a Kashgar-to-Sust overnight stop in either direction. You'll probably be deposited at the *Jiaotong Binguan* ('Bus Station Hotel') with plain quads at Y12 for a bed and doubles at about Y20 per bed.

Groups go to the *Pamir Hotel*, where a clean double with bath and hot water is at least Y50 FEC. Staff are dedicated to doing as little work as possible. The Pamir also has medieval five-bed dorms at about Y10 FEC per bed, with washing water from a barrel in the hallway, and genuinely disgusting pit toilets in the yard.

Individuals might also have some luck at a government resthouse called *Shi Ping Gongsi Lüshe*, which has cheap four-bed rooms. There's no English sign but it's in a courtyard behind a pair of restaurants west of the Pamir Hotel.

Places to Eat

Food is a misery here, and grossly over-priced. At the *Pamir Hotel*, set Chinese meals are priced for groups (eg Y20 for dinner); if there are no groups about, they may have nothing at all. The restaurant at the *Jiaotong Binguan* is adequate. Two side-by-side restaurants with questionable hygiene and predatory prices (eg Y5 for a Y1 bowl of noodles) are halfway down the main street; the one on the left is marginally better. A few grotty Tajik places have noodles or gummy steamed bread stuffed with meat or vegetables. In the morning the bazaar has hot bread, melons and some vegetables.

In 1987-88 hepatitis was epidemic in southern Xinjiang. This has now been brought under control, but Tashkurghan may still be one of the easiest places on the KKH to catch a stomach infection.

Getting There & Away

A Y15 public bus goes from Kashgar to Tashkurghan two or three times a week, returning the following day. Empty seats as far as Tashkurghan on the Kashgar-Sust bus are sold on a 'standby' basis. If you want to take a bus from here to Pakistan on a later day, you can expect a sour face from that driver, who won't have you on his customs manifest, but that can be sorted out at Pirali.

You might hitch a lift to Pirali but from there you'll probably have to wait for an empty seat on the bus. Jeeps returning empty from Pakistan may give you a lift to Kashgar for perhaps Y100 to Y200 per person.

TASHKURGHAN TO PIRALI

This level stretch along the Tashkurghan River is grand and picturesque in fine weather, with muscular-looking peaks along the west side of the valley and lots of horse and camel traffic.

About 1½ hours south of Tashkurghan (1¼ hours north of Pirali) is **Dabdar**, the largest permanent Tajik settlement along the highway. Except for a mosque and the occasional camel, it looks a little like the 19th-century American west: adobe houses, brown ponies with bright blankets parked outside, sheep and goats grazing near the road.

South of Dabdar, the road passes the mouth of an enormous opening westward into the Pamir. This is the **Mintaka Valley**, once a major Silk Road branch and historically one of the main routes to the Hunza Valley and on to Kashmir. About 75 km up the Mintaka Valley, a jeep track enters Afghanistan's Wakhan Corridor.

Two hours from Tashkurghan, **Pirali** is, in effect, the outer rim of China. South of the customs and immigration post there (described in the next chapter) the Pamir gradually becomes the Karakoram.

PAMIR RANGE

Tashkurghan

Tashkurghan River

Xinjiang
Autonomous
Region

TAJIKISTAN

AFGHANISTAN

Dabdar

CHINA

Mintaka River

Khunjerab River

Kilik Pass

Pirali

Mintaka
Pass

PAKISTAN

Dih

KKH

Northern
Areas

Khunjerab
Pass

KARAKORAM RANGE

Sust

Tashkurghan to Sust

0   25   50 km

To Gilgit &
Rawalpindi

The Khunjerab Pass

At 4730 metres, the road over the Khunjerab Pass is said to be the highest public highway in the world. *Khunjerab* is Wakhi (Tajik) for 'Blood Valley'. Nobody is sure where the name came from, although the area swarmed with Wakhi and Hunza bandits until the 1890s, stalking caravans between Kashgar and Kashmir.

A steady trickle of horseback commerce crossed the Khunjerab (*Hong-qi-la-pu* to the Chinese) until the 1950s, when China-Pakistan hostility closed the border. But relations improved and by the mid-1960s the two countries had agreed to cooperate on a Friendship Highway over the mountains. Work began in 1966, and the KKH was inaugurated in 1980. In 1982 the pass was formally opened to official traffic and cross-border trade. It was opened to tourism at a media event in 1986, though travellers had long since discovered it.

The crossing is not only between countries but between two of the world's major mountain ranges, the Pamir and the Karakoram. In the 135 km from Pirali to Sust the transition is evident, from the rounded *pamir* valleys to the deep, angular gorge of the Khunjerab River.

The alpine region between Pirali and the Pakistan security post at Dih is the only habitat of the rare, big-horned Marco Polo sheep, of which there are now only a few hundred in the world. The pass is also home to ibex, Himalayan marmot, brown bear, fox and, according to some, snow leopard.

Both countries have set aside game preserves here. On the Pakistan side, in a 20 km by 100 km strip along the border called the Karakoram National Park, hunting has been banned and grazing restricted since 1975, though little money and manpower have been allocated for surveys or enforcement. On their side the Chinese in 1984 established the 15,000-sq km Tashkurghan Nature Reserve (the KKH is within it from about Tashkurghan to the border).

Time Zones

You reset your watch here, but it's not simple. All China uses Beijing time, though Xinjiang also runs on unofficial local time, two hours earlier. China sets its clocks ahead one hour during the summer, but Pakistan doesn't. Consequently, from mid-May to mid-September, Pakistan time is two hours earlier than Xinjiang time and four hours earlier than Beijing time. For the rest of the year, Pakistan is one hour earlier than Xinjiang and three hours earlier than Beijing.

PIRALI

There is no town at Pirali ('peer-a-LEE'), just China customs and immigration, a Bank of China branch and, in the tourist season, a small guesthouse, noodle shop and post office. Though foreigners can stay in the cheap guesthouse at a pinch, they're encouraged to move on. A public toilet is about 100 metres west of the gate.

Cyclists' Notes, Khunjerab Pass

Pirali to Khunjerab Pass, about 40 km Pirali has very basic food and accommodation. If you're north-bound you get a paper from the Chinese security post four km below the top of the pass, to present at Pirali. The friendly soldiers at the security post might offer biscuits and tea to chilled cyclists. See the notes in the Kashgar to Tashkurghan chapter about cycling north out of Pirali.

Khunjerab Pass to Dih, 50 km The road near the top is a series of tight switch-backs, rarely very steep. Kukshal (15 km below the summit) or other abandoned KKH work camps make good camping spots. Even without camping gear you might be able to stay the night at a road-works camp or the Dih security post.

Dih to Sust, 35 km The 'rumour-book' at the Mountain Refuge Hotel in Sust includes current comments from cyclists.

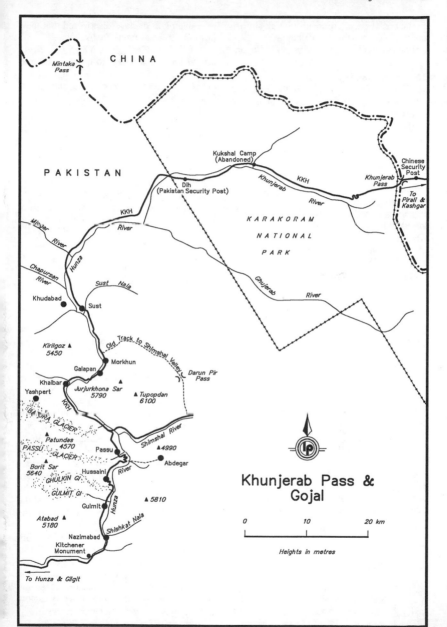

CHINA

Mintaka
Pass

PAKISTAN

Kukshal Camp
(Abandoned)

KKH

Khunjerab

Chinese
Security
Post

Dih
(Pakistan Security Post)

Khunjerab
Pass

River

To
Pirali &
Kashgar

KKH

River

KARAKORAM

Misgar

River

Hunza

NATIONAL

PARK

Chapursan
River

Sust Nala

Ghujerab

River

Khudabad

Sust

Kirilgoz ▲
5450

Old Track to Shimshal Valley

Galapan

Morkhun

Darun Pir
Pass

Khaibar

Jurjurkhona Sar
5790

Yashpert

▲ Tupopdan
6100

BATURA GLACIER

KKH

Patundas
4570

PASSU

GLACIER

Shimshal River

Passu

▲ 4990

Borit Sar
5640

Hussaini

River

Abdegar

GHULKIN GI

GULMIT GI

Gulmit

Hunza

▲ 5810

Atabad ▲
5180

Shishkat Nala

Nazimabad

Kitchener
Monument

To Hunza & Gilgit

Khunjerab Pass &
Gojal

0   10   20 km

Heights in metres

The bank here charges substantial, almost horrific, commissions so change as little money as possible until you reach Kashgar.

Border Formalities
See Customs & Immigration in the Facts for the Visitor chapter for more about border procedures.

Entering China Queue up for an entry-exit card and health form. Passports are inspected and stamped. China does not issue transit visas at the border. Fill out a customs declaration; you must present your copy when you leave China. Baggage inspection is usually cursory for foreigners but they like to see saleable hi-tech items like cameras and Walkmans. The bank accepts most major currencies and gives you FEC. Get some of it in small bills because you'll only get change in RMB between here and Kashgar.

Leaving China At customs, turn in the declaration form you filled out when you entered China. Baggage inspection is usually cursory for foreigners, though Pakistanis get done over. Visit the bank next because immigration will keep your passport until the bus leaves. The bank gives only US dollars and accepts only FEC; swap your RMB with north-bound travellers at Sust (or some Sust merchants will trade RMB for rupees at poor rates). At immigration, turn in your passport and the entry-exit card you got when you entered China. If you don't have a card you may be charged Y1 for a new one.

Officials here have occasionally used expired visas and lost customs declarations or entry-exit cards as excuses for impromptu fines. They demanded US$50 from one traveller whose visa had expired the day before, and the bus was sent on to Sust without him. He refused to give in and they finally settled for Y20 to issue a visa extension.

Getting There & Away
If you're Kashgar-bound, a Chinese bus normally leaves when formalities are completed, although some travellers have been stranded here overnight or have discovered that their bus only went as far as Tashkurghan.

The fare to Kashgar is Y80 FEC. *Don't pay in RMB*; it's illegal to bring RMB into China, and if the driver tells a customs officer, your RMB may be confiscated (away from the border you're unlikely to have such problems).

Occasionally jeeps returning from taking tourists to Sust may give you a lift to Kashgar, for around Y100 to Y200 per person.

PIRALI TO SUST
The Khunjerab Pass region has historically been admired for pastures rather than passage, and from Pirali to the top you're likely to see herds of shaggy wild yaks or domesticated dzu, a cross between yak and cow. Another creature you'll see (and hear) is the whistling Himalayan marmot.

A few km before the top, at what must be China's loneliest security post, the People's Liberation Army counts you and looks you over.

The pass itself is long and flat. At the summit are a plaque commemorating the 1982 opening and a cheerful Pakistani security post. At this point you're about 400 km from Kashgar and 880 km from Rawalpindi.

Scattered down the Pakistan side are deserted concrete buildings with sculpted gables: hostels for Chinese KKH workers, built in the late 1960s when the road was being laid to Gulmit. At **Kukshal**, about 45 minutes below the top, the ruins of a Chinese work-camp straddle the river at a large side-canyon. Below Kukshal the valley walls are 'black, crumbling rock' (this is how the Uyghur words *kara koram* translate) and the river cuts through deep beds of gravel, the residue of repeated mud and rock slides.

About 50 km below the top (35 km from Sust) is the Pakistan security post of **Dih**. If you're coming from China you'll get a warm welcome that may bring tears to your eyes. It's an hour from Dih to Sust, through some of the narrowest gorges on the KKH. Below the tributary Misgar and Chapursan valleys, whose streams rise near the Afghan border, the Khunjerab River becomes the Hunza River.

SUST

Although it's mainly a customs and immigration post, Sust (pronounced 'sost'), at 3100 metres, has long walks, grand scenery, even a hot spring. You can also visit the Khunjerab Pass from here as a day trip. Local people are mostly Wakhi (Tajik) and speak the Wakhi language. People from here to Hunza are nearly all Ismaili Muslims, followers of the Aga Khan.

The opening of the pass forced development on Sust, and hotels have popped up faster than the services to support them. Electricity only arrived in 1987.

Orientation

Along the road are the tourist facilities. Customs, immigration, bank, post office, ticket office and some hotels are clustered near the gate, and more hotels are up the road in the Pakistan direction. Customs and immigration will eventually move to a new site about one km upstream.

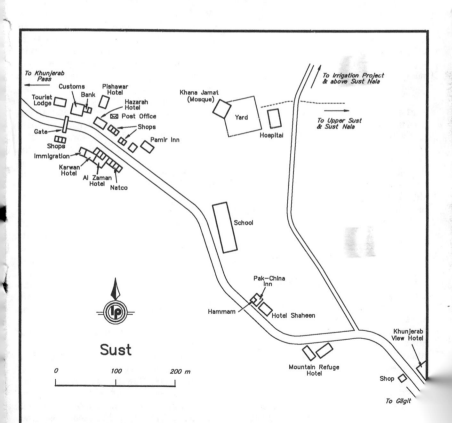

Most people never see the village itself, on a ledge above the highway. Across the river (via a bridge just upstream) is the village of Khudabad. The razor-sharp ridge above Khudabad is Kirilgoz (5450 metres) and the big peak straight down the road into Pakistan is Jurjurkhona Sar (5790 metres).

By an odd orientation of the KKH here, you go north-west to China and south-east into Pakistan.

Information

Bank & Moneychangers The tiny National Bank of Pakistan near customs accepts US dollars and pounds sterling (cash or travellers' cheques) and sometimes other currencies. They claim to be open from 9 am to 2 pm and from 3 to 6 pm. If they're closed you might change a few dollars cash at immigration or your hotel. If you're north-bound you can sell your rupees here.

Post & Telecommunications A post office is set back from the road near customs; from here you can also cable or telephone within Pakistan.

Hospital A village clinic dispenses medications and first aid. Take the track near the Mountain Refuge Hotel for about 400 metres and turn left. The clinic is the last gate on the left before a walled yard.

Hot Wash There is a *hammam* (a kind of barber shop and bath-house found all over Pakistan) at the corner of the Pak-China Inn. For Rs 10 you get a bucket of hot water and a bar of soap in a grotty private stall. This is usually for men but they'll make arrangements for women.

Shops There are one or two bread shops and others with biscuits, jam, juice, toilet paper and souvenirs.

?rder Formalities

? is probably the most casual border post ?istan. But it must be a rough posting – ?tion from Pakistan and the proximity ?se foreigners, especially women,

has clearly knocked a few moral screws loose, so stay awake. See Customs & Immigration in the Facts for the Visitor chapter for more about border procedures.

Entering Pakistan You fill out an entry-exit card and get an entry stamp as soon as you arrive. If you don't have a Pakistan visa you get a 'landing permit' (transit visa) good for 72 hours – barely time to dash to Islamabad and extend it. In the past, officials here have been somewhat arbitrary in issuing these, though the law obliges them to do so.

Most ports of entry give you a Temporary Certificate of Registration (Form C) which you return when you leave Pakistan. If you're staying more than 30 days you're supposed to register with the police and trade Form C for a residence permit. Immigration may not give you Form C here; save yourself later headaches by asking for one.

After you've cleared immigration your bags are inspected. For foreigners this usually consists of: 'What's in there? ... OK'. On arrival once by jeep I was asked to sign an impromptu declaration that none of the passengers were carrying anything 'objectionable', and nobody looked at our bags at all.

Leaving Pakistan It's almost essential to stay at Sust the night before you go. You must have a bus ticket before going through customs; the ticket office opens at 8 am. At immigration you present your entry-exit card or fill out a new one, and get an exit stamp. You must have a China visa or you'll be sent back from Pirali. China does not issue transit visas at the border.

Day Trip to the Khunjerab Pass

The air at 4730 metres is very dry, cold and thin, but it feels like the top of the world. For safety's sake have a good idea how you'll get back down! For Rs 800 you can hire a Suzuki for an eight-hour round trip. Natco sells an overpriced Rs 300 return-trip ticket – to the pass on the China-bound bus and back on the empty returning Natco bus, which *usually* crosses the pass between 3 and 6 pm. There's also the full Chinese bus from Kashgar, which *usually* crosses between noon and 3 pm. Immigration keeps your passport while you're gone, and will check for you that the buses from Pirali are running. Take lots of water.

Hot Spring

Six km upstream from Sust, rock piles mark a steep path to the river, where there are several shallow pools near the bank. You must leave your passport with immigration. A Suzuki is about Rs 100 for the round-trip, but agree on how long he'll stay – or stay away – while you soak.

'Hot spring' is *theen kook* in Wakhi, and *garam chashma* in Urdu.

Hikes Above Sust

At the intersection near the clinic, turn right on a path through fields to upper Sust and Sust Nala (a nala is a tributary canyon). The compact houses and walled fields, the poplars and fruit orchards, and the dramatic canyon are very different from the scene along the road.

If instead you go straight at the intersection it's three km up to a 400-metre irrigation tunnel dug by villagers in 1985, one of hundreds of Northern Areas self-help projects started with the aid of the Aga Khan Rural Support Programme or AKRSP (see Facts about the Region – Rural Development). From here you can take several excellent, half to full-day walks above Sust Nala, with fine views of the Hunza River valley.

Khudabad

Across the Hunza River is Khudabad village and the narrow Khudabad Nala. A bridge spans the river 1½ km upstream of Sust. A walk to the village and back takes an hour; the nala can be a full day's trek.

Chapursan & Misgar Valleys

These valleys, dropping from near Afghanistan's Wakhan Corridor, are said to be very beautiful and their villages still very

Marco Polo sheep

traditional. Unfortunately, they are now in a Restricted Area, full of soldiers. For information about permits, inquire at the office of the Northern Areas Administrator in Gilgit.

Places to Stay

Most hotels will let you pitch a tent and use their toilets and water for a fraction of the room cost. In fact, you could throw a bag down almost anywhere, but keep in mind that most open space near the road is used as a toilet too!

The *Mountain Refuge Hotel* is the best cheap bet, with Rs 25 beds in grotty dorms, Rs 100 doubles with attached toilet and cold shower, and good food. They also have a 'rumour-book' with current news and comments by travellers. For similar prices you can also choose from several noisy inns with dreary food, no privacy and lots of cheerful Pakistanis – the *Hazarah, Pishawar, Karwan* and *Al Zaman* hotels near customs and *Pak-China Inn* and *Hotel Shaheen* up the hill.

The *Khunjerab View Hotel* has Rs 30 dorm beds, doubles with cold showers from Rs 100 and doubles with hot showers for Rs 400. They also have a spartan 40-bed dorm in a local house. Beside customs, the *Tourist Lodge* (☎ 46210) has Rs 35 bed dorms with cold showers and overpriced Rs 350 doubles with hot showers – possibly negotiable in the off-season.

The group-oriented *Dreamland Hotel* (☎ 46212) has doubles with hot showers for about Rs 150, but it's two km south of town. Their Rs 25-per-bed dorms are a poor bargain.

Places to Eat

The *Mountain Refuge Hotel* has good sit-down Hunza- style dinners – rice, noodle soup, meat and vegetables – for Rs 25. This is normally for guests only; if you're staying elsewhere see them in advance. They also do Western-style breakfasts. The *Tourist Lodge* has a Rs 80 buffet when groups are staying there. Most hotels have basic Pakistani road food: gosht (curried mutton), dhal (overcooked lentils), chapatti and tea.

Getting There & Away

Kashgar The government-run Northern Areas Transport Company (Natco) runs buses to Pirali, a four-hour trip for Rs 300. From there, Chinese buses take you to Kashgar for Y80 FEC, with an overnight stop at Tashkurghan.

Get a ticket to Pirali from the Natco office first thing in the morning; you'll need to show it at customs. The bus leaves when formalities are done, usually by 11 am. From June to September they routinely lay on as many buses as necessary, so it's not essential to book very far ahead. Earlier or later in the season, there may not be buses on the days. Landslides can cancel these trips even in summer. Baggage goes on the roof, out of reach even on the overnight stop, so plan your carry-ons. The overall best views are from the right side of the bus.

The Khunjerab Pass is closed for all but official business from 30 November to 1 May, and snow often closes it several weeks sooner. In the Northern Areas only the immigration chief at Sust or Natco managers at Sust or Gilgit know for sure when this will happen, and only within a week or so of the actual date. After mid-November Sust immigration may limit or prohibit departures to Kashgar.

Food can be a problem, especially near the end of the season. There's no lunch stop; the Pirali noodle shop may be closed; the bus may get to Tashkurghan too late for dinner and leave too early for breakfast; and it's all aggravated by the time change. Carrying a day's water and snacks is a good idea.

You can also hire a Natco van or Land Cruiser to Pirali, and if you can fill it up the per-person cost can be as little as the bus fare.

Gojal, Hunza & Gilgit A clapped-out Natco bus leaves daily for Gilgit at 6 am in summer, 7 am in spring and autumn and 8 am in winter, taking four to five hours. The fare is about Rs 60, and is paid on board. Passu and Gulmit are about a quarter of the Gilgit fare, and Ganesh (on the KKH below Karimabad) about half. In summer there are also private vans for a bit more, usually leaving before the Natco bus does. Passu is six to seven hours away on foot, and the hitching is good from here to Gilgit.

'Specials' To points in Pakistan you can hire an entire vehicle and driver, at least in summer. At the time of writing a hired Suzuki to Karimabad was about Rs 600, and to Gilgit Rs 1200. Natco will also rent you a Land Cruiser, van or even a bus; a Toyota Coaster (seats 21) one-way from Sust to Karimabad, for example, would be about Rs 1800.

Some private operators may tell you Natco is not running and offer their own very high rates. Don't panic: Natco goes every day, and Sust is not a bad place to spend some time.

Gojal

The region known locally as Gojal ('go-JAAL' or 'gu-JAAL') extends for about 60 km from Sust to where the Hunza River turns west (see the Khunjerab Pass & Gojal map on page 95). This is the only river that cuts across the high spine of the Karakoram, and it does so in southern Gojal. As a result the High Karakoram is more accessible here than anywhere else on the KKH. At Passu and Gulmit several major glaciers reach nearly to the highway.

'The scenery is stern and impressive, but too gloomy and harsh to be really sublime,' wrote the British explorer Reginald Schomberg in 1935. Mountains with razor-edge summits and bare walls drop sheer to the river, and the wind drives up the valley even on brilliant days. Nevertheless, if you are fit, this is the place to climb up and get a feeling for the highlands. The clearest and most storm-free weather is in early autumn.

The river picks its way among great fans of alluvium brought down by the smaller streams; most villages are built on these fertile deposits. The larger tributaries also carry down soil and rocks, but often suddenly and destructively. Huge floods have periodically destroyed river-front fields and orchards. In 1974, a mudslide from Shishkat Nala backed up the Hunza River for 20 km, despite Pakistan air force attempts to bomb it loose. The resulting lake lasted for over three years, during which time the once deep valley practically filled up with sand and gravel, leaving much of it grimmer than when Schomberg saw it.

Gojal is usually described as 'upper Hunza'. Like the people of Hunza proper, Gojalis are Ismaili Muslims and were loyal subjects of the Mir of Hunza. But their Persian-influenced language is unrelated to Hunza speech, and the people are Wakhi (Tajik), descendants of nomadic herders from what is now eastern Afghanistan, China's Tarim Basin and the former Soviet republic of Tajikistan. They're probably the most warm-hearted people on the KKH, with easy greetings and hospitality for both men and women.

Gojal Food

Gojal specialities are similar to those of Hunza (see the Hunza-Nagar chapter) but with Wakhi names. One of the best local items is whole-wheat bread, available in some hotels, though not for sale in shops. *Kamishdoon* (called *phitti* in Hunza) is a heavy round loaf baked under coals. *Dildungi* is a slightly risen tandoor-style flat-bread. *Kulcha* is a Kashmiri-style flat-bread made with lots of milk and eggs, mainly for ceremonial occasions.

Celebrations & Holidays

Once an important part of life, community celebrations are giving way to 'progress'. But some, either Ismaili holidays or very old seasonal rituals, are still held in Gojal.

Cyclists' Notes, Gojal

The KKH drops steadily but not steeply from Sust into Hunza, but strong winds can make cycling very hard or very easy! There are numerous hotels and camping options at Sust, Passu and Gulmit.

Sust to Passu, about 40 km An easy, beautiful ride. The Greenland Hotel, seven km south of Sust, avoids the crowds and has hot showers. At Khaibar, about 20 km from Sust, is a small inn with basic food. The Batura Inn at Passu has good 'rumour-books' including current cyclists' comments.

Passu to Gulmit, 16 km Near Hussaini village, about nine km from Passu, a link road climbs to a small hotel at Borit Lake, with a few cheap rooms and free camping.

Gulmit to Ganesh, 34 km Karimabad is a steep climb on a link road from Ganesh; see cyclists' notes in the Hunza & Nagar chapter.

Late February

Kitdit, the 'First Festival', for the coming of spring. Houses are decorated and there are public gatherings with food, music and dancing.

Early March

Taghun ('sowing' in Wakhi). Families celebrate privately when the first seeds are cast, offering prayers and preparing *samn*, a sweet delicacy made from fermented wheat flour.

21 March

Nauroz ('New Days'), a Shia and Ismaili festival celebrating the succession of the Prophet's son-in-law Ali. In Gojal this is a spring festival too; villagers visit one another and there may be music and dancing.

Early July

Chinir, the first (wheat) harvest. Farmers may celebrate privately, as at first sowing, and there are some community celebrations too.

11 July

Taqt Nashina ('taking of the seat'), the day the present Aga Khan assumed leadership of the Ismaili community. In Gojal this may include parades, games, music, dancing and fireworks on the mountain-sides.

* 31 August (1993), 20 August (1994), 10 August (1995), 29 July (1996)

Eid-Milad-un-Nabi, the Prophet's birthday. Some businesses may be closed.

18 November

First visit by the Aga Khan to Gojal in 1987, celebrated in Gojal only. Festivities are similar to *Taqt Nashina*.

13 December

The Aga Khan's Birthday, celebrated by Ismailis with gatherings and speeches.

* approximate dates

SUST TO PASSU

Several village projects supported by the AKRSP (see Facts about the Region – Rural Development) are visible along the highway, including tree plantations at **Morkhun**, orchards at **Galapan**, irrigation channels and orchards just south of **Khaibar** (or Khyber) and an irrigation channel from the Batura Glacier near Passu.

As the valley widens near Passu the highway crosses a makeshift girder bridge over the **Batura Glacier** stream. The glacier itself comes nearly to the road, although its dirty grey ice looks more like rocky soil. Its lower end is accessible on a day hike from Passu. This is one of the larger glaciers of the

Karakoram, extending 60 km back into the cluster of 6000-to-7000 metre peaks called the Batura Muztagh.

The Batura advances and retreats from year to year. In 1976 its 30-metre-high front ground up the original Chinese bridge (the ruins are still visible nearby), which was then replaced by the 'permanently temporary' girder bridge. There are also two steel bridges across the Hunza River, one for access to the other side and one to complete a KKH bypass next time the glacier eats up the highway.

East of the bridge is the yawning **Shimshal Valley**, once one of the remotest places in the old state of Hunza. It was from upper Shimshal, even in the last century, that Hunza raiders plundered caravans heading to Kashmir. In 1985, an Aga Khan-funded road was begun and will eventually reach 45 km to Shimshal village at the valley's head.

Ten minutes from the bridge, at the north end of Passu, is a windy plain full of broken-down buildings. From 1968 until 1979 this was a camp for Chinese KKH workers. Now it's a mostly deserted Pakistan army post.

Places to Stay & Eat

About seven km south of Sust near Morkhun is the *Greenland Hotel*, where a double with hot shower is a negotiable Rs 150. At Khaibar, the *Khaibar Inn* has tea, light food and a few rooms.

PASSU

Sitting between the black Batura Glacier and the white Passu Glacier, this is the place to stop if you like to walk. Passu, at 2400 metres, is the base for many dramatic day hikes, overnights and long treks.

Although it's one of the oldest settlements in Hunza and Gojal, a kind of geographical curse has prevented Passu from growing into a town. As glaciers in the Shimshal Valley periodically dammed the Shimshal River and then broke, floods have gradually torn away Passu's river-front land. The 1974 mudslide at Shishkat Nala in southern Gojal created a lake that submerged parts of the village and choked the valley with sand and

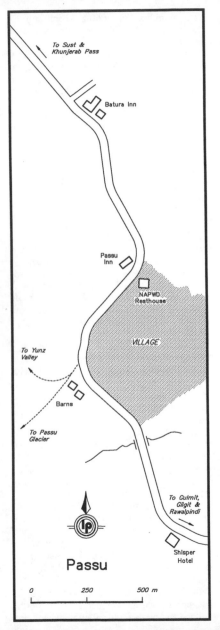

Passu

0   250   500 m

gravel. Passu at one time had extensive orchards, a polo field and nearly five times its present population, mostly on land that is no longer there.

The 'cathedral' ridge across the river from Passu is called Tupopdan (Wakhi for 'hot rock', because in winter its slopes shed the snow quickly).

High on the valley walls are messages (spelled out with painted rocks) associated with the 1987 visit of the Aga Khan to Gojal.

Orientation & Information

The present village is below the Passu Inn, where KKH buses usually stop. Buses will also drop you 1½ km south at the Shisper Hotel, or 800 metres north at the Batura Inn, on the edge of the old KKH road-camp.

The nearest post offices are in Sust and Gulmit. Telephone calls within Pakistan can be placed from the Passu Inn. The village has a tiny dispensary.

Hikes

Though many fine treks start from Passu, only day hikes and a few overnight trips are described here. Except for Shimshal, all can be done without a guide or porter and with minimal equipment.

However, no excursion longer than a few days should be undertaken without sound advice, weather information and a reliable guide. If you need budget-minded help finding a guide, ask any of Passu's wise hotel-wallahs. They might also be able to find tents, sleeping bags and other items to rent.

Hiring help is a tricky business. Porterage is based on *stages*, very roughly corresponding to steps in elevation – so, for example, porters' wages for an overnight trip to Abdegar ridge (six stages) would be more than for three days into Shimshal (five stages). Guides (who don't carry your gear) are normally paid per *day*, though many people in this area unfairly demand per-stage fees as guides too. A local student might want at least Rs 150 per *stage* to show you trails and act as an interpreter – a pretty poor bargain. More reasonable would be Rs 150 to Rs 250 per *day*.

For more on hiring help for long treks, see Trekking & Other Sports in the Facts for the Visitor chapter. Those considering a serious high-country trek, eg up the Batura Glacier, should refer to the Trekking chapter in the new (4th) edition of LP's *Pakistan – a travel survival kit*.

A cheerful source of local tips is the team of Manchester University hydrology students based at the Batura Inn each summer, slightly mad from too much Gojal sun and not enough beer.

Glacier Views An easy trail goes to the lake below Passu Glacier from the stone barns half a km south of the Passu Inn. Better views of this beautiful glacier are from the Yunz Valley and Passu Gar trails.

The toe of the Batura Glacier is four km north of the Batura Inn. The views improve as you climb the moraine (glacial rubble) along its south side.

Yunz Valley The massive caramel-coloured rock behind Passu is called Skazart (Wakhi for 'high-yellow'). A vigorous six to seven-hour loop climbs to the Yunz Valley behind Skazart, offering excellent views of both the Batura and Passu glaciers. This is a hot, strenuous walk with no water along the trail.

South of the Passu Inn, where an old channel comes to ground level, the trail immediately begins climbing the wall to the right (if you end up at the Passu Glacier lake, you began too far to the left).

From the Yunz Valley a 1½-hour detour goes to a view-point over the Hunza River. At the north end of the valley, bear left by some shepherds' huts and descend steeply to the moraine beside the Batura Glacier. At the toe of the glacier cross the low plateau to the right, back to Passu.

An overnight option is to climb the far side of Yunz Valley onto 4300-metre Patundas ('arid plain'), the first rise on the ridge separating the Passu and Batura glaciers.

Passu Gar This hike climbs to shepherds'

huts along the south side of the Passu Glacier and back, in six to seven hours. The trail leaves the KKH at a highway sign half a km beyond the Shisper Hotel, where power lines cross the road. The huts are about two hours beyond the bottom of the glacier.

An option from here is a steep traverse toward Borit Sar (Borit Peak), with almost 360° views of the Passu Glacier, Ghulkin Glacier to the south, Borit Lake below and the Karakoram crest behind. This adds at least 1½ hours to the trip.

Borit Lake A walk from Passu to Borit Lake and back takes four to five hours. From the Passu Gar trail, branch left near the bottom of the glacier. Near the lake is a summer village. Beside the lake, the basic *Borit Lake Hotel* has a few beds for Rs 25 and Rs 30 in summer, and free camping. The once-big lake has grown swampy and brackish (*borit* is Wakhi for 'salty') over the years, possibly because the underground seepage that feeds it has decreased as the glaciers have receded. From the lake it's an additional two-hour climb to Ghulkin Glacier.

A return option is to walk 20 minutes down the jeep road to the KKH and hitch back to Passu. The lake also makes a good overnight stop on a walk from Passu to Gulmit.

Zarabad & Hussaini This trip crosses the Hunza River on two long suspension bridges, and has fine views of the Passu and Ghulkin glaciers from the other side. It takes four to five hours from Passu to Hussaini, plus a hitch-hike or walk back (eight to 10 km along the KKH or via Borit Lake).

From the KKH, at the first hairpin turn past the Shisper Hotel, a trail drops to the right of a hamlet called Ashvendan. Go on up the far side of the ravine, following a path (marked by stone piles) to the river bed, then up another path on the bank, to the first bridge. It's just a cluster of cables with planks and branches woven in; on a windy day it will make you feel like Indiana Jones.

On the far side a trail branches left at a pile of stones, but you should continue straight

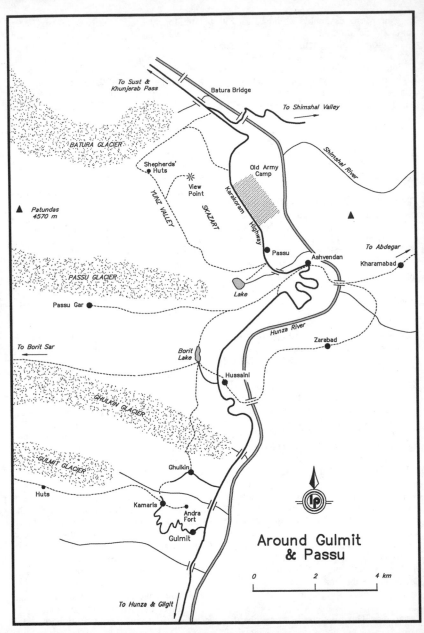

*To Sust &
Khunjerab Pass*

Batura Bridge

To Shimshal Valley

BATURA GLACIER

Shepherds'
Huts

Old Army
Camp

Shimshal River

View
Point

Karakoram Highway

▲ Patundas
4570 m

YUNZ VALLEY

SKAZART

Passu

Ashvendan

To Abdegar

Kharamabad

PASSU GLACIER

Passu Gar ●

Lake

Hunza River

Zarabad

To Borit Sar

Borit
Lake

Hussaini

GHULKIN GLACIER

GULMIT GLACIER

Ghulkin

Huts

Kamaris

Andra
Fort

Gulmit

Around Gulmit
& Passu

0   2   4 km

To Hunza & Gilgit

on. Climb toward the canyon walls and cross the shallow valley as high as possible, to the small village of Zarabad. A dramatic narrow track then crosses a sheer rock face to the second bridge.

Hussaini, back on the other side, is in a hollow below the KKH. It has a warm spring by the river's edge, used by Hussaini women for doing their wash, but they don't like travellers soaking in it!

On the north end of the village is a white shrine to Shah Talib, a Muslim missionary active around the 14th century. A path climbs to the highway near the shrine.

Abdegar East across the river is a 4900-metre ridge offering stupendous views from Sust to Shishkat, the entire length (over 20 km) of the Passu Glacier, and the highest peaks of the Batura Muztagh.

It's possible, in a strenuous, dry and very vertical day trip, to enjoy pretty amazing views from the tree-dotted 'meadow' about halfway up the ridge and return to Passu in about 10 hours. I drank 3½ litres of water on this trip. Start at dawn to avoid the harsh mid-day sun on the way up.

At the top of the ridge – almost as high as the Khunjerab Pass – is a shallow pass called Abdegar. Getting there is a very demanding trip; you will almost certainly have to spend the night there, and the nights are cold, but it's a sublime place to see the sun come up. It's probably best done in early autumn when the risk of sudden storms is low. Talk to local people before you go in any case.

Cross the bridge, as to Zarabad, and bear left toward the scattered houses of Kharamabad village. A trail above Kharamabad heads left and up to a deep ravine, where there is a fresh spring just below a waterfall plunge-pool (another spring further up dries up in autumn). Cross the stream about 100 metres below the pool to find the upward trail. Higher up, the way is very easy to lose among yak tracks or, near the top, in scree.

Yashpert This pasture and summer encampment up the north side of Batura Glacier is

accessible in a day from Passu. Above, on a moderate grade, are further meadows. You begin by climbing the south moraine and crossing the glacier, for which you might want local guidance.

The poor herders and villagers you will meet are hospitable, though the smaller your group, the warmer the welcome. A locally known companion can smooth the way. Carry all the food you'll need, and consider taking items like sugar, salt, tea, oil, matches, etc as gifts.

A three-day trek goes on from Yashpert to Khaibar village, northward near the KKH. Khaibar has a small inn. For detailed information on Batura trekking consult the Trekking chapter in *Pakistan – a travel survival kit*.

Kipgar This is the island in the river downstream from Passu. It's said to have some petroglyphs and the scattered remains of an old fortification. But getting there is probably more trouble than it's worth. Once there was a footbridge from Passu, but now you must cross the footbridge below Ashvendan, walk back up the other side and walk or wade out to the island.

Shimshal Valley It's feasible to take a three-day round trip by jeep (or a hitch on a tractor) plus walking, past Dut and Ziarat to Malunguti Glacier. An experienced guide is recommended, and a guide is essential on and beyond the Malunguti. From the KKH, at the hairpin turn 1½ km north of the Batura Inn, a track crosses a jeep bridge into the valley. *Stay away* on rainy or windy days, when rockfall hazard is high.

Places to Stay
The very spartan but cheerful *Batura Inn* occupies a corner of the old KKH work camp, and started out in 1974 as a canteen for Chinese officers. Camping is free, four-bed dorms without toilet are Rs 25 per bed, and doubles are Rs 60 and up. Izatullah Beg's food is abundant and delicious, and he has a small shop. Check out the psychedelic 'rumour books' full of good (and bad) advice about the area.

The *Passu Inn* (☎ 1), above the village, has doubles for Rs 100, comfortable hot-shower doubles for Rs 250 and up, and good food. Owner Ghulam Mohammed also has a dorm in traditional Gojal style (with an un-traditional attached toilet) for Rs 50 per bed. There are a few shops next door.

Isolated but with magnificent views and several hours' more sunshine than the others, the *Shisper Hotel* is on the highway below the Passu Glacier. Owner Azim Shah has clean doubles with toilet and cold shower for Rs 70 and up.

An *NAPWD Resthouse* is opposite the Passu Inn. Doubles are Rs 150. Take a chance, or book through the Chief Engineer in Gilgit.

Getting There & Away

Sust-to-Gilgit buses pass around 6.30 to 7 am, Gilgit-to-Sust buses around 1 to 2 pm, and vans sooner. Just put your bags beside the road and they'll stop. If there are enough people to fill it, a wagon might be arranged through your hotel. You could even walk to Gulmit, about 15 km (four hours) via Borit Lake and Hussaini, or about two km longer along the KKH. Sust is six to seven hours on foot.

GULMIT

With a library, a museum and the mirs' traditional second home, Gulmit ('GOOL-mit') is the closest thing to a town in Gojal, and its unofficial capital. It's very picturesque in spring and early summer when the fruit trees bloom. There are many good walks, though these are less monumental than Passu's.

Orientation & Information

Gulmit is centred on its old polo ground, 700 metres up a track from the KKH, although several hotels and the post office are on the highway. For medications or routine matters, Gulmit has a small civil hospital (but the Health Centre is only for child and maternity care). A police post is south of the village on the KKH.

Cultural Museum

A unique collection of Hunza history is packed into a dusty traditional-style house near the Marco Polo Inn. It contains maps, utensils, musical instruments, a stuffed snow leopard, gems and firearms (including the matchlock gun said to have injured the British commander at the Battle of Nilt in 1891). If it isn't open, ask next door or at the Marco Polo Inn. Admission is Rs 10.

Old Gulmit

The mir's palace is at the north end of the polo ground. Until the early 1970s the Mir of Hunza lived here for three months of the year, presiding over local *durbars* (councils); now it's locked up and rarely used.

A cluster of houses to the left of the palace is the original village. The tallest of these houses is said to be Gulmit's oldest, probably 100 to 200 years old; before the palace was built the mir stayed in it on his Gulmit sojourns. To the left of this are the carved lintels of an old Shia mosque, from the early 1800s before Gojalis converted to Ismailism.

Library

Adjacent to the *jamat khana* (Ismaili meeting hall) is a library that includes English-language books on history, education and religious studies. If it's closed the librarian, Mohammed Rahbar, can be contacted at the Tourist Cottage.

Hikes

Only day hikes and some overnight options are described here; all can be done with minimal equipment and no assistance. If you want to hire a guide, any able-bodied Gulmiti can help, though they tend to grossly underestimate walking times for a downlander! For some comments on hiring, see Trekking under Passu, and Trekking & Other Sports in the Facts for the Visitor chapter.

Kamaris, Andra Fort & Gulmit Glacier A

twisting track behind Gulmit climbs for an hour to the village of Kamaris, with views up and down the valley. A half-hour walk north-east from Kamaris brings you to the ruins of Andra Fort, built about 200 years ago to defend Gulmit in Hunza's war with the

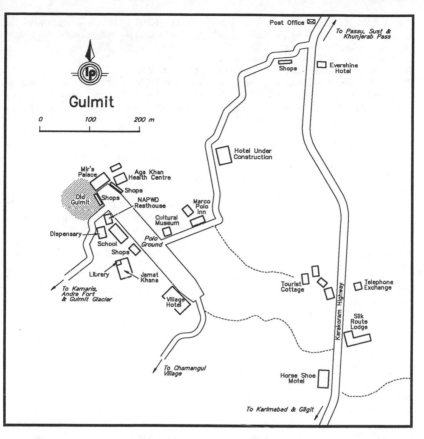

Gulmit

neighbouring state of Nagar. Ask local people for Andra Gelah ('geh-LA').

The jeep track continues past Kamaris for another hour, north-west to the base of the Gulmit Glacier. A long-day or overnight option is to continue on the footpath along the south side of the glacier, an area known locally as *Zherav* ('white glacier', as the ice here is no longer dirty), where there are some shepherds' huts.

High winds increase the rockfall hazard along here. This is also the starting point for more rigorous treks into the high country.

Ghulkin Village From Kamaris a footpath crosses the stream below Gulmit Glacier, then becomes a jeep track up to Ghulkin village, and returns to the KKH. The entire loop from Gulmit takes four to five hours.

Ghulkin Glacier, Borit Lake & Passu From Ghulkin a footpath crosses the grey Ghulkin Glacier to Borit Lake, two hours away. It's about 1¼ km across the glacier; although the way is marked by a rock pile on the south moraine and a big cleft in the north moraine, it's easy to lose your bearings. Kids in Ghulkin will show you across for a few rupees. Ask in Gulmit about seasonal conditions on the glacier.

Borit Lake is altogether about five hours (about 12 km) from Gulmit via Kamaris, or two to three hours (about eight km) via the KKH to Ghulkin or Hussaini. You can spend the night at the lake, hitch back from Hussaini or walk on to Passu. The little *Borit Lake Hotel*, with a few beds for Rs 25 and Rs 30 in summer, and free camping, is beside the lake. Passu is two to three hours from the lake.

Shishkat Nala A three-hour loop goes down the far side of the Hunza River past Shishkat Nala (locally called Baltbar) and returns on the KKH. Shishkat is the source of the 1974 slide that dammed the Hunza River for three years.

Cross a footbridge below the Horse Shoe Motel. A few km downstream is the original KKH section leading to the Friendship Bridge that is still buried under 25 metres of sediment from the slide. The track passes Nazimabad village on both sides of Shishkat Nala. Cross back on the new KKH bridge at Lower Nazimabad.

Places to Stay – bottom end
The *Tourist Cottage* (☎ 19), on the highway, has a traditional-style dorm (a raised sleeping area surrounding a stove) for Rs 40 a bed, and clean doubles with shared toilet for Rs 150. This is a good place for information on local trips too.

The *Village Hotel* (☎ 12), by the polo ground, has a few quiet doubles with shared loo for Rs 70 per bed. The *Evershine Hotel* on the highway has Rs 30 dorm beds and overpriced Rs 150 doubles and triples.

Places to Stay – top end
The friendly *Village Hotel's* comfortable doubles in an old Gojal-style building are good value at Rs 200 and Rs 250. A run-down *NAPWD Resthouse* with Rs 150 doubles can be booked through the Chief Engineer in Gilgit. The *Marco Polo Inn* (☎ 7) has evening videos and Rs 400 doubles. Deluxe doubles at the *Silk Route Lodge* (☎ 18) and its annexe, the *Horse Shoe Motel,* are priced for tour groups – Rs 500 and up.

On the KKH, by the Ghulkin link road, the small *Al Rahim Hotel* has doubles for a negotiable Rs 250.

Places to Eat
Every hotel has a dining room, with food prices in line with room prices. The bazaar at the polo field has fruit and snacks. By request the *Tourist Cottage* serves Gojal-style whole-wheat bread and home-made apricot jam at breakfast, and (for a price) traditional Hunza and Gojal dishes at dinner.

Getting There & Away
Sust-to-Gilgit buses pass around 7.30 to 8 am, Gilgit-to-Sust buses around 1 pm, and vans sooner. In summer, a Gilgit-bound van reportedly goes directly from Gulmit in the early morning for about Rs 40. You can book jeeps or Suzukis through your hotel. It's a four to five-hour walk to Passu – about 15 km via Borit Lake or about two km longer along the KKH. To Karimabad on foot along the KKH is said to take at least nine hours.

GULMIT TO GANESH
At the Shishkat Bridge south of Gulmit, Nazimabad village is the southernmost settlement of Wakhi people and the end of Gojal.

Perhaps the most obscure monument in British history is about 15 minutes south of the bridge (or opposite km-post 19 from Ganesh) where the gorge turns west. Across the river, a small white stone tablet marks the passage in August 1903 of Lord Kitchener, on a tour of the frontier areas of British India as the army's new Commander-in-Chief. The stone was erected by Nazim Khan (great-grandfather of the present mir), probably to flatter the British, who had installed him as mir following their invasion of Hunza in 1891. It's even with the highway, about three metres above the tenuous old track – forerunner of the KKH – that Kitchener took.

Fifteen minutes on (10 minutes east of Ganesh), Ahmedabad village clings to the opposite wall, illustrating the extremes of 'vertical agriculture' made possible by Hunza's distinctive irrigation channels.

Hunza & Nagar

For pure natural beauty, the Hunza Valley is the centre-piece of the KKH. In spring everything is green shoots and white blossoms in endless tiers, and autumn is a riot of yellow poplars, reddening orchards and maize drying on rooftops. Above are broad brown mountain sides and higher yet, the snowy peaks.

Added to this, for a Westerner, is a kind of mythology about Hunza's isolation and purity, spawned by James Hilton's 1933 novel *Lost Horizon*, nourished in films about the lost kingdom of Shangri-la, and fostered in the 1970s by media stories of extraordinary health and longevity.

The KKH itself has put an end to Hunza's isolation, and the Garden-of-Eden image ignores a rather bloody and disreputable history. But this hardly alters its appeal. Western visitors find more in common culturally with Hunzakuts than with anyone else in Pakistan, and the feeling seems mutual.

'Hunza' is commonly (and inaccurately) used in reference to the entire broad valley below Baltit. Two former princely states, Hunza and Nagar ('NAH-gr'), with a shared language and shared ancestry, face one another across this valley. Hunza, including its one-time satellite, Gojal, extends north and north-east to the China border.

The smaller but more populous Nagar actually occupies more of the main valley (the entire south side and some of the north side near Chalt) and includes 7790-metre Rakaposhi and the lower Hispar Glacier. Although it has enjoyed less media fame, Nagar is home to some of the best treks in the Karakoram.

The Valley

Hunza-Nagar is a place of great 'geo-drama'. The very edge of the ancient Asian continent is exposed near Chalt (see Facts about the Region – Geology). The continuous sweep from the valley floor to the summit of Rakaposhi, which seems to loom everywhere, is a reminder of the river's deep slice across the Karakoram.

Snaking across the slopes are Hunza's hallmark, the precision-made stone channels on which its life depends. Carrying water from canyons to fields and orchards as much as eight km away, they have transformed a dry valley with few horizontal surfaces into a breadbasket. Their paths on the high rock faces are revealed by thin lines of vegetation, and patches of green can be seen on the most improbable walls and ledges.

Irrigation sustains orchards of Hunza's famous apricots, as well as peaches, plums, apples, grapes, cherries and walnuts; fields of corn and wheat; and the ever-present poplars, a fast-growing source of fodder, firewood and timber.

History

The Hunza Valley lies on a branch of the Silk Road from Kashgar to Kashmir. Just east of Ganesh a cluster of boulders called Haldekish bears prayers, pictures and graffiti scratched in by passers-by over a period of 2000 years.

The origins of the Hunza-Nagar Kingdom are lost in legend, but it is probably an 11th-century offshoot of the Trakhan Dynasty of Gilgit. In perhaps the early 1600s the king or *mir* divided the realm between two sons. They immediately fell to fighting and one killed the other. Over the years their royal descendants have continued the feud, even as they intermarried. Until a century ago, murder was a routine solution to questions of succession.

Islam came with Arab armies to the south of Pakistan in the 8th century, but only later to the mountains. Shia missionaries were probably at work in the Hunza Valley from the 12th century to as late as the 17th. In the mid-1800s Hunza's ruling family and most of their subjects converted to Ismailism.

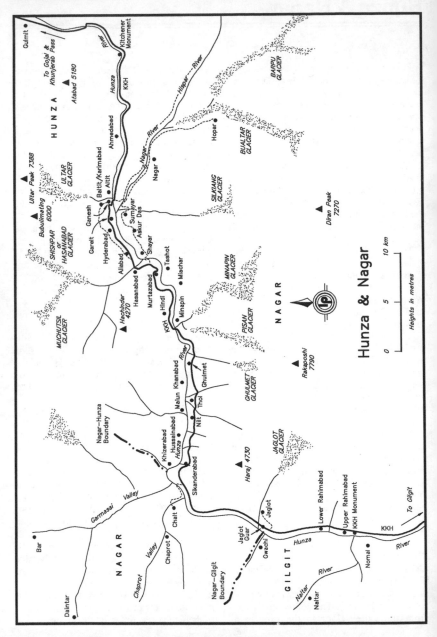

Hunza & Nagar

Heights in metres

0   5   10 km

Top Left: View from the roof of Baltit Fort, Hunza (JW)
Top Right: Musician, Gilgit (JW)
Bottom: Khunjerab Pass from the Pakistan side (JK)

Top & Middle Centre: Decorated trucks, Gilgit (JK)
Middle Left: KKH Memorial plaque, Pattan (JK)
Middle Right: KKH Memorial plaque, Rahimabad (JK)
Bottom: Rajah Bazaar Bus Stand, Rawalpindi (JK)

The 'Pacification' of Hunza & Nagar In the early 1800s Hunza had a political tilt toward China. Annual tributes of gold dust went to the governor of Xinjiang, and in 1847 the mir helped put down a rebellion in Yarkand. At the same time, the valley's modest agricultural output was supplemented by raids on caravans between Kashgar and Kashmir and by slave trading.

Yaqub Beg, who proclaimed an independent Turkestan republic in Xinjiang in 1865, put a temporary end to the caravan raids. This economic blow led Hunza and Nagar to declare allegiance to the British-aligned Maharajah of Kashmir, probably for the subsidy they got in return. Kashmiri troops occupied Chalt.

In 1886 Safdar Ali Khan became Mir of Hunza by murdering his father and three brothers (his father had inherited the throne in much the same fashion). Within two years he conspired to eject the Kashmiris from Chalt, resumed the caravan raids and played host in Baltit Fort to a party of Russian 'explorers'.

British India, spreading north from Kashmir, had grown aware of Russia expanding into Central Asia. Hunza began to look like a liability, and Britain decided to improve supply lines from Kashmir and to reopen its old agency at Gilgit. The Crown's representative was Captain Algernon Durand, who apparently believed that, to counter foreign influence in India, sooner or later all its frontier tribes would have to be subjugated or bought off.

In 1889 Durand visited Mir Safdar Ali Khan of Hunza and Mir Zafar Khan of Nagar and proposed British access up to Shimshal and an end to the caravan raids, in exchange for more subsidies. Both agreed, but the irrepressible valley men couldn't control themselves. The following year Hunza plundered a Kirghiz camp in the Pamirs, and in 1891 Uzar Khan, eldest son of the Mir of Nagar, began making threatening noises towards the British. Moreover, he had just had two of his 12 brothers murdered and was plotting against the others.

Durand moved troops to Chalt and built a sturdy bridge across the Hunza River. The mirs protested, but they were already undone: both royal families were increasingly terrorised by Uzar Khan and both mirs had already advised several sons and nephews to take refuge with the British. Durand in fact arrived at Chalt with Uzar Khan's youngest brother, Sikander.

On 21 December 1891 a combined British and Kashmiri force crossed the river and next day, at Nilt, encountered Uzar Khan's Hunza-Nagar irregulars at a fort beside a deep ravine. After dynamiting the gate the invaders rushed in, and the defenders fled through hidden passages beneath the fort. The British, despite some casualties, congratulated themselves on a splendid little fight.

Durand, seeking a view of the action, had stood up and received a shot in the groin – made, he later discovered, of a garnet slug encased in lead, standard issue in Hunza. The gun allegedly used for this deed is in the Gulmit Museum.

Then it was discovered that the men of the valley had destroyed the trails by which they escaped across the ravine, and had regrouped in a stronger position on the other side. For 17 miserable days the British, unable to advance, sat in the fort trying this and that. Finally, a party of Kashmiris slipped out at night and stormed the far side before breakfast, and opposition evaporated. Zafar Khan surrendered at Tashot and Durand's army marched into Baltit.

While they languished at Nilt, the British had received, and rejected, an appeal for negotiations from Safdar Ali, who then fled into Xinjiang with Uzar Khan and several hundred others.

Arriving at Baltit Fort, the mir's castle, the British found most of its treasure already gone, though they ransacked what was left. The spoils from years of plunder included antique chain armour, a Parisian music box, Dutch engravings, even a European armchair, as well as an extensive library and a cache of guns, powder and garnet bullets.

Overlooking superior British firepower and the embarrassing layover at Nilt, a

London *Times* correspondent, E F Knight (who had already forsaken his objectivity by volunteering for a command at Nilt), declared the episode 'one of the most brilliant little campaigns in military history'.

The ageing Zafar Khan was reinstated as ruler of Nagar; his grandson is the present Mir of Nagar. As ruler of Hunza the British installed Nazim Khan, Safdar Ali's stepbrother and the great-grandfather of the present Mir of Hunza. Uzar Khan was sent back by the Chinese authorities and jailed in Kashmir. Safdar Ali was allowed to stay in Xinjiang and died a poor man at Yarkand in 1930.

A British garrison stayed at Aliabad until 1897, after which Hunza and Nagar carried on in relative peace for three-quarters of a century.

After Partition Within weeks of the formal partition of India and Pakistan in August 1947, an uprising in Gilgit against the Maharajah of Kashmir, who had opted to join India, brought Hunza and Nagar into Pakistan. But they remained semi-autonomous until 1969 when General Yahya Khan – probably mindful of the political sensitivity of the future KKH – declared them merged with Pakistan, reducing the mirs to district officials.

People

Although Nagaris and Hunzakuts have common ancestors, there is no consensus on the place of their origin; scholarly suggestions include Kashmir, Baltistan, Persia, Russia and Mongolia. A persistent legend is of descent from Alexander the Great ('Sikander') or some of his soldiers who are said to have stayed behind in the 4th century BC. There is little to support this but it's startling to occasionally see 'Mediterranean' features, sandy hair and blue eyes.

Most people here still think of themselves as subjects of their mirs, rather than as Pakistanis. They are not fond of the downland Pakistanis that the KKH has brought, but even in remote areas they are very hospitable to foreigners.

The two kingdoms also have a common language, Burushaski, but nobody is sure where that came from either. Wakhi is spoken in upper Hunza (Gojal); in lower Nagar (in common with Gilgit) Shina is also used. Many people speak Urdu and English.

Hunza and Nagar once also shared the Shia Islamic faith, but in the last three or four generations Hunza has become almost entirely Ismaili (except for Ganesh and a few other pockets). Older shamanistic beliefs also linger, especially about mountain spirits or fairies who supposedly live on the highest peaks and behave capriciously toward humans. You can still see children and young women with dark eye make-up, to ward off spirits that may enter the eyes and other body orifices.

Hunza men and women wear the long shirt and baggy trousers called shalwar qamiz. The women's outfits are brightly coloured and many wear embroidered pillbox caps with a dupatta or shawl thrown over them. Men wear the distinctive Hunza wool cap, essentially a tube of cloth with the edges rolled tightly up, and in cold weather they may put on a *chogha*, a handsome embroidered woollen cloak with oversize sleeves.

Food

Hunza food is closer to Western food than anything else on the KKH. Typical items are potatoes, rice, *daudoh* (a noodle soup with vegetables, thickened with egg and whole wheat flour) and *phitti* (thick whole wheat bread). Oil and spices are used sparingly.

Milk products include yoghurt and *diltar*, a cultured buttermilk left after yoghurt is churned for butter. A soft cheese called *burus* ('broose') settles to the bottom of diltar kept warm for several days; it's very easy on upset stomachs. *Kurut* is a sour, hard cheese made by boiling and drying diltar.

Though not sold commercially (because they take so long to make), phitti and yoghurt are available at some hotels, and you can often special-order them through your hotel or from villagers.

Most of the Northern Areas' dried fruit comes from here, and dried Hunza apricots are found in bazaars all over Asia. There are at least 22 varieties of apricots, and the best trees are said to be heirlooms. Apricot season is July and early August. (Note that they are not always handled hygienically and should first be soaked in boiling water.)

Early autumn produce includes peaches, plums, apples, grapes, cherries and walnuts. A great travel snack is dried mulberries. If you're China-bound, Karimabad is a good place to stock up for the trip.

Alcohol

Despite Muslim prohibition and disapproval from the Aga Khan, some Hunzakuts carry on pre-Muslim traditions by brewing a rough grape wine called mel and a potent mulberry firewater called arak. This so-called 'Hunza water' may be offered to you by friends or hustlers.

Aga Khan Programmes

The loss of sovereignty in 1969 (and further loss of government subsidies in 1974) deprived Hunza, Nagar and other areas of the mirs' traditional power to initiate public works. Since then the private Aga Khan Rural Support Programme (AKRSP) has helped build an alternative infrastructure by which villages carry out their own revenue-producing projects, the most visible ones being irrigation and flood-control schemes, link roads and plantations. AKRSP signs sprout weekly by the roadsides, announcing new projects.

Other programmes include Aga Khan Health Services (AKHS), establishing rural primary-care projects and maternity and child health centres, and Aga Khan Educational Services (AKES), operating teacher-development schemes and scores of schools, mostly for girls. The Community Basic Services programme (CBS) is a joint project by the Pakistan government and UNICEF to improve rural drinking water and sanitation. The government's low-profile Local Bodies & Rural Development (LB&RD) agency also carries out its own projects.

For additional information about these programmes see Rural Development in the Facts about the Region chapter.

Celebrations & Holidays

Traditional seasonal festivals are hard to find now, though they are held privately. Locals

---

Cyclists' Notes, Hunza & Nagar

In addition to inns noted here, there are numerous hotels at Karimabad and Gilgit.

Ganesh to Minapin turning, about 25 km Karimabad is a steep two-km climb above Ganesh. The Kisar Inn at nearby Altit has a 'rumour-book' with current news from travellers. If you aren't stopping at Karimabad, the mid-range Garelt Hotel is 1½ km west of Ganesh, and there is a campsite and cheap inns at Aliabad, about eight km west of Ganesh. The easiest route between Karimabad and Aliabad is the link road that meets the KKH two km west of Aliabad bazaar; though still partly unpaved, it can be cycled. Murtazabad, about 15 km from Ganesh, has a peaceful small hotel. About nine km further and across the Hunza River is Pisan, from where it's 2½ km off the KKH to Minapin, with camping and cheap beds.

Minapin turning to Chalt turning, about 25 km There are two tent camps at Ghulmet, about five km west of Pisan, and grotty local inns at Ghulmet Das, three km further. On the KKH three km before Sikanderabad is the Snow White Hotel, and in the village is a government resthouse. Chalt, about three km on and 3½ km off the KKH, has a pleasant resthouse and small hotel.

Chalt turning to Gilgit, about 55 km Basic food and rope-beds are available at Jaglot Guar, about 14 km from the Chalt turning or 42 km from Gilgit. The shortest route into Gilgit from Hunza is over two swinging suspension bridges (turn off the KKH at Dainyor). Good 'rumour-books' are at Tourist Cottage and North Inn in Gilgit.

speak of the 'dreamful times' when people enjoyed community gatherings, music, dancing, courtship, and a little drink. Ismaili holidays are big events in Hunza. Nagaris and people of Ganesh celebrate Shia holy days, to which non-Muslims are usually not welcome.

*12 February to 15 March (1994), 1 February to 4 March (1995), 22 January to 22 February (1996) (Nagar, Ganesh)

Ramadan, a month of daytime fasting. Food is hard to find in Shia villages, though not in most of Hunza.

Late February or early March

Bo Pho, the first wheat sowing. Families may celebrate in their fields, with food and prayers.

21 March

Nauroz ('New Days'), a spring festival, and a Shia and Ismaili celebration of the succession of the Prophet's son-in-law Ali. People visit family and friends, and there may be music, dancing and, in Chalt, possibly polo matches

*15 March (1994), 4 March (1995), 22 February (1996) (Nagar, Ganesh)

Eid-ul-Fitr, the end of *Ramadan*. This may include elaborate meals, visits to relatives, exchange of gifts.

Late June or early July

Ginani, the first harvest. Before cutting the first wheat, farmers may celebrate in their fields. Community celebrations may include music and dancing, the slaughter of sheep and, in Chalt, sometimes polo.

*1 July (1993), 20 June (1994), 9 June (1995), 29 May (1996) (Nagar, Ganesh)

Ashura. Shias mourn the death of Hussain; in village processions men and boys perform ritual self-punishment.

11 July (Hunza)

Taqt Nashina ('taking the seat'). Ismailis celebrate the day the present Aga Khan became leader of their community; there may be games, music, dancing and fireworks.

*10 August (1993), 30 July (1994), 19 July (1995), 8 July (1996) (Nagar, Ganesh)

Chhelum, occurs 40 days after *Ashura*, with similar processions.

*31 August (1993), 20 August (1994), 10 August (1995), 29 July (1996)

Eid-Milad-un-Nabi, the Prophet's birthday. Some shops may close.

23 October (Hunza)

The Aga Khan's first visit to Hunza in 1960; similar to *Taqt Nashina*.

13 December (Hunza)

The Aga Khan's Birthday, celebrated by Ismailis with gatherings and speeches.

21 December

Tumishaling, a festival of renewal, celebrating the death of the cannibal-king Sri Badat of Gilgit. According to local legend he put the writing on the Sacred Rocks of Hunza with his bare fingers. His daughter plotted with his subjects to trap him in a pit and burn him to death. Bonfires are built in some villages, and people carry fire from their own homes; there may also be music, dancing and the slaughter of sheep or goats.

Late December

Nosalo. This usually begins at *Tumishaling* and goes on for 15 days. Each household slaughters a sheep or goat and hangs it up for all to see. This practical occasion assures a winter supply of protein and fat, and is soon enough to allow the meat to dry without spoiling.

* approximate dates

GANESH

Most travellers know Ganesh ('GUN-ish') only as Karimabad's bus stop. But this is probably the oldest settlement in Hunza-Nagar, and despite having been cut to pieces by the KKH, it has a lovely village centre full of classic Hunza architecture.

Ganeshkuts were once famous for their raids against Nagar. In the 1800s, Ganesh was the main Hunza hold-out against Ismailism and is today 100% Shia. With cultural ties to Hunza and religious ties to Nagar, the village is, nowadays, almost friendless.

Orientation & Information

The bus drops you at a clutch of shops and cafes near a monument to KKH construction-worker 'martyrs' (casualties). Have a cup of tea before the two-km climb up to Karimabad. If you want a ride up, first see Baltit & Karimabad – Getting Around.

Ganesh Village

Older Ganeshkuts frown on outsiders but if you ask around you may be welcomed into the village, one of the least modernised in Hunza. Around a central pond are several richly carved wooden mosques, 100 to 200 years old, each donated by a Ganesh clan,

Shepherds' summer hut at Ultar Glacier, Hunza (JK)

and a timber-&-stone watchtower from the days of war with Nagar.

West across the fields is a flag-decked ziarat (shrine) to an early Muslim holy man named Bulja Toko – who never came to Hunza, but featured in a villager's dream. On Fridays food is left here for the poor to take.

Two km west, Ganesh's sister-village of Tsil Ganesh has a Balti-style *imam barga*, a hall used for the Shias' Ashura and Chhelum observances.

Sacred Rocks of Hunza

About 1½ km east of Ganesh on the KKH are several stony rises marked by a sign with this name (which was probably invented at the Ministry of Tourism). Locally the site is called Haldekish ('hal-DAY-keesh'). The rocks, with pictures and writing from as early as the 1st century AD, are a kind of 'guest book' of the valley. In addition to local traditions they tell of Buddhist pilgrims, kings of the Kushan Empire at Taxila, a 6th-century Chinese ambassador, 8th-century Tibetan conquerors and even KKH workers!

Places to Stay & Eat

A small hotel is under construction at Ganesh bazaar. At Garelt, 1½ km west on the KKH, the friendly *Garelt Hotel* has doubles for about Rs 200. Nearby is PTDC's *Hunza Motel*, marring the valley view from almost any angle, like graffiti on the Sistine Chapel; singles/doubles are Rs 450/550.

Getting There & Away

Wagons leave Ganesh for Gilgit early in the morning for about Rs 35. Vans and the bus from Sust come through late in the morning but may be full; the bus is about Rs 25 to Gilgit. Passenger Suzukis ply between here and Aliabad for Rs 3. For Sust, the Natco bus from Gilgit passes after 10 am, and private vans pass sooner.

BALTIT & KARIMABAD

Baltit has always been the capital of Hunza. It consists mostly of Baltit Fort and a compact village at its feet. The fort was the royal palace until the 1940s, when sounder quarters were built in Karimabad, just below. Karimabad (named for Prince Karim, the present Aga Khan) is just a latter-day extension of Baltit with hotels, cafes and a bazaar.

Orientation

From the KKH, a rough link road climbs two km up from Ganesh to Karimabad bazaar, and another weaves up the valley from west of Aliabad. A branch of the road from Ganesh goes round to Mominabad and Altit villages, and another is being cut down to the KKH at Garelt, west of Ganesh. A link road also descends from the Karimabad bazaar to Altit, and a track near the Rainbow Hotel leads up to Baltit.

Information

There's no tourist office but a shopkeeper named Mujibullah has local maps and lots of information. The post office, near the New Hunza Tourist Hotel, is open from 8.30 am to 2 pm for general business, to 4.30 pm for stamps. For domestic calls, there is a public call office on the road from Ganesh, but it's quicker to use the Aliabad telephone exchange.

Change money at the National Bank or a few doors down at the shop of Karimabad's cheerful tycoon, Mr Ali Gohar Shah. The tiny Hunza Book Centre has some works on local history and culture, plus charming educational posters. There are also some books for sale at the Hilltop Hotel's souvenir shop. A small hospital is on the road from Ganesh.

Until Baltit and Karimabad get 24-hour electricity, the evening calm will be shattered by the sound of hotel generators.

Baltit Fort

Tibetan-style Baltit Fort, on a throne-like ridge in front of Ultar Nala, was built in its original form some 600 to 800 years ago for a princess of Baltistan (hence its name) who married a mir. She brought her own artisans to do the work.

In about 1900, balconies and interior comforts were added. It was the royal residence until the 1940s, and the mir held his councils on the roof, from where the view of the

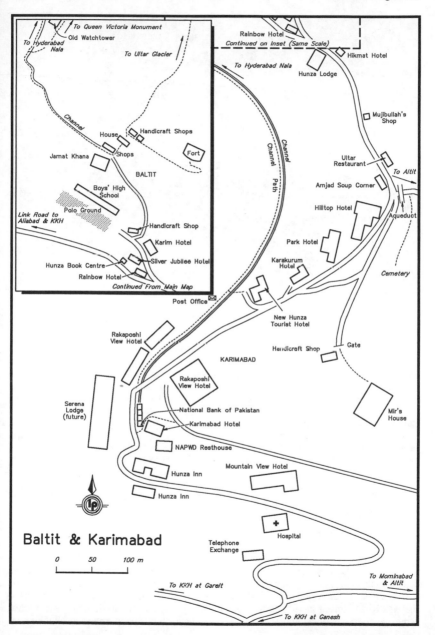

To Queen Victoria Monument
Old Watchtower
To Hyderabad Nala
To Ultar Glacier
Rainbow Hotel
Continued on Inset (Same Scale)
Hikmat Hotel
To Hyderabad Nala
Hunza Lodge
Channel
Mujibullah's Shop
House
Handicraft Shops
Shops
Fort
Jamat Khana
BALTIT
Ultar Restaurant
To Altit
Channel
Channel Path
Amjad Soup Corner
Boys' High School
Hilltop Hotel
Aqueduct
Link Road to Aliabad & KKH
Polo Ground
Handicraft Shop
Park Hotel
Karim Hotel
Cemetery
Karakurum Hotel
Hunza Book Centre
Silver Jubilee Hotel
Rainbow Hotel
Continued From Main Map
Post Office
New Hunza Tourist Hotel
Rakaposhi View Hotel
KARIMABAD
Handicraft Shop
Gate
Rakaposhi View Hotel
Serena Lodge (future)
National Bank of Pakistan
Karimabad Hotel
Mir's House
NAPWD Resthouse
Hunza Inn
Mountain View Hotel
Hunza Inn
Hospital
Telephone Exchange

Baltit & Karimabad

0   50   100 m

To KKH at Garelt
To Mominabad & Altit
To KKH at Ganesh

Tibetan-style tower on the roof of Baltit Fort (JK)

valley is superb. The fort was near collapse when restoration was begun a few years ago by a joint British-Pakistani team. It's temporarily closed to the public. There is talk of making it into a cultural museum.

The track to the fort begins near the Rainbow Hotel. Turn right at the polo field; 150 metres further, turn right on a path that runs under a house, then right again. Kids along here hawk 'rubies' (garnets) to the tourists.

Around Karimabad

Above the Park Hotel a road leads to the modern residence of the Mir of Hunza. Just beyond the aqueduct near the Hilltop Hotel a right turn takes you to a cemetery, with good low-altitude valley views. About one km out on the Aliabad link road is Hunza's pride and joy, the surprisingly modern, fort-like Aga Khan Girls' Academy, dedicated by the Aga Khan himself in 1987 (boys of the same age go to school in Gilgit).

Altit Fort

The small fort at Altit, with its carved lintels and window-frames, is older than Baltit's. In front is an apricot orchard, and behind is a vertical 300-metre drop to the Hunza River. It's a three-km walk down from Karimabad and across the Ultar stream. An alternative route is via Mominabad. Ask anyone for the chowkidar with the keys (who may appreciate Rs 15 or so for showing you around). Fort is *gela* ('geh-LAH') in Burushaski.

The village is said to have its own small library, near the pool, with a few English-language titles.

Mominabad

In the Northern Areas are traces of an ancient caste system, in which musicians and other craftspeople rank low. In the past they were often segregated in their own villages. Mominabad (old name Berichal), though quite ordinary-looking, was such a village, and its people even speak their own language, Beriski. A road leads there from a turn on the Ganesh-Karimabad road, and continues down to Altit. With tourism on the rise, local musicians may be low-caste but they're getting rich.

Channel Walks

It's amazing how many irrigation channels come out of a single canyon, and how far they go. A three or four-hour walk along the main channels (*gotsil*) from Ultar Nala is a good way to see Hunza. Try to avoid the more delicate side-channels.

Climb past the polo field, bearing left beside the channel. The path goes down the valley all the way to Hyderabad Nala. There, scramble down the stream-bed to the link road. Turning back to Karimabad, you can soon drop to another channel that goes all the way back. By now you may have 'canal fever', and you can go right on around Karimabad, past Mominabad, to the channel's headworks behind Baltit Fort.

Both channels distribute water from Ultar. There are two more above these, and at least two on the other side of the nala. The velvety appearance of the Ultar water is the result of minute flakes of mica.

Melishkar & Duikar

These are side-by-side summer villages 300 metres above Altit; Melishkar is said to be Hunza's highest village. The five or six-hour round trip includes a hard, dry climb past friendly hamlets and gravity-defying terraced fields, up to huge valley views. The best views are from a promontory above Melishkar called Tok.

Just before reaching Altit's polo ground from Karimabad, branch left for the trail up. A return option is to cross from just above Melishkar, directly across the valley wall to Ultar Nala. The path is below the upper water channel and points roughly toward Baltit Fort. A trail then descends into the nala behind Baltit Fort. Climb to the far side, where the path leads into the village.

Ultar Nala & Ultar Glacier

A climb to the Ultar icefall will give you an appreciation for how vertical things are here. It's a strenuous day trip, or the sort of thing you might want to spend longer on. Some people hire a local guide for around Rs 250 per day – useful but not necessary.

Enter Ultar Nala from the top of Baltit village and follow a sometimes-indistinct trail up the steep moraines. There is a spring 15 minutes beyond the village, just past the channel headworks.

Three to four hours up at the foot of the rumbling icefall is a meadow in an amphitheatre of peaks. One black pinnacle, Bubulimating (named for the hapless Princess Bubuli, left there by a demon king), is so sheer that snow doesn't stick to it. To its right, on the backbone of the Karakoram and 4½ vertical km above you, is Ultar peak (7388 metres). Until it was scaled in September 1991 by a British team, this was one of the world's highest unclimbed mountains.

Shepherds drive flocks up to the meadow and live in the stone huts all summer. You should ask before camping near their animals. With tea, salt, sugar, cigarettes or matches you might bargain with them for fresh milk (*mamu*), yoghurt (*dumanu-mamu*), buttermilk (diltar) or cheese (*burus*).

West, and up from the huts, is a 4500-metre ridge called Hon with incredible views across to Nagar, Golden Peak and Rakaposhi – but it takes up to four hours more and probably shouldn't be attempted unless you're staying the night. The ridge is not a technical climb but does require great care. A less vertical alternative above the shepherds' huts is to turn right off the trail, about two-thirds of the way down to the ridge, crossing a stream coming down from the right. About a km up is a campsite with equally fine views.

On the return trip, high water channels look like good trails but they aren't, because they leave you with some dangerous descents, and may pose a rockfall hazard below. If you must use a channel, walk *in* it if you can, so as not to damage it.

Carry water; the glacier's thrashing stream can be hard to approach, and there is no water at Hon. Take extra layers, even on a hot day, against the icy wind off the glacier. Rockfall hazard is high after prolonged rain, high winds or a thaw. In July and August, thunderstorms may roll through. Streams are swollen then, and some are dicey to cross. See LP's *Pakistan – a travel survival* kit for more information on this walk.

Queen Victoria Monument

At the top of the rock face behind Baltit is a monument to Queen Victoria (probably erected by the mir's sycophantic grandfather Nazim Khan) which can be reached in an hour from Baltit.

Take the channel path above the polo ground. Five minutes out, cross the channel and climb stone steps beside an old watchtower. At the top of the village, scramble to a shallow cleft with some very large boulders (you'll find garnets among the rocks here). Go straight up to the base of the cliff before crossing over to the monument; avoid a diagonal crossing of the face because the top Ultar water channel spills down it.

In Burushaski, the monument is referred to as *Malikamu Shikari* ('ma-li-KA-mu shi-KA-ri').

Places to Stay – bottom end

The cheerful *New Hunza Tourist Hotel* has Rs 30 dorm beds and crumbling doubles with toilets for about Rs 75, negotiable in the off-season. The cook has the longest face in Hunza but his food is pretty good. They also run a shuttle-jeep from Ganesh.

Another good bet is the *Karim Hotel* at the top of the hill, with Hunza-style dorm, very spartan doubles/quads for Rs 40/125, and mid-range doubles and a sunny roof with a view. Both places have generators and evening electricity.

The *Silver Jubilee Hotel* has Rs 50 dorm beds (but another traveller reported Rs 25) and pricier rooms, and service is said to be good. The *Hunza Lodge* (☎ 61), with sunny doubles for a negotiable Rs 80, has erratic service but great views. Less appealing are *Hunza Inn*, *Karimabad Hotel* and *Rainbow Hotel* with rooms for Rs 20 to Rs 45 per bed.

At Altit's friendly *Kisar Inn* (☎ 41)

doubles are Rs 60 to Rs 150 (but avoid Altit's so-called 'spring water'). They also have a shuttle-jeep from Ganesh, and a 'rumour-book' with useful and current travellers' comments.

At some hotels you can pitch a tent and use the facilities for a fee. See Ganesh for other options.

Places to Stay – middle

An *NAPWD Resthouse* with Rs 150 doubles can be booked with the Chief Engineer in Gilgit. The bottom-end *Karim* and *Silver Jubilee* hotels have doubles for about the same price. The *Karakurum Hotel's* clean doubles are Rs 200. A friendly hotel with similar prices is at Garelt, west of Ganesh on the KKH (see Ganesh).

Places to Stay – top end

Doubles with cold showers are Rs 250 at the *Park Hotel* (☎ 45), and Rs 300 at the group-oriented *Hilltop Hotel* (☎ 10).

The mir's own *Rakaposhi View Hotel* (☎ 12) has singles/doubles with fine valley views for Rs 200/300; some rooms have a hot shower, and prices are negotiable in the off-season. A monster extension is under construction above the road. You can even stay at the mir's house for a mere Rs 800 per deluxe double.

The *Mountain View Hotel* (☎ 17) has doubles/triples for Rs 350/450; visitors say the food is overpriced. The concrete megalith opposite the bank will eventually be a four-star *Serena Lodge*. PTDC has an eyesore of a motel down on the KKH (see Ganesh).

These places all have their own generators and evening electricity.

Places to Eat

Hotel Food *New Hunza Tourist Hotel* has a bargain Hunza-style meal for Rs 25 (if you're not a guest, book it in the morning). Food at the *Park Hotel* is good too. Most other hotels serve up something, but more often than not it is the usually dreary chicken curry, dhal and boiled potatoes.

Cafes Best in the bazaar is *Ultar Restaurant*, with meat and vegetables, chips and tasty soup, and Cokes chilled in the stream. Try authentic daudoh at the *Hikmat Hotel*. *Amjad Soup Corner* serves peppery chicken soup and is a meeting place for local adults, kids and most of the flies in the village.

Drinks Offers of 'Hunza water' are not uncommon. Some shops sell non-alcoholic beer. If you don't like the look of Karimabad's murky water, fill your bottle at a clear spring 15 minutes beyond Baltit village on the Ultar trail, just past the channel headworks.

Entertainment

Traditional Hunza sword dances are occasionally performed at the Hilltop Hotel by local musicians.

Things to Buy

Hunza-Nagar wool is renowned for durability, though it's being displaced by factory imitations. The best deals are in small general shops (but selection is larger in Gilgit). A handicrafts shop run by the Karimabad Women's Welfare Centre is just inside the gate to the mir's house. Other souvenir shops are at the Hilltop Hotel and on the way to Baltit Fort.

Getting There & Away

Wagons leave for Gilgit's Jamat Khana Bazaar from near Hunza Lodge in the morning, from about 6 am, for Rs 35; in summer there are at least three a day. An alternative is to catch the Sust-to-Gilgit bus at Ganesh. When the Karimabad-Aliabad link road is fully paved there is certain to be more service this way.

The cheapest way to Sust is potluck at Ganesh (see Ganesh). There's nothing convenient from Karimabad except to hire a jeep or van through your hotel for around Rs 200 to Rs 300 per person.

Getting Around

New Hunza Tourist Hotel and Altit's Kisar Inn run free jeep shuttles up from Ganesh.

Other jeeps lurking at Ganesh may ask Rs 100 per person but prices quickly collapse to Rs 20.

ALIABAD

Aliabad's characterless bazaar, strung for 1½ km along the KKH, is a transport hub and administrative centre. Until the Karimabad-Aliabad link road has regular transport, this is an awkward place to stay unless you want to trek in Hasanabad Nala.

Orientation & Information

By the police post in the centre of the bazaar is a road to a small civil hospital, probably Hunza's best (they also have basic dental facilities). The post office is 200 metres east of the petrol station. The link road to Karimabad joins the KKH two km west of the bazaar.

Places to Stay

At a yard called *Hunza Rakaposhi Tentage Accommodation* you can pitch a tent for Rs 30 or sleep in theirs for Rs 60; toilets and washing facilities are on site. It's aimed at pre-booked groups but you can inquire next door at the *Dumani View Hotel* – where doubles with cold shower are overpriced at Rs 200. West of town is the top-end *Rakaposhi Inn*.

Places to Eat

The fairly clean *Prince Hotel* has Pakistani food and ersatz daudoh. The *Moonland Hotel* in the centre has Pakistani dishes, and there are various grotty cafes with soup, meat and chapattis.

Getting There & Away

Several wagons leave Aliabad for Gilgit between 5 and 8 am, for Rs 30. Natco and private vehicles come through between Gilgit and Sust. Suzukis go to/from Ganesh all day for Rs 3, and some go to Murtazabad.

HASANABAD NALA

Three km west of Aliabad is the deep Hasanabad Nala. In a sense this is the perfect short excursion: step off the KKH and walk up a gradual trail through varied terrain, with good views of high country and glaciers, and good camping just hours away. No guide is needed unless you're planning a multi-day trek (for information on treks here, see LP's totally revised *Pakistan – a travel survival kit*).

One option is the trail up the east side of the nala, from near a highway maintenance camp. The best place to camp is a sandy spot near the river, just below the mouth of the Shishpar Glacier (also called Shisper or Hasanabad Glacier), two to three hours from the KKH. You could go further but this site has a spring nearby. From here the trail gets difficult and includes a bit of glacier-walking.

A trail also goes up the west side of the nala. Turn left after three km into the first side canyon, left again after 3½ to four km, and climb to the beautiful pastures called Hachindar. The walk is about five hours one way. Water is available but purity is unknown. There's good camping and you may meet shepherds with whom you can barter for food.

Back in the main nala, you can also climb past the snout of Shishpar Glacier to the tributary Muchutsil Glacier.

MURTAZABAD

Other than Ganesh, Murtazabad is one of the few villages in Hunza with a sizeable Shia population. The village centre is just off the KKH eight km down-river from Aliabad.

Hot Springs

There are several hot springs near the village, regularly used by local people for bathing. For information, ask at the Eagle Nest Hotel. 'Hot spring' is *garum bul* (gah-ROOM bool) in Burushaski, *garam chashma* in Urdu.

Places to Stay & Eat

In an orchard 100 metres east of the village centre is the plain, peaceful *Eagle Nest Hotel* (☎ 45089), whose three clean doubles with loo and shower are a negotiable Rs 140.

Getting There & Away

Some passenger Suzukis come to Murtazabad from Aliabad for Rs 3, or from Ganesh. For-hire Suzukis between Ganesh and Murtazabad would be about Rs 40. Wagons from Gilgit will take you to Karimabad for Rs 10.

UPPER NAGAR

That part of Nagar visible from Karimabad is strung together by a jeep road from the Hasanabad-Shayar suspension bridge up to the glaciers at Hopar. Much of it is in the shadow of its own peaks, giving it a slightly gloomy atmosphere. It's more densely populated than Hunza. But the location gives Nagar heavier snows and more water, so there's no need for Hunza's meticulous irrigation and husbandry.

Orientation & Information

Opposite Ganesh the Nagar (also called Hispar) River joins the Hunza River. About 12 km upstream the valley divides, south to the fertile Hopar Nala and south-east to the remote Hispar Nala. Hopar's glaciers reach nearly to this confluence.

In addition to the main jeep road from the KKH at Hasanabad, a track climbs from the KKH east of Ganesh, up the dry east side of the Nagar River. At a bridge one branch continues toward Hispar Glacier and the other crosses to the main road near Nagar village. There is also a tenuous jeep track along the south bank of the Hunza River from Minapin to Shayar.

This area has few of the conveniences found along the KKH. Reliably clean water is rare at lower levels.

Hasanabad to Sumayar

At the promontory down-river from Hasanabad Nala a jeep track drops from the KKH to a suspension bridge across the Hunza River. Except for the crossing, it's a fairly level two-hour walk to Sumayar, with wide views of Hunza and a close look at the villages of Nagar. There are stories of stone-throwing kids along here, though Nagaris dismiss them as 'Hunza propaganda'.

En route, Askur Das has a tea shop and a tiny cafe, and villagers say there's a room to rent. Other lodging options include camping in Sumayar Nala, pressing on to Nagar village, three hours past Sumayar, or backtracking to Murtazabad on the KKH.

Sumayar Nala
This is the narrow canyon you look into from Karimabad, just west of the Nagar Valley. Camping is not advisable near Sumayar village but it's excellent at the meadows three hours up the nala, with views of 7270-metre Diran Peak and the Silkiang Glacier. In summer you may find shepherds there. A footpath leaves the road near the powerhouse and initially follows the powerhouse channel. In the afternoon after freezing nights there is a rockfall hazard in the nala.

Nagar Village
This was the capital of the state of Nagar, and the old mir still lives here. It has a few shops, a hospital and a police post. An *NAPWD Resthouse* has doubles for Rs 150 (book with the Chief Engineer in Gilgit). Apart from the resthouse there are no other obvious places to eat.

Hopar
After the hard-scrabble agriculture below, the stretch from Nagar village to Hopar looks fertile and lovely in spring. Hopar is a cluster of villages around a natural bowl at a bend of the Bualtar Glacier. Opposite Hopar the white Bualtar is joined by the Barpu Glacier. Jeeploads of tourists come up on summer mornings, click-click and drive away.

From Hopar you can hike beside the Bualtar or cross it and climb to summer villages along both glaciers. This is also a base for treks into the high, glacier-draped peaks called the Hispar Muztagh.

At the end of the road is a soup-kitchen called the *Hopar Hilton* where you can pitch your tent or take a bed in one of theirs. A two-room *NAPWD Resthouse* is under renovation. The managers of both can help with information (including glacier crossings)

and local guides, but beware of other 'friends' who later demand a guide fee.

Getting There & Away
There is no regular transport to the Nagar side. From Bank Rd in Gilgit, cargo jeeps go in via Hasanabad or Ganesh, but they're usually loaded to the gunwales. Most go only to Nagar village, heading back early the next morning. Some vans may go to Nagar from Bank Rd. At the time of writing, a hired jeep from Ganesh or Karimabad was Rs 700 for a day trip to Hopar, and Rs 900 overnight.

Walking from Karimabad, via the Sacred Rocks and the jeep road up the east side of the Nagar Valley, Nagar village is about three hours, and Hopar is about five to six hours. A footpath over the ridge on the Nagar side of the KKH bridge shortens this a bit. Or you can ride to Hasanabad, cross the suspension bridge and walk up the Nagar side. This way, Hopar is a very long day's hike from Hasanabad.

When the Nagar River is low (mostly in winter) a makeshift footbridge crosses it where it joins the Hunza River. This way it's only a one-hour hike from Ganesh to Sumayar. Footpaths descend to this point from the Nagar end of the KKH bridge and from the jeep road above Sumayar.

MINAPIN
Down-river from Murtazabad the KKH crosses into Nagar, over a Chinese bridge with little stone lions. Just on the Nagar side, at Pisan, a jeep track turns east, and up it is 40 minutes' walk to Minapin. Literally at the foot of Rakaposhi, Minapin is the start of a glacier-side climb to one of the mountain's expedition base camps, and to longer treks toward Diran Peak.

Rakaposhi Base Camp via Minapin Glacier
The well-used, very steep trail starts behind the resthouse. The first few km climb the Minapin Glacier's terminal moraine to the path along its west side. The path gives wide views of the glacier, and eventually of the entire Rakaposhi-Diran crest-line.

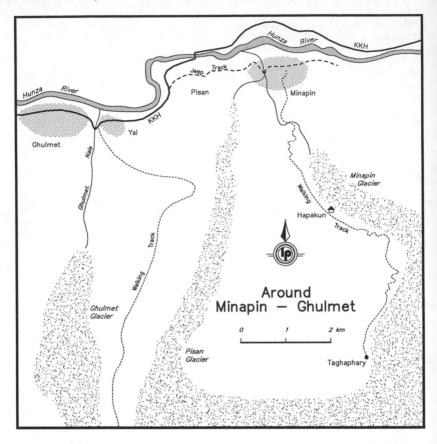

Around
Minapin — Ghulmet

One day up is a hut at Hapakun. Day two gets you to Rakaposhi base camp, 1500 metres above Minapin in a meadow called Taghaphary overlooking the glacier's upper icefields. Rakaposhi (7790 metres) is south-west and Diran (7270 metres) is south-east. In another day you could reach Diran base camp at Kacheli.

This trek is best done between July and September when days are long and water is available, but even then nights are cold. Rakaposhi is also subject to sudden, chilling storms. A local guide is a good idea – especially in the spring when the trail is eroded and treacherous. Beyond Taghaphary meadow, a guide is essential at any time.

Places to Stay & Eat

You can camp, eat, shower and get help with equipment, food, guide, porter or a pony, at *Alpine Camping* in Minapin. Across the road is an *NAPWD Resthouse*, which can be booked through the Chief Engineer in Gilgit.

Getting There & Away

Occasional wagons go directly between Minapin and lower Bank Rd in Gilgit, or you can get off a long-haul bus at Pisan.

GHULMET

The starting point for another Rakaposhi climb is the village of Ghulmet (pronounced 'ghool-MET'; this spelling is used instead of the often-seen 'Gulmit', to avoid confusion with the village in Gojal). At its eastern end is Ghulmet Nala, out of which Rakaposhi rises in a single unobscured sweep, begging to be photographed. In fact, a thoughtful sign points out this stupendous view, in case you overlook (underlook?) it.

Rakaposhi Base Camp via Ghulmet Glacier

Although there's a base camp up this trail (used by a Japanese expedition in 1979) and the views are outstanding, it's a long, steep hike with no water and poor camping on the way.

The trail begins behind the hamlet of Yal east of Ghulmet Nala and climbs a high ridge between the Ghulmet and Pisan glaciers. As with the Minapin hike, July through September are the best months, and even then cold storms can blow in. For more information ask at the Rakaposhi View Hotel, whose owner was a guide for the Japanese team.

Places to Stay

For cyclists or trekking freaks, on both sides of the nala are makeshift inns with ultra-basic food and cheap beds in tents – the original *Rakaposhi View Hotel* and copycat *Rakaposhi Mountain Hotel*. They open in late May and close down in October, like a travelling circus. Alternatives are the campsite and resthouse at Minapin or a couple of seedy inns, three km west in Ghulmet Das.

GHULMET TO CHALT

The nala and village west of Ghulmet are called **Thol** ('tole'). A prominent landmark is the blue-roofed shrine to Shah Wali, a Shia preacher from Afghanistan who settled here in, perhaps, the 1600s. Roadside flags remind travellers to leave a few coins for upkeep. Nearby is a small timber-and-stone house with carved door and a 'skylight' in the Balti-Tibetan style of Baltit Fort. Local people claim this was Shah Wali's house.

West of Thol (or about 20 minutes' drive east of Chalt) are the nala and stone fort at **Nilt** that nearly derailed the British invasion of 1891. A path on the south side of the KKH is east of a stone tablet reading 'Mountaineering Institute & Alpine Club'. The fort, 300 metres up the path, is a nondescript low structure now used as homes, closed to the public.

The nearby 'Mountaineering Institute' is a kind of club house where some army officers have run training programmes for Pakistani mountaineers. The 'institute' is affiliated with the Adventure Foundation of Pakistan (see Abbottabad). Local mountain guides report little useful activity here.

West of Nilt the KKH arches around fertile **Sikanderabad**, with basic accommodation and a small civil hospital. Across the river is **Khizerabad** and west of it a small nala marks the western end of Hunza. Further west, scratched into the valley walls hundreds of metres high, is the 'road' that was once Hunza's link to the outside.

Here the KKH runs along the southern edge of the primordial 'Asian Plate' into which the Indian subcontinent crashed 50 million years ago, giving rise to the Himalaya chain. Although there's no simple line, Asia roughly speaking is to the north, and to the south are remnants of a chain of volcanic islands trapped between the two continents. See Geology in the Facts about the Region chapter.

Places to Stay

On the KKH three km east of Sikanderabad you may find the small *Snow White Hotel* open. There is also an *NAPWD Resthouse* in the village, booked through the Chief Engineer in Gilgit.

CHALT

In a wide bowl where the Hunza River turns south, Chalt sits across the mouths of two large valley systems. The only part of Nagar north of the river, this is probably the most well-endowed area from the Chinese border to Kohistan in terms of weather, water, fire-

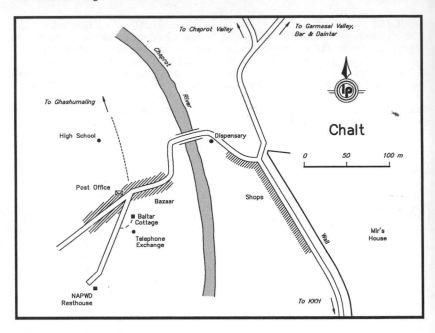

wood, pasture and tillable land. The Mir of Nagar still keeps a house here.

The Chaprot Valley, with some fine day-hikes, has brought out the poet in visitors and residents alike. The misanthropic explorer Schomberg called it 'lovely, more beautiful than any other valley in the Gilgit Agency'. Safdar Ali, the Mir of Hunza at the time of the British invasion, said Chalt and Chaprot were 'more precious to us than the strings of our wives' pyjamas'. Excellent long treks start in both valleys.

People in the Chalt area speak Shina (in common with Gilgit, Chilas and Kohistan), Burushaski, Urdu and sometimes English.

Orientation & Information

From the KKH, one km west of a lonely petrol station, at the east end of a large rock outcrop, a jeep road crosses the river to Chalt. Three to four km along it a left fork crosses the Chaprot River and climbs to the small bazaar. Here are shops, post office (at the only intersection) and a telephone exchange. There is a dispensary on the east side of the river.

For information about the area, ask at the NAPWD resthouse or the high school – or in Bank Road in Gilgit, where many Chalt people have shops.

Ghashumaling

Ghashumaling ('ga-SHU-ma-ling') is a lovely area in a lower Chaprot tributary. With easy trails and mulberry, peach, apple and walnut orchards, even local people come up for picnics. A walk can take from two hours to all day.

Take the path past the high school and up the south side of Chaprot Valley, through the village of Rahbat. Bear left into the canyon and cross a footbridge. At the head of the canyon, about 12 km from the bazaar, are pine forests and the small Kacheli Glacier. A return option is via Chaprot village and the jeep track down the north side of the valley.

Top: Hunzakut men at rest, Karimabad (JK)
Bottom Left: Altit Fort & Hunza Valley, from Melishkar Village (JK)
Bottom Right: Baltit Fort, Hunza (JK)

Top & Middle Right: Sunday Market, Kashgar (RI'A)
Middle Left: Fruit vendors, Green Chowk, Mingora (JK)
Middle Centre: Selling fish fry, Abbottabad (JK)
Bottom: Confectioner, Saddar Bazaar, Rawalpindi (JK)

Chaprot Valley

From the bazaar, cross the Chaprot River and turn left. About 150 metres up take the left fork, which climbs the north side of Chaprot Valley. It's an hour's walk to Chaprot village (actually a collection of hamlets).

From there it's three to four hours on a mule track through summer villages to pastures at the head of the valley, a good overnight destination. This is also the start of a five to six-day trek to the Naltar Valley north of Gilgit, said to be one of the most beautiful medium-size treks in the Northern Areas. In the summer, horses can be hired at Chaprot.

Garmasai Valley

From the bazaar, cross the river and turn left, but at the next fork keep right into Garmasai ('gar-ma-SAY') Valley, also called Bar or Budalas Valley (not to be confused with the Chaprot village of Bola Das). After four km a path continues up the west side of the valley while the jeep road crosses to Budalas.

Four to five km up the west side was a popular sulphurous hot spring. It's been washed out by a flood but may eventually be rebuilt. If you do find local people there, note that men and women soak separately. 'Hot spring' in Burushaski is *garum bul*, 'ga-ROOM bool'; in Shina it is *tato uts*, 'TAII-to oots'; and, in Urdu, it is *garam chashma*.

For longer trips, continue up the west side to Torbuto Das village at the confluence of the Bar and Daintar nalas. Northward is Bar village, trailhead for long treks to the upper Batura Glacier. Westward is Daintar village, from where you can return to Chaprot in one or two days, or take the trek to Naltar or a longer one to the Ishkoman Valley.

Shutinbar Nala

On the east side of Garmasai Valley, about three km upstream from the Budalas jeep bridge, the road briefly enters Shutinbar Nala. It's a steep eight to 10 km to a glacier at its head, and there are said to be abandoned ruby mines in the canyon.

Places to Stay & Eat

Baltar Cottage in the bazaar has a few rope-beds and double rooms. In an apricot orchard beyond the hotel a pleasant *NAPWD Resthouse* has Rs 150 doubles and a friendly chowkidar; book it with the Chief Engineer in Gilgit. In addition to meals here by arrangement, there are cafes in the bazaar and stalls on the road east of the bridge.

Getting There & Away

In addition to buses from Gilgit to Hunza and Sust, Chalt-bound vans and passenger jeeps often go in the early morning from lower Bank Rd in Gilgit for Rs 20, returning next morning.

CHALT TO GILGIT

Below Chalt the Hunza River turns south. Ten minutes' drive down-river from the Chalt turn-off, the road cuts above the highway are early 1960s attempts at a highway by Pakistan army engineers. Across the river is the KKH's precarious precursor, a now-abandoned jeep road that follows the oldest caravan trails.

A few minutes southward the highway passes several cafes and a road-maintenance base called Jaglot Guar (Jaglot Camp). Two or three km later, a jeep road climbs up to Jaglot village, the starting point for another Rakaposhi base camp trek, a day's climb up the north side of Jaglot Nala toward 4730-metre Haraj Peak, Rakaposhi's western arm. Accommodation in the area is scarce, though the cafes at Jaglot Guar have rope beds and basic food. (There's another Jaglot on the KKH south of Gilgit.)

Across the river from Jaglot Guar is an imaginative AKRSP irrigation scheme by the villagers of Gwachi: where a channel down the Gwachi Nala was impossible they have suspended a water pipe right across it.

About 25 minutes down-river from Chalt, at the south end of Rahimabad village – and almost exactly midway between Kashgar and Rawalpindi – is a monument to KKH workers, topped with an old pneumatic drill used for setting explosives. In Urdu script on the pedestal are the words of Pakistan's

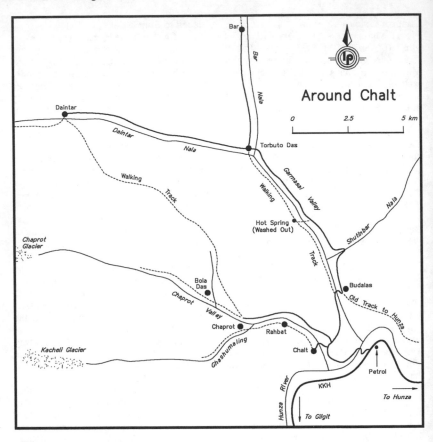

favourite philospher-poet, Alama Moham-med Iqbal (who in the 1930s first proposed a Muslim state in India): 'God has given man integrity, faith, and a strong mind, and if he sets himself to it he can kick a mountain to powder or stop a river in its tracks.'

Two minutes south of the monument the highway crosses a nala on a Chinese bridge decorated with the characters for 'double happiness'.

Across the Hunza River is Nomal, the base

for day trips and treks into the beautiful Naltar Valley (described in the chapter on Gilgit, and in detail in the Trekking chapter of *Pakistan – a travel survival kit*).

As the road comes out into the basin where the Hunza River joins the Gilgit River, the view back up the Hunza Valley is dominated by 7140-metre Kampire Dior, 70 km north on the crest of the Karakoram. Dainyor, at the confluence, is the southern-most Ismaili village on the KKH.

Gilgit

Gilgit is the hub of the KKH: services, information, transport and relative luxury; easy access to over half the KKH on the Pakistan side; and a web of valleys fingering Rakaposhi, Nanga Parbat and other giants. Not surprisingly it swarms with travellers, trekkers and climbers from May to October.

The scenery around Gilgit Town (at 1500 metres) is austere and brown, except for spring blossoms and autumn colours. But, typical of the Karakoram, the higher you go the better it looks; many glacier-fed valleys above 2000 metres harbour pine and juniper forests and luxuriant meadows.

Gilgit is administrative headquarters for the 70,000-sq km Northern Areas, a federally administered quasi-province extending north-east to the Khunjerab Pass; west up the Gilgit River into the Hindu Kush; south-east up the Indus River to the highest peaks of the Karakoram; and south to the Nanga Parbat massif. For the Pakistan government it's a ticklish place, bordering on India, China and Afghanistan, and a stone's throw from the former Soviet republic of Tajikistan.

History

Early History From the 1st century AD, Gilgit was part of the Buddhist Kushan Empire at Taxila, and remained Buddhist after the Kushans' demise in the 3rd century. The Chinese pilgrim Fa-Hsien found hundreds of active monasteries on his way from Xinjiang to Taxila in 403 AD. A few traces remain, including the great bas-relief Buddha on a cliff-face near Gilgit and pictures scratched onto riverside rocks at Chilas.

Sanskrit inscriptions on a boulder at Dainyor list local Tibetan rulers of the 7th and 8th centuries. In the 8th century a Tang Chinese army occupied Chitral and the upper Gilgit basin for three years before the Tibetans drove them out. According to the Dainyor stone, local rulers in turn expelled the Tibetans.

The last Buddhist ruler was the cruel Sri Badat in the 7th century. Legend says he ate a baby every day, and that his slayer and successor was a Persian adventurer named Azur Jamshed who married Sri Badat's daughter and introduced Islam. In fact it was only after preachers came from Afghanistan and Persia in the 12th century or later that Islam began to catch on here.

Gilgit was ruled more or less continuously from the 10th to the 19th century by the so-called Trakhan Dynasty, possibly of Turkic origin. The dominant tribe or caste was the Shins, who may have originally been Hindu and come from the lower Indus valley. Their language, Shina, is still the common speech.

Around 1240 Taj Mughal, king of Badakhshan in north-east Afghanistan, seized Chitral and Gilgit. To commemorate his victory at Gilgit he built a stone monument above Jutial and tried to convert everyone to Ismailism. He was turned out after about 30 years, but the monument is still there and the upper Gilgit basin is still Ismaili.

As the Silk Road finally fell out of use in the 16th century the region split into feuding mini-kingdoms, the main ones being Gilgit, Hunza, Nagar and four in the upper Gilgit basin – Punial, Ishkoman, Yasin and Ghizar. In the 17th century most were vassal to Baltistan.

The Dogras & the British The last local ruler at Gilgit was a tyrant from Yasin named Gohar Aman, famous for selling a large part of the town's population into slavery. He was dethroned in 1841 by Dogra soldiers of Kashmir on behalf of the Sikh Empire in the Punjab, but they proved so disagreeable that he made a comeback in 1848. He fortified the town (a remnant is the yellow tower at the present militia barracks) and ruled until he died, 10 years later.

After that the Dogras came back, under

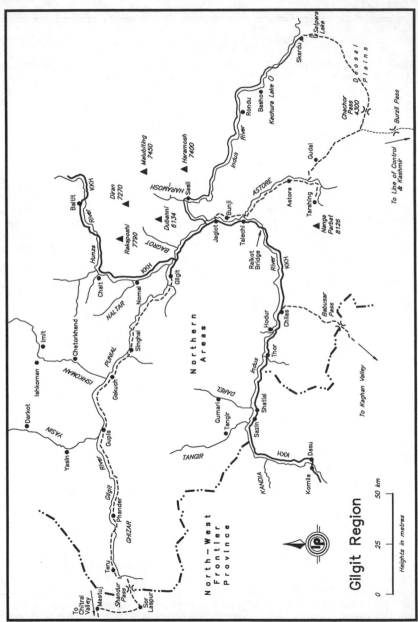

Gilgit Region

new management. In 1846 the British had won the first of two quick wars with the Sikhs and annexed Sikh territories in the Kashmir Valley, Ladakh, Baltistan and the vassal state of Gilgit. Packaging them up as 'the State of Jammu and Kashmir', they sold it for £750,000 to a Dogra prince named Gulab Singh and declared him the first Maharajah of Kashmir. Thus Muslim Gilgit found itself with a Hindu master, who received grudging tributes from local rulers, and maintained his garrisons.

Then Britain discovered Russians snooping in the Pamirs and Afghanistan, and began to have doubts about the Maharajah. In 1877 Kashmir was put under control of the Indian Foreign Office and a British 'political agent' arrived in Gilgit to look over the Kashmiri governor's shoulder. This arrangement proved awkward and the Agency was closed down after a few years – only to reopen in 1889 as Britain's anxiety mounted. The new 'PA' was a no-nonsense soldier named Algernon Durand, who lost no time in taking charge and putting everyone in their places.

Durand conducted his own foreign policy in the region. Soon after his invasion of Hunza in 1891 (see the Hunza & Nagar chapter) he put a garrison at Chilas to control the Babusar Pass to the Kaghan Valley, one of two tenuous supply routes for Gilgit (the other was the Burzil Pass from Kashmir). The troops had barely arrived when Indus Valley tribes attacked and nearly overran them. This inspired some quick improvements to the Chilas Fort, which still stands today.

Gilgit, like Kashgar, was an outpost in the Great Game, the imperial hide-and-seek between Britain and Russia, well into the 20th century. A succession of political agents managed by grace or guile to stay in charge, and in 1935 Britain actually leased back the entire Agency from Kashmir.

A local militia, the Gilgit Scouts, drawn heavily from sons of local royalty, was raised and dressed in their own tartan. They were probably as much a symbolic warning to the Russians and a vehicle for intrigue, as a defence force.

Partition & the Gilgit Uprising In the 1930s and 1940s demands mounted both for Indian independence and for a separate Muslim homeland. In the end, Britain agreed to split the Raj into two separate countries, a Muslim-majority Pakistan and a Hindu-majority India.

An awkward problem was the hundreds of princely states with direct allegiance to Britain, who theoretically stood to regain their original sovereignty. Most were coaxed to join India or Pakistan. Kashmir – with a Hindu ruler, a Muslim majority and its lovely vale beloved by both Hindus and Muslims – was the biggest hot-potato of all. Maharajah Hari Singh, hoping for his own independence, stalled.

Two weeks before the 14 August 1947 end of the empire, the last political agent handed over the Gilgit Agency to a new Kashmiri governor, Ghansar Singh. As 14 August came and went, Gilgit held its breath while the Maharajah dithered. Then, on 26 October, a band of Pathan (Pashtun) Afridi tribesmen from the North-West Frontier Province marched into Kashmir proclaiming a *jihad* or holy war, and everything came unglued. Hari Singh fled to Delhi, acceded to India and asked for military help. India accepted, subject to an eventual vote by the people of Kashmir.

Several groups had anticipated this. A clique of Muslim officers in the Maharajah's own army, led by Colonel Mirza Hassan Khan, had been conspiring to seize Kashmir for Pakistan, but word had got out and Hassan was transferred to Kashmir's 'Siberia', the Bunji garrison south of Gilgit.

Meanwhile, Major Mohammed Babar Khan of the Gilgit Scouts and several fellow-officers (and, according to some, their British commander) had hatched their own rebellion.

Within days of the Maharajah's decision, a mob collected in Gilgit from neighbouring valleys. The governor called Bunji for help, and who should be among the reinforcements but Colonel Hassan. On 1 November Babar Khan arrested Ghansar Singh and the rebels asked to join Pakistan. Within a few days the Scouts, and Muslim soldiers of the Kashmiri army, joined an already ongoing war with India. In the following months the Scouts took Baltistan and Hassan got to the outskirts of Srinagar.

The fledgeling Indian air force at one point bombed Gilgit, no easy task in the narrow valleys. Gilgitis like to tell the story of the Scouts' pipe band, who mocked the Indian pilots by defiantly tootling up and down the airfield the whole time.

In January 1949 the war ended with a United Nations cease-fire. Pakistan was given temporary control over what is now the Northern Areas, and a slice of western Kashmir it calls Azad ('Free') Kashmir. India got Ladakh and the Kashmir Valley. The cease-fire line across Kashmir became the de facto border.

Memories of the 'Uprising' are still alive in Gilgit. Babar and Hassan are buried in the town's maple-shaded municipal park, Chinar Bagh. One of Babar's sons is a chief of police and one of Hassan's sons is a local politician. A Pakistani officer later put in charge of Babar and Hassan has become something of a local villain in Hunza: Brigadier Aslam, purveyor of the Shangri-La resorts.

Of course it's not 14 August but 1 November that Gilgit celebrates as Independence Day, with spontaneous music and dancing and a week-long polo tournament. One of the best polo teams every year is from the Gilgit garrison of the Northern Light Infantry, descendants of the Gilgit Scouts.

After Partition India and Pakistan again fought over Kashmir in 1965 and 1971 (the latter war also led to the secession of East Pakistan as Bangladesh), and almost again in 1991 over Indian actions in Kashmir. Pakistan stands officially by its position that, until the referendum promised by India is held, Kashmir doesn't belong to anyone. But the chances seem to have faded away.

The Burzil Pass was closed by the 1948 cease-fire, leaving only the Babusar Pass to link the Northern Areas with Pakistan. It's surprising to realise that Gilgit was only firmly linked to the outside world some 25 years ago, by a civilian air corridor and the first stages of the KKH.

The Northern Areas' 850,000 people are in limbo. To make it a province would concede the status quo of a divided Kashmir. It is instead a 'Federally Administered Area' governed by the Northern Areas Council, with 16 elected members but headed by a federally appointed commissioner answerable only to Islamabad. Although the government is generous with development money, the inhabitants of the Northern Areas cannot, for example, vote in national elections or take cases to the Supreme Court. Having fought to join Pakistan, many now feel excluded and exploited.

Cyclists' Notes, Gilgit

The Gilgit-Chitral crossing via the Shandur Pass takes about eight days, though it's too rough for anything but a mountain bike. The Chitral side is the steepest. For notes on crossing the Babusar Pass between Chilas and the Kaghan Valley, see the Hazara chapter.

Gilgit to Raikot Bridge, 80 km Gilgit is about 10 km off the KKH. Useful 'rumour-books' are at Tourist Cottage and North Inn in Gilgit. Jaglot, about 20 km south of Gilgit, has cheap serais and a small hotel. The best overnight stop between Gilgit and Chilas is the run-down but scenic NAPWD Resthouse at Talechi, 67 km from Gilgit. Cyclists report astronomical prices and shifty staff at the Shangri-La Motel by the bridge.

Raikot Bridge to Chilas turning, 54 km No food is available on this stretch, and it's oven-like in summer. At several slide-zones, the road is bumpy and occasionally washed out.

Chilas turning to Shatial, 63 km Cyclists have stayed at Shatial's basic inn, stashing bikes on the roof, and at its primitive NAPWD Forestry Resthouse.

People

The Shins provide a major pedigree in the Gilgit Valley and Indus Kohistan and their language, Shina ('shee-NA'), is spoken by everyone. Gilgit's crossroads position has filled its bazaar (and enlivened its genetic pool) with people from all over Asia, and forced Gilgitis to be multilingual. It is not unusual to hear Uyghur, Wakhi, Burushaski, Pashto or even Persian; Urdu and English are widely spoken.

All brands of Islam are represented: Ismailis in the Gilgit, Ghizar and Hunza valleys; Shias in Nagar, Punial, Bagrot and Haramosh; Sunnis in Chilas and southward. They all overlap in Gilgit Town, where sectarian tension is just below the surface. In 1988 Sunni-Shia hostility burst into virtual warfare around Jalalabad in Bagrot. Over 100 were killed, and there have been aftershocks ever since. Despite a beefed-up police presence (including numerous highway checkpoints) and serious efforts at reconciliation, relations remain sour, casting a shadow over the whole region. At least 10 died in two attacks in September 1991.

Festivals

*12 February to 15 March (1994), 1 February to 4 March (1995), 22 January to 22 February (1996)
Ramadan, a month of day-time fasting for Shias and Sunnis. Many restaurants and markets are closed until sunset, though foreigners can find food at tourist hotels and in Ismaili neighbourhoods such as Jamat Khana Bazaar.

Late February – Early March
First (Wheat) Sowing. In remote valleys like Bagrot, farmers, before breaking ground, may celebrate in their fields with their families and neighbours.

21 March
Nauroz ('New Days'), a spring festival and a Shia and Ismaili celebration of the succession of the Prophet's son-in-law Ali. In Gilgit there may be polo, but many shopkeepers close down and celebrate in their home villages.

*15 March (1994), 4 March (1995), 22 Feb (1996)
Eid-ul-Fitr, two days of celebrations at the end of Ramadan, including feasting and gift-giving. Many shops are closed.

April
Polo matches are often held in Gilgit or towns of the upper Gilgit basin during this month.

Late June – Early July
First (Wheat) Harvest. In remote valleys some farmers have private ceremonies, similar to First Sowing.

*1 July (1993), 20 June (1994), 9 June (1995), 29 May (1996)
Ashura, the 10th day of Muharram. Shias mourn the death of Hussain at Karbala. In an awesome procession through the west end of Gilgit, men and boys pound their chests and chant the names of the dead at Karbala; some flail their backs with blade-tipped chains. Shia-Sunni hostility has sometimes flared at this time, and police have begun keeping tourists away. In other Shia villages, tourists are not welcome.

*10 Aug (1993), 30 July (1994), 19 July (1995), 8 July (1996)
Chhelum, 40 days after Ashura, with similar but smaller processions.

*31 August (1993), 20 August (1994), 10 August (1995), 29 July (1996)
Eid-Milad-un-Nabi, the Prophet's birthday. Some shops are closed. This may be celebrated on different days by Sunnis and Shias, which tends to be a source of tension.

1 November
Uprising Day or *Jashan-i-Gilgit*, 'Gilgit Festival'. For Gilgitis this is the biggest event of the year, celebrating the 1947 uprising against the Maharajah of Kashmir. People stream into town for a week-long tournament of thunderous 'no-rules' polo at the main polo ground, kicked off by a tartan-clad pipe band and much good-humoured pomp. You can also see practice matches at the old polo ground for weeks beforehand.

*15 December
Nos. In Bagrot and Haramosh, each household slaughters a goat and hangs it up for all to see, thus insuring a winter food supply, and in time for the meat to dry without spoiling. In Bagrot, Nos is an occasion for music and dancing.

* approximate dates

GILGIT TOWN

Gilgit Town is of interest mainly for its people, though there are historical spots and good walks within day-trip distance, and the bazaar is eclectic and lively. The shopkeepers, from all over Pakistan and Xinjiang, are part of its attraction. In search of a sale or a chat, it's their 'Muslim duty' to ask you in and serve you sweet tea till your kidneys burst.

The town wakes up early, to muezzins in scores of mosques, calling the faithful to

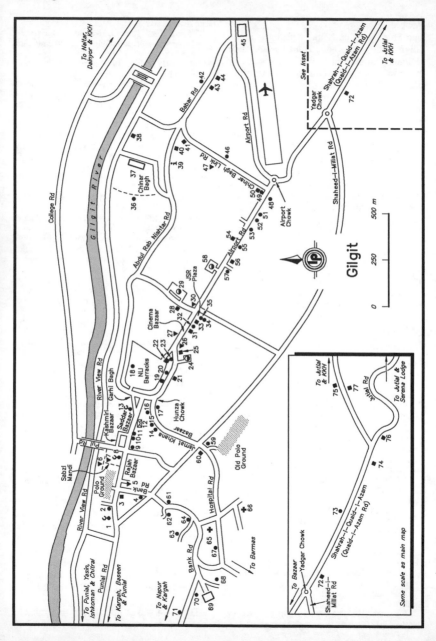

Gilgit

dawn prayers. Plaintive and charming for the first few days, the overlapping, amplified chants soon lose their appeal for the average infidel. The faithful presumably cope by going to bed early; except for a few cafes and barbershops, the bazaar is dark soon after sunset.

There are very few local women on the streets. Young men, fed on cinematic stereotypes, often seem unable to take foreign women seriously. There are stories of low-level sexual harassment, eg in passenger Suzukis after dark. More often, women are simply patronised or ignored.

■ PLACES TO STAY

3	NAPWD Resthouse
19	Kashgar Inn
21	Mt Balore Motel
22	Madina Guesthouse
25	Indus Hotel
28	Alflah Hotel
31	Skyways Hotel
33	JSR Hotel
38	Riverside Lodge
39	PTDC Chinar Inn
40	Hunza Inn
41	Chinese Lodge
43	Golden Peak Inn camping
44	Hunza Tourist House
50	Park Hotel
54	Karakorum Inn
56	Vershigoom Inn
60	New Lahore Hotel
72	Golden Peak Inn
74	North Inn
75	Tourist Cottage
76	Future Hotel
77	Rupal Hotel

▼ PLACES TO EAT

5	Haidry Tea Shop
6	Yoghurt Stall
7	Turkistan Restaurant
26	Madina Cafe
27	Pathan Hotel
30	Baig's Restaurant
33	JSR Hotel
44	Hunza Tourist Office
47	New Tabaq Restaurant
50	Park Hotel
74	North Inn
75	Tourist Cottage

OTHER

1	Imamia Mosque
2	Mr Pakistani's Shop
4	British Cemetery
8	Jama Mosque
9	Police Post & Foreigners' Registration
10	Allied Bank
11	Habib Bank
12	Post Office
13	Moti Mosque
14	Hunza Photo Studio
15	Hunza Gift House
16	Jamat Khana
17	Mohammad Book Stall
18	Gohar Aman's Tower
20	National Music Centre
23	Petrol Station
24	Mashabrum Tours Bus Yard
29	General Bus Stand
32	Cinema
34	PIA Booking Office
35	Pamir Tours
36	Uprising Memorial
37	Town Hall
39	PTDC Tourist Information (Chinar Inn)
42	Aga Khan Rural Support Programme Office
45	Airport Terminal
46	Himalaya Nature Tours
48	Mountain Movers
49	Hunza Handicrafts
51	Walji's Adventure Pakistan
52	Xama Shop
53	Petrol Station
55	Petrol Station
57	Hunza-Gojal Transport
58	Natco Bus Yard
59	Cinema
61	NAPWD Office
62	National Bank
63	Library
64	Gilgit Book Centre
65	District Hospital
66	Women's Hospital
67	Telephone Exchange
68	Deputy Commissioner's Office
69	Commissioner's Office
70	Deputy Commissioner's House
71	Fisheries Office
73	Police Headquarters

On the cards is an extension of the airport runway, which will allow jets to land and make the region more accessible for more of the year. Gilgit is on the way to becoming a city, though its infrastructure can't keep up – public services aren't multiplying as fast as hotels, and electricity and water are unreliable and vulnerable to heavy weather.

Orientation

Gilgit is on the south bank of the Gilgit River, 10 km west off the KKH via the cantonment at Jutial (these tidy military sectors are a colonial holdover in large towns of India and Pakistan). A back road also comes from the KKH at Dainyor via bridges over the Hunza and Gilgit rivers.

The bazaar is essentially a single two-km street full of shops. South-west up Bank Rd are government offices, and further up are several villages, the biggest of which is Barmas. The airport is east of the bazaar. The flat ground across the river is appropriately named Konodas, Shina for 'scrubby plain'.

Gilgit is growing east toward Jutial along Quaid-i-Azam Rd. When the airport runway is extended west, traffic from the KKH to the bazaar will be deflected down Shaheed-i-Millat Rd and/or east around the airport to River View Rd.

Many larger streets have two names, one common and one official. These include (official name in parentheses) Jamat Khana Bazaar (Sir Aga Khan Rd), Bank Rd (Khazana Rd; *khazana* is Urdu for 'bank'), Hospital Rd (Alama Mohammed Iqbal Rd) and Jutial Rd (Quaid-i-Azam Rd or Shahrah-i-Quaid-i-Azam).

Information

Tourist Office The Pakistan Tourism Development Corporation (PTDC, ☎ 2562), at the Chinar Inn on Babar Rd, has Northern Areas brochures and can help with bookings and tours. Oddly enough, there's no Gilgit map.

To book any of the Northern Areas Public Works Department (NAPWD) resthouses between Chilas and the Khunjerab Pass, see the Administrative Officer, office of the Chief Engineer (☎ 3375), on Bank Rd opposite the National Bank.

Guides, Equipment & Transport You don't need a guide unless you're trekking, though remoter valleys can be easier with a locally-known person who speaks some English. Agencies have multiplied like rabbits. Old ones like Mohammad Book Stall (now also called Adventure Centre) in Jamat Khana Bazaar (☎ 2409), and Pamir Tours in JSR Plaza (☎ 3939), use local guides and can accommodate low-budget customers. Guides for up-scale outfits like Walji's Adventure Pakistan on Airport Rd (☎ 3848) are reliable and speak English well but don't always know local valleys.

Some of these agencies and some hotels also rent equipment (though sleeping bags are scarce). Hunza Handicrafts, by the Park Hotel, occasionally has sleeping mats, stoves, clothing and climbing gear for rent or sale. Hunza Gift House in Jamat Khana Bazaar sells cheap backpacks. Himalaya Nature Tours, Chinar Bagh Link Rd (☎ 2946), rents mountain bikes and runs bike tours.

For jeep rental or other transport try these same agencies, or Mountain Movers or the Xama shop in Airport Rd, or your hotel-wallah. It's worth shopping around. At the time of writing you could hire a jeep for about Rs 8 per km plus Rs 150 per day or Rs 200 per overnight, or fixed totals for common destinations, or unlimited-mileage rates within a certain radius. Pamir Tours will rent you a car (for paved roads only) but to drive it yourself you need an International Driver's Licence and a large security deposit.

Money National Bank is off Bank Rd; Habib and Allied banks are in Saddar Bazaar. Hours are 9 am to 1 pm Monday to Thursday, and to 11 am Sunday. US dollar and pound Sterling travellers' cheques or cash are the most acceptable. Ask for encashment receipts, which may come in handy later, eg for airline-ticket paperwork. To be of any use they must have the amounts in both currencies, the exchange rate, an official signature and the bank's stamp.

At a pinch, some merchants will change US dollar cash. From here, the closest other places to change money are Karimabad (Hunza), Skardu, Abbottabad and Swat.

Post & Telecommunications The post office is in Saddar Bazaar. Hours are 8 am to 2 pm, Saturday through Wednesday. A window out front sells stamps. Poste restante is at the rear; this is also the place to get outgoing mail franked while you wait (to avoid the risk of stamp theft). Except for things like papers, parcels must be sewed up in cloth (a tailor will do it for a few rupees); leave it open for postal inspection.

You can make overseas calls and send telegrams from the telephone exchange in upper Hospital Rd. It's open 24 hours a day. Some hotels can place calls for you at a higher rate. Gilgit has overseas direct-dialling (area code 0572). The Serena Lodge (fax 2525) will send and accept faxes.

Library Off upper Bank Rd, in the home of the early British political agents, is the Gilgit Municipal Library. Many of its 20,000 volumes are in English, heavy on colonial tastes and modern Americana, and you can browse through some Western magazines and English-language Pakistani papers. Senior Librarian Ashraf Ali is a good source of local knowledge. Hours are 11 am to 5 pm, Sunday to Thursday, 8 am to noon Friday, with earlier hours in winter.

There is a small library in the Ismaili Study Centre, by the jamat khana (prayer hall) in Jamat Khana Bazaar.

Bookshops The Northern Areas' best known shop is Mohammad Book Stall (☎ 2409) in Jamat Khana Bazaar, with hard-to-find books on the region plus postcards and newspapers. Near the library is the Gilgit Book Centre, specialising in Northern Areas literature. Hunza Handicrafts, by the Park Hotel, has books among the curios and camping gear. The bookshop at the Serena

Lodge is said to have a good selection of trekking maps.

Foreigners' Registration If you're coming from China and didn't get a Temporary Certificate of Registration (Form C) at Sust, or if you plan to be in Pakistan more than 30 days, registering at the Saddar Bazaar police post and getting a residence permit will reduce later headaches.

Hospitals The District Hospital is in upper Hospital Rd. Nearby is a Women's Hospital, with female doctors. Foreign women can go to either, though the District Hospital apparently has more specialists. The Punjab Medical Store, 50 metres west of Mashabrum Tours, stocks every antibiotic known to science at reasonable prices.

Photo Shop Hunza Photo Studio in Jamat Khana Bazaar sells major-brand colour-print film and Fujichrome slide film and can do passport-size photos in an hour or two. There are other shops in the bazaar too.

Hot Wash If your hotel hasn't got hot water, you can wash at a hammam, a barbershop-cum-bathhouse easily recognisable by the line of towels drying outside. For Rs 10 you get soap, towel and bucket in a tiny booth with hot water on tap; bring your own towel if a recycled one doesn't appeal to you.

Normally men-only, some will clear the premises for women customers. They're open early and late, and closed only one day a month.

Gohar Aman's Tower

On the grounds of the NLI barracks (Northern Light Infantry, once the Gilgit Scouts) a yellow tower is all that remains of a fort built by Gohar Aman in the 1850s. The sentries won't let you in but you can see it from the west gate.

British Cemetery

In lower Bank Rd is an overgrown old graveyard, surrounded by barbed wire. Among those buried there is Captain George

Hayward, a British explorer murdered in Yasin in 1870 by a son of Gohar Aman. Ask for the key in the shop of Sarwar the tailor across the street (key is *chabi* in Urdu).

Uprising Memorial

By Chinar Bagh, the municipal park, is a rather touching memorial to those who rose against the Maharajah in 1947. On either side are the graves of the local heroes, Mohammed Babar Khan of the Gilgit Scouts and Mirza Hassan Khan of the Kashmir Infantry.

Places to Stay – bottom end

Bottom-end best bets are the Rs 25 to Rs 30 dorm beds at *Tourist Cottage*, *Golden Peak Inn*, *Hunza Inn* and *Madina Guesthouse*. Tourist Cottage (☎ 2376), three km out on Quaid-i-Azam Rd, also has singles/doubles for about Rs 55/80, a garden and good cheap dinners (see Places to Eat). Check out their 'rumour book' too.

Golden Peak Inn (☎ 3538) once occupied a villa of the Mir of Nagar but when the landlord knocked it to pieces, manager Latif Anwar took the hotel to Quaid-i-Azam Rd, east of Airport Chowk. Besides dorms he has Rs 150 triples, Rs 100 and Rs 200 doubles and a garden – plus a campsite on Babar Rd. (Meanwhile the old place on Bank Rd has ripped off the name, calling itself New Golden Peak Hotel. Vote with your feet.)

Madina Guesthouse by the NLI barracks has spartan doubles/triples for Rs 60/80, and their meals get high marks since two NZ women taught the cook how to prepare Western dishes.

Near the park, the Hunza Inn (☎ 2814) has cold-shower doubles for Rs 100, luxury ones for Rs 300, plus trekking information, guide and transport services, and a garden. At the *Park Hotel*, dorm beds (with morning hot water) are Rs 50. The *Chinese Lodge* on Chinar Bagh Link Rd has doubles for Rs 120 and dorm beds for Rs 35.

The *New Lahore Hotel* (☎ 3327), in lower Hospital Rd, has doubles/triples for about Rs 100/120 and quads with shared loo for Rs 125. The *Kashgar Inn* in Cinema Bazaar has noisy doubles for Rs 60 and Rs 80. Doubles

at the seedy *Karakorum Inn* and the gloomy *Vershigoom Inn* on Airport Rd, and the miserable *Indus Hotel* in Cinema Bazaar, are all about Rs 70.

Places to Stay – middle

Mt Balore Motel (☎ 2709), run by sons of Colonel Hassan, hero of the 1947 Uprising, has a quiet garden behind a wall right in the middle of town. Doubles with cold shower are Rs 150, or pitch a tent for Rs 25 per person. Doubles at *Skyways Hotel* and *JSR Hotel* (☎ 3971) are Rs 150 but JSR's toilets and showers are communal. JSR's carpeted doubles/triples/quads with shower are Rs 250/300/350.

A clean, comfortable *NAPWD Resthouse* is on Bank Rd at Punial Rd, but its Rs 150 doubles are usually booked out in the summer; check with the Chief Engineer's office on Bank Rd.

Far away on River View Rd is the tranquil *River View Hotel* (☎ 3568) with three doubles for Rs 130; camping is possible. Doubles in the dreary *Alflah Hotel*, by the general bus stand, are Rs 150.

Pricier but very good value is the *North Inn* (☎ 2887) on Quaid-i-Azam Rd. Doubles with 24-hour hot showers are Rs 300; and some without hot showers are Rs 200. Staff are helpful and the food is first-rate. Another well-run place is *Hunza Tourist House* (☎ 2338) on Babar Rd, with a big garden and clean singles/doubles for Rs 250/350. The mammoth *Park Hotel* (☎ 2379), on Airport Rd, has poorly maintained doubles with hot shower for Rs 250 and up – and a loud, smelly generator.

Places to Stay – top end

PTDC's *Chinar Inn* (☎ 2562) has singles/doubles for Rs 450/550 and a damp restaurant. In Jutial, *Serena Lodge* (☎ 2330, 2331), with deluxe singles/doubles for about Rs 700/950, may not be the place for budget travellers to stay but, with free video movies, all-you-can-eat buffet dinners and a free shuttle bus, it might be a good place to visit. Several other top-end places are on the main road opposite Jutial Cantonment, but public transport to them is awkward.

Places to Eat

Hygiene is problematic if you have to eat with your fingers or scraps of chapatti, but even the lowliest place has a washstand somewhere, and something on the menu that's steaming hot. Probably a bigger risk is drinking tap water from communal tumblers.

Vegetarians can get by, but meatless fare tends to be dreary. Some hotels will stir something up by request, especially if you bring the ingredients.

In this angler's paradise, it's a pity nobody serves fish (commercial fishing is illegal), although they'll cook it if you catch it.

Cheap & Good Gilgit's most visible eatery is the *Pathan Hotel* in Cinema Bazaar, its back room full of men tucking into chapli kebabs ('mutton-burgers') and other Pathan favourites. Highly recommended is half a braised chicken (karahi murgi), enough for two for Rs 50. You'll find similar food at the gloomy *Vershigoom Inn* on Airport Rd. Hygiene at both is dicey so stick to hot-off-the-fire items.

Friendly *Madina Cafe* in Cinema Bazaar has Pakistani and Western items. Beside the alley into the Mashabrum Tours bus yard is a tiny, nameless cafe offering only karahi gosht – mutton braised with vegetables, served in its own cooking pan (and thus very hygenic).

Opposite JSR Plaza is *Baig's Restaurant* – gloomy but clean, with good Pakistani dishes. The *New Tabaq Restaurant* on Chinar Bagh Link Rd has meaty Pakistani and Chinese dishes. In the vegetable market by Jama Mosque is the *Turkistan Restaurant*, a cavernous local hang-out, medium-clean and greasy.

Hotel Restaurants *Tourist Cottage* (☎ 2376) serves a filling Hunza-style evening meal (thick noodle soup, rice, vegetable, meat and dessert) for Rs 35. If you're not staying there, book by 4 pm.

The best mid-range hotel food – Pakistani,

Chinese, even Italian! – comes from the *North Inn's* legendary cook. *Hunza Tourist House* has good but pricey Pakistani and Chinese dishes. *JSR Hotel's* and *Park Hotel's* clean restaurants have ho-hum food.

Serena Lodge has all-you-can-eat buffets on Monday, Wednesday and Friday for Rs 145, and the food is first-class. They have a free shuttle service from the bazaar; see Getting Around.

Self-Catering Stands on Airport Rd sell fruit and vegetables, especially in the evening. A vegetable market (*sabzi mandi*) is along the west side of Jama Mosque.

Apricot season is July and early August. The best dried apricots are not in the big-volume wholesale shops (which bring out their best only after the rest have gone to down-country buyers) but in small general stores. Good ones are at least Rs 30 a kg. Wholesalers sort their dried apricots on the floor and may walk all over them, so you should soak them in boiling water (or one traveller suggested soaking them in water while iodine-treating it). Apples, pomegranates, walnuts and Gilgit's own peaches appear in autumn.

Fresh nan bread is sold right out of the tandoor ovens in the sabzi mandi and elsewhere, but it disappears soon after 7 am. You can find yoghurt (*dahi*) in a stall at the back of the sabzi mandi; tell him *pita* or *jata* (to drink there or to take away). It's tastiest (and probably safest) when it's still warm, about the same time the nan is ready.

Numerous general stores have sweets, jam, cornflakes, long-life milk, tinned processed cheese and, reportedly, tuna fish.

Best Teashop in Town The *Haidry Tea Shop* is in an alley off Rajah Bazaar, around the corner from Bank Rd. This tiny one-man operation serves fresh black tea with milk, sugar, cardamom and ginger, in meticulously washed glasses, for Rs 1.

Alcohol There is none available, even in the top-end hotels.

Entertainment

The Serena Lodge screens free Western videos on most evenings at 5.30 and 8.30 pm, and provides a free shuttle service (see Getting Around).

Things to Buy

A Northern Areas bargain is the coarse, durable wool *(patti* or *pattu)* of Hunza and Nagar. 'Handicraft' shops around Hunza Chowk have hats, waistcoats and embroidered cloaks called *choghas*, though some are of cheap, machine-woven wool and some shopkeepers will tell you anything. Good hand-made wool is thick and tight with an uneven grain. Brown and white are best, as colours fade quickly. Try the smaller shops of Jamat Khana Bazaar, Rajah Bazaar, Bank Rd and Punial Rd.

If you buy your own wool and take it to a tailor you'll get a better garment but you won't save any money. Good hand-made local wool is at least Rs 50 per metre. You can also have a shalwar qamiz (the standard baggy trousers and long shirt) made, or your own clothes copied.

The Xama shop in Airport Rd has a great collection of old jewellery, rugs and flintlocks. A few curios and antiques are among the books at Mohammad Book Stall in Jamat Khana Bazaar and at Hunza Handicrafts on Airport Rd. National Music Centre is a tape- shop in Cinema Bazaar with interesting Pakistani music, both traditional and modern fusion.

Getting There & Away

Air The PIA booking office is in JSR Plaza in Cinema Bazaar. The spectacular daily flights to Islamabad and weekly ones to Skardu are very weather-dependent, so all bookings are standby. Confirm by leaving your ticket at PIA by 12.30 pm on the day before you're scheduled to go. At 2 pm they give it back and tell you the check-in time. The flight decision is only made next morning.

The 1¼-hour, Rs 570 Islamabad flight follows the Indus, Babusar Pass and Kaghan Valley; from Gilgit, a left-side seat looks out at Nanga Parbat. If it's cancelled you're waitlisted for the next flight. You may have to book ahead a month or more in summer.

The 40-minute, Rs 410 Skardu flight – Gilgit-Skardu Thursday, Skardu-Gilgit Sunday – is equally amazing. From Gilgit, Nanga Parbat is on the right. If this one is cancelled you get your money back. Demand is usually light.

There are two tourist-priority seats on each flight so if PIA says it's full, ask PTDC for a 'special booking' (a confirmation letter to give PIA). If, after waiting weeks for a booking, you board and find empty seats, it may be because the old Fokkers get less lift in hot summer air and can't take a full load.

An upcoming 600-metre runway extension will allow jets to land here even in cloudy weather. Pakistan has also opened the door to competition on domestic routes, and

at the time of writing an Aga Khan-funded airline was in the planning stages, to serve at least the Northern Areas and Chitral.

Bus, Wagon & Van Long-distance operators are Natco and Hunza-Gojal Transport on Airport Rd, Mashabrum Tours in Cinema Bazaar, Sargin Travel at the JSR Hotel and Hamid Travel at the Skyways Hotel. The general bus stand is up a link road from JSR Plaza, with buses and wagons for Nomal, Naltar, Chilas, Hunza-Nagar, Jaglot and sometimes Astore.

Much regional transport tends to start where people from outlying towns have shops – Jamat Khana Bazaar for Hunza; lower Bank Rd for Nagar; Punial Rd for Punial, Ishkoman, Yasin and Chitral; Garhi Bagh (the little slice of park at the east end of Saddar Bazaar) for Haramosh and Bagrot valleys. There is talk of a future Natco station at Jutial.

Rawalpindi This takes 14 to 17 hours. Natco and Mashabrum go to Pir Wadhai and Sargin goes to Rawalpindi's Rajah Bazaar.

Mashabrum's comfortable small buses go at 11 am, 3.30 and 7 pm for Rs 157. Sargin's vans go at 2 and 4 pm for Rs 180; Hamid Travel also has vans. Natco's miserable buses go at 4 and 9 am, 1, 6 and 9 pm. The 'deluxe' 9 am bus is Rs 180, the others Rs 157, with a 50% student discount on all except the deluxe.

These times may vary with the season. Buy tickets the day before if possible. For the best views most of the time, sit on left unless you're squeamish about heights.

Hunza, Nagar & Sust A Natco bus goes to Sust at 8 am, a four to five-hour trip for about Rs 60. Hunza-Gojal Transport runs vans to Sust at 7.30 am and 2 pm for about Rs 70, plus others to intermediate points. In the mornings, wagons go directly from Jamat Khana Bazaar to Karimabad, and from lower Bank Rd to Chalt and Nagar (and cargo jeeps sometimes go on to Hopar).

Skardu This takes seven to eight hours.

Mashabrum has a bus at 7 am for Rs 70 and vans or small buses later in the morning for Rs 100. Natco's clapped-out bus goes at 6 am. The best views are on the right side going to Skardu.

Jaglot, Astore & Chilas From the general bus stand, wagons go all day to Jaglot for about Rs 20 and to Chilas for about Rs 50. Occasional wagons go directly from Gilgit to Astore, or it's easy to catch a wagon or jeep from Jaglot to Astore.

Punial, Ishkoman, Yasin, Chitral You can get as far as Gakuch by bus or Gupis by Natco pickup. Otherwise you must hire a jeep, or hop a cargo jeep with the help of shopkeepers in Punial Rd. Many agencies have jeeps for hire (see Gilgit – Information) and private drivers going to Chitral scout the hotels for riders. For more information see Gilgit River Basin in this chapter.

Getting Around
To/From the Airport The cheapest way is a passenger Suzuki to Airport Chowk plus a 15-minute walk. To hire a Suzuki, figure on paying Rs 20 to Rs 30 between terminal and bazaar.

Passenger Suzukis Suzukis go from near the post office through the bazaar to Jutial (Serena Lodge) and to Dainyor and can be flagged down anywhere, though they don't run much after dark. They're Rs 2 to Airport Chowk, and Rs 3 beyond. Suzukis also run west from Punial Rd. To signal a stop while you're riding, stomp on the floor.

Serena Shuttle Serena Lodge runs a free pick-up and return service from Hunza Chowk at 6.20 pm, near Hunza Inn at 6.30 and near the Park Hotel at 6.45, and up to the Serena. It heads back at 9 and 10.45 pm. It's not restricted to the Serena's overnight guests.

Bicycles Bikes can be hired for about Rs 8 an hour (sometimes plus a security deposit) from shops near Hunza Chowk and Yadgar Chowk, from the Hunza Inn and elsewhere.

AROUND GILGIT
The Kargah Buddha & Kargah Nala
A Buddhist survivor is the large standing Buddha carved on a cliff-face in Kargah Nala, west of Gilgit. It may date from the 7th century. From Punial Rd catch a passenger Suzuki toward Baseen and get off at Kargah (or it's a five-km hike). Ten minutes' walk up the left side of Kargah Nala is a gully called Shuko Gah (*gah* means tributary valley in Shina), and the Buddha is high above this gully. Small boys will try to 'guide' you there. A Suzuki can be hired for a three-hour excursion for about Rs 150.

On up Shuko Gah is Napur village, the ruins of a monastery and stupa, and a cave where Buddhist birch-bark texts (now called the Gilgit Manuscripts) were found in the 1930s. Cave is *kor* in Shina, and *gufa* in Urdu.

A return option with good valley views is to continue on this high path to Barmas village, and then back down into Gilgit, in about two hours.

The jeep track on up Kargah Nala passes a series of hydroelectric stations generating Gilgit's electricity supply. Beyond the last one a trail climbs past small villages and side-canyons. The canyon eventually opens up, the river now meandering past a large village and cultivated fields. Beyond the village a crumbling guard tower marks the old boundary between British control and the territory of Darel.

From here there are trails over 4000 to 5000-metre passes, east down the Sai Valley to Jaglot on the KKH, south into the Indus Valley or south-west into the Darel Valley. But the peoples of these valleys have a reputation for lawlessness and these treks are definitely not recommended.

Jutial Nala & Taj Mughal Monument
The Gilgit Valley is actually rather grand, but it's impossible to appreciate it from town. A fairly easy hike from Jutial along a high water channel gives a fine panorama of the valley, plus Rakaposhi and other peaks.

Take a Jutial Suzuki from Saddar Bazaar to the end of the line, below Serena Lodge. Half a km uphill past the Serena, turn right and then left up the nala. Climb till you see a stream going off to the right – the headworks of the water channel. Several km along the channel, you can scramble 100 metres up to Taj Mughal's monument. At Barmas village, near some water tanks, descend on Hospital Rd back into Gilgit.

From the Serena to the bazaar takes under two hours. A variation is to climb into Jutial Nala, two hours up to pine forests and excellent Rakaposhi views. Another is to continue on the channel to Napur and the Kargah Buddha, three-plus hours from the Serena.

If there have been more than a few hours of rain in recent days, *stay away*, as the hillsides are very prone to rockslides.

Dainyor
A small village at Gilgit's back door, and perhaps Pakistan's southernmost Ismaili village, Dainyor makes a good day-trip for some interesting historical items. From Saddar Bazaar, Suzukis go to Dainyor bazaar on the KKH, via two dramatic bridges. Some Gilgitis claim the one over the Gilgit River is the longest suspension bridge negotiable by jeep in Asia, although the one over the Hunza River is more hair-raising.

Overlooking the Hunza River is a *ziarat* (shrine) to a 14th-century Shia preacher named Sultan Alib, complete with Balti-style 'skylight' like the one on Hunza's Baltit Fort. Villagers will show you inside, and ask you to leave a few coins for upkeep. Get off the Suzuki when it tops the climb on the east side of the Hunza River, and double back by foot on a path above the road.

From the Dainyor bazaar it's 1½ km south on the KKH to a melancholy cemetery, on the left behind a large gate, with the graves of 88 Chinese KKH workers who never made it home.

In Dainyor village is a huge rock with Sanskrit inscriptions about a line of Tibetan princes who ruled here in the 7th and 8th centuries. It's on the property of one Rafid Ullah, who'll show it to visitors for a few rupees. From the Dainyor bazaar go one km north on the KKH to a jeep road on the right; if you cross a bridge you've gone too far. Up the road about three-quarters of a km, Rafid Ullah's house is on the left. If you get lost ask for 'old writing stone' – *likitu giri* in Shina or *girminum bun* in Burushaski.

Local people say there are other inscriptions and an excavation of a 'very old' village about one km further up the jeep road. Travellers also say Dainyor Nala above the village is good for walking.

Trout Fishing

Streams and lakes all over northern Pakistan are stocked with trout. Good reaches near Gilgit are Kargah Nala, Naltar Valley and Singhal Nala in Punial. The season is from 10 March to 9 October. Information and licences (Rs 42 a day) are available at the Fisheries office in upper Bank Rd in Gilgit. Tackle can be hired there (for Rs 15 per day plus a deposit) or bought at shops in Bank Rd below the National Bank. Some agencies have package deals.

White-Water Boating

Local stretches open to visitors include the Gilgit River in Punial, the Hunza River from Nomal to Gilgit and the Indus from Jaglot to Thakot. Mountain Movers on Airport Rd organises trips.

NALTAR VALLEY

Naltar was Gilgit Agency's 'hill station', where British colonial administrators went when summer heat grew oppressive. Most guides who know the valleys around Gilgit call this the loveliest. Its perfect alpine scenery is accessible for overnights or as the start of treks to Chalt or Ishkoman, or even on a fast day trip by jeep from Gilgit. It's crowded in summer.

The valley meets the Hunza River at Nomal, 25 km north of Gilgit. A jeep road climbs 16 km (five to six hours on foot) to Naltar village, where the valley opens up. From Naltar it's a beautiful half-day (12-km)

hike up to Naltar Lake and dense pine forests. Near Naltar is a Pakistan air force winter survival school.

Beyond the lake, a day's walking takes you to summer pastures at Shani, where you may meet nomadic Gujar shepherds. Another half-day up is the foot of the 4800-metre pass to Daintar and Chalt, five to six days from Nomal. A six-day trek also crosses a 4700-metre pass west to Phakor, north of Chatorkhand in the Ishkoman Valley. A guide is recommended for either of these trips. See the Trekking chapter in Lonely Planet's *Pakistan – a travel survival kit* for more information.

Places to Stay & Eat

Nomal has a run-down *NAPWD Resthouse* with two doubles at Rs 150, and the simple *Prince Hotel* and *Aliar Hotel* are open in summer. There are two heavily used *NAPWD resthouses* at Naltar village with doubles at Rs 150 and Rs 200, or you can pitch a tent on the lawn. Book them with the Chief Engineer in Gilgit. There's a stone hut above Naltar Lake. Local people may let you camp on their land, though some are greedy.

During the summer a few Nomal and Naltar cafes have basic food. The resthouse caretakers can do meals with what they can find or what you bring.

Getting There & Away

At least one bus goes to Nomal from Gilgit's general bus stand before mid-day for Rs 10, returning next morning. A hired jeep to Naltar village is at least Rs 700 one way or Rs 900 for a day trip.

An alternative is to get off any northbound bus at Rahimabad on the KKH, climb down to the river, walk south about 1½ km and catch an ox-skin raft across to Nomal for a few rupees (set the price before you go). Raft is *jalo* in Shina. There is also a ropebridge to Nomal.

GILGIT RIVER BASIN

The Gilgit River basin (except for its Hunza River branch) is mainly familiar to trekkers and anglers. Once a nest of feuding kingdoms, it's still a surprising patchwork of people and languages, with hardly anything big enough to be called a town.

The old valley-kingdoms are Punial ('poon-YAAL'), above Gilgit; Ishkoman ('ish-KO-man'), entering from the north about 80 km up the Gilgit River; Yasin ('ya-SEEN'), which enters at about 110 km; and Ghizar ('GHUH-zr'), stretching west to the Shandur Pass into Chitral. See the Gilgit Region map on page 132 and the Naltar Valley & Punial map below.

The mountains are the Hindu Raj, an arm of the Hindu Kush (the Karakoram formally begin east of Ishkoman). The lower reaches are hot in summer and unexceptional to look at, but the upper valleys are grandly beautiful. The route is dotted with ancient petroglyphs of ibex and other animals.

Punialis are a mix of Sunnis, Ismailis and a few Shias. Most of the good-natured people of the further valleys have been Ismaili for six or seven centuries. Women dress in bright colours and pillbox caps (which get taller the farther west you go) and are unveiled and relaxed in public.

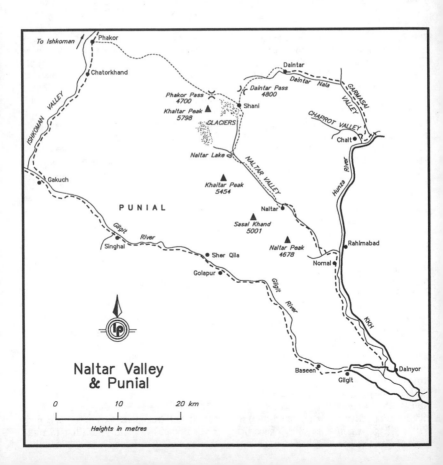

Naltar Valley & Punial

0   10   20 km

Heights in metres

Most Punialis speak Shina (as in Gilgit). In Ishkoman you can hear Shina, Wakhi (as in Gojal), and Chitrali. Yasinis speak the purest form of Burushaski, the tongue of Hunza, which suggests that this obscure language was once used across a wide area. Chitrali is the speech of Ghizar. Little English is spoken.

Punial

Properous-looking **Sher Qila**, 1¼ hours from Gilgit and across the river, has a watchtower and a big Aga Khan-funded girls' school. At **Singhal**, 40 minutes further, Singhal Gah (Singhal Canyon) is a well-known trout reach. About 45 minutes on, the valley broadens at the district headquarters of **Gakuch** (also with good trout fishing), and just beyond it is the mouth of the Ishkoman Valley. After 1½ more hours on the worst roads in the basin, Yasin Valley enters.

Ishkoman

Chatorkhand, 25 km from Gakuch, is the traditional seat of the Pir of Chatorkhand, head of a line of hereditary religious leaders who came from Bukhara in Central Asia in the early 19th century. With headwaters near the Afghan border, Ishkoman is best known for treks.

A six-day hike climbs to 4700 metres from **Phakor**, upstream of Chatorkhand, east to Naltar Valley. See Lonely Planet's *Pakistan – a travel survival kit* for more on this one. Others go west to Yasin, and a spectacular long one – lately closed – runs near the Afghan border to the Chapursan Valley, which enters the Hunza River valley near Sust.

Yasin

The Yasin and Ghizar rivers join near **Gupis** to form the Gilgit River. **Yasin** village is 25 km north of Gupis. From there it's about 40 km to the valley's highest village, **Darkot**, beyond which is the now-closed Darkot Pass into far northern Chitral. At his death in 1857 the Yasini ruler Gohar Aman held everything down to Astore, but six years later Kashmiri soldiers retook it all and massacred some 1200 people at Yasin village.

Ghizar (Gupis)

This ruggedly beautiful valley is sometimes called Gupis, after the village at its junction with the Yasin Valley. About 3½ hours above Gupis, to the south behind **Chashi**, is Chashi Gol (*gol* is Chitrali for a side-valley). Half an hour later, where the valley opens wide, is friendly **Phander**. An hour on at **Gulagmuli** village, Handrap Gol gapes to the south. If you want to linger, places to do it are Phander and **Teru**, six hours from Gupis, 3100 metres high and at the foot of the Shandur Pass.

Shandur Pass

The 3810-metre pass is actually broad enough to have several lakes, and a polo ground where the best players from Gilgit and Chitral meet every summer, part of a four-day festival of polo and merry-making. It's usually in July or early August, with dates set only a month or so ahead. The Ministry of Tourism wants to fix it in the last week in June and tart it up for tourists. The first Chitrali settlements beyond the pass are Sor Laspur, three to four hours from Teru by jeep, and Mastuj, six to seven hours from Teru.

Places to Stay & Eat

In the basin there are nine NAPWD resthouses (booked with the Chief Engineer in Gilgit) and a few cheap hotels. You can pitch a tent in hotel gardens, or by the river anywhere above Gakuch, with no worries.

Punial
> Heavily-used *resthouses* at Golapur, Singhal and Gakuch; *Pakeeza Hotel* at Singhal; and two seedy inns at Gakuch.

Ishkoman
> *Resthouses* at Chatorkhand and Imit (about 30 km beyond Chatorkand).

Yasin
> *Resthouse* at Yasin village.

Ghizar
> *Resthouses* at Gupis, Phander and Teru; two cheap inns at Gupis; *Tourest Hotel No 1* at Phander; and the tiny *Sarhad Hotel* at Teru.

Decent food is scarce; consider carrying your own, especially in Ishkoman or Yasin, and even to the resthouses toward the end of the season.

Getting There & Away

The three resthouses in Punial are within half a day by jeep from Gilgit; those in Ishkoman, Yasin and at Gupis are within a day. The 400-km Gilgit-Chitral trip can take as little as two or three days, depending on connections. The Shandur Pass is normally open from June through October. No permits are necessary except for trekking in the extreme north of Ishkoman and Yasin.

Cargo Jeeps In summer, cargo jeeps go from Gilgit's Punial Rd to up-valley villages on most days, and to Sor Laspur or Mastuj every few days. Ask shopkeepers in Punial Rd and the lane to the cemetery, or a Pathan named Mr Pakistani on the corner west of the polo ground. If you get a seat at all, you'll share it with petrol cans, sacks of flour and lots of cheerful people.

Figure about Rs 200 from Gilgit to Teru, and Rs 200 from there to Mastuj. In Mastuj, there's a daily 6 am passenger jeep to Chitral town for Rs 60. Few cargo jeeps set out westward from intermediate points, so going in short hops can mean long waits and midnight departures on whatever comes through.

Hired Jeep At the time of writing Gilgit-Chitral was Rs 6000 in a hired jeep for four or five passengers. But drivers returning to Chitral may scout the hotels and offer substantial discounts if you deal directly with them. From Teru a hired jeep to Sor Laspur is at least Rs 800, and to Mastuj about Rs 1200.

Bus & Pickup A daily bus goes from Gilgit to Gakuch for Rs 30, and Natco runs 4WD pickups between Gilgit and Gupis.

Foot If you get to Teru and the pass is closed by snow or nobody's driving, you could walk the roughly 40 km on to Sor Laspur or hire a horse and guide, a 1½-day trip for about Rs 500.

BAGROT VALLEY

Fifteen km down-river from Gilgit, a broad alluvial fan marks the Bagrot ('ba-GROTE') Valley. Its lower reaches are like a marbled moonscape, and a ride up the narrow, perched road in an overloaded cargo jeep is unforgettable. The upper valley is huge, rugged and densely cultivated. The Shina-speaking, Shia Muslim Bagrotis see few foreigners except passing trekkers.

Jalalabad, opposite the KKH, was the scene of the heaviest fighting in the 1988 Shia-Sunni violence. Bagrot's main village is **Sinakkar**, two hours from Gilgit. At the end of the jeep road 1½ hours on is the last year-round village, **Chirah**, with a view of Hinarche Glacier and a series of ridges culminating in Diran Peak (on the other side are Nagar and Hunza).

Half a day's walk above Chirah are summer villages where a large part of the valley's population goes with their goats and sheep each year. Seven to eight hours from Chirah are shepherds' huts and good camping, and a 4600-metre crossing past the Barche Glacier into Haramosh Valley. The prominent peak to the south-east is 6134-metre Dubanni.

A local guide is essential for treks to Haramosh or toward Diran. Ask among the Bagrot and Haramosh shopkeepers at Garhi Bagh in Gilgit's Saddar Bazaar.

Places to Stay

The old *NAPWD Resthouse* at Chirah looks abandoned. The best bet is to camp out above Chirah.

Getting There & Away

Cargo jeeps go to Chirah from Gilgit's Garhi Bagh around mid-day, returning early next morning. The ride alone is worth the price, for the valley view and the adrenalin rush. Don't take the bus to Jalalabad, which has no up-valley connections.

HARAMOSH VALLEY

An hour south of Gilgit the Skardu road leaves the KKH and heads up the Indus

Gilgit 149

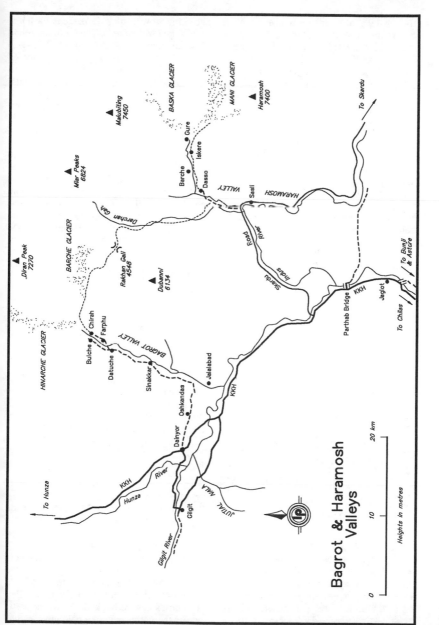

Bagrot & Haramosh Valleys

River. After arcing north the road and canyon turn south to skirt 7400-metre Haramosh Peak; this region is locally called Haramosh Valley. Like Bagrotis, its Shina-speaking people are unused to foreigners and haven't much to offer visitors. There's no food or lodging, but alpine meadows and the glaciers of Haramosh Peak are a strenuous day's walk from the highway.

Sasli (or Sassi) village is a bus stop on the Skardu road, 1½ hours from Gilgit. By a bridge a km or two down-river a jeep track climbs north; take the right (lower) fork. After about eight level km a bridge crosses the canyon. **Dasso** village is on the bluff above. From there a footpath climbs four steep km to **Iskere** ('ISS-keh-reh') at 2500 metres, where most of Dasso's population lives from May until December, grazing goats and cutting timber.

About one km above Iskere, near the toe of the Mani Glacier, are good tent sites and views of Haramosh (source of the glacier), Lyla Peak across the glacier, Baska Glacier and Malubiting peak (7450 metres) to the north. Three km above Iskere there are shepherds' huts.

Places to Stay & Eat
There are none beyond the highway. Sasli has a cafe and several seedy road houses.

Getting There & Away
Skardu-bound buses stop at Sasli, 1½ hours from Gilgit. The early bus is the best way to get into the high country the same day. A daily wagon (Rs 25) goes to Sasli in mid-afternoon from Garhi Bagh in Gilgit, returning around 7 am next morning. A local guide would be a big help here; ask Haramosh shopkeepers at Garhi Bagh.

ASTORE VALLEY & NANGA PARBAT
Strictly speaking, the Karakoram ends at the Indus River. On the other side is the western end of the Great Himalaya, crowned by 8126-metre Nanga Parbat, eighth highest mountain in the world and still growing. Its south-east face is a 4500-metre wall, too steep for snow to stick (its name is Kashmiri for 'Naked Mountain'). The north side steps down an incredible 7000 metres to the Indus.

Pre-Islamic traditions blame many of life's misfortunes on mountain fairies, and Nanga Parbat (or Diamar, 'DYA-mr', as it's known locally) is said to be a fairy citadel, topped by a crystal palace and guarded by snow serpents. The caprice of these spirits is manifest in the mountain itself: many climbers have died here.

The hair-raising track beside Nanga Parbat, up the Astore Valley and over the Burzil Pass, was an ancient caravan route, and was the only link between British India and Gilgit until the Babusar Pass route was opened in 1892. The Indo-Pak cease-fire line has closed the Burzil, but Astore is still the best way to get up close to the mountain. Until the track was improved in 1987, jeeps regularly fell off it; now it's safer, though probably no more comfortable.

Astore Valley is about 75% Sunni and 25% Shia, the latter mainly in the upper tributaries. Everyone speaks Shina and almost nobody speaks English. Some food is available in Astore but if you're camping it's a good idea to bring your own.

Jaglot to Astore Village
The spine-wrenching track from Jaglot to the mouth of the valley passes through Bunji, once the Maharajah of Kashmir's local garrison, and now headquarters of the Northern Light Infantry (NLI). The lower valley is barren, slide-prone and oven-like in summer, but grows lovelier as you climb.

Astore Village
The village is perched at 2450 metres astride Rama Gah. The bazaar is up a steep track on the north side of the ravine, and the valley road continues on the south side.

The police, a jolly bunch, ask foreigners to register on arrival; the station is in the bazaar. Above the bazaar is the NAPWD Executive Engineer (☎ 11), where valley resthouses can be booked. A post office is across the ravine, near the polo ground.

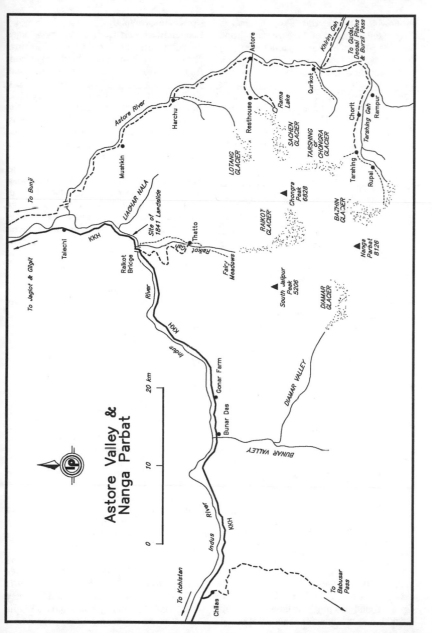

Astore Valley & Nanga Parbat

Places to Stay & Eat The *Dreamland Tourist Inn* at the top of the bazaar has good food, Rs 50 dorm beds and a garden for tents; doubles with shared loo are Rs 200. Other hotels are cheaper but dreary; the *Rama* in the bazaar and the *Tourist Cottage*, across Rama Gah past the polo ground, have dark doubles with toilet for about Rs 70, and basic restaurants. An *NAPWD Resthouse*, with doubles for Rs 150, is south of Rama Gah, and can be booked with the Executive Engineer here or the Chief Engineer in Gilgit.

Getting There & Away Occasional wagons go directly to Astore village from Gilgit's bus yard but there are frequent wagons and passenger jeeps from Jaglot on the KKH, for about Rs 50. Most return from Astore next morning. A hired jeep from Gilgit is about Rs 1600 one way. Astore is four hours from Jaglot, and about six hours from Gilgit.

Rama Lake
Above Astore village is the steep and very beautiful Rama Gah, with scattered hamlets and thick pine and birch forest. There's no village, only an idyllic resthouse two to 2½ hours' steep walk above Astore. In the meadow beyond the resthouse, take the left-hand track, one to 1½ hours up past the tree-line to Rama Lake, about one vertical km higher than Astore village and considerably cooler in all seasons.

From here you can see Rama Ridge, a minor shoulder of Nanga Parbat, and the Sachen Glacier (not to be confused with the Siachen in the High Karakoram). No guide is necessary unless you're trekking further.

Places to Stay Book the small *NAPWD Resthouse* with the Executive Engineer in Astore, or in Gilgit. There is excellent camping near the resthouse and at the lake.

Getting There & Away The track starts from Astore bazaar. You can hire a jeep in Astore for the round-trip to the resthouse for about Rs 500, or to the lake for about Rs 600.

Upper Astore Valley
Longer treks start from up-valley villages including Gurikot, Rampur and Tarshing. Tarshing is up Rupal Gah, about 40 km from Astore. From there a rigorous day trip puts you within sight of Nanga Parbat's naked south-east face. Guides might be found in Astore or Tarshing. The old track toward the Burzil Pass goes up Khirim Gah, just above Gurikot. For more detailed information see the Trekking chapter in Lonely Planet's *Pakistan – a travel survival kit.*

Places to Stay Tarshing has a small hotel with fairly clean rooms for about Rs 50 a bed, flush toilet, and a garden for camping. The owner is a good cook and can help with porters, etc. Beyond Tarshing, bring a tent. At Gudai, about 15 km up Khirim Gah, is an *NAPWD Resthouse*, which is booked at Astore or Gilgit.

Getting There & Away Passenger jeeps go to Tarshing from Astore, more or less daily if there are enough passengers. A hired jeep from Gilgit is about Rs 2700 one way, or you might be able to hire one in Astore.

FAIRY MEADOWS
This is a lovely high plateau with level upon level of meadows and direct views up Nanga Parbat's north side, and it is isolated by a gruelling climb from the Indus. The solitude may soon be broken by the redoubtable Brigadier Aslam, who is driving a private road up the mountain, apparently to build a resort at the meadows.

Two hours south of Gilgit the KKH crosses the Indus on the Raikot (or Rakhiot) Bridge. On the south side is Aslam's road and his Shangri-La Motel. For the trail, walk up-river (east), cross Raikot Gah and up you go. It's six hours of switchbacks to the village of Thatto and another steep four hours to the meadows, 3200 metres above sea level and two vertical km above the river. There's no water until Thatto.

At the time of writing the road had been completed to Thatto, so you could walk (four hours) or drive that way. Local people have imposed a Rs 500 toll on vehicles (but not on pedestrians). Thatto kids have sticky fingers, so camp well above the village.

Above Fairy Meadows are numerous day hikes and more strenuous climbs, including six hours up the west side of the valley to an old expedition base camp at 4000 metres. For more information see the Trekking chapter in Lonely Planet's *Pakistan – a travel survival kit*.

Places to Stay

The *Shangri-La Motel's* prices are staggering. Better alternatives near the highway are camping in Raikot Gah or staying at the *NAPWD Resthouse* 13 km north on the KKH at Talechi.

Getting There & Away

Take any Chilas or Rawalpindi-bound bus from Gilgit to Raikot Bridge.

SKARDU & BALTISTAN

Rising at Mt Kailas in Tibet, the Indus flows north-west almost to Gilgit in a deep trench dividing the Himalaya from the Karakoram, and the Indian subcontinent from Asia. Before turning south it drains Baltistan or 'Little Tibet', an arid land inhabited by people who today speak classical Tibetan and in the 17th century were masters of the Northern Areas.

Near the Balti capital of Skardu the Indus is joined by the Shigar and Shyok rivers, flowing down from the Baltoro Muztagh, a segment of the Karakoram backbone containing the densest mass of glaciers and high mountains on earth, including 8611-metre K2, second only to Mt Everest.

Since 1949, after the first India-Pakistan war, Baltistan has been a sub-division of the Northern Areas. In recent years specially trained Indian and Pakistani troops have been fighting for the peaks around the Siachen Glacier in Baltistan's eastern corner. But away from this zone there are fine treks, mind-bending scenery and villages that hardly seem touched by the 20th century.

Until an air route was opened from Islamabad in the 1960s Baltistan was still almost medieval in its isolation. From 1972 to 1985, simultaneously with construction of the KKH, Pakistan army engineers cut a road up the Rondu Gorge of the Indus that is even more harrowing than the KKH, and often littered with rocks from the peeling mountainsides. In rainy weather (eg summer storms and winter drizzle) multiple slides may block it completely. Ride this road to feel genuinely small.

People

Balti people are a mix of Tibetan, Mongol and the descendants of Northern Areas peoples taken prisoner in Baltistan's 17th-century heyday. They stand out with their short stature, leathery hide and friendly disposition. Nowadays, Skardu is also full of Gilgiti bureaucrats and traders.

Baltis speak an archaic form of Tibetan, seasoned with Arabic and Persian; a few Balti phrases are included in the Language glossary at the back of the book.

The villagers of the Satpara Valley above Skardu, whose ancestors probably came from Astore, speak Shina. Urdu and some English are spoken in Skardu and larger villages.

Everyone is Shia Muslim and not a woman is visible in Skardu. Men and women visitors alike should dress conservatively. Shorts are out; even bare arms on women will put orthodox local backs up.

The Gilgit-Skardu Road

An hour south of Gilgit the road leaves the KKH and crosses a bridge and a spit of rock into the Indus Gorge. Ten minutes from the bridge is a perfect panorama of the entire Nanga Parbat massif. Fifteen minutes later the Indus is at its very northernmost point. Another 15 minutes on is the fuel stop of **Sasli**.

About 3½ hours from the KKH (2½ hours from Skardu) is the regional centre of **Thowar**. Across the river is **Rondu**, capital of the ancient Rondu kingdom. Below **Basho** the canyon opens into the vast Skardu valley, and an hour later you're in the Skardu bazaar.

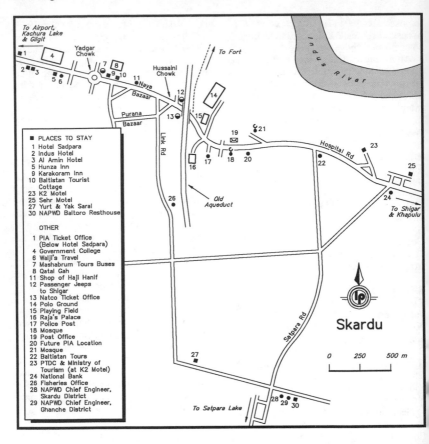

To Airport, Kachura Lake & Gilgit

Yadgar Chowk

To Fort

Hussaini Chowk

Indus River

Naya Bazaar

Purana Bazaar

Link Rd

Old Aqueduct

Hospital Rd

To Shigar & Khapulu

Satpara Rd

Skardu

0   250   500 m

To Satpara Lake

■ PLACES TO STAY
1 Hotel Sadpara
2 Indus Hotel
3 Al Amin Hotel
5 Hunza Inn
9 Karakoram Inn
10 Baltistan Tourist
   Cottage
23 K2 Motel
25 Sehr Motel
27 Yurt & Yak Sarai
30 NAPWD Baltoro Resthouse

OTHER
1 PIA Ticket Office
  (Below Hotel Sadpara)
4 Government College
6 Walji's Travel
7 Mashabrum Tours Buses
8 Qatal Gah
11 Shop of Haji Hanif
12 Passenger Jeeps
   to Shigar
13 Natco Ticket Office
14 Polo Ground
15 Playing Field
16 Raja's Palace
17 Police Post
18 Mosque
19 Post Office
20 Future PIA Location
21 Mosque
22 Baltistan Tours
23 PTDC & Ministry of
   Tourism (at K2 Motel)
24 National Bank
26 Fisheries Office
28 NAPWD Chief Engineer,
   Skardu District
29 NAPWD Chief Engineer,
   Ghanche District

Places to Stay & Eat Rondu has a *NAPWD Resthouse* with Rs 160 doubles, booked with the Skardu District Chief Engineer (in Skardu). Bring your own snacks and water – food stops are dismal.

Skardu

The vast, flat Skardu valley is 40 km long, 10 km wide and carpeted with sand dunes, and a gritty wind always seems to be blowing. The brown mountains give no hint of the white giants beyond. Skardu, at 2290 metres, is on a ledge at the foot of Karpochu, a rock sticking 300 metres out of the plain.

The town has been a mountaineer's haunt for years, but it's also a base for many classic treks and even day trips. It's hot in mid-summer, though sudden chilling storms are common. From November to March, temperatures drop to freezing. Summer is prime mountaineering season so jeeps and hotel space may be hard to find then.

Orientation Along the main road is Naya (or New) Bazaar and in the back streets the more interesting Purana (or Old) Bazaar. Reference points are Yadgar Chowk, with a monument to the uprising against the Maharajah of

Kashmir, and Hussaini Chowk near the 17th-century aqueduct. The cheaper hotels are near Yadgar. Government offices are well east or south of the bazaar. The airport is 14 km away on the road to Gilgit.

Information PTDC (☎ 104) is at the K2 Motel, but you'll get more help from your hotel-wallah. Other sources of help here are Walji's Travel and Baltistan Tours. Baltistan's NAPWD resthouses may be booked through the Chief Engineers for the districts of Skardu (☎ 788) and Ghanche (☎ 406, 433). Both are south of the centre. National Bank, two km east of the centre, does foreign exchange.

Karpochu The 17th-century fort on the east end of this rock (also called Askandria) is a 45-minute climb from the bazaar. The Dogra soldiers of the Sikh Empire trashed and rebuilt it a few years before they moved into Gilgit. From the polo ground there is also a track around the base of the rock. The summit is a steep, dicey, dry, two to three-hour scramble up the west end from near the Hotel Sadpara.

Qatal Gah The brightly painted complex behind the Tourist Cottage hotel includes a mosque and an *imam burga*, a hall used during the Shia festivals of Ashura and Chhelum.

Satpara Lake & Buddha Nine km south of Skardu is beautiful Satpara Lake, a moderately steep 2½-hour walk from Skardu. En route is a big sitting Buddha carved on a rock in about the 7th century, in the same style as the one near Gilgit. Where the jeep road and irrigation channel cross near Skardu Public School, a side-track crosses the nala to the rock. Six km beyond the lake is Satpara village.

The *Satpara Lake Inn* has two doubles with shower for a negotiable Rs 100, tents for Rs 50 and a lakeside cafe where you can get chips or complete meals. There is another inn nearby. PTDC's *Satpara Hut* has Rs 300 doubles; these are booked at the K2 Motel in Skardu.

Kachura Lake Thirty km west of Skardu, off the road to Gilgit, this small lake is known mostly for the hyper-expensive *Shangri-La Tourist Resort* with its ersatz Chinese architecture and a DC-3 fuselage converted into luxury suites. There is also a smaller mid-range hotel. There are petroglyphs up Shigarthang Nala, above the lake.

Places to Stay *Baltistan Tourist Cottage* (☎ 707) has cold-water doubles and a dorm with outside toilet for Rs 30 a bed, and hot-water doubles for Rs 150 and Rs 200; it's also a good place for local information. The *Hunza Inn* (☎ 570) has doubles with shared toilet for Rs 50 and cold-shower doubles and triples for about Rs 100 a room.

The *Karakoram Inn* (☎ 449) has doubles/triples for Rs 150/200, and a VIP double for about Rs 450. West of Yadgar Chowk are the *Sadpara* and *Al Amin* hotels with the same rates, and the *Indus Hotel* with doubles for Rs 250. Far south is NAPWD's *Baltoro Resthouse* where doubles with hot shower are Rs 160, but public transport is non-existent. Book it two doors up with the Skardu District Chief Engineer.

The *Sehr Motel* (☎ 841) has comfortable singles/doubles for about Rs 400/550. PTDC's *K2 Motel* (☎ 946) is about Rs 500/600. Both are a long walk from the bazaar. The *Yurt & Yak Sarai* (☎ 856) has two-bed 'luxury yurts' with electricity, toilets and hot showers for Rs 400, though it's a 15-minute walk from the bazaar and there's no public transport.

Places to Eat Street-cafe food is suspect but travellers recommend the chips and burgers at *Tibet Fast Food* beside Natco. *Baltistan Tourist Cottage's* restaurant does chips, roast and karahi chicken, and other Pakistani standards. Other decent hotel restaurants are at the *Karakoram Inn* and *Sadpara Hotel*. The *Sehr Motel's* food is pricey but very good. It's hard work for vegetarians here, though there's fruit in the bazaar in summer.

Getting There & Away – air PIA is below the Hotel Sadpara, but a new office is planned opposite the post office. Weather permitting, Boeing-737s fly daily from Islamabad, going fairly often even in winter. Prop-driven Fokkers make the Islamabad, Skardu, Gilgit, Islamabad loop on Sundays and the reverse on Thursdays. Islamabad is Rs 680, and Gilgit is Rs 410. From a Fokker you look *up* at Nanga Parbat; from a Boeing in clear weather you can look right out across the Karakoram.

The weather-dependent flights are effectively standby and must be tediously confirmed with PIA the morning of the day before departure. The final decision is made on departure day. There are two tourist-priority seats per flight; to get one, ask PTDC for a letter to show PIA at confirmation time. In summer, without a previous booking you might have to wait a week for a seat out to Islamabad.

Getting There & Away – road Mashabrum Tours is near Yadgar, and Natco has a ticket office by the aqueduct. Clapped-out Natco and Mashabrum buses go to Gilgit around 5 am, for Rs 70. Mashabrum also has comfortable vans for Rs 100. In good weather the 170-km road trip from Gilgit to Skardu takes seven to eight hours. For the best views, sit on the right side heading for Skardu.

Shigar

One of two routes from Skardu into the High Karakoram is the huge, lush Shigar Valley. A tributary of the Shigar River, the Braldu, flows down from the mighty Baltoro Glacier, surrounded by 10 of the world's 30 highest peaks. LP's *Pakistan – a travel survival kit* includes details on the trek up the Baltoro Glacier to Concordia and K2.

In Shigar village, at the mouth of the Bauma Lungma side valley, is a crumbling old royal palace, in the same timber-and-stones style as Baltit and Altit forts in Hunza, from the days when this was an independent kingdom. Along the Shigar Valley wall, down-river of Bauma Lungma, are recently excavated Buddhist ruins, including monastery foundations and rock inscriptions from as early as the 5th century.

Places to Stay Shigar village has a grubby inn and a peaceful stream-side *NAPWD Resthouse*, booked with the Skardu District Chief Engineer.

Getting There & Away The village is 1¼ hours from Skardu on a rough track, by morning passenger jeep (Rs 20) or hired jeep (about Rs 800).

Khapulu

Above Skardu the Indus is joined by the Shyok River, flowing down from the border between Ladakh and Xinjiang. This is the axis of Khapulu, biggest of Baltistan's ancient kingdoms. Khapulu village, 100 km from Skardu on a spine-jerking road, has an old royal palace and an even older mosque, and from the village you can look (or walk) into the heart of the Karakoram, up the Hushe Valley towards Masherbrum.

Places to Stay Khapulu has two rudimentary inns, and there are NAPWD resthouses (booked with the Ghanche District Chief Engineer in Skardu) at Khapulu and at Keris, en route.

Getting There & Away Cargo jeeps (about Rs 60) and a Natco bus (Rs 35) go from Skardu each morning.

GILGIT TO CHILAS

Ten minutes south of the Skardu turn-off, say hello to the Indus River, one of the longest in the world; the KKH runs beside it for the next 340 km, through Kohistan to Thakot.

Just below the confluence is the Parthab Bridge, on the old jeep (and pre-jeep) road to Skardu. Ten minutes on is **Jaglot** ('jh-GLOTE') bazaar, and just downstream, the bridge across the Indus toward Astore. Across the river is **Bunji**, once a garrison of the Maharajah of Kashmir's army; above it is the Matterhorn-like Mushkin Peak.

A good place to keep your eyes open is 15 minutes beyond Jaglot, 1½ hours from either

Gilgit or Chilas, at **Talechi** ('TA-li-chee') village, the only place on the road where both Rakaposhi and Nanga Parbat are visible. Along here are the best views of the largest number of snowy peaks anywhere on the KKH. From the north, the prominent ones are the Karakoram peaks of Rakaposhi (7790 metres, a sharp point above a broad white base), Dubanni (6134 metres, a blunt pyramid) and Haramosh (7400 metres, a series of glaciated ridges), and the Himalayan massif of Nanga Parbat (8126 metres, eighth highest in the world).

From here, the closer you get to Nanga Parbat the more it hides behind its own lower reaches. Opposite Talechi is the deep Astore Valley, which winds around to Nanga Parbat's sheer south-east (Rupal) face.

Soon the gorge closes in, the vistas disappear and about 10 minutes in (or five minutes north of the Raikot Bridge), **Liachar Nala** enters the Indus across from the highway. In

1841 an earthquake caused an entire valley wall to collapse into the Indus here, damming it up and creating a lake that stretched nearly to Gilgit. When the dam broke, a wall of water roared down the canyon, washing away scores of villages and drowning thousands of people, including an entire Sikh army battalion camped at Attock, almost 500 km downstream.

By now the Indus has turned west, deflected by Nanga Parbat. At a narrow spot the KKH crosses on the **Raikot Bridge** (also referred to as Rakhiot Bridge). From the south side a private road is being driven up the mountain toward the alpine plateau called Fairy Meadows, beneath the north (or Raikot) face of Nanga Parbat.

Except for road-weeds, the river and a few irrigated plateaux, the Indus Valley west of the bridge for 100 km is 'a barren dewless country; the very river with its black water looks hot', in the words of the late-1880s

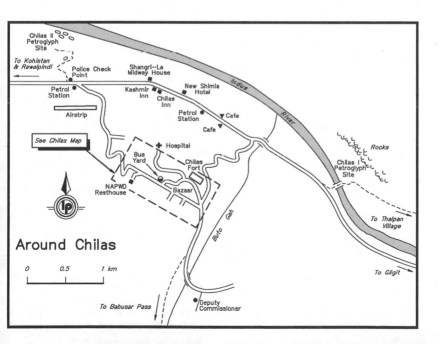

Around Chilas

Imperial Gazetteer of India. In a series of landslide zones beneath eroded sandstone cliffs, the highway resembles the little make-believe roads that kids make in dirt-piles.

Half an hour west of the bridge is a small tree-lined bazaar at **Gonar Farm**. Five minutes further (half an hour east of Chilas) is the new village of **Bunar Das** (Bunar Plain), on a plateau below the Bunar Valley, the main access to Nanga Parbat's western (Diamar) face.

A jeep-bridge spans the Indus just east of Chilas. Here, on both sides of the river, are the best known of the extraordinary rock inscriptions made by 2000 years of travellers through the Indus Valley and the Karakoram. About three minutes westward, near a petrol station, is a dramatic view of Chilas Fort in the distance.

Places to Stay

Jaglot has several grotty inns and a small hotel with private rooms. At Raikot Bridge is a *Shangri-La Motel*, almost certainly the worst rip-off on the KKH.

It is better to stop 13 km north at Talechi's run-down but beautifully located *NAPWD Resthouse*, where a double is Rs 150; it can be booked through the Executive Engineer in Chilas and possibly with the Chief Engineer in Gilgit.

CHILAS

Most visitors are here to look at the petroglyphs or to cross the Babusar Pass (see The Kaghan Valley in the Hazara chapter). There are few other good reasons to stop in this sullen place. Western women especially may feel unwelcome.

Even after Kashmiri-British rule was imposed a century ago the Indus Valley west of Chilas – called Shinaki for its Shina-speaking people – was a hornets' nest of tiny republics, one in almost every side-valley, each loosely guided by a *jirga* (assembly) but effectively leaderless, all at war with one another and feuding internally. Administratively lumped with Gilgit, Chilas and its neighbours are temperamentally more like Kohistan, possibly owing to a similar hostile

environment and the same Sunni Muslim orthodoxy (their ancestors were forcibly converted six centuries ago by Pathan crusaders, whereas hardly anyone north of Gilgit is Sunni).

The huge Chilas Fort was first garrisoned to protect British supply lines over the Babusar Pass, and beefed up after local tribes, in a rare case of collective action, nearly overran it in 1893. Now a police post, it has put a lid on Chilas, though not on the Darel and Tangir valleys to the west.

Chilasis are Shina-speakers, with some Pathan settlers speaking Pashto. Urdu and some English are also spoken.

Orientation

Some hotels are on the KKH but the town is on a plateau above. You can flag a pickup three km up to the bazaar from the police checkpoint, or walk up Buto Gah past the old village. The bazaar huddles by the fort, with newer development on Ranoi Rd. South of the bazaar a left fork drops to district offices and the right fork climbs toward Babusar Pass.

Information

On Ranoi Rd is the NAPWD Executive Engineer (☎ 515), where resthouses in the area can be booked. The post office is opposite the fort. The police post *is* the fort.

A government hospital is at the bottom of Hospital Rd.

Petroglyphs

The ancient routes through the Karakoram are dotted with places where travellers pecked graffiti into the rocks: names, pictures or prayers for safe passage, merit in the afterlife or good luck on the next hunting trip. The desolation around Chilas must have moved many to special fervour, and several sites by the highway are rich with inscriptions on the 'desert-varnished' stones.

Near the KKH checkpoint is a sign to the 'Chilas II' site. About ¾ km down a jeep track a huge rock is covered with hunting and battle scenes and Buddhist stupas. A common image is the long-horned ibex,

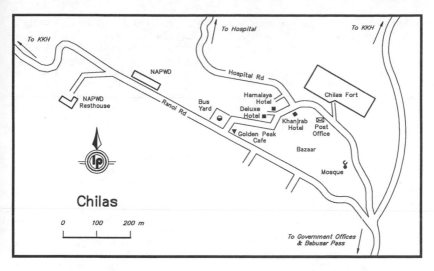

Chilas

ancient symbol of fertility and abundance, and an elusive trophy animal even now. On a rocky knoll facing the river are the oldest inscriptions, from the 1st century AD – scenes of conquest and stories of the Buddha's life.

Four km east beside the jeep bridge to Thalpan is the 'Chilas I' site, on both sides of the highway and the river. The most striking pictures are a large stupa with banners flying, close to the highway, and mythical animals, battle scenes, royal lineages and Buddhist tales across the river on dozens of rocks west of the track. The serene, 2000-year-old Buddha figures seem incongruous at this goatherds' crossing in the middle of nowhere.

Other petroglyphs are at Hodur, Thor and Shatial (see Chilas to Shatial); all can be reached by passenger pickups from Chilas. Details of these and other sites are in two books you might find in Gilgit or Islamabad bookshops: Dr A H Dani's *Human Records on Karakorum Highway* and Dr Karl Jettmar's *Rockcarvings & Inscriptions in the Northern Areas of Pakistan*.

Take water; in summer the banks of the Indus are like an oven.

Places to Stay – bottom end

Three cheapos in the old bazaar have squalid doubles for Rs 40 to Rs 60 – the un-deluxe *Deluxe Hotel* (☎ 208), the *Hamalaya* (☎ 209) next door and the *Khanjrab* (☎ 290, no English sign) at the top of Hospital Rd.

Places to Stay – middle

A *NAPWD Resthouse*, west of the bazaar, has clean doubles with toilet and shower for Rs 150, but it's popular in summer. Others are at Gonar Farm and Jalipur (west of Chilas), Gini (east of Chilas and off the highway) and a primitive one at Babusar village (the only one that closes in winter). All can be booked through the NAWPD Executive Engineer in Chilas.

Best bet down on the highway is the *Kashmir Inn* (☎ 315) with doubles/triples with toilet and cold shower for Rs 100/150. Nearby is the similar *New Shimla Hotel* (☎ 212) at a negotiable Rs 120/180.

Places to Stay – top end

The hospitable *Chilas Inn* (☎ 211) on the KKH has plush hot-shower doubles from Rs 400. Across the road and surrounded by barbed wire is *Shangri-La Midway House*, owned by the infamous Brigadier Aslam.

Places to Eat

A selection of decent food is at the clean *Golden Peak Cafe* in the bazaar. The lower-end hotels, and two cafes on the KKH, serve meat-dhal-and-chapatti and rubber chicken; the *Khanjrab* also has karahi gosht (braised mutton). More elaborate (and expensive) meals at the NAPWD Resthouse are by arrangement.

Getting There & Away

Gilgit Wagons leave from the bus yard every few hours for about Rs 40, or you can flag a through bus on the highway.

Babusar Pass & Kaghan Valley In summer, a Natco 4WD pickup goes up to Babusar village from near the post office at around 8 am, for Rs 30. You may be able to hire a jeep to Naran (in the Kaghan Valley) for about Rs 2500, from the bus yard. A surer way is to hire one in Gilgit. For information about crossing the Babusar Pass, see The Kaghan Valley in the Hazara chapter.

Getting Around

Local pickups will take you from the bus yard to the KKH for a few rupees, Hodur for Rs 10, Thor for Rs 15, and Shatial for Rs 30.

CHILAS TO SHATIAL

West of Chilas the Indus is flat and meandering. On the south side the Lesser Himalaya stretch 80 km south toward the Punjab. On the north side are the Hindu Raj, eastern arm of the Hindu Kush.

From **Hodur**, 20 minutes west of Chilas, take your last (or first) look at Nanga Parbat. Across the river, the remains of a 1000-year-old fort are on a ridge to the right of a ravine called Hodur Gah. The rocks below the fort are covered with old inscriptions. Twenty minutes on (or an hour east of Shatial) is **Thor** ('tore'), site of more inscriptions, below the bridge over Thor Gah.

Fifteen minutes west of Thor, the KKH crosses from the Northern Areas into the North-West Frontier Province (NWFP), passing a line drawn on a map by Sir Cyril Radcliffe in the feverish fortnight before Partition in 1947. This was the intended border between India and Pakistan, disarranged by the Gilgit Uprising. Ten minutes west another line, an ominous string of little white markers, prefigures 'Basha Dam', according to a sign.

SHATIAL

Shatial was once the centre of a little republic, though from the road it seems an ad hoc collection of cafes, wagons, and idle men. If you're travelling on local transport you may have to change here.

Stash your bags in a teahouse and have a look at the petroglyphs east of the bazaar, near the bridge over the Indus. They include a detailed Buddhist tableau and lots of travellers' names (imagine: *Yaqub Qarim of Yarkand was here, 21 June 346. Turkestan Rules!*).

West of Shatial the landscape darkens as the Indus cuts a deep gorge into Kohistan.

Places to Stay

The bazaar has an ultra-basic inn with rope-beds, and a primitive *Forestry Resthouse* (bring your own bedding?), booked with the NAPWD District Forestry Officer at Dasu or the Conservator of Forests in Abbottabad.

Getting There & Away

Datsuns go up-river to Chilas (1½ hours away), wagons down-river to Besham (five to six hours), all day. This is also the transfer point for the Darel and Tangir valleys.

DAREL & TANGIR

Two of the old unruly valley-states that have stayed unruly are Darel ('da-REL') and Tangir ('tahn-GEER'), which meet the Indus across from Shatial. They only voluntarily joined Pakistan in 1952, and even today have the Northern Areas' worst reputation for lawlessness. 'Administration' from Chilas mostly means police garrisons to keep the customary blood feuds from boiling over.

Reports of gun-battles between locals and

Top Left: Dasso Village, Haramosh Valley (JK)
Top Right: Rama Lake & Nanga Parbat, Astore Valley (JK)
Bottom: Farphu villagers, Bagrot Valley (JK)

Top: Shop in bazaar, Gilgit (JK)
Middle: Rice threshing, Alai Valley (JK)
Bottom: Barbers, Sunday Market, Kashgar (RI'A)

police are common, and well-worn travellers' stories tell of theft and even rape. It's hard to separate fact from legend but this clearly isn't a very safe place to go, and outsiders aren't warmly welcomed. It's a pity, because the valleys are said to be rich in natural beauty and archaeological remains. Darel was the site of some important Buddhist monasteries.

Oddly enough, despite their murderous reputation the valley males didn't always measure up to the standards of colonial machismo. One official wrote in 1907:

Their dislike for bloodshed is most marked: where amongst Pathans the disputants would betake themselves to their rifles, here they throw a few stones at each other or indulge in a biting match. If this does not settle matters, recourse is had to ... entertaining the community to dinner on alternate days.

Places to Stay
NAPWD resthouses at Tangir village and Gumari (the main village of Darel), can be booked with the NAPWD Executive Engineer in Chilas.

Getting There & Away
You can hire a pickup at Shatial or a jeep at Chilas. Your first stop should be the Assistant Commissioner or the Chief of Police at Tangir or Gumari. Both are about 20 km from Shatial.

Indus Kohistan

Skirting the western end of the Himalaya at Nanga Parbat, the Indus River cuts a gorge so deep and narrow that some parts see only a few hours of sunlight in a day, and so inhospitable that even the caravan routes bypassed it. When the forerunner of the KKH was driven into the remote canyon in the early 1960s, highway engineers were offered hay to feed their jeeps!

Kohistan, meaning 'land of mountains', refers to the expanse of sub-6000-metre peaks enclosing the upper Swat and Indus valleys. In administrative terms Indus Kohistan includes the Kohistan District and a stretch below Besham where the KKH briefly enters Swat District – both in the North-West Frontier Province (NWFP).

Its yawning, crumbling terrain made Indus Kohistan one of the most harrowing passages in Asia. The intrepid Chinese Buddhist pilgrim Fa-Hsien, having already crossed most of China, the Tarim Basin and the Karakoram on foot, was awestruck. In 403 AD he wrote about the passage down the Indus from Darel to Swat:

The road is difficult and broken, with steep crags and precipices in the way. The mountainside is like a stone wall 10,000 feet high. Looking down, the sight is confused and there is no sure foothold ... In old days men bored through the walls to make a way, and spread out ladders, of which there are 700 in all to pass. Having passed these, we proceed by a hanging rope bridge to cross the river.

Kohistanis live, literally and figuratively, in the shadow of their surroundings. Nanga Parbat in its slow upheaval has dealt them a steady stream of catastrophes. The worst in modern times were the floods following the 1841 landslide near Raikot Bridge (see Gilgit to Chilas in the previous chapter) and a massive earthquake at Pattan in 1974 that buried entire villages and killed more than 7000 people (and wrecked some 60 km of the KKH).

The region's old nickname was *Yaghistan*, 'land of the ungoverned'. Outlaws could hide here without fear of capture; tribal warfare and blood-feuds were commonplace. Stone watchtowers and fortified houses can still be seen in the older villages. The Sikhs, the British and then the Pakistanis left Kohistan more or less alone.

But in 1976, as the KKH was nearing completion, Pakistan took an interest in these semi-autonomous areas and a Kohistan District was created from them, partly at least to protect the highway. The district government relies heavily on the police and the NWFP's Frontier Constabulary, whose large forts dot the valley. Away from the KKH, outside authority diminishes quickly.

Not surprisingly, travellers tend to rush through. The highway bazaars are depressing even on a sunny day, and on the road, sometimes hundreds of metres above the thrashing Indus, you can empathise with Fa-Hsien. And the setting seems to induce a kind of nihilistic abandon in bus drivers.

But this is one of the most dramatic of all Pakistan's mountain roads, and especially in the early morning its side-canyons and corduroy hillsides are magnificent. As usual, the best is off the highway. It would be madness to go off at random into the hills, but there are some safe and beautiful detours. Outsiders tend to be treated with reserve, though hospitality turns up everywhere.

Armed tribesman, Kohistan

162

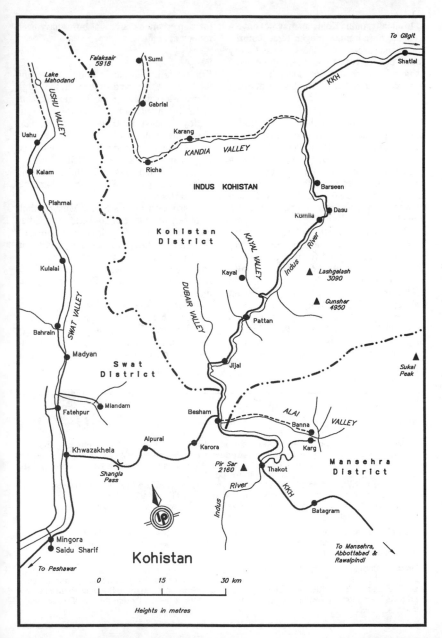

Kohistan

0   15   30 km

Heights in metres

Ironically, Indus Kohistan may not have a living river in it much longer. Near Komila, Kayal and several other spots, signs identify future dam sites that could turn the narrow canyon into a chain of lakes (on the face of it a pretty stupid idea, in this earthquake zone).

A Word of Caution Off the KKH, Indus Kohistan is fairly lawless. Locals may advise you not to go into the hills alone; the police will advise you not to go at all, reciting stories of robbery, assault or rape. Many travellers do indeed find the vibes bad. On top of a reputation for anarchy, many local men have skewed ideas about Western women.

It's tempting to see the police as an occupying army, but of course if they weren't there, we couldn't go. If you plan to get more than a few hours off the KKH, especially between Shatial and Pattan, you should inform the local Chief of Police or District Officer of the Frontier Constabulary.

Even if you're just passing through, you may find the police delaying vehicles travelling after dark (possibly as far south as Mansehra) until enough have collected to form an escorted convoy, as buses have been robbed at night.

People

Kohistanis are an ethnic hodge-podge and the faces are as varied as those in the Gilgit bazaar. Most are thought to be Shins, descendants of invaders from the lower Indus Valley at least 1000 years ago. Pathans (Pashtuns), whose tribes straddle the Pakistan-Afghanistan border and who have ruled in lower Swat since the 15th century, expanded into Kohistan in the 1700s and 1800s. Along the KKH they predominate around Besham.

Nearly everyone is Sunni Muslim, their forebears having been converted by Pathan missionaries from the 14th century onward. Five times a day you'll see men setting out their prayer mats wherever they are – in cornfields, motel courtyards, by the roadside; your own bus driver may stop at a local mosque.

In their harsh environment Shins eke out a living where others couldn't, by a strenuous hybrid of nomadic and sedentary lifestyles. Shepherds drive animals to high summer meadows in most south Asian

**Cyclists' Notes,
Indus Kohistan**

Cyclists – with their obviously expensive gear, skin-tight clothing that may offend orthodox Muslims, and a tendency to explore where others can't – are especially vulnerable in Indus Kohistan. There are unverified stories of theft and assault (and a rape of a lone woman cyclist near Dasu), though in fact very few report any problems.

At Dasu's C&W Executive Engineer's office you can book the good C&W resthouses at Dasu, Pattan, Besham and Chattar Plain in Hazara. At the District Forestry Office in Dasu you can book decent Forestry resthouses at Shatial, Kayal Valley and Dubair Valley. Booking will greatly improve your chances of getting in.

Shatial to Dasu, 63 km Shatial has a basic inn and primitive resthouse. PTDC has an expensive motel at Barseen, about 15 km north of Dasu, but it's more pleasant to stay at Dasu, which has a few hotels and a good C&W Resthouse.

Dasu to Besham, 78 km The road climbs high on the canyon wall. Pleasant resthouses and basic food are at Kayal Valley, Pattan and Dubair Valley, respectively about 30, 40 and 60 km south of Dasu. On the KKH at Pattan is a filthy but friendly inn with food. South of Pattan some hamlets have stone-throwing kids. Besham has numerous hotels, though the C&W Resthouse there is superb.

mountain valleys, but here nearly *everyone* moves up and down, and many riverside villages are little more than places to wait out the winter. A typical cycle takes villagers from the river to higher farmland (maize is the staple crop) in April-May, on to high pastures in early June and to higher pastures (as much as 3000 metres above the river) in July, then down starting in mid-September.

Kohistani speech is a mixture of Shina, Pashto, Urdu and even Arabic. Pashto, the speech of the Pathans, is spoken around Besham and in the upper Kandia Valley. Beyond the Komila and Besham bazaars, little English is spoken except by officials.

SHATIAL TO DASU & KOMILA

West of Shatial the Indus suddenly turns south. Ten minutes south of the bend (40 minutes north of Dasu) is the confluence with the 80-km-long **Kandia Valley**, a major Indus tributary and until the 1800s a prominent kingdom of Kohistan. For almost a km the Kandia River runs parallel to the Indus behind a razor-sharp ridge before emerging, emerald-green.

To the north of Dasu, the road clings to increasingly vertical canyon walls, until in places it's just an amazing notch in a sheer granite face. Highway workers became mountaineers here, often lowered on ropes to drill and set charges. Massive blasting loosened the mountains for several km up and down the valley. This stretch took a year to carve and cost more workers' lives per km than any other part of the KKH.

Strangely enough, across the river are broad, shallow slopes where a highway would be much easier to build. In fact, that was the original plan. But villagers whose marginal landholdings were threatened put up such fierce resistance – sabotaging equipment, stealing supplies, harassing workers – that in the end the road was realigned.

Places to Stay

About 15 km north of Dasu at Barseen is a four-room *PTDC Motel* with doubles for Rs 475. Travellers say it's miserable, with noisy generator, problematic water, etc.

DASU & KOMILA

A century ago, a fugitive from one side of the Indus only had to cross to the other side to be safe, and even 20 years ago towns like Dasu and Komila were worlds apart. Since being linked by the KKH bridge they have become a single extended town, the biggest between Chilas and Besham.

Dasu, headquarters of Kohistan District, has government offices and resthouses. Komila has the bazaar and regional transport. Opposite Komila, tiny Jalkot was once the main village of the area but has faded away since the KKH arrived.

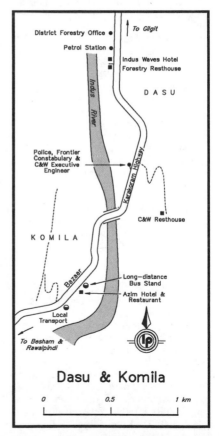

Dasu & Komila

Information

Komila has a tiny upstairs post office. North of the bridge in Dasu are police, Frontier Constabulary and the office of the Executive Engineer, NAPWD Construction & Works Department (☎ 25), where you can book C&W resthouses here and at Pattan, Besham and Chattar Plain. The District Forestry Office, where you can book Forestry resthouses here and at Shatial, Kayal, Sharakot and Dubair, is in Dasu, 100 metres north of the petrol station.

Kandia Valley

This deep valley north of Dasu was an independent princely state until the 1800s, when Pathan influence and Sunni orthodoxy began percolating in from lower Swat. In 1939 Swat annexed it, but lost it in 1976 to Pakistan's new Kohistan District.

Kandia has a scattering of villages, the largest of which is Karang, 30 km from the Indus. From Gabrial, 65 km in, a track crosses west to the Ushu River in upper Swat. From Sumi, near the head of the valley, another trek into Swat is a loop around 5918-metre Falaksair.

However, multi-day trips should *not* be attempted without a guide who is known in the valley, and without informing the police or Frontier Constabulary at Dasu.

A long day trip looks feasible by passenger Suzuki from Komila bazaar. Start early to allow enough time to get a ride back; Sumi is four hours from Komila.

Places to Stay & Eat

Decent budget accommodation and food on the Komila side are at the big green *Azim Hotel & Restaurant* and general store (☎ 31). Doubles/triples with toilet are Rs 60/80 and there are cheaper rooms with shared loo. Other meat-and-chapatti cafes have rope-beds but aren't eager for Western guests.

On the Dasu side, air-conditioned doubles with hot shower at the quiet *C&W Resthouse*, up a track north of the police station, are a bargain at Rs 150 (but some travellers were told Rs 300). The Kohistani cook is first-rate.

Book with the Executive Engineer here or the Senior Divisional Officer at Besham.

Doubles at the *Forestry Resthouse*, 1¼ km north of the bridge are overpriced at Rs 200. A better deal is the cheerful *Indus Waves Hotel* next door, where a double with shared toilet is Rs 60, and a triple with attached bath is Rs 100. North of the petrol station the *Azeem Golden Hotel* has dreary triples for Rs 60.

Getting There & Away

Catch regional transport in upper Komila bazaar. Passenger Suzukis go all day to Sumi in the Kandia Valley for Rs 30.

Long-distance buses and vans use a wide space below the Azim Hotel, and may also stop at the petrol station or the Indus Waves Hotel in Dasu. Wagons to Pattan are Rs 15, and to Besham Rs 30. GTS buses go to Besham at 5.30 and 6 am for about Rs 20. For Chilas, change at Shatial (Rs 25).

DASU & KOMILA TO PATTAN

The pyramid peak south of Dasu is Lashgelash (3090 metres); soon saw-tooth Gunsher (4950 metres) looms south of it. In spring or after rain the dark gorge lined with white peaks is powerfully photogenic – and hair-raising: the crumbly walls slide regularly and the Indus looks miles away below. Across the river, houses cling to isolated, impossible slopes as if banished there.

Kayal Valley

About 50 minutes south of Komila (20 minutes north of Pattan) the highway slithers into a nala so narrow the traffic on the other side seems within reach. At the end, south of the bridge, a jeep road climbs seven km to Kayal village. Above that the valley divides and a track up the right fork continues for 15 km to pastures at 3000 metres. Do not venture very far in without good local advice, as outsiders may not be warmly welcomed.

Places to Stay & Eat Just up a track north of the bridge is a *Forestry Resthouse*, with two doubles with cold shower for Rs 200; it

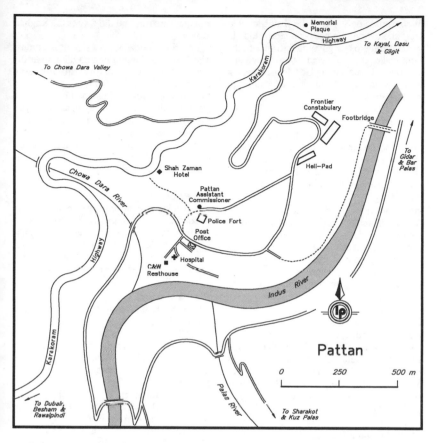

Pattan

can be booked in Dasu (District Forestry Officer) or Abbottabad (Conservator of Forests). The caretaker lives at the back of the resthouse. It would be easy to stay here for weeks. But the KKH shacks have only meat-and-chapatti and snacks, so bring your own food.

Getting There & Away Passenger Suzukis and Datsuns pass frequently between Pattan and Komila. Occasional passenger jeeps go to Kayal village from Pattan bazaar.

PATTAN

Pattan ('PAH-tahn') sits in a fertile bowl where the Indus is joined by the Chowa Dara and Palas rivers. The Indus snakes through a cross-grain of ridgelines, making for multi-layered scenery and many tributaries.

This was the centre of the catastrophic earthquake of 1974 in which entire sections of valley wall collapsed, burying whole villages and killing thousands of people. A vast amount of relief money poured in, which accounts for the 'new' look of the place. There are no ruins; arable land is too scarce (it comprises only 4% of the Kohistan District) and everything has been redeveloped.

According to one government worker, the earthquake was followed by a noticeable upsurge in virtue among God-fearing locals, so that even today Pattan is a safer area for travel than, say, Dasu.

Orientation

The village is far below the highway. A link road descends from near a KKH memorial, but buses drop you almost a km south on a bluff above the village, from where you can short-cut straight down like everyone else.

Information

A small hospital is next to the C&W Resthouse. The Assistant Commissioner is a good source of information on roads, villages and people in the upper valleys. His office, near the police fort, is a good place to stop before doing anything more than a day trip here.

Chowa Dara Valley

The steep Chowa Dara ('CHO-wa da-RA') Valley makes a fine day hike, with channels and terraced fields, and hamlets every few km. A jeep road from the KKH north of the bus stop will eventually reach 15 km (and climb 1400 metres) to Chowa Dara village at the head of the valley.

Old Indus Jeep Road

A two-hour loop, with views of the Chowa Dara Valley, takes in a few km of the pre-KKH jeep road on the other side of the Indus. At the west end of the Pattan bazaar, the lower road crosses the Chowa Dara, the Indus and the Palas River. Up-river, a footbridge connects to a path back to the bazaar.

Palas Valley

The canyon across the Indus from Pattan offers some strenuous day hiking and possible overnight stops. About 12 km up a jeep road (less by a steep mule track) is Sharakot village. Beyond it, the pastures of Kuz Palas (Lower Palas) are said to be very beautiful,

and there are trails all the way to the Kaghan Valley.

Few foreigners visit this side of the Indus. The Assistant Commissioner will have information on the road and the Forestry Resthouse at Sharakot, as well as advice on local protocol (eg paying a call on Sharakot elders would be a good idea). In any case you should call in at the Sharakot police post.

Cross the Indus on the road west from the Pattan bazaar or by the footbridge up-river. Occasional jeeps to Sharakot from the bazaar are around Rs 25. Bring your own food.

Bar Palas

A longer jeep trip on the east side of the Indus looks possible. About 15 km north on the old road a track turns up into the Gidar ('guh-DAHR') Valley. It's 20 km more up to Gidar village, above which are meadows beneath a glacier at Bar Palas (Upper Palas).

Places to Stay

At the KKH bus stop is the friendly *Shah Zaman Hotel*, with pretty disgusting four-charpoy rooms with attached loo for Rs 60. A peaceful *C&W Resthouse* is on the banks of the Indus below the bazaar; comfortable doubles with hot shower are Rs 150. It's popular so book it if you can, with the Executive Engineer in Dasu or the Senior Divisional Officer at Besham. The caretaker lives to the right of the gate.

Forestry resthouses in the Kayal and Dubair valleys are within reach by passenger Suzuki.

Places to Eat

The chowkidar at the resthouse will fix a very basic meal at cost. The *Shah Zaman Hotel* has meat and dhal. Shops in the poor bazaar have biscuits and occasional fruit.

Getting There & Away

The climb from the bazaar to the highway is a killer and there is no regular transport. From the highway, passenger Suzukis and Datsuns go to Dubair Valley, Besham, Kayal and Komila for under Rs 10.

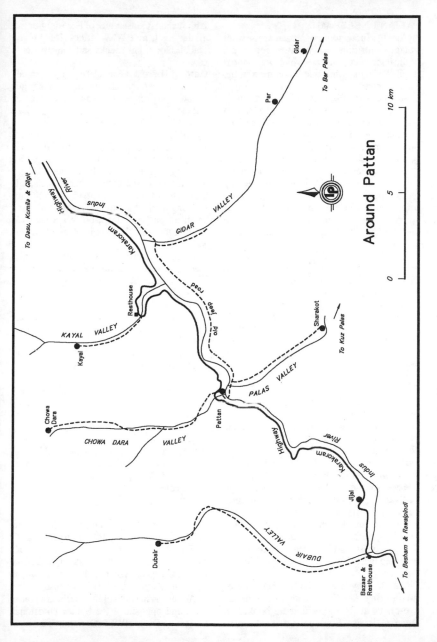

Around Pattan

PATTAN TO BESHAM

Across the Indus south of Pattan are several villages with stone watchtowers, reminders of the inter-valley warfare which was typical of pre-KKH days and is still common in the high country.

At **Jijal** (or Jajial), 20 minutes south of Pattan, the KKH crosses onto the Indian subcontinent, geologically speaking. The Himalaya and Karakoram were born some 50 million years ago in a cataclysmic slow-motion collision between a drifting 'Indian plate' and the Asian landmass. The green rocks at Jijal were part of a chain of volcanic islands trapped against Asia, and the contorted white and grey material 100 metres south belongs to the subcontinent. See Geology in the Facts about the Region chapter.

The canyon walls are very slide-prone here. Frontier Works Organisation crews in their tan overalls are a common sight, endlessly rebuilding the scarred road.

A few minutes south of Jijal a startling bright blue plume in the muddy Indus is actually its confluence with the clear Dubair River. Across the Indus are your last (or first) road views of permanent snow on the angular summits of the Lesser Himalaya.

Dubair Valley

Half an hour south of Pattan (¾ hour north of Besham) is a rambling highway bazaar at Dubair ('doo-BARE') Valley. South of the bridge a jeep track climbs up beside a fast, clear stream, past terraced fields irrigated by wooden aqueducts and guarded by scarecrows with Chitrali hats.

The lower end of the valley looks too cultivated and well-trafficked for camping, but it would make a good day hike. Dubair village is about 15 km in, and a mule track reaches a further 20 km to the valley head, though you should get local advice before going up there.

Places to Stay Just off the KKH is a peaceful *Forestry Resthouse* with two doubles, overpriced at Rs 200, which are booked in Dasu (District Forestry Officer) or in Abbottabad (Conservator of Forests) – or ask at the Besham PTDC office. The ragged Dubair bazaar has snacks and some fruit.

Getting There & Away Get off any Besham-Pattan transport. Occasional passenger Datsuns go on up the canyon to Dubair village.

BESHAM

Besham ('beh-SHAAM' or 'beh-SHUM') is a long-distance transport junction about midway between Rawalpindi and Gilgit, with a few tourist hotels, cheap serais, all-night shops and a main road choked with honking trucks and buses. This is no place to catch up on your sleep, but it's a base for visiting the Alai Valley, and pleasant Dubair Valley is not far away.

Besham is actually in Swat District, which reaches east to the Indus here. Swat, once a princely state like Hunza, was conquered during the 15th to 17th centuries by Pathans (Pashtuns). Besham is now mostly a Pathan town, and the common speech is Pashto. Pathans call the Indus *Abaseen*, 'father of rivers'.

The forerunner of the Karakoram Highway was the Indus Valley Rd, meant to link the Northern Areas, not south to Hazara but west to Swat over the scenic Shangla Pass. Besham is still the junction for buses to Swat.

Orientation

Nearly everything is right on the KKH. Most transport in every direction starts from near the fork to Swat, where the serais and teahouses are too.

Information

For Northern Areas brochures and current information on road conditions try the PTDC (☎ 92), 2½ km south of town at the PTDC Motel, accessible by local passenger Suzuki for a few rupees (you may have to ask for it by its old name, the KDB Resthouse).

About ¾ km south of the bazaar is a police post, and opposite it the Senior Divisional Officer (SDO), NWFP Communication &

Works Department (☎ 52), where you can book C&W resthouses here and at Dasu, Pattan and Chattar Plain. Also south of the bazaar are a post office and telephone exchange. The District Hospital is down a side road near the Swat junction.

Besham Qila

Some maps call the town Besham Qila, Pashto for Besham Fort, referring to a fortified villa built here by the former Wali of Swat around 1945. On the KKH, 400 metres north of the Swat junction, it's now a private residence – probably for offspring of the old royal family.

Fa-Hsien's Crossing

The Chinese pilgrim Fa-Hsien described a harrowing passage through Indus Kohistan, ending with 'a bridge of ropes, by which the river was crossed, its banks there being 80 paces apart'. In 1941 the Hungarian-English explorer Sir Aurel Stein concluded that the site of this bridge was near Kunshe village, south of Besham, where the Indus squeezes between vertical rock walls. The spot is just below the Kund Bridge, up-river from the PTDC Motel.

Stein also mentions the ruins of a watchtower on an outcrop above the bridge, probably on the west side.

KDB Road-Marker

By the road south of town, below an obelisk honouring the Kohistan Development Board (which oversaw development of this area after the 1974 Pattan earthquake), is a great stone marker that includes the distances to Karachi, Kashgar, Beijing and other points. It's 20 minutes out, a few rupees on a Thakot-bound Suzuki, and flagging a ride back is easy.

Dubair Valley

This long valley, ¾ hour north of Besham, has a peaceful resthouse. See Pattan to Besham in this chapter.

Places to Stay – bottom end

Serais near the Swat junction have grotty

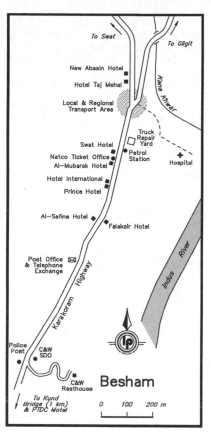

doubles for around Rs 30 and rope-beds in the open for less. Two that welcome foreigners are the *Swat Hotel* and the *Al-Mubarak Hotel*.

The *Hotel International* (☎ 65) has adequate doubles with shower and 'flushsistom' for Rs 50 and Rs 80. The *Prince Hotel* (☎ 56) next door is a bit cheaper. Both are cursed with a loud music shop nearby. Marginally quieter are the *Al-Safina Hotel* (☎ 64), with doubles/triples for Rs 50/70, and the *Falaksir Hotel* (☎ 30) across the road, with doubles from Rs 80. Too far to walk is the *Al-Madina*, 1½ km south of the bazaar.

The friendly *New Abasin Hotel* (☎ 38) just north of the Swat junction has plain, clean doubles/triples with loo and shower for around Rs 90/120 (but with upper windows that can act like mirrors to the hallway outside). The *Hotel Taj Mehal* next door is more or less equivalent.

Prices seem to vary a lot with the season. All but the serais have generator electricity.

Places to Stay – middle

Five minutes' walk down a track near the police post is a quiet, comfortable *C&W Resthouse* with doubles for Rs 150 and a friendly chowkidar. Book it with the C&W Senior Divisional Officer (☎ 52) up on the main road, or the Executive Engineer in Dasu.

Places to Stay – top end

The *PTDC Motel* has clean bed linen, tiled bathrooms and high prices (eg doubles for Rs 600).

Places to Eat

The serais have cheap meat, vegetables and omelettes, and the *Swat Hotel* also has good chapli kebabs. In the morning, try deep-fried puri pastry with sweet orange halwa. The best hotel restaurants are probably at the *Taj Mehal* and *New Abasin*. A long way south of town is the *Indus View Restaurant*. Shops have snacks, fruit and basic supplies.

Getting There & Away

Rawalpindi-Gilgit Buses Natco and Mashabrum Tours stop near the Swat Hotel but may not have empty seats. 'Pindi-bound buses come through eight to 10 hours after leaving Gilgit, and are about Rs 65 from Besham, except the Natco 'deluxe' around 5 to 6 pm, which is a little more.

Gilgit-bound buses come through six to seven hours after leaving 'Pindi, and are about Rs 105, except Natco's 'deluxe' around 3 to 4 pm. The Prince Hotel runs three minibuses a day to Gilgit, leaving when they're full, for Rs 110.

Mansehra Wagons go frequently from beside the Swat Hotel for about Rs 30.

North-Bound Local Suzukis, Datsuns and wagons leave from Swat junction when they're full, for Pattan (Rs 15) and Dasu (Rs 30).

ALAI VALLEY

The 100,000 or so people of the beautiful Alai ('ah-LYE') Valley are Pathans whose forebears were probably driven out of Swat in the 16th century. They had their own ruler or nawab and were mostly left alone until the late 1970s, when the area was brought under NWFP control (enforced from the huge Frontier Constabulary stockade in the middle of the valley) and Nawab Ayub Khan was demoted to a parliamentary delegate.

In spite of the Pathans' love of independence and the fact that everyone here is armed to the teeth, the change apparently came without bloodshed. In fact Ayub Khan (who lives in the village of Biarai) remains the valley's effective leader.

Though surprised to see foreigners, people are instinctively hospitable. Try out *asalaam aleikhum* and a few Pashto words. If you show your respect for their Sunni orthodoxy – particularly by dressing modestly – you may enjoy some legendary Pathan hospitality. Only the present generation (and mainly boys) are learning English; if you need a translator, watch for schoolboys in their berets.

You get to Alai from Thakot on a road so lofty that near the top you can see 20 km of the Indus in one sweep – reason enough to go, with the valley as a bonus, lush with maize, rice terraces and orchards and rising to pine-clad mountains. The optimal visit is probably a long day trip from Besham, but since transport is unpredictable a back-up resthouse booking is a good idea.

Down in Besham people may advise you to avoid Alai, or at least to register with the police when you get there. The police may ask you to accept an escort – sound advice in many parts of Indus Kohistan but inappropriate for a respectful visitor here.

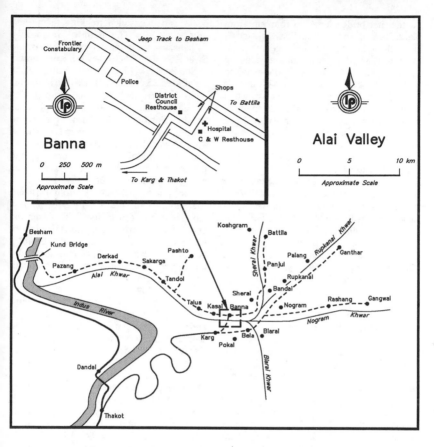

The valley is cool even in summer, so take an extra layer. From November to April it's very cold, with snow by December.

Orientation & Information

The 29-km Thakot-Alai road rises more than one vertical km. A single hamlet, Kanai, is about halfway up. From the end of the bus line at Karg, walk half a km back for good views of the Indus. A long way down-river you can see Thakot bridge, and above it flat-topped Pir Sar.

At the east end of Karg, fork left to the main village of Banna across the Alai River, with a red-roofed District Council Resthouse, C&W Resthouse and a small hospital. Left from Banna is the police post, Frontier Constabulary fort and a jeep track running 30 km down-valley directly to Besham.

Things to See

The road from Banna up Sherai Khwar (*khwar* is Pashto for river or canyon) offers the best up-valley views. The right fork at Karg eventually takes you into Rupkanai Khwar, at the head of which is Sukai Peak.

At the first bridge, three to four km from Karg, look up toward Biarai, which locals say is the valley's prettiest village.

Choar is a vast alpine meadow area, as big as Alai itself, a long day's walk (one-way) up both the Rupkanai and Nogram khwars. It's accessible only from May to August, when herds are driven up to it. You can camp there, even trek across to the Kaghan Valley, but a local guide is essential; try asking at Pokal village.

Places to Stay & Eat
There are two resthouses and some tea shops but no hotels or restaurants. The *C&W Resthouse* in Banna, with doubles for Rs 150, is under the jurisdiction of the Executive Engineer in Mansehra but you might get help from PTDC or the Executive Engineer in Besham. You can arrange meals with the chowkidar, or bring your own food. There are also said to be *Forestry Resthouses* here and up Nogram Khwar at Gangwal.

Getting There & Away
Alai is actually in Mansehra District, not Kohistan, but its road access is from the Indus. Occasional cargo jeeps make the two-hour trip up the jeep track from Kund Bridge south of Besham, but there's no passenger service that way yet.

Until there is, you must go the long way via Thakot ('ta-KOTE'), 28 km south of Besham on the KKH, Rs 10 on a Suzuki or wagon. From there several buses climb to Karg every day, a two to three-hour trip for Rs 15. Datsun pickups go when they're full for Rs 20. You can hire a Datsun for about Rs 250 one way.

Getting Around
The occasional cargo jeep will take you to Alai's upper villages for a few rupees.

SWAT VALLEY
The Swat Valley parallels the Indus to the west. The upper end (see the Kohistan map on page 163) is known for its rough natural beauty and deodar-forested, snow-capped peaks, and for excellent trekking, fishing and winter skiing. The people are mainly Pathans, except in the extreme north, called Swat Kohistan, where they are Kohistanis.

Southern Swat has been a civilised place for at least 35 centuries. It was the northernmost end of the Buddhist empires of Gandhara, and probably the birthplace of Vajrayana or Tantric Buddhism which, in the 7th century, took root directly in Ladakh and Tibet. A wealth of ruined stupas, monasteries and non-Buddhist sites are open to the public, and the Swat museum has artefacts dating from the 2nd century BC.

The year-round passage from Besham, four hours over the 2134-metre Shangla Pass, is a fine trip in itself. This was the ancient route from the Indus Valley to Peshawar and the plains. In fact, if you're bound for Peshawar, Swat is quicker and more interesting than going via Rawalpindi.

Places to Stay
Forestry resthouses at Alpurai and Yakhtangai on the east side of the Shangla, and another near the summit, can be booked with the Conservator of Forests in Saidu Sharif or District Forestry Officer in Mingora.

Mingora & Saidu Sharif
Swat's traditional seat of government is Saidu Sharif, while its sister city, Mingora, is mainly a market town and long-distance transport hub. This is the most urbanised centre in the northern mountains, and its noise, pollution and manic pace will come as a shock if you've just come down from the Northern Areas.

Orientation Mingora is on the south bank of the Swat River beside the main Swat Valley road. Saidu Sharif's Swat Museum is about one km south of the Mingora bazaar and the Swat Serena Hotel just over a km further. Passenger Suzukis and motor-rickshaws are plentiful. The airport is about four km northwest of Mingora.

Information The helpful PTDC office

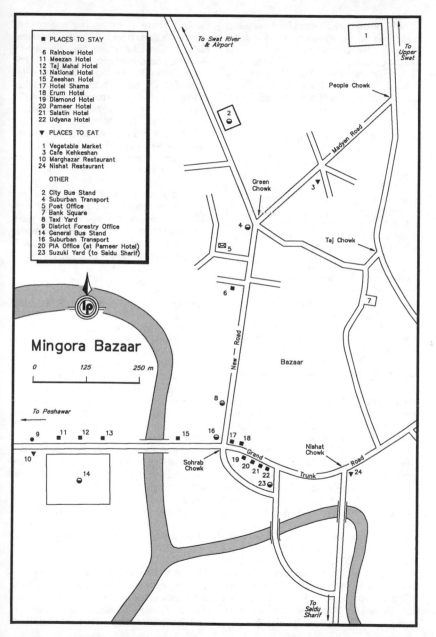

(☎ 5007) at the Swat Serena Hotel has information on hotels, transport, local archaeology, the museum and the upper valley. At Mingora's Bank Square several banks will do foreign exchange. The Mingora post office is behind the Suzuki yard at Green Chowk; in Saidu Sharif it's on the main road, south of the Swat Serena.

Museum & Buddhist Sites in the City The Swat Museum is stuffed with artefacts from Swat's pre-Buddhist and Buddhist sites.

Several excavations are right in Saidu Sharif. Butkara No 1, one km east of the museum and centred on an enormous 3rd-century stupa, has yielded one of Swat's richest harvests of artefacts. The remains of another large stupa and monastery are behind Central Hospital.

Nearby Sites The most interesting site near Saidu Sharif is to the south at Udegram, with remains of the Buddhist town of Ora (defeated by Alexander the Great in the 4th century BC), the mountainside citadel of the region's last Hindu raja and a mosque from the time of Mahmud of Ghazni.

A serene 7th-century Buddha carved on a rockface is north of Mingora at Jehanabad.

Places to Stay There are dozens of hotels, mostly in Mingora. Three noisy bottom-end places are opposite the general bus stand. Marginally quieter ones are nearby on the Grand Trunk or GT Rd – the *Shams, Erum, Diamond, Salatin* and *Udyana*, with singles/doubles for around Rs 50/80 and pricier rooms with hot showers. The *Udyana* is probably the best of the lot. Off New Rd the friendly, quiet *Rainbow* has doubles for Rs 80.

A decent mid-range place on GT Rd is the *Zeeshan Hotel* with singles/doubles for Rs 80/120 (Rs 200/300 with hot showers). At the top end are the centrally located *Pameer Hotel* on GT Rd (Rs 450/550) and Saidu Sharif's luxurious *Swat Serena Hotel* at Rs 683/920 and up. The Serena's food is first-class.

Getting There & Away The general bus stand is on the GT Rd in Mingora. Vans and buses go there all day from Swat junction in Besham, a three-hour trip for Rs 20 to Rs 25. Some, including Government Transport Service (GTS) buses, may go to a smaller station on New Rd. Transport is plentiful from Mingora on to Peshawar (three hours) and Rawalpindi (five hours).

PIA flies to Saidu Sharif daily from Islamabad (for Rs 505) and Peshawar (Rs 215) and, weather permitting, on Saturdays from Chitral (Rs 460).

Getting Around Passenger Suzukis ply between Mingora bazaar and Saidu Sharif Rd for a rupee or two, and there are many motor-rickshaws. There may be occasional buses to the airport from the city bus stand, though the easiest airport transport is to hire a Suzuki for about Rs 50.

Upper Swat
Miandam is a touristy resort at 1820 metres, an hour's drive north of Mingora and 10 km up a side-valley. **Madyan**, by the Swat River 1¼ hours from Mingora, was a hippy haven in the 1960s and 1970s and is still a popular place to relax. Just north of it is **Bahrain**, a good place to shop for Swat's famous carved furniture. At 2070 metres and 100 km from Mingora on a gradually disintegrating road is the glum Kohistani village of **Kalam**, centre of an independent state in the 19th century.

Beyond Kalam, up the heavily forested Utrot and Ushu river valleys, is legendary trout fishing and world-class trekking, but although new hotels continue to spring up like weeds, the area is not safe to trek without a trustworthy (and armed) local guide.

About 25 km up the Ushu Valley is Lake Mahodand and views of Swat's highest peak, Falaksair.

Places to Stay In Upper swat, hotel prices are *very* seasonal, with absurd bargains in the off-season. There are a few plain but nicely located *Forestry resthouses* at Rs 200, 300 and 400 per double, some booked through

Top: Pattan Village on the Indus River, Indus Kohistan (JK)
Bottom Left: Komila bazaar & KKH bridge, Indus Kohistan (JK)
Bottom Right: Indus River, south of Dassu, Indus Kohistan (JK)

Top: Goatherd, near Karimabad (JK)
Middle: Blacksmith, Kashgar (RI'A)
Bottom: Polo match, Gilgit (JK)

the Conservator of Forests in Saidu Sharif or the District Forestry Officer in Mingora. Camping is safe as far north as Madyan.

Miandam

Doubles at the *Nizara* and *Karashma* hotels start at about Rs 150. At the *Green Peaks* they're Rs 300 and up.

Madyan

For cheap rope-beds in a village house, ask at Muambar Khan's shop. The best mid-range choice is *Caravans Guesthouse*, where rooms with cold shower are about Rs 75/bed. The *Imran Hotel* in the bazaar has doubles from Rs 100.

Bahrain Hot-water doubles start about Rs 70 at the *Bahrain* and *Decent* hotels and Rs 150 at the *Deluxe Hotel*

Kalam

The prominent cold-water cheapo in the bazaar is the *Khalid Hotel* with doubles from Rs 100. Decent mid-range places include the *Shangrilla* and *Falak Naz*, with doubles for Rs 150 to Rs 200. Best at the top end (Rs 300 to Rs 500/double) are the *Manano Inn*, *Pameer Hotel* and *Motel Sangam*.

Ushu

The *Ushu Hotel* has doubles for Rs 150 to Rs 300 in mid-summer. There are resthouses at Ushu, Utrot and Gabral.

Getting There & Away Mingora's general bus stand has plentiful up-valley transport. To go directly from the KKH to upper Swat, change at Khwazakhela.

BESHAM TO THAKOT

Forty minutes south of Besham the KKH crosses the Indus on an elegant suspension bridge decorated with stone lions and a big sign, 'Welcome to the Karakoram Highway'. In 1976 a lively party was held here, with Pakistani and Chinese music and dance, to open the bridge and celebrate the completion of the Indus Valley Rd. On either side are seedy roadside bazaars, **Dandai** on the west and **Thakot** on the east.

This is the southernmost of the Chinese bridges, and in many respects the real southern end of the KKH is at Thakot, not at the railhead at Havelian. The highway has run beside one or another branch of the Indus since the first trickle at the Khunjerab. A few km from here it leaves the wide and heavy 'Father of Rivers' behind, and soon climbs down out of the mountains as well.

Hazara

Below Thakot the KKH leaves the Indus Valley, climbs briefly and then descends through progressively gentler countryside to the upland plateau of Rawalpindi and Islamabad. This is a region of forested mountains below 4000 metres, with a series of broad, fertile valleys up its middle. Ease of travel through these valleys has for centuries made this a gateway from the south into the mountains, toward Kashmir and Gilgit.

The region's historical name is Hazara. Its natural boundaries are the Indus River on the west, the Margalla and Murree hills on the south and east, and the peaks of the Lesser Himalaya to the north. In administrative terms it includes the Abbottabad and Mansehra districts of North-West Frontier Province (NWFP).

If you're south-bound, Hazara is a way to ease back into civilisation, though it may feel like you've left the real KKH behind – no more Chinese bridges, no more outlaws, no more fickle, harrowing high-road. If you're north-bound, Hazara will be your first escape from the thick air of the Punjab.

History
As the strength of the Moghul Empire waned in the 1700s the region was for a time under the control of various Afghan chieftains. One of them in 1799 granted the governorship of Lahore to Ranjit Singh, a Sikh warlord from the Punjab. Ranjit expanded his domain into a small empire that by the time of his death in 1839 included most of the Punjab, Kashmir, Hazara and Peshawar.

An early treaty with the British had barred his expansion south-east, but in 1845 this was violated by the regent who succeeded him. Following the short and bloody Sikh Wars of 1846 and 1849 the British annexed the entire state, including Hazara. At Partition in 1947, Hazara's Sikhs fled to India.

Many Hazara and Punjab towns still have buildings from this time, including fortifications from before the Sikh Wars and

---

Cyclists' Notes, Hazara

In addition to accommodation noted here, there are numerous hotels in Besham, Mansehra and Abbottabad. Further cyclists' notes are in the Kaghan Valley section of this chapter.

Besham to Chattar Plain, 70 km The KKH climbs out of the Indus Valley at Thakot, 28 km south of Besham. Batagram, 20 km up from Thakot, has a few cheap hotels. The road climbs for 16 km beyond Batagram to a 1670-metre pass with a pricey PTDC Motel. But just beyond the pass is a peaceful C&W Resthouse overlooking Chattar Plain (book it at Dasu, Besham or Mansehra).

Chattar Plain to Mansehra, about 55 km About 20 km from Chattar Plain, just north of Shinkiari, is the isolated (and pricey?) Jangal Mangal tourist restaurant. There is cheap food along the road south of Shinkiari. An alternative route is on the back road via Batal village and Dadar.

Mansehra to Hasan Abdal, about 100 km Traffic is very heavy and drivers are reckless. Abbottabad is about 25 km from Mansehra. In the 15 km from Abbottabad to Haripur the KKH drops almost 500 metres. South of Haripur the road is flat for 35 km to Hasan Abdal. Alternative routes to Rawalpindi are the very hilly road from Abbottabad via Murree, and the rough road from Haripur directly to Taxila. Taxila bazaar is horribly congested.

Hasan Abdal to Rawalpindi, about 50 km This follows the Grand Trunk Rd, a high-speed divided highway that is neither enjoyable nor very safe for cyclists.

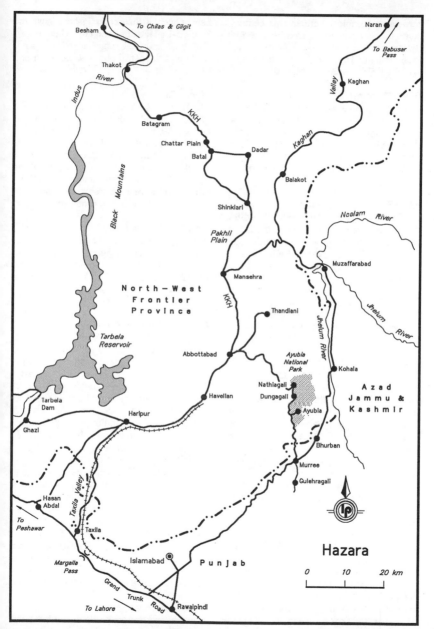

Hazara

0   10   20 km

gurdwaras (temples) built in this century. Some towns have names from this period: Haripur and Mansehra, for example, were strongholds of Hari Singh and Man Singh, two of Ranjit's governors-general.

Travel Warning
Buses have occasionally been robbed at night on the KKH from Indus Kohistan as far south as Mansehra. Police may delay vehicles travelling after dark until enough have collected to form an escorted convoy. Try to avoid travelling after dark in northern Hazara.

BATAGRAM
The Pathan village of Batagram, straddling the Nandhiar River 20 km above the Indus, has little to offer but picturesque walks in the fields, and some hard-to-find Buddhist ruins in the hills near Pishora. Little English is spoken.

Across the river 15 minutes north on the KKH is the village of Kotgala, tarted up like an amusement park. Local people claim the gaudy paint-jobs are by villagers showing off fat remittances from overseas work.

Pishora & Kala Tassa
Archaeological researchers say there are Buddhist ruins by a spring near Pishora village, eight km north of Batagram. With local help I found a narrow hole in a hillside that – according to someone who allegedly went in – leads to a deep underground grotto with two large stone figures. Unfortunately, getting into such a place would be a major caving expedition.

In the same area, which is called Kala Tassa, is a rock overhang beneath which are inscriptions depicting hunters, animals and a Buddhist stupa. The writing refers to a monastery in the time of a Kushan king of the 1st and 2nd century AD. There may be other things to find.

This isn't a leisurely trip, but a two-km climb in a steep ravine just south of the village. It does, however, give fine views of the Nandhiar River Valley. You would certainly need to ask someone in the village for help. Catch a Suzuki to Pishora near the Shangri-La Hotel in Batagram. There is also a six-km track to the ridge above Kala Tassa, starting at the petrol pump at the north end of Batagram.

Places to Stay & Eat
The *Shangri-La Hotel*, by the bus stop north of the bridge, has damp doubles for Rs 50 and up. Across the bridge, the *Tarand Hotel*, 200 metres off the KKH up Kutchery Rd, is about the same. The quieter *Al-Fakhar Hotel*, on the KKH half a km south of the bridge, is a few rupees more and a long climb. All have restaurants and there are street-side cafes and fruit vendors in the area.

Getting There & Away
About 200 metres south of the bridge is a bus yard from which wagons go all day to Besham (1½ hours) and Mansehra (two hours) for about Rs 15. You can catch a long-distance bus by the Shangri-La Hotel, if it stops.

BATAGRAM TO MANSEHRA
South from Batagram the highway climbs steeply through pine plantations, out of the Nandhiar River basin. Dipping for a while into the picturesque bowl called **Chattar Plain** (after Chattar Singh, yet another Sikh general), it then enters the basin of the Siran River. The land flattens as you descend, through cornfields and the precision terracing of rice paddies, into the Pakhli Plain surrounding Mansehra.

Half an hour south of Chattar Plain (45 minutes north of Mansehra) is the village of **Shinkiari**. A few wagons from Mansehra continue from here up the picturesque Siran River valley to pine-scented **Dadar**. You can walk over the mountains into the Kaghan Valley in a few days – from Shinkiari to Balakot, or from Dadar to Balakot or Sharan. But the hills still harbour a few black bears and wild cats (and outlaws, according to some), so a local guide is a good idea.

Places to Stay
Dadar has a *Forestry Resthouse* with doubles

for Rs 200, booked with the Conservator of Forests in Abbottabad. There is said to be a *Forestry hut* on the trek from Dadar to Sharan; ask at the District Forestry Office in Mansehra.

There's a fine *C&W Resthouse* in the woods above Chattar Plain with doubles for Rs 150; it is booked with the C&W Executive Engineer in Mansehra. The PTDC has also built a four-room motel just above the resthouse, with doubles for about Rs 500.

MANSEHRA

Tourists don't pay much attention to Mansehra ('mahn-SEH-ra') except to get out and squint at three big rocks on the northern outskirts, on which the Mauryan King Ashoka inscribed a set of edicts over 2200 years ago. But the town itself, on high ground (975 metres) in the fertile Pakhli Plain, is an interesting place too, with traces of its history as a Sikh garrison town in the early 1800s.

It's also a good place for people-watching, with a rich mix of Pathans, Punjabis, Kashmiris and Afghan refugees (there are several refugee camps in the area). The Afghan men stand out because of their stature and their big, loosely-wrapped turbans, and the women (when not veiled) because of their beauty and their bright and elaborate clothing. The most common language is Pashto, with some Hindko Punjabi (similar to Urdu).

Mansehra is a major transportation junction for Rawalpindi, Azad Jammu & Kashmir, the Kaghan and Swat valleys, and the KKH.

Orientation

The KKH goes around Mansehra but the local roads come through. The three main streets, named for their destinations – Abbottabad, Shinkiari village, and Kashmir – converge on the bridge in the middle of town. Arriving buses stop at the GTS and general bus stands on Abbottabad Rd. Some long-distance buses only stop on the KKH near the Ashoka Rocks, a one-km walk to the bazaar on Shinkiari Rd.

Information

The telephone exchange and post office are a fair way out on Kashmir Rd. No banks here will change money; if you're broke, spend your last Rs 5 on the bus to Abbottabad and do it there. A newsstand up the street from the Zam Zam Hotel has Pakistani English-language newspapers.

Ashoka Rocks

On the north side of town is Mansehra's tourist attraction, three granite boulders on which 14 edicts were engraved by order of the Mauryan King Ashoka in the 3rd century BC. Appalled by the suffering his military campaigns caused, Ashoka became interested in Buddhism and tried to dictate a new morality based on piety, moderation, tolerance and respect for life.

He was greatly revered but his reforms (and his empire) didn't last much longer than he did. The inscriptions have done better, but they too are fading away; the ancient Kharoshthi script is now almost impossible to see.

Sikh Temple

Up Kashmir Rd is a gaudy three-storey building, a pastiche of colours and styles. Built in 1937 as a Sikh gurdwara, it's now the police station. The interior hasn't been altered much either, and they might let you in for a look.

Sikh Fort

Up an alley 300 metres past the police station is a fort, built in the early 1800s by Sikh governor-general Man Singh (after whom Mansehra is named) and rebuilt by the British in 1857 after the annexation of the Sikh state. It now houses government offices and a jail. A few traces of the original mud-and-rock structure can be seen inside.

Further up the side-street under pine, eucalyptus and maple trees, are old British garrison buildings, district courts and the homes of government officials.

Bazaars

Shinkiari Rd and Kashmir Rd curve round a

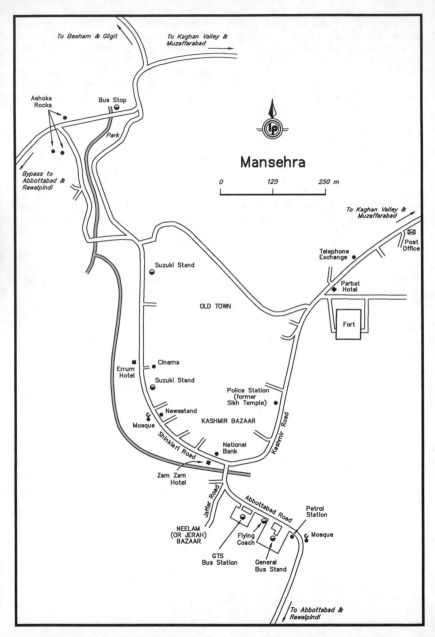

To Besham & Gilgit

To Kaghan Valley &
Muzaffarabad

Ashoka
Rocks

Bus Stop

Park

Bypass to
Abbottabad &
Rawalpindi

Mansehra

0   125   250 m

To Kaghan Valley &
Muzaffarabad

Post
Office

Telephone
Exchange

Parbat
Hotel

Suzuki Stand

OLD TOWN

Fort

Cinema

Errum
Hotel

Suzuki Stand

Police Station
(former
Sikh Temple)

Newsstand

Mosque

KASHMIR BAZAAR

Shinkiari Road

Kashmir Road

National
Bank

Zam Zam
Hotel

Jaffar Road

Abbottabad Road

Petrol
Station

NEELAM
(OR JERAH)
BAZAAR

Flying
Coach

Mosque

GTS
Bus Station

General
Bus Stand

To Abbottabad &
Rawalpindi

hill in the middle of town, and Kashmir Bazaar sprawls across the top. It's a warren of shops and homes, its narrow lanes in semi-permanent shadow. Across the bridge along Jaffar Rd is the smaller, older Neelam (or Jerah) Bazaar, with spice vendors and confectioners.

Other Things to Do

If you're feeling active, there look to be some good hill walks, with views of the Pakhli Plain and the Black Mountains, starting about two km out Kashmir Rd.

If you're not feeling active, the grotty, baroque old Friends Hotel is good for people-watching or reading the paper over tea; climb the stairs on the right. Women may be asked (but not required) to go to the 'family' area on the top floor.

Places to Stay – bottom end

Serais near the bus stands and on Kashmir Rd, recognisable by their big upstairs balconies, have rope beds for about Rs 15 but aren't interested in Westerners. The *Zam Zam Hotel* (☎ 2521) has doubles for Rs 60 (Rs 80 with a loo), a windowless single for Rs 40, communal cold shower, and good service. It's hidden off Shinkiari Rd 50 metres west of the bridge.

Places to Stay – top end

The *Errum Hotel* (☎ 2809), further up Shinkiari Rd, has quiet, clean doubles with toilet and shower for Rs 150 and Rs 200, and a rooftop patio. On Kashmir Rd beyond the fort the newish *Parbat Hotel* has doubles/triples with attached shower for Rs 120/185.

Places to Eat

Food along Abbottabad Rd is cheap and good. Little cafes serve braised mutton, chapli kebabs, qeema (mince), omelettes and thick northern-style noodle soup. In the morning some have the Pakistani 'continental breakfast': tea and light, deep-fried halwa puri pastry. There are enough vegetable and fruit stalls to keep vegetarians going.

The best (and cleanest) restaurants are in the hotels. As one of its highway signs says, the *Zam Zam's* food is 'very cheap and testy'.

Getting There & Away

On Abbottabad Rd are the Government Transport Service (GTS) bus stand and the chaotic general bus stand. GTS buses depart on a schedule; buy tickets at the window. From the general bus stand, some operators have schedules but most go when they're full; buy tickets on board or in one of the little rooms at the front of the yard.

Abbottabad Both stands have departures all day for Rs 5.

Besham Vans go frequently from the general bus stand for about Rs 30, a 3½-hour trip. The slightly cheaper GTS service goes once in the morning.

Gilgit There's no direct service. Natco and Mashabrum Tours drop passengers at the Ashoka Rocks. The alternative is a hop to Besham where there are local and direct options to Gilgit.

Kaghan Valley Wagons from the general bus stand go to Balakot for Rs 10, sometimes as far as Naran for Rs 50. GTS goes to Balakot several times a day.

Muzaffarabad Wagons take two hours and leave from the general bus stand all day for Rs 13.

Rawalpindi Wagons go from the general bus stand to Saddar Bazaar all day, and GTS goes to Pir Wadhai hourly. The trip takes three to 3½ hours and costs about Rs 25. Flying Coach, a ticket office between the two bus stands, has minibuses to Liaquat Chowk in the evening (they also go to Lahore). A slow, scenic alternative is to catch a bus from Abbottabad via the hill-station towns around Murree.

Getting Around

Passenger and for-hire Suzuki pickups start

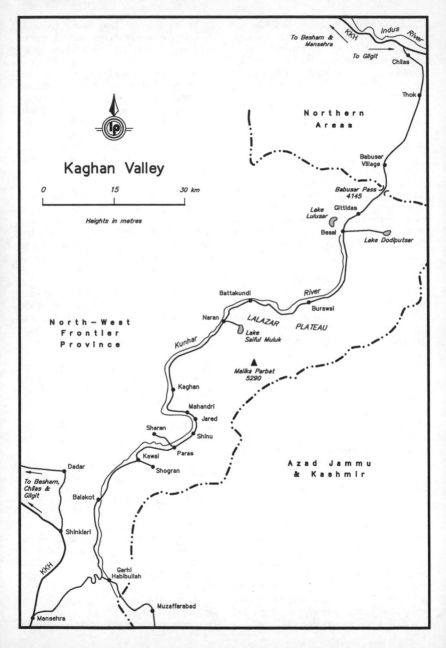

Kaghan Valley

Heights in metres

0   15   30 km

from the general bus stand and from two small yards on Shinkiari Rd.

THE KAGHAN VALLEY

Embraced by forested peaks of the Lesser Himalaya and drained by the Kunhar River, this 160-km-long valley is one of Pakistan's most popular holiday spots. For all its accessibility and rugged beauty, however, it's surprisingly undeveloped.

At its head is the 4145-metre Babusar Pass over to the Indus Valley at Chilas. In 1892 the British opened a supply line across the pass, one of only two links to Gilgit from the outside world. After Partition the Babusar was Pakistan's only reliable overland route to the Northern Areas until the KKH was built. For about six weeks each summer a jeep road over the pass is a challenging

alternative to the KKH between Chilas and Mansehra.

The valley has photogenic treks of all sizes, and the Kunhar River from Naran to Kaghan is open for white-water boating.

The valley population consists of a string of villages along the river (Hindko-speaking up to Gittidas, Kohistani from there), plus a bi-annual migration of Gujars, the 'cowboys' of northern Pakistan. After wintering in Kashmir and the Punjab, these nomads fan out with their animals to the high pastures of Chitral, Kohistan and Hazara. In Kaghan you'll find the roads full of them, heading up in May-June and back down in September-October.

Orientation Balakot is 50 km from Mansehra on a snakey paved road. The

**Cyclists' Notes,
Kaghan Valley & Babusar Pass**

The road north from Balakot averages about 20 metres' climb per km, steeper near the Babusar Pass. Some who have cycled over the pass say it is only sensible on a lightly loaded mountain bike, and only if you're in very good shape. See the main text for more about the road and when it's open.

Balakot and Naran have hotels in all price ranges. Food from Naran to Chilas is very basic – dhal, chapatti, sometimes rice.

Mansehra to Balakot, about 50 km The road is hilly and twisting, and drivers tend to be reckless. Garhi Habibullah, the junction for the road to Muzaffarabad, has some food stalls.

Balakot to Naran, 84 km At Kawai, 24 km from Balakot, is a turn-off for Shogran (on a rutty 10 or 15-km jeep track that climbs 1300 metres); Kawai and Shogran have resthouses, and Shogran has a few hotels. At Paras, eight km on from Kawai, is a jeep track to Sharan (a steep 15 to 20 km away); there is a youth hostel and resthouse here. Kaghan village, 30 km north of Paras (22 km south of Naran) has cheap inns, a resthouse and two pricey hotels. The road is paved to Kaghan, though ravaged by winter weather.

Naran to Babusar Pass, about 75 km Above Naran the road deteriorates. Battakundi, 16 km beyond Naran, has a resthouse and a Forestry hut, and on a left turn there is a cheap cafe. At Burawai, 15 km on, is another resthouse. There may be a cafe open at Besal, about 20 km beyond Burawai and a few km before Lake Lulusar. You can camp safely from Naran to Lulusar. From there on, some Kohistani villages have stone-throwing kids, and camping is not advisable all the way to Chilas. The pass is about 15 km past Besal, and the track over it is awful.

Babusar Pass to Chilas, 52 km Babusar village, with a primitive resthouse and a few cheap inns and shops, is 13 km north of the pass; the route is very rocky. There is a rutty jeep track for 39 km from there to Chilas.

valley road is more or less paved up to Kaghan village, 62 km from Balakot, and gravelled to Naran, 22 km further on. From Naran to Babusar Pass it's 70 km of gradually deteriorating jeep track. Regular buses and passenger pickups go up and down the valley, and jeeps and other vehicles can be hired in Balakot or Naran, with rates dropping in the off-season.

Information Change money in Abbottabad or Muzaffarabad; no banks in the valley will do it.

When to Go By May, Shogran and Naran are accessible by 4WD. Tourist season begins at Naran in June. The monsoon brings rain and delays in July and August but up-valley travel is possible; in fact, mid-July through August is the only reliable time for a jeep crossing of the Babusar Pass. Fine weather returns in September. In October, the upper valley again becomes 4WD-only. From late November to early April snow blocks the road beyond Kaghan, and upper villages are mostly deserted. Conditions vary widely from year to year.

Places to Stay Hotels overflow in tourist season, but in May and in September-October they'll fall all over themselves for your business and you can negotiate some real bargains. There are several *Pakistan Youth Hostels* where IYHA members pay Rs 25 a bed (Rs 15 if you have a student card too), but they tend to be run-down, packed with Pakistani students in summer and closed the rest of the time.

Some government resthouses are available on the rare occasions when officials aren't using them. Most *Forestry resthouses* here are Rs 300 for a double; some can be booked with the Kaghan Valley Project Director in Abbottabad (☎ 2893), but the best ones are only obtainable through the Forest Ministry in Peshawar (☎ 217025). A few spartan huts in remote spots can apparently be booked with the District Forestry Officer at Balakot. Most *C&W resthouses* in the valley, with doubles for Rs 150, must be

arranged with the Construction & Works Ministry in Peshawar (☎ 70455).

Balakot
Balakot (982 metres) looks better from a distance than up close. Aside from a small bazaar there's little of interest except information and transport.

Orientation & Information PTDC, in the PTDC Motel at the south end of town, can arrange jeeps and has information on weather, road conditions and jeep availability in the upper valley. The police, post office, telephone exchange and hospital are a short walk south of PTDC.

Bazaar The market, from the main road down to the old river bridge, is called Brelwi Bazaar for Ahmed Shah Brelwi, a local 'freedom fighter' who stood up to the Sikhs here in the 1830s and lost.

By the river is the surprisingly big Syed Ahmad Shaheed Mosque, dedicated to a 19th-century missionary from Kashmir.

Places to Stay – bottom end A *Pakistan Youth Hostel* is down a path south of the hospital. The *Mashriq Hotel* is the cheapest in town, but overpriced like the rest; a barren double without loo is about Rs 50. On the main road some serais have rope beds in open rooms, but they aren't interested in foreigners.

Places to Stay – middle The *Koh-i-Toor* (☎ 63) and *Taj Mahal* (☎ 121) hotels have simple doubles for about Rs 100. Carpeted doubles with cold shower start around Rs 150 at the *Balakot Hotel* (☎ 180). The *Park Hotel* (☎ 23), across the river and up the road, is more expensive. In summer, these places get booked out but before and after the season they may drop their rates by 50% or more.

Places to Stay – top end At the *PTDC Motel* (☎ 8) a single/double is a non-negotiable Rs 450/550 plus 10% excise tax.

Hazara 187

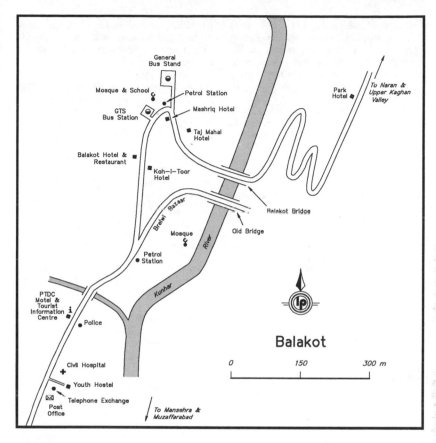

Getting There & Away The GTS and general bus stands are opposite the Mashriq Hotel. Buses, wagons and cargo jeeps go up to Kaghan and Naran all day in summer; Naran is about Rs 20 by bus, and double that by wagon. GTS goes at least to Kaghan.

Buses or wagons go to Mansehra every hour or two until mid-afternoon from the general bus stand, for about Rs 10. GTS has several morning departures.

For Muzaffarabad, take a bus or Suzuki for a few rupees from the general bus stand to Garhi Habibullah ('ha-BEE-bu-la') and catch a Mansehra-Muzaffarabad bus.

Hire Your Own You can hire a Suzuki for a day trip or a jeep for longer. Some PTDC jeep rates are: Shogran, Rs 350 return with a few hours there; and Naran, Rs 600 one way. A full Suzuki is cheaper per person but drivers are less reliable in the face of problems and dislike waiting around whilst you enjoy the view. For trips beyond Naran you can hire a private jeep there.

Shogran
At Kawai, an hour north of Balakot by bus, a jeep track climbs eastward for 10 or 15 km onto the Shogran Plateau. With views down

to a carpet of forest and up to majestic peaks – including 5290-metre Malika Parbat ('Queen of Mountains'), tallest in the Kaghan Valley – this is a great place to walk the soles off your boots or snooze away a few days.

Places to Stay An older *Forestry Resthouse* at Shogran can be booked with the Kaghan Valley Project Director at Abbottabad, or with Abbottabad PTDC; the VIP one can only be booked in Peshawar. There are also some mid-range hotels. To beat the crowds, pitch a tent in higher pastures, two to three hours up. Kawai has a *C&W Resthouse*, booked with the C&W Executive Engineer (☎ 2710) in Mansehra.

Getting There & Away A passenger pickup is about Rs 10 from Balakot to Kawai, from where it may be possible to hire a jeep.

Sharan
At Paras ('pa-RAHS'), about 20 minutes north of Kawai, a rough track crosses the river and climbs 15 to 20 km to Sharan, in the middle of nowhere at 2400 metres. From there you can hike through the forest, or trek overnight across to the Siran Valley, north of Mansehra (a local guide can help you find the trail and avoid the occasional bear or wild cat).

Places to Stay Sharan's *Pakistan Youth Hostel* was under repair at the time of writing. You may be able to book a *Forestry resthouse* there with the Kaghan Valley Project Director at Abbottabad.

Shinu
At Shinu, just beyond Paras, is a NWFP Fisheries Department hatchery, from which the upper Kunhar River and lakes Saiful Muluk, Lulusar and Dodiputsar are stocked with brown and rainbow trout. You can also buy a fishing licence.

Jared
The NWFP government operates a 'handicrafts development centre' at Jared ('ja-RED'), two hours from Balakot. State-run and private shops sell traditional-style carved furniture, hand-made woollen shawls and other work.

Places to Stay Just past Jared at Mahandri is a *Forestry Resthouse*, booked with the Kaghan Valley Project Director in Abbottabad.

Kaghan
This is a dreary place whose only advantage is that it's usually open year-round and so makes a base for winter trips. Any other time, move on to Naran if you can.

Places to Stay There are a few bottom-end local hotels. A VIP *Forestry Resthouse* can only be booked in Peshawar. The huge *Lalazar Hotel* (☎ 22) has doubles for Rs 400 and up. The equally bloated *Vershigoom Hotel* (☎ 12) may have some cheaper rooms.

Getting There & Away From Balakot, a bus is about Rs 15, a Datsun or wagon Rs 25, and there are frequent departures.

Naran
At 2400 metres, Naran is the summertime base for exploring the valley. Just a one-road bazaar full of hotels, it's a beehive in tourist season, choked with jeeps and wagons. The most popular destination from here is the picture-postcard Lake Saiful Muluk.

Summer accommodation is dicey unless you have a tent (Naran visitors sometimes have to stay in Kaghan), but in October hotels may ask less than a *fifth* of the summer price. From December to April, snow shuts Naran down.

Information PTDC tourist information is at the PTDC Motel. They have guides for hire and can help you negotiate a jeep. Fishing licences are sold at the Fisheries office, near the road on the track to Lake Saiful Muluk. The only equipment for rent is tackle in some shops during fishing season.

Places to Stay – bottom end By the road, several km south of town, is a *Pakistan Youth Hostel*, scheduled for repairs. Some mid-range places may let you pitch a tent and use their water and toilets for a small fee.

Places to Stay – middle The *Sarhad* (☎ 13), *Zam Zam* (☎ 14), *Pakistan* and *Shalimar* (☎ 4) in the centre, and the *Madina* and *Frontier* further south, ask from Rs 200 to whatever the traffic will bear for a double. The Sarhad and Zam Zam, with plain rooms with attached toilet, look the best of the lot.

Naran has two *C&W resthouses*, which can be booked in Peshawar (though Abbottabad PTDC says they can book one). There are two *Forestry resthouses*; the older one is booked with the Kaghan Valley Project Director in Abbottabad, and the new one only in Peshawar.

Places to Stay – top end The monster *Lalazar Hotel* (☎ 1) has doubles for Rs 400 and up; the *Naran* and *New Park* are about the same. The *PTDC Motel* complex (☎ 2) has overpriced two-bed tents with shared loo and cold shower for Rs 150; you cannot pitch your own. Doubles with shared loo are Rs 300, and those with bath are Rs 600 and up. To this add 10% excise duty. They say you must book through Islamabad or Rawalpindi PTDC in peak season.

Places to Eat All but the cheapest hotels have restaurants with basic meat, dhal and chappatis.

Getting There & Away Buses to/from Balakot are about Rs 20, and wagons or pickups about Rs 40; they go every hour or two. Outside July, August and September you may have to change at Kaghan, or hire a jeep. Naran PTDC has no jeeps for hire but they'll help you bargain with greedy local drivers. You can hire a pony for about Rs 200 per day.

Lake Saiful Muluk & Other Walks
Lake Saiful Muluk is an easy uphill walk, two to three hours east from Naran; the path

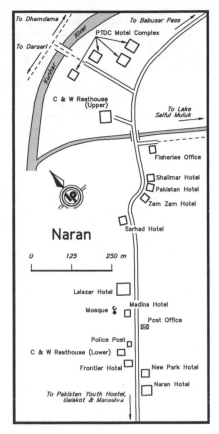

starts just above the bazaar. At 3200 metres, surrounded by moody, snowy mountains, it's said to be inhabited by mountain spirits. Legend has it that in ancient times a mortal, Prince Saiful Muluk, fell in love with one and married her.

The best way to have it to yourself is to camp. A *Forestry Resthouse* at the lake can be booked through the Kaghan Valley Project Director in Abbottabad. A day's further walking takes you to the edge of the Lalazar Plateau (though this is more easily reached from Battakundi). There is said to be a WAPDA (Water & Power Development

Administration) hut at Lalazar, which is booked with WAPDA in Abbottabad. You can make a day trip by jeep from Naran to the lake for Rs 350 or to Lalazar for Rs 500.

Local people suggest other walks across the Kunhar River from Naran. Cross the footbridge by PTDC. Turning left, you can walk to Darseri village opposite Naran. If instead you turn right, it's three km to Dhamdama village. Or you can climb right up the hill in front of you, an all-day outing, for excellent views.

Babusar Pass

The Kaghan Valley's most dramatic scenery is beyond Naran. Travel is by 4WD, pony, mountain bike or foot. At **Battakundi**, 16 km up the valley, you can detour up to summer pastures on Lalazar Plateau. Battakundi has a Forestry hut, booked with the District Forestry Officer in Balakot; a *Pakistan Youth Hostel* here is apparently in a state of collapse. There are said to be *C&W resthouses* here and 15 km up-valley at **Burawai**; check with the Abbottabad or Balakot PTDC.

The road degenerates to a barely 'jeepable' track 20 km beyond Burawai, at **Besal** ('BEH-sal'). From there you may detour about 15 km east up to beautiful, green **Lake Dodiputsar**, or stay on the main track about three km to **Lake Lulusar**, the biggest natural lake in Hazara and the source of the Kunhar River.

Gittidas, about six km north of Lake Lulusar, is the southernmost Kohistani village in the region, and apparently not a friendly place to stay the night without a guide from the area. From there it's about eight km to Babusar 'top'. If the weather is clear you can walk about a km east from the summit for views of the Kaghan Valley behind you and Nanga Parbat to the east.

Babusar village is 13 km north of the pass on the track, or about half that far on a short-cut footpath. In summer there are a few shops and serais open, and a spartan *NAPWD* (Northern Areas Public Works Department) *Resthouse* with two doubles at about Rs 100 (coming from the north, try to book it at Chilas NAPWD). Folks are not very hospitable along here, so camping is not recommended.

It's 39 km from Babusar village to **Chilas** on a rutty jeep track. Natco (Northern Areas Transport Company) 4WD cargo pickups make this trip daily in summer for Rs 30.

Getting There & Away A small 4WD jeep can manage the narrow, rocky track over the pass in July and August, though even then monsoon rains make it problematic. One-way jeep rental from Naran to Chilas at the time of writing was about Rs 2400. The pass is also feasible as a day trip from Naran and back, for about Rs 2000. Cargo jeeps sometimes go up as far as Besal.

On foot, give yourself at least a week from Naran to Babusar village, which allows some sidetrips. It may be possible to trek across as early as mid-June (though you'll still find snow) and until early October (though most villagers will be gone for the winter by then). Snow normally begins in November. A local guide might be helpful, as not everyone is friendly en route. There are apparently many springs along the way.

Any way you do it, get some local advice before crossing the pass. PTDC is a good source in Naran; in Chilas try field officers at the NAPWD office, or Natco drivers on the Babusar village run. Naran to Chilas is 130 km. Allow for wide variations in the seasonal changes noted in this chapter.

ABBOTTABAD

Abbottabad ('AB-it-uh-bahd') is the headquarters of NWFP's Hazara Division and its biggest town. Named after James Abbott, a British officer in the Sikh Wars and Hazara's first deputy commissioner, it was established as a British military cantonment in the 1850s.

Its continuing military importance (home to Pakistan's National Military Academy at nearby Kakul, and to several elite regiments) has preserved some colonial-era flavour. Shady gardens and clean streets seem lifted from the 19th century, and it's not unusual to hear church bells or a military band. Beside the cantonment is a robust old bazaar. At 1220 metres, it has a cool climate, and one of Pakistan's finest hill-station retreats is an hour away at Thandiani.

The town has a sizeable Christian minority and three active churches. Abbottabad's Muslims are mostly Sunni, with large numbers of Shias and some Ismailis. The language of the region is Hindko Punjabi, but English and Urdu are spoken.

Orientation

Below the general bus stand is a roundabout, Fowara Chowk. Down the right fork is The Mall (or Mansehra Rd). The left fork is Jinnah Rd, the town's axis, running past the bazaar and cantonment and rejoining The Mall. From either end roads climb toward Shimla Peak.

Information

Tourist Office PTDC (☎ 4946), across from Cantonment Park, is open 9 am to 1 pm and 2 to 4.30 pm Saturday through Wednesday, and 9 am to 1.30 pm Thursday.

To book Forestry resthouses at Thandiani, Dadar, Kaghan Valley or Indus Kohistan, see the Conservator of Forests (☎ 2728) or the Forestry Project Director (☎ 2893), both of them in a compound on Jail Rd. PTDC may be able to help with some Kaghan Valley resthouses.

Foreigners nearing a month in Pakistan and planning to stay longer can register with the Senior Superintendent of Police by the district courts, south of Kutchery (Kechehri) Rd.

Post & Telecommunications The post office is at Club and Central Rds. Overseas calls can be placed, and cables sent, from the telegraph office on Pine View Rd.

Banks The main office of the National Bank of Pakistan (near the courts) and the Pine View Rd office of United Bank will do foreign exchange.

Emergency A police post is on Jinnah Rd near the bazaar. The small Cantonment General Hospital is on Pine View Rd and the big District Headquarters Teaching Hospital is on Id Gah Rd east of The Mall.

Bookshops The best of several neighbouring bookshops is Variety Book Stall, south of the post office, with foreign magazines, novels and postcards.

Abbottabad Town

Abbottabad's historical heart is the cantonment, with its orderly streets, European architecture and grand parade ground. St Luke's Church, opposite Cantonment Public Park, is as old as the town. A melancholy Christian cemetery is half a km up Circular (Sabir Sharif) Rd.

Abbottabad's other persona is the bazaar, 10 square blocks of crumbling colonial architecture, full of noise and the smells of incense and lime. In Gurdwara Bazaar, beneath the arch off Jinnah Rd, is a former Sikh gurdwara (temple) built in 1943, abandoned at Partition and now used as municipal offices.

Two slightly unkempt parks are in the cantonment and south-east of the bazaar. In warm weather you might find itinerant performers or a travelling circus in one.

Shimla Peak

The hills cradling Abbottabad are Shimla Peak to the north-west and Sarban Peak to the south. Shimla's cool, piney summit is full of trails with fine panoramas of the town and its surroundings. You can walk up (three steep km) or take a Rs 2 passenger Suzuki from upper Pine View Rd; ask for *Shimla Pahari* ('pah- REE').

Ilyasi Mosque

Near Nawan Sheher village, five km east on the Murree road, is this striking mosque, which includes a complex of spring-fed bathhouses and pools. A small bazaar has teashops and cafes. Catch a Rs 2 Suzuki to Nawan Sheher from Id Gah Rd.

Places to Stay – bottom end

A *Pakistan Youth Hostel* is north of Abbottabad at Mandian, quite isolated

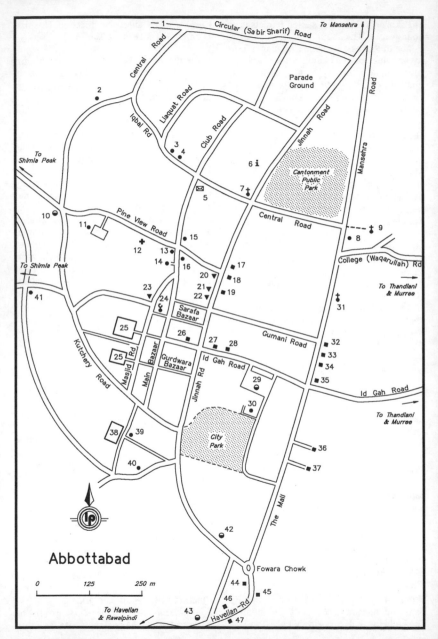

Abbottabad

0   125   250 m

unless you're biking or driving. Take a Rs 3 Suzuki to Mandian from Id Gah Rd. At the end of the line turn left at the 'Ayub Medical College' sign, go 700 metres to a T-junction, and then left for 300 metres. IYHA members pay Rs 25, and students Rs 15.

The *Bolan Hotel* (☎ 4623) near the general bus stand is good value with basic singles/doubles with loo and hot shower for Rs 60/100 and up. The *Park Hotel* nearby is cheaper, if you don't mind a snooker hall downstairs. In Id Gah Rd, for the same price, are the *Marhaba Hotel* (☎ 2925) with pleasant atrium, rooftop access and hot showers, and the miserable *Mount View* and *Asia* hotels. North on Jinnah Rd, the *Kohisar, Pineview* and *Model* hotels are around Rs 50/70. Prices drop in spring and autumn.

Places to Stay – middle
At Fowara Chowk the *Ramlina Hotel* (☎ 5431) has comfortable singles/doubles for Rs 125/200 but pricey food. The grandiose *Al-Zahra* behind it is Rs 200/250. Hotels in the same range on The Mall are the small, clean *Faisal* and *Falcon* (☎ 4169) and the big *Zarbat* (☎ 2608). Set back and peaceful is the *New Palm Hotel*, with damp rooms for Rs 150/250 and up. All have hot showers. Prices tend to drop in the off-season.

Places to Stay – top end
On The Mall, doubles at the *Springfield Hotel* (☎ 4770) start from Rs 350 and at the *Sarban Hotel* (☎ 4876) from Rs 500.

Places to Eat
The *Rainbow Cafe, New Friends Cafe* and *Wood Lock Restaurant* on Jinnah Rd serve curries, braised meat, rice and vegetables in fairly clean surroundings. Most have butcher stalls out front – not very appetising but it keeps the flies outside. Among bottom-end hotel restaurants, the *Marhaba* has the best

■ PLACES TO STAY

17	Pineview Hotel
18	Model Hotel & Cafe
19	Hotel Kohisar
26	Marhaba Hotel
27	Asia Hotel
28	Mount View Hotel
32	Zarbat Hotel
33	Falcon Hotel
34	Faisal Hotel
35	Sarban Hotel
36	New Palm Hotel
37	Springfield Hotel
44	Ramlina Hotel
45	Bolan Hotel
46	Al-Zahra Hotel
47	Park Hotel

▼ PLACES TO EAT

20	Wood Lock Restaurant
21	New Friends Cafe
22	Rainbow Cafe
23	Iqbal Restaurant
25	Vegetable markets

OTHER

1	Cemetery
2	C&W Executive Engineer
3	Public Library
4	Commissioner's Office
5	Post Office
6	PTDC Tourist Information Centre
7	St Luke's Church
8	Petrol Station
9	Presbyterian Church
10	Shimla Peak Suzuki Yard
11	Telegraph Office
12	Cantonment General Hospital
13	Kashmir Gift House
14	Cinema
15	Variety Book Stall
16	United Bank
24	Mosque
29	Regional Bus Yard
30	City Hall
31	Catholic Church
38	District Courts
39	Senior Superintendent of Police
40	National Bank
41	Conservator of Forests
42	GTS Bus Station
43	General Bus Stand

atmosphere. In the bazaar the *Iqbal Restaurant* has an elegant interior but so-so food, and always seems to be full of Pathans watching the television.

Things to Buy
A local speciality is Hazara embroidery. Good deals on shawls and other items are in small shops, but bigger selections (and higher prices) are in Kashmir Gift House near the United Bank and Threadlines Gallery, two km out on the Mansehra Rd.

Getting There & Away
The GTS bus station is on Jinnah Rd near Fowara Chowk. The general bus stand is south of Fowara Chowk on the Havelian road. For regional trips (eg Thandiani) there is a bus yard down an alley east of the Mount View Hotel on Id Gah Rd.

Private buses and vans go to Rawalpindi's Pir Wadhai stand all day for Rs 20. GTS goes several times a day for a little less. 'Flying Coach' Mansehra-Rawalpindi minibuses may stop at the plaza in front of the Springfield Hotel. All go via Havelian in two to three hours.

A slow, scenic alternative route to Rawalpindi is via Murree (see the Rawalpindi & Islamabad chapter). Buses go to Murree all day for Rs 15, a five-hour trip.

GTS goes to Balakot in the Kaghan Valley two or three times a day, but there are more options from Mansehra. Both stands have departures to Mansehra all day for Rs 5.

There are no direct connections to Gilgit, but GTS makes the five-hour trip to Besham at 8 am for about Rs 30.

Getting Around
Regional passenger Suzukis clog Id Gah Rd all day.

THANDIANI
Thandiani ('tahn-dee-AH-nee'), a series of 2700-metre forested ridges north-east of Abbottabad, is the northernmost of the hill-station retreats called the Galis (the others are described in the Rawalpindi & Islamabad chapter). The air is cool and clean,

development is minimal and there are fine views east across the Pir Panjal Range and north even to Nanga Parbat in clear weather. *Thandiani* means 'cool place', so bring an extra layer or two. It's possible as a long day trip.

Places to Stay & Eat
To stay cheaply, bring a tent. The little *Far Pavilions Hotel* at the bus terminus has two doubles for Rs 400 and some two or four-person tents for about Rs 300, which you can book through the Sarban Hotel in Abbottabad. They may also have cheaper rope-beds or tent sites. A cafe and snack shops are open in summer.

One km south by the TV tower is a *C&W Resthouse*, where a double with bath is Rs 150. Theoretically, you can only book it in Peshawar (NWFP Minister for Construction & Works (☎ 70455)) but travellers report booking it with the Executive Engineer in Abbottabad. One km further, a *Forestry Resthouse* has doubles for Rs 300, booked with the Conservator of Forests in Abbottabad.

Getting There & Away
Thandiani is an hour's ride on a winding road beside the Kalapani River, through terraced fields and pine and deodar forest. A Datsun or Suzuki is Rs 15, and a bus is Rs 10, from the back of Abbottabad's regional bus yard. Departures are frequent until mid-afternoon.

HAVELIAN
This dusty, nondescript market town has only one claim to fame: it's the official southern end of the KKH, 790 km from the Chinese border and 1200 km from Kashgar. No signs announce it, and there was already a road through to Abbottabad before the KKH was even an idea. It's a strange choice, except that Havelian is a railhead.

But there actually is a kind of geographical boundary here. The road fairly falls out of the hills to the banks of the Dor River beside Havelian. Southward, the road and railway proceed almost horizontally to Rawalpindi. This certainly feels like the southern end of the mountains.

There's no reason to stop here unless you want to go on to Rawalpindi by rail.

Places to Stay & Eat
The *Indus Hotel* has cheap rooms and a little cafe. Nobody speaks much English.

Getting There & Away
Three creaky trains a day go to/from Rawalpindi for Rs 12, taking three hours. If you've come from Rawalpindi on the train, you'll probably find a bus at the station – half an hour to Abbottabad or an hour to Mansehra, for a few rupees. Or keep right at the fork, and at the end of the bazaar you'll find more buses, leaving about every 30 minutes. Buses to Rawalpindi stop at the petrol station down the left fork.

HAVELIAN TO THE GRAND TRUNK ROAD
From Havelian southward it's flat and warm. Half an hour away is **Haripur**, once the centre of Hazara. It was founded in 1822 as the headquarters of the Sikh General Hari Singh, after whom it's named. In 1853 its administrative functions were all moved to Abbottabad and now it's just a big market town.

From Haripur the road crosses the wide, sandy **Taxila Valley**. It's odd to reflect that this quiet plain was for almost five centuries a world centre of Buddhist philosophy and art, the Buddhist 'Holy Land'. Taxila was the cultural capital of the Mauryan and Kushan empires – from the 3rd century BC to the 3rd century AD – and the valley still has abundant evidence of this extraordinary period, at archaeological sites and in a fine museum. This makes a worthwhile one or two-day trip from Rawalpindi, as described in the next chapter.

At Taxila Town or at Hasan Abdal (there are several routes from Haripur) you arrive at the **Grand Trunk Road**, the old axis of the Moghul Empire and the British Raj – Rudyard Kipling's 'broad, smiling river of life' that once ran 2500 km from Kabul to Calcutta. Now the 'GT Road' is a thunderous stream of chrome-plated trucks and buses, and the Karakoram Highway seems pretty far away.

Rawalpindi & Islamabad

This is the business end of the KKH. Going or coming, you're likely to pass through but unlikely to linger. But there's plenty to do while waiting for your visa, trekking permit or plane out.

Rawalpindi only came into its own after the Sikh wars of the 1840s, as the largest cantonment in Asia (cantonments were the tidy residential-military-administrative enclaves built next to major British colonial towns). Astride the Grand Trunk Rd, Rawalpindi 'Cantt' is today the headquarters of the Pakistan army. Islamabad may be the capital, but in a country with a nearly unbroken line of military rulers – up front or behind the scenes – since 1958, 'Pindi is still the centre.

By contrast, where Islamabad stands there was nothing 35 years ago. Karachi being too far from everything, it was decided in the 1950s to build a new capital near Rawalpindi and the summer hill stations. To avoid urban chaos and decay, architect-planner Konstantinos Doxiades' idea was to let it grow in only one direction, sector by sector across a grid, each sector having its own residences, shops and parks. Construction began in 1961 and will go on for decades.

Subdued and suburban, Islamabad couldn't be less like Rawalpindi. So far only half a dozen sectors are done, but in the long term they'll swallow up 'Pindi itself.

Orientation

The two cities, 15 km apart, are effectively a single mega-town with bazaars at one end and bureaucrats at the other. Buses between them are tedious but straightforward. If you're only here for the paperwork you can stay cheaply at Aabpara in Islamabad. The rest of Islamabad is expensive, spread out and fairly boring. In Rawalpindi, Saddar Bazaar is the sensible choice, with cheap hotels and transport to everywhere.

Rawalpindi The axes are Murree Rd and The

Mall (also called Shahrah-i-Quaid-i-Azam). The cheaper hotels are in Saddar and Rajah bazaars and along Murree Rd at Liaquat ('LYAH-kut') Chowk and Committee Chowk. The railway station is in Saddar, the Pir Wadhai bus stand is north-west of town, and the airport is north-east.

South of Saddar, the Cantonment has top-end hotels and traces of colonial life. At Rajah, the biggest bazaar, six-way Fowara Chowk has 'spoke' roads to Saddar, Pir Wadhai and Murree Rd. The city's growing end is Satellite Town, touching Islamabad at the local transport junction of Faizabad.

Islamabad Islamabad has no axis or centre. Each sector, built around a commercial area *or markaz*, has a letter-number designation, eg F-7, with quarters numbered clockwise, eg F-7/1 in the south-west corner, F-7/2 north-west, etc. These Orwellian coordinates also have names; F and G are Shalimar and Ramna, so F-7 is also Shalimar-7, and so on. Numbered streets run within sectors, while avenues and *khayabans* (meaning avenue or boulevard) run between sectors.

But as a practical matter sectors are called by the names of their markets. The main ones, in sequence on the bus line, are Aabpara ('AH-pa-ra', south-west G-6), Melody or Civic Centre (G-6), Super Market (F-6), Jinnah or Jinnah Super (F-7) and Ayub Market (F-8).

Between the Fs and Gs is a commercial belt called the Blue Area. Federal offices (Parliament, the President's and Prime Minister's houses, and ministries in the Secretariat) and most foreign embassies are on the east side of the city.

Information

Tourist Offices In Rawalpindi, PTDC has a marginally useful information office (☎ 581480) at Flashman's Hotel, which is open 9 am to 1 pm and 2 to 4 pm, and closed Friday. A better one is in Islamabad at the

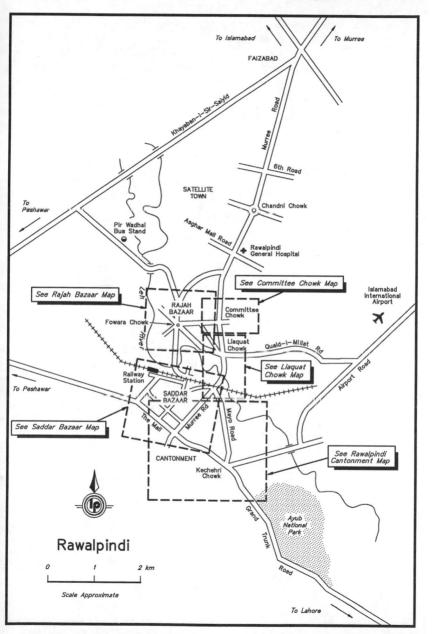

To Islamabad

To Murree

FAIZABAD

Khayaban-i-Sir-Saiyid

Murree Road

6th Road

To Peshawar

SATELLITE TOWN

Chandni Chowk

Asghar Mall Road

Pir Wadhai Bus Stand

Rawalpindi General Hospital

See Rajah Bazaar Map

Leh River

See Committee Chowk Map

Islamabad International Airport

RAJAH BAZAAR

Committee Chowk

Fowara Chowk

Liaquat Chowk

Quaid-i-Millat Rd

See Liaquat Chowk Map

Airport Road

Railway Station

To Peshawar

SADDAR BAZAAR

Murree Rd

Mayo Road

See Saddar Bazaar Map

The Mall

See Rawalpindi Cantonment Map

CANTONMENT

Kechehri Chowk

Grand Trunk Road

Ayub National Park

Rawalpindi

0   1   2 km

Scale Approximate

To Lahore

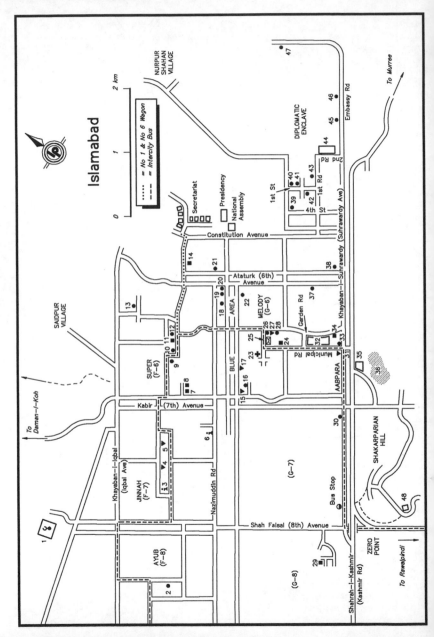

Islamabad

········· = No 1 & No 6 Wagon
– – – = Intercity Bus

NURPUR SHAHAN VILLAGE

To Murree

DIPLOMATIC ENCLAVE

Embassy Rd

2nd Rd

1st Rd

1st St

4th St

Secretariat

Presidency

National Assembly

Constitution Avenue

SAIDPUR VILLAGE

Ataturk (6th) Avenue

AREA

MELODY (G-6)

BLUE

Garden Rd

Khayaban-i-Suhrawardy (Suhrawardy Ave)

Municipal Rd

AABPARA

SUPER (F-6)

To Daman-i-Koh

Kabir (7th) Avenue

Khayaban-i-Iqbal (Iqbal Ave)

JINNAH (F-7)

Nazimuddin Rd

(G-7)

Bus Stop

SHAKARPARIAN HILL

Shah Faisal (8th) Avenue

ZERO POINT

To Rawalpindi

AYUB (F-8)

(G-8)

Shahrah-i-Kashmir (Kashmir Rd)

Ministry of Tourism (☎ 816932) in Jinnah Market. This is also the starting point for trekking permits (see Trekking & Other Sports in the Facts for the Visitor chapter). A third office (☎ 816815) is at 52 Nazimuddin Rd (F-7/4).

TDCP, the Tourist Development Corporation of the Punjab (☎ 564824), at 44 Mall Plaza (corner of Kashmir Rd and The Mall), has a few brochures, plus buses to Murree and Lahore.

The Survey of Pakistan sells a detailed but dated *Islamabad & Rawalpindi Guide Map* for about Rs 25 in bigger bookshops.

Foreign Embassies & Visas For Pakistan and China visa regulations, and information on getting foreign visas in Pakistan, see Visas & Embassies in the Facts for the Visitor chapter. Most embassies are in the Diplomatic Enclave (G-5) at the east end of Islamabad.

From Aabpara, pickups and wagons to Quaid-i-Azam University pass the American, Chinese, Russian and Australian embassies. Those to Bari Imam (Nurpur Shahan village), and the No 1 wagon from Saddar, pass near the Canadian, Iranian, Indian and British embassies.

Afghanistan
  House 14, St 83, G-6/4 (☎ 822566)
Australia
  Diplomatic Enclave (☎ 822111)
Canada
  Diplomatic Enclave (☎ 821101/4)
China
  Diplomatic Enclave (☎ 821114, visa office)
France
  University Rd, Diplomatic Enclave (☎ 823981)
Germany
  Diplomatic Enclave (☎ 822151)
India
  Diplomatic Enclave (☎ 814371, visa office)
Iran
  House 222-238, Street 2, G-5/1 (☎ 822694)

■ PLACES TO STAY

7 VIP Guesthouse
8 Host Guesthouse
11 Shehrazad Hotel
14 Holiday Inn
24 Islamabad Hotel
29 Blue Star Motel
34 Pakistan Youth Hostel
35 Tourist Campsite

▼ PLACES TO EAT

4 Kabul Restaurant
5 Pappasalli's Italian Restaurant
15 Omar Khayam Restaurant
17 Usmania Restaurant
27 Bakery
31 Kamran Restaurant

OTHER

1 Shah Faisal Mosque
2 Foreigners' Registration Office
3 Ministry of Tourism & PTDC Tourist Information Centre
6 PTDC Tourist Information Centre
9 Passenger Datsuns to Saidpur
10 Lok Virsa Bookstore
12 Mr Books
13 London Book Company
16 PIA Booking Office
18 American Centre
19 Bank of America
20 American Express
21 Central Telegraph Office
22 American Book Company
23 Capital Hospital
25 General Post Office
26 Pakistan Railways Booking Office
28 British Council Library
30 Capital Development Authority
32 Juma Bazaar
33 GTS Bus Stand
36 Rose & Jasmine Garden
37 Afghan Embassy
38 US Consular Office
39 German Embassy
40 Canadian High Commission
41 Iranian Embassy
42 Indian High Commission
43 British High Commission
44 US Embassy
45 Chinese Embassy
46 Russian Embassy
47 Australian High Commission
48 Lok Virsa Museum

Italy
54 Khayaban-i-Margalla, F-6/3 (☎ 825791)
New Zealand
(go to the UK Embassy)
Russia
Diplomatic Enclave (☎ 824604)
UK
Diplomatic Enclave (☎ 822131)
USA
Consular office in USAID Bldg, 6 Ataturk Ave, G-5/1 (☎ 824071, ext 258 or 378);
Embassy in Diplomatic Enclave (☎ 826161)

Pakistan Visa Extension or Replacement
Islamabad is the only place in Pakistan to extend a visa or landing permit or deal with expired visas and lost documents. For how to do it, see Visas & Embassies in the Facts for the Visitor chapter.

Foreigners' Registration If you register here, do it in the city where your hotel is. Rawalpindi's office is in the Civil Courts beside the Senior Superintendent of Police (SSP). Catch an airport Suzuki on Adamjee Rd and get off just past Kechehri ('kuh-CHEH-ree') Chowk; see the Rawalpindi Cantonment map on page 207. The Islamabad office is by the SSP in Ayub Market. The best time to go is 9 am to 1 pm.

Bring two passport-size photos and the Temporary Certificate of Registration (Form C) if you got one when entering Pakistan; there's no fee.

Money In Saddar Bazaar, National Bank, behind the shops on Bank Rd, and Habib's Cantonment branch on Haider Rd do foreign exchange. In Rajah it's Habib's City branch in Bara Market. Habib can arrange telegraphic transfers from overseas. In Islamabad, go to United Bank beside the Islamabad Hotel, or to the National Bank behind the hotel.

American Express on Murree Rd, Rawalpindi (☎ 582864), and in the Blue Area, Islamabad (☎ 812753), cash travellers' cheques and major currencies and can arrange cash from Amex cards. They're open 9 am to 5 pm Sunday to Thursday, and 9 am to 1 pm Saturday. Bank of America

(☎ 828801), near American Express in the Blue Area, Islamabad, can arrange cash from major credit cards. Other foreign banks are Citibank and Grindlays in Saddar Bazaar, Rawalpindi.

Post & Telecommunications The Rawalpindi general post office (GPO) is on Kashmir Rd; poste restante is in the rear building. The Islamabad GPO is at the north end of Melody Market. American Express card-holders can have mail sent to the Rawalpindi American Express office.

For overseas calls, cables, telex and fax, the central telegraph office (☎ 580276) is in Rawalpindi, on Kashmir Rd south of The Mall. The Islamabad office (☎ 821579) is on Ataturk Ave. Both are open 24 hours a day.

Travel Agencies Some trusty agencies are:

American Express Travel Service, Rawalpindi office (☎ 582864, 565766), Rahim Plaza, Murree Rd; Islamabad office (☎ 812753, 829422), 1-E Ali Plaza, Blue Area, Islamabad
Shakil Express, Haider Rd between Canning & Kashmir Rds, Saddar, Rawalpindi
Rohtas Travel Consultants (☎ 563224, 566434), 60 Canning Rd, Saddar, Rawalpindi
Travel Walji's Ltd (☎ 812151, 823963), 10 Khayaban-i-Suhrawardy, Aabpara, Islamabad

Bookshops In Rawalpindi, the Book Centre (☎ 565234) on Saddar Rd has maps, overseas periodicals, used books and lots of Lonely Planet titles. Capri Bookshop on Haider Rd and Pak-American Commercial Ltd on Kashmir Rd (upstairs) have foreign magazines.

In Islamabad, the good London Book Company (☎ 823852) has a big Pakistan section, maps, periodicals and used books. To get there from Super Market walk north on 14th St and turn right at 10th St to Kohsar Market. The Lok Virsa Bookstore in Super Market has books on Pakistani folk art and history and tapes of folk music. It's open from 9 am to 5 pm, Saturday to Thursday.

Mr Books in Super Market has a good selection of overseas magazines and newspapers. At the Old Book Corner, behind Mr

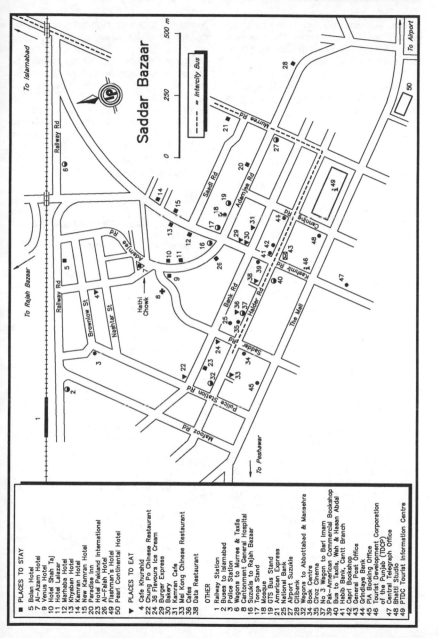

Saddar Bazaar

- - - = Intercity Bus

■ PLACES TO STAY
5 Bolan Hotel
7 Al-Azam Hotel
9 Venus Hotel
10 Hotel Shah Taj
11 Hotel Lalazar
12 Marhaba Hotel
13 Khyaban Hotel
14 Kamran Hotel
15 New Kamran Hotel
20 Paradise Inn
26 Hotel Pakland International
49 Al-Falah Hotel
49 Flashman's Hotel
50 Pearl Continental Hotel

▼ PLACES TO EAT
4 Cafe Khurshid
22 Chung Po Chinese Restaurant
24 36 Flavours Ice Cream
29 Burger Express
30 Bakery
31 Kamran Cafe
33 Mei Kong Chinese Restaurant
36 Cafes
38 Data Restaurant

OTHER
1 Railway Station
2 Buses to Islamabad
3 Police Station
6 Wagons to Murree & Taxila
8 Cantonment General Hospital
16 Suzukis to Rajah Bazaar
17 Tonga Stand
18 Mosque
19 GTS Bus Stand
21 American Express
25 National Bank
27 Airport Suzukis
28 Citibank
32 Wagons to Abbottabad & Mansehra
34 Book Centre
35 Ciroz Cinema
37 No 3 Wagon to Barl Imam
39 Pak-American Commercial Bookshop
40 Bus to Taxila, Wah & Hasan Abdal
41 Habib Bank, Cantt Branch
42 Capri Bookshop
43 General Post Office
44 Grindlays Bank
45 PIA Booking Office
46 Tourist Development Corporation
   of the Punjab (TDCP)
47 Central Telegraph Office
48 Bhatti Studio
49 PTDC Tourist Information Centre

Books, you can trade two of your second-hand books for one of theirs. The American Book Company is opposite American Express in the Blue Area.

Libraries The American Centre (☎ 824051) in the Blue Area of Islamabad has a posh library of periodicals, videotapes and US Information Service propaganda, but they're a paranoid lot. The British Council Library (☎ 822505) in Melody Market, Islamabad, is for UK citizens. Both are open from Sunday to Thursday.

The Asian Study Group was started in 1973 to help expatriate residents get acquainted with the area. They have programmes on history, art and so on, a tiny but well-thumbed library and a file of hand-drawn maps of local trails, available for photocopying at your expense. Volunteer-run and not geared to transients, they're nevertheless available to help with specific interests. Contact them through your embassy (they have no formal office but every Western embassy has a few members); their address is PO Box 1552, Islamabad.

Police Saddar Bazaar police station (☎ 564760) is on Police Station Rd near the railway. Pir Wadhai has a police post (☎ 863787). In Islamabad there are stations in Melody Market and in south-west Ayub Market. Police emergency numbers are ☎ 823333 and 810222.

Hospitals In an emergency you might first want to call your embassy. Hospitals open to foreigners include Rawalpindi General Hospital (☎ 847761, Murree Rd at Ashgar Mall Rd) and Cantonment General (☎ 562254, Saddar Rd in Saddar Bazaar). In Islamabad, Capital Hospital (☎ 825691) is a few blocks west of the GPO and the Government Poly Clinic is in G-6 near the Blue Area.

Film & Photography A good place for film and processing is Bhatti Studio (☎ 568771) on Canning Rd in Rawalpindi. A Fuji lab is below American Express on Murree Rd.

Numerous shops do passport-size pictures, eg Quick Foto on Adamjee Rd.

Luggage Storage The railway station left-luggage room, open seven days a week, will store baggage at Rs 3 per piece per day.

Festivals & Holidays In addition to the following events of local interest, the Muslim holidays of Ramadan, Eid-ul-Fitr, Ashura and Eid-Milad-un-Nabi (see Holidays & Festivals in the Facts for the Visitor chapter) are important throughout Pakistan.

March
    Rose Festival, Rose & Jasmine Garden
April
    Spring Flower Show, Rose & Jasmine Garden
13 to 15 April
    Baisakhi, when Sikh pilgrims from India visit Panja Sahib shrine at Hasan Abdal
1st week in May
    Urs (death anniversary) of Bari Shah Latif at Nurpur Shahan village. Pilgrims come from the Punjab and NWFP, in a carnival mood. Foreigners are tolerated.
November
    Chrysanthemum Show, Rose & Jasmine Garden.

Rajah Bazaar (Rawalpindi)

The biggest of Rawalpindi's bazaars, Rajah is a kaleidoscope of people and markets spreading in every direction from Fowara Chowk. Dotted around are crumbling stone towers marking old Hindu temples. Get there by Suzuki from Kashmir Rd in Saddar or from Committee Chowk. For some bigger markets (here and elsewhere) see Things to Buy in this chapter.

Shakarparian Park & Lok Virsa Museum (Islamabad)

In this urban wilderness south of Islamabad is Shakarparian Hill, with sculpted gardens and panoramas of both cities from its east viewpoint. Down below is the 20-hectare Rose & Jasmine Garden, site of several annual flower shows.

On Garden Rd is Lok Virsa, the National Institute of Folk & Traditional Heritage (☎ 812675, 823883), with a first-rate ethnographic museum including traditional

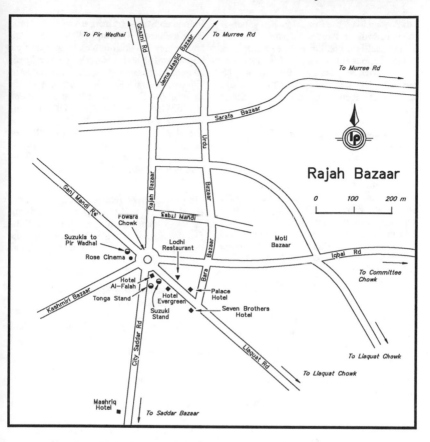

handicrafts, the best of which are the textiles and carved wood. It's open from 9 am to 1 pm and 2 to 5 pm, and is closed Friday and Monday. Next door is a book and tape library, open from 9 am to 3 pm, except on Friday.

There's no public transport. The cheapest way is to get off the bus at the Zero Point stop, where a path climbs 20 minutes up the hill. For Lok Virsa you can walk on over the hill; or from the bus stop cross the road, bear right and enter the woods on a path where an approach road joins the Rawalpindi road, a 15-minute walk. A taxi from Aabpara is about Rs 25.

Shah Faisal Mosque (Islamabad)
This incredibly opulent, marble-faced mosque is said to be Asia's biggest, with room for 100,000 worshippers. Most of its US$50 million cost was a gift of King Faisal of Saudi Arabia. The late President Zia ul-Haq is buried on the grounds. Get off an intercity bus at 8th Ave.

Daman-i-Koh & Saidpur (Islamabad)
Daman-i-Koh ('DAH-ma-ni-ko') is a picnic spot in the Margalla Hills with great views over Islamabad and, on clear days, south to the Salt Range. Get off the intercity bus at

7th Ave and catch a Suzuki at Khayaban-i-Iqbal, or walk up the nearby path.

Just east is a one-km road to Saidpur, a village famous for pottery shops and workshops. Take a No 8 bus from the Saddar GTS bus stand. Datsun passenger pickups are said to go there from the west end of Super Market.

Nurpur Shahan & Bari Imam Shrine (Islamabad)

North of the Diplomatic Enclave at Nurpur Shahan village is a shrine to Shah Abdul Latif Kazmi, also known as Bari Shah Latif or 'Bari Imam', a 17th century Sufi mystic and Islamabad's unofficial patron saint. Thursday evenings are quite festive, with pilgrims and trance-like Qawwali music, and in the first week of May the carnival-like *urs* (death anniversary) of Bari Shah Latif is celebrated here. A No 3 wagon goes from Haider Rd in Saddar Bazaar via Aabpara.

Margalla Hills

The hills north of Islamabad are full of hiking trails and resthouses, as described in the Capital Development Authority's map-brochure, *Trekking in the Margalla Hills*, available from CDA's public relations office (☎ 828301) on Khayaban-i-Suhrawardy west of Aabpara. Planning is underway for a Margalla Hills National Park, stretching west as far as Haripur.

Ayub National Park (Rawalpindi)

Named after General Ayub Khan, the first of Pakistan's martial law administrators, this staid park south of the Cantonment has 900 hectares of paths, gardens and lakes. Get off an airport Suzuki at Kechehri Chowk and take the right fork about one km.

Army Museum (Rawalpindi)

If you're interested in military matters, there's an Army Museum in the Cantonment, on Iftikhar Rd, 1½ blocks south of the Pearl Continental Hotel. Summer hours are 8 am to noon and 5.30 to 7 pm; winter hours are 9 am to 3 pm.

Places to Stay – bottom end

Saddar Bazaar (Rawalpindi) Several hotels have noisy singles/doubles with part-time hot water for about Rs 50/80 – the *Venus* (☎ 566501, best of the lot), *Lalazar* and *Shah Taj* on Adamjee Rd, the old wing of the *Kamran Hotel* on Kashmir Rd and the *Bolan* (☎ 563416) on Railway Rd. Others along Railway Rd are not recommended. The friendly *Al-Azam Hotel* (☎ 565901), on Adamjee Rd, has rooms with shower for Rs 60/100 and decent food; the *Al-Falah Hotel* nearby has similar rates.

Liaquat Chowk (Rawalpindi) The *Park Hotel* (☎ 70594) is said to have clean dorms at Rs 50/bed, and hot showers. The *Shangrila Hotel* is said to be very noisy into the night because of the minibus stand outside.

Rajah Bazaar (Rawalpindi) Recommended is the friendly *Hotel Al-Falah* (☎ 553206) behind the tonga stand at Fowara Chowk, with hot water and singles/doubles for about Rs 40/70. The *Hotel Evergreen* on Liaquat Rd has similar rates.

Islamabad Cheapest of all is the *Tourist Campsite* near Aabpara. A tent platform or space in a concrete 'bungalow' (no beds) is Rs 15, and a spot on the ground is Rs 8 with a tent or Rs 3 without. Locked storage is available. The maximum stay is two weeks.

Nearby, on Garden Rd, is a new *Pakistan Youth Hostel* (☎ 826899) with dozens of four-bed rooms, communal toilets and cold showers – but no cooking facilities and no camping. Beds are Rs 35 for IYHA cardholders, and Rs 25 if you have a student card too. It's popular with Pakistani students in summer. Maximum stay is three days if it's crowded.

Pir Wadhai (Rawalpindi) Hotels here are sleazy and not keen on foreigners, but in a pinch try the grotty *Al-Medina Hotel* at the west end.

Places to Stay – middle
Saddar Bazaar (Rawalpindi) On Kashmir Rd the *New Kamran Hotel* (☎ 582040) has good service and clean doubles/triples with hot shower for Rs 130/150. Opposite is the slightly pricier *Khyaban Hotel*. Nearby, at the *Marhaba Hotel* (☎ 566021), there are damp doubles for Rs 300.

Several travellers have written to praise the *Paradise Inn* (☎ 568594) on Adamjee Rd, with comfortable singles/ doubles for Rs 225/275, or Rs 400/500 with TV and air-conditioning. For Rs 330 you can have a double with air-conditioning, telephone and muzak at the *Hotel Pakland International* (☎ 566080) on Bank Rd.

Rajah Bazaar (Rawalpindi) Half a km south of Fowara Chowk is the *Mashriq Hotel* (☎ 556161), where hot-water doubles/triples are Rs 160/200. On Liaquat Rd, the *Palace Hotel* (☎ 70672) has Rs 120 doubles; the friendly *Seven Brothers Hotel* (☎ 551112) opposite is slightly more.

Liaquat Chowk (Rawalpindi) A good bet is the tidy *City Hotel* (☎ 73503) on College Rd, with Rs 50 dorm beds, doubles/triples for Rs 150/175 and morning hot water. On Murree Rd, the friendly *Faisal* (☎ 73210) and *Al-Hayat* (☎ 70979) have doubles for about Rs 100; the *Citizen* is about Rs 150. Up a notch are the *Park* (☎ 70594) and *National City* (☎ 71411) with doubles from Rs 250.

Committee Chowk (Rawalpindi) Recommended is the *Mushtaq Hotel* (☎ 553998) on Murree Rd, where doubles/triples/quads with loo and hot water are Rs 250/300/350 and the food is good. Doubles at the *Al-Farooq Hotel* (☎ 556200) and *Queen's Hotel* (☎ 73240) are about Rs 160.

Islamabad *Shehrazad Hotel* (☎ 822295) at Super Market has overpriced doubles with hot shower for Rs 200. In an awkward neighbourhood near Zero Point is the *Blue Star Motel* (☎ 852717) with damp doubles for the same rate.

Places to Stay – top end
Rawalpindi Cantonment Travellers recommend the *Hotel Holiday* (☎ 568068), on Iftikhar Rd behind State Bank of Pakistan, for its good service and clean doubles for about Rs 400. Many rate PTDC's *Flashman's Hotel* (☎ 581480) a bad deal, with shabby doubles for a ridiculous Rs 1050 and up. The *Pearl Continental* (☎ 566011) is 'Pindi's primo hotel; for the price of a night there you could stay in the bazaar for a month.

Islamabad In a residential street near Super Market, the *VIP Guesthouse* and *Host Guesthouse* are converted homes with posh doubles for Rs 500 and up, and meals are included. The address is Street 28, F-6/1. Bigwigs stay at the *Islamabad Hotel* (☎ 827311) in Civic Centre or the *Holiday Inn* (☎ 826121) near the Secretariat.

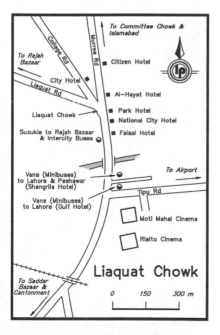

Liaquat Chowk

To Committee Chowk & Islamabad

To Rajah Bazaar

College Rd
Murree Rd
Liaquat Rd

City Hotel
Citizen Hotel
Al–Hayat Hotel
Park Hotel
National City Hotel
Faisal Hotel

Liaquat Chowk

Suzukis to Rajah Bazaar & Intercity Buses

Vans (Minibuses) to Lahore & Peshawar (Shangrila Hotel)

Vans (Minibuses) to Lahore (Gulf Hotel)

To Airport

Tipu Rd

Moti Mahal Cinema

Rialto Cinema

To Saddar Bazaar & Cantonment

0   150   300 m

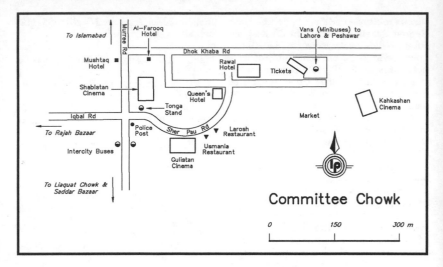

Committee Chowk

0   150   300 m

Places to Eat

Quick & Cheap Quick-service stalls are plentiful around markets and transport stops. Typical items are samosas (fried pastries stuffed with spiced potato or chickpeas), pulau (rice fried with vegetable bits), tikkas (barbecued meat pieces) and shami kebabs (lentil-and-mutton 'pancakes').

Saddar Bazaar (Rawalpindi) A recommended cheapo with good Pakistani dishes is the *Data Restaurant* in an alley off Haider Rd. Other decent places are *Cafe Khurshid*, north of Hathi Chowk, and *Kamran Cafe*, on Bank Rd. Two Chinese restaurants – *Mei Kong*, off Haider Rd, and *Chung Po*, on Bank Rd – are overpriced and mediocre.

Fast-food places with hot sandwiches, French fries and the like are everywhere – eg *Burger Express* on Kashmir Rd. Rumour has it there's a *Pizza Hut* on The Mall. Get good ice cream at *36 Flavours* on Bank Rd. If you've developed a craving for a banana split or a good cup of coffee, you can find it at the *Pearl Continental Hotel*.

A Pakistani-style breakfast of tea, yoghurt, cholla (spicy chickpeas), fried paratha bread or halwa puri pastry is available from street-side cafes that materialise at 6 am and close by mid-morning. One is opposite the mosque on Kashmir Rd.

Rajah Bazaar (Rawalpindi) The restaurant upstairs at the *Lodhi Hotel* on Liaquat Rd has cheap curries and fried chicken. The *Palace* and *Seven Brothers* hotels have so-so restaurants.

Committee Chowk (Rawalpindi) Travellers give *Hotel Mushtaq* good marks for food. *Usmania Restaurant* isn't cheap but the Pakistani dishes are varied and good; eat well for Rs 80. Almost as good is the *Larosh Restaurant* next door.

Islamabad Aabpara and Melody Market have kebab stands and cafes with cheap curries and shami kebabs. Pakistani items at Aabpara's *Kamran Restaurant* are not too pricey. At a fantastic bakery in Melody Market you can ruin your budget with brownies, banana bread, pizza and imported cheese.

Expats say *Omar Khayam* Iranian restaurant in the Blue Area is very good; it's open from 7 pm. Nearby is an *Usmania* like the one in Committee Chowk. The *Holiday Inn* is reported to have an expensive but all-you-can-eat dinner buffet.

Super and Jinnah markets are full of fast-food cafes. Jinnah also has some good restaurants, including the *Kabul Restaurant* at the west end of the market, with Pakistani and Afghan dishes, and pricey *Pappasalli's Italian Restaurant* at the east end. Others spotted but not sampled are *Kim Mun Chinese*, *New Afghan* and *Jakarta*.

Alcohol

In unmarked lounges or back-rooms in top-end hotels (Pearl, Flashman's, Islamabad Hotel, Holiday Inn) you can sign a form saying you aren't a Muslim, pay a fee and get a one-day permit allowing you to buy spirits or lager brewed in Pakistan for non-Muslims.

You can get a longer-term liquor permit, as foreign residents do, from the Excise & Tax Office, beside Foreigners' Registration in either city. The Rawalpindi permit is supposedly good throughout Pakistan, though along the KKH you won't find anything to buy with it.

Entertainment

The Australian Club (☎ 822115), at the Australian Embassy, has a social night for all Australian visitors (and guests by permission) on *most* Thursdays from 4.30 to 7.30 pm; bring your passport. On Tuesday evening the Canadian Club on Embassy Rd admits Canadian visitors who are guests of members.

Things to Buy

Juma Bazaar, the block between Municipal and Garden Rds in Aabpara, comes to life on Fridays as a huge handicrafts market with carpets, leather, jewellery, pottery and clothing. On evenings and holidays, Saddar

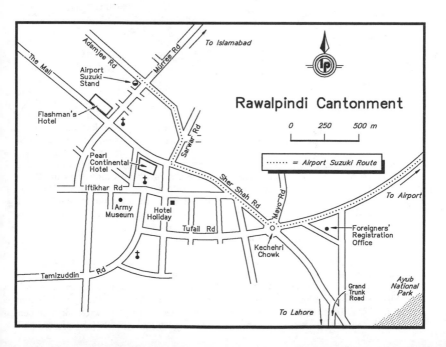

Bazaar fills with tape, book and clothes hawkers.

Tourist shops – on The Mall, in Islamabad's shopping centres and in top-end hotel arcades – have pricey carpets, brasswork, jewellery, Kashmiri shawls, carving and antiques. If you prefer hunting in the bazaars, following are some prominent markets. You can knock a third off a merchant's opening price if you're firm and friendly about it.

Pottery – try Bara Bazaar (Rajah Bazaar), Faizabad Bazaar (north end of Rawalpindi) or Saidpur village.

Jewellery & Brasswork – try Sarafa Bazaar (Rajah Bazaar) or Murree Rd around Asghar Mall Rd

Clothing & Tailors These are all over Rajah and Saddar bazaars. Off-the-shelf shalwar qamiz start at about Rs 200.

Spices – the main spice area is between Rajah Bazaar and Ganj Mandi Rd.

Fruit & Vegetables – go to the Sabzi Mandi ('vegetable market') in Rajah Bazaar.

For Western-style supplies and fast-food, toiletries and tampons, go to the shops in Jinnah or Super markets.

Getting There & Away – air

PIA's Rawalpindi booking office (☎ 567011 for Northern Areas; ☎ 568071 for other destinations) is on The Mall. The Islamabad office (☎ 815041) is in the Blue Area at 7th Ave; take a No 6 wagon. Both are open seven days a week.

Gilgit & Skardu These cheap and spectacular flights must be booked at the Rawalpindi office. Because they are so weather-dependent, all bookings are on a standby basis. Confirm by leaving your ticket with PIA the morning of the day before departure; at 3 pm they give it back. The final decision is made next morning. If it's cancelled you're waitlisted for the next flight.

Schedules are seasonal but there's at least one flight a day, weather permitting. Gilgit (Rs 570) is 1¼ hours by prop-driven Fokker, and Skardu (Rs 680) is 1½ hours by Boeing 737. A further weekly Fokker flight takes in

both. Travel agents cannot offer discounts on these flights.

Pakistan recently opened its domestic corridors to competition, and an Aga Khan-funded airline is said to be in the works, at least for the Northern Areas and Chitral.

Other Pakistan Destinations PIA has flights almost every day to Saidu Sharif (Swat), Peshawar-Chitral, Lahore, Quetta, Karachi and other cities. For these you'll get the lowest fares from a travel agent, not PIA; for the names of some reliable ones, see Information in this chapter. The 'Night Coach' to Karachi, departing around 11 pm, costs 25% less than the day-time fare of Rs 2070.

International Flights Only PIA, British Airways and Saudia have direct Islamabad connections. These and other carriers have booking offices along The Mall, in the Blue Area and in top-end hotels, but you'll do better at a reputable travel agent. Airline booking numbers are listed in the Getting There & Away chapter.

Getting There & Away – train

Pakistan Railways' booking & information office (☎ 827474) is at Melody Market in Islamabad; it's open from 9 am to 1 pm and 2 to 5 pm, except 9 am to 2.30 pm on Friday. A less user-friendly booking office is at the railway station in Saddar Bazaar.

You can ride to Havelian, the KKH's official southern end, in an ancient 2nd-class carriage on a lightly used spur from Taxila. There are three trains a day and the three-hour ride is Rs 12. For other Pakistan destinations, and information on tourist and student discounts, see the Getting There & Away chapter.

Getting There & Away – buses, vans & wagons

Pir Wadhai general bus stand is in north-west Rawalpindi. Between there and Saddar Bazaar (Kashmir Rd) passenger Suzukis cost a few rupees and take 25 to 50 minutes with

Top Left: Mansehra police station, formerly a Sikh temple (JK)
Top Right: Rajah Bazaar, Rawalpindi (JK)
Bottom: Street vendor, Rawalpindi (JK)

Top: Drying apricots, Hunza Valley (RI'A)
Middle Left: Waiter in restaurant, Xinjiang (RI'A)
Middle Centre: Dyer's shop, Gurdwara Bazaar, Abbottabad (JK)
Middle Right: Fruit vendors at Sunday Market, Kashgar (RI'A)
Bottom: Chinese Army workers on KKH, Xinjiang (JK)

a change at Fowara Chowk in Rajah Bazaar. Pir Wadhai's Suzuki conductors are aggressive; if you've just arrived in Rawalpindi, fight your way through them to an almost-full Suzuki or you may wait a long time before yours goes. Tongas are a laid-back alternative. The cheapest way from Pir Wadhai to Islamabad is by bus, changing at Faizabad.

Other long-distance transport is at Committee Chowk (behind the Rawal Hotel), Liaquat Chowk (on Murree Rd), and in the bazaars.

Gilgit This takes at least 15 hours in a bus, less in a van. Natco (☎ 860283) goes from Pir Wadhai daily at 4 and 9 am, and 1, 5, 8 and 11 pm (summer timings). The 9 am 'deluxe' is Rs 180, the others Rs 157; buy tickets from the window. A 50% student discount is available on all but the deluxe. Mashabrum Tours (☎ 863595) has daily

buses from Pir Wadhai for Rs 157 at 2, 6 and 9 pm; the 'office' is a man in a chair at the end of the yard. These buses cannot be booked ahead.

The Hameed Travel Service runs vans in the afternoon from the Mashriq Hotel (☎ 556161) south of Fowara Chowk, for Rs 180; you can book in advance.

Sit on the right for overall best views, unless you're subject to vertigo!

Mansehra via Abbottabad Simplest are vans from Haider Rd in Saddar for about Rs 25, which take three hours. GTS and private buses go from Pir Wadhai all day for about the same.

Murree Each morning TDCP (☎ 564824) runs comfortable buses from the corner of Kashmir Rd and The Mall; they're about Rs 20 and can be booked ahead. Wagons go all day from Railway Rd in Saddar Bazaar for

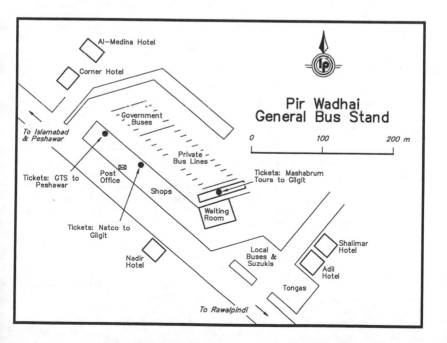

Rs 15, and buses go from Pir Wadhai and Faizabad for less.

Swat PTDC has a daily air-conditioned 25-seater at 9 am from Flashman's Hotel to Saidu Sharif, for Rs 100.

Taxila, Wah Gardens & Hasan Abdal Buses from Haider Rd in Saddar are about Rs 5; wagons also run from Railway Rd.

Other Pakistan Destinations See the Getting There & Away chapter.

Getting Around

To/From the Airport Suzukis to the airport go from Adamjee Rd in Saddar Bazaar and from Fowara Chowk in Rajah Bazaar. They're Rs 3 and take under half an hour in normal traffic.

To catch one *from* the airport, go out the gate and turn right. Those to Rajah Bazaar are near a petrol station on the left, about 100 metres up; those to Saddar Bazaar are 100 metres further at a fork on the right. For Islamabad, take a Rajah Bazaar Suzuki and change at Liaquat Chowk.

There's no bus service. A taxi is about Rs 50 to Rawalpindi, and Rs 70 to Islamabad.

Intercity Buses & Wagons Gaudy Bedford buses link Saddar Bazaar (Haider Rd), Murree Rd, Aabpara and Islamabad's markets in a tedious line (see the Islamabad and Saddar Bazaar maps). Saddar to Super Market takes one to 1½ hours, and costs Rs 4. Buses also go from the railway station to Islamabad.

Ford wagons have numbered routes, a bit quicker and about the same price as the Bedfords. The No 1 and No 6 from Haider Rd go via Aabpara to Super Market, then east to the Secretariat.

Other Ways In Rawalpindi, fixed-route passenger Suzukis are a few rupees. Black-and-yellow taxis have meters but, as most are 'broken', fix a price before you get in; Rawalpindi-Islamabad is at least Rs 80. Snarling motor-rickshaws are common in Rajah Bazaar, Pir Wadhai, Committee Chowk and Satellite Town; they're not much cheaper than a taxi and a lot less comfortable. Horse-drawn tongas are a relaxing way to get around the same area; some are fixed-fare, some for hire.

Around Rawalpindi & Islamabad

MARGALLA PASS

Twenty minutes from Rawalpindi the Grand Trunk Rd crosses the low Margalla Pass. At the top is a monument to John Nicholson, a British soldier-administrator who at age 25 led Pathan (Pashtun) tribesmen against the Sikhs here in 1848, and died a hero at the Siege of Delhi in 1857.

TAXILA

The Peshawar Plain, known historically as Gandhara, has attracted invaders since the 6th century BC when the Achaemenians built a city called Takshasila here. In 326 BC Alexander the Great rested at Takshasila – he called it Taxila – in his drive toward India. Half a century later, the Mauryan Emperor Ashoka, a patron of Buddhism, built a university at Taxila, to which pilgrims and scholars came from all over Asia. After about 180 BC, Bactrian Greeks moved in, and later Scythians and Parthians.

In the 1st century AD, the Kushans built their own city. Until the 3rd century this was the cultured capital of an empire stretching across the subcontinent and into Central Asia, the place from which Buddhism spread into China, and the birthplace of a striking fusion of Greek and Indian art. The city fell into obscurity after it was destroyed by White Huns in the 5th century.

The various excavations at Taxila are open to the public, along with many smaller sites over a 25-sq-km area. Tools and ornaments, temple friezes and Buddha-figures with Mediterranean faces are on display in the excellent Taxila Museum. A long day of

walking from the museum should include
Sirkap, Jandial Temple and Dharmarajika
stupa, though two days would be better.

Taxila Museum & Information Centre

The museum is open daily (except the first
Monday of each month) from 8.30 am to
12.30 pm and 2.30 to 5.30 pm in summer,
and 9 am to 4 pm in winter. The useful
*Gandhara, An Instant Guide to Pakistan's
Heritage* is for sale in an information centre
(☎ 2344) at the PTDC Motel opposite the
museum.

Bhir Mound

This Achaemenian site from the 6th to 2nd
centuries BC is a mostly unexcavated
mound, 300 metres from the museum. What
has been excavated shows twisting streets
and tiny stone houses or shops.

Sirkap

The Bactrians began 'their' Taxila, an
orderly walled city, in the 2nd century BC. It
was later adapted by Scythians and
Parthians; in fact most of what you can see
is Parthian. Along half a km of the wide main

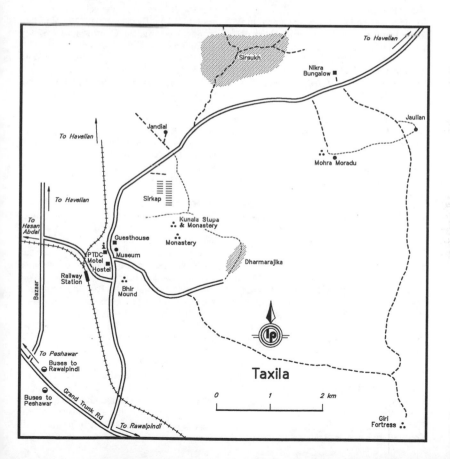

street are foundations of houses, stupas and a Buddhist temple; at the south end were wealthier homes. South of the town are Kunala Stupa, named for Emporer Ashoka's son, and the remains of two Kushan-era monasteries.

Jandial

Near the road just north of Sirkap are the ruins of a classical Greek temple, a rather haunting place with Ionic columns in front and the base of what may have been a Zoroastrian tower in the rear.

Dharmarajika

Within the huge Dharmara-jika stupa, three km east of the museum, is an original, smaller stupa built by Ashoka, possibly to house ashes of the Buddha. Around it are the bases of statues and small votive stupas and the remains of a monastery complex.

Sirsukh

Little of the Kushan city, started in the 1st century AD, has been excavated, and there isn't much to see.

Mohra Moradu

In a hollow about five km north-east of the museum and one km off the road is the isolated Mohra Moradu monastery, dating from the 3rd to 5th centuries. In one monk's cell is a small complete stupa.

Jaulian

At this site, on a hill east of Mohra Moradu, the stupas are gone but the courtyard and foundations are in good condition. In a security enclosure are the bases of several 5th-century votive stupas, which are ornamented with Buddhas and other figures. Other stupa bases have equally vivid carvings.

East of the courtyard is a monastery with dozens of closet-sized meditation cells. The caretaker might appreciate a few rupees for letting you in.

Places to Stay

Near the museum, a *Pakistan Youth Hostel* has Rs 25 beds for IYHA members (Rs 15 if you also have a student card). On the museum grounds is a deluxe *guesthouse*, very good value at Rs 160 per double with hot water. Near the Jaulian turn-off is *Nikra Bungalow* at the same price. Both can be booked through the museum (☎ (0596) 2495). The *PTDC Motel's* doubles are about Rs 250.

Getting There & Away

Taxila is half an hour from Rawalpindi's Saddar Bazaar by bus or wagon, but the half-hour, Rs 7 train ride is a far pleasanter way to get here. From the permanently congested Taxila Bazaar, buses, Suzukis and tongas pass Taxila Cantonment railway station en route to the museum.

Going back to Rawalpindi via the Grand Trunk Rd, check whether your bus is going to Saddar, Rajah or Pir Wadhai. Some Saddar-bound wagons originate at Taxila Bazaar.

Getting Around

Some buses and Suzukis from Taxila Bazaar go on up the road past Sirsukh, Mohra Moradu and Jaulian, or you can hire one of the tongas lurking around the museum.

WAH GARDENS

West of Taxila is the site of a Moghul camp developed by Emperor Akbar into a pleasure-ground of pools and gardens. It's gone to seed but the rows of ancient cypress and plane trees, the empty canals and run-down pavilions are still stately. Unfortunately, Wah Town is the site of a Pakistan Ordnance Factory too, and the peace is frequently shattered by explosions from across the highway. This makes a good addition to Taxila but is dubious as a day trip on its own.

Getting There & Away

On any bus to Hasan Abdal or Peshawar, ask for Wah Gardens, not Wah. Fifteen minutes beyond Taxila a 'Mughal Garden Wah' sign marks a road on the south side of the highway. The gardens are a 10-minute walk down this road.

HASAN ABDAL

This town on the GT Rd is a city of shrines. Pilgrims have been visiting since the 7th century when it was a Buddhist holy place. On a hill east of the village is a ziarat (shrine) to Baba Wali Kandahari, a 15th-century Sufi preacher. And Sikhs still come from India to Panja Sahib, a shrine to Baba Wali's contemporary Guru Nanak, founder of Sikhism – especially in mid-April for the *Baisakhi* festival. Also in the old walled town are abandoned Hindu temples and several Moghul tombs.

Orientation & Information

From the highway, walk 150 metres to a fork, bearing right past a post office and a playing field, half a km to another fork. Panja Sahib is left and around the corner; the Moghul tombs are to the right. Beyond the playing field a path climbs for an hour to Baba Wali's ziarat.

Panja Sahib

You may not be allowed into the yellow and white gurdwara. A central temple is surrounded by pools and shade trees, and around that several storeys of rooms, probably a pilgrims' hostel.

Moghul Tombs

The first tomb, built by a Punjab governor for himself, was commandeered by Emperor Akbar for a couple of his own favourites. Beyond this, in a tiny garden, is the mysterious tombstone of one Lala Rukh.

Baba Wali

The hilltop has an undramatic 360° view that includes Wah Gardens below, and on a clear day Taxila and the Margalla Pass.

Getting There & Away

Hasan Abdal is 20 minutes beyond Taxila by bus.

MURREE & THE GALIS

A few hours north of Islamabad is a maze of cool, forested ridges. As in other hilly bits of colonial India, the British developed many villages as 'hill stations' – beat-the-heat resorts for bureaucrats and army officers. In summer, the entire Punjab administration moved up to Murree, and anyone who was anyone had a villa at Nathiagali or one of the other hamlets whose names mostly end in *gali* (Hindko Punjabi for 'pass').

All still show the colonial imprint: prim bungalows, guesthouses and churches on the heights, roads and noisy bazaars below. Nowadays they bulge with middle-class Punjabi tourists all summer and on winter weekends. Summer season is May to September, and demand is heaviest in July and August. There seems to be no limit to summer hotel prices, but before and after that you can strike good bargains. Youth hostels at Khanspur and Bhurban are open to IYHA members but are also beloved by Pakistani students.

Murree

Murree sits high above its surroundings so the views are impressive, but there's little to do but stroll around or shop. A faint colonial aroma lingers along The Mall but it's pretty modern and touristy now.

Orientation Climb Cart Rd from the general bus stand. Past the Blue Pines Hotel, shortcut up through a small bazaar to The Mall. British-era Murree rambles for four km along the ridge-top. The downhill transport junctions of Sunny Bank, Kuldana Chowk and Jhikagali are effectively suburbs of Murree.

Information The best source for tourist information is TDCP, the Tourist Development Corporation of the Punjab, with an office (☎ 2729) below the Blue Pines Hotel on Cart Rd and a kiosk (☎ 2730) on The Mall. Murree maps are for sale at the Book Gallery on The Mall. No banks do foreign exchange.

Walks From Pindi Point you can look out toward the Punjab or ride a chairlift three km down to the road and back for about Rs 20. Kashmir Point (the highest place in Murree,

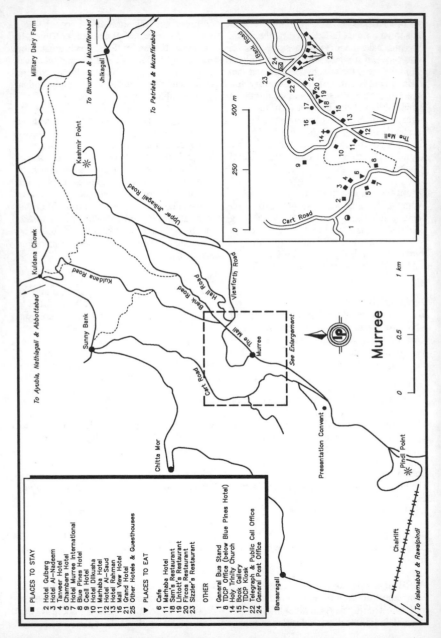

Murree

PLACES TO STAY
2 Hotel Gulberg
3 Hotel Al-Nadeem
4 Tanveer Hotel
5 Chambers Hotel
7 Hotel Murree International
8 Blue Pines Hotel
9 Cecil Hotel
10 Hotel Dilkusha
11 Marhaba Hotel
12 Hotel Al-Saud
13 Hotel Rehman
16 Mall View Hotel
21 Grand Hotel
25 Other Hotels & Guesthouses

PLACES TO EAT
6 Cafe
11 Marhaba Hotel
18 Sam's Restaurant
19 Lintott's Restaurant
20 Fircos Restaurant
23 Sizzler's Restaurant

OTHER
1 General Bus Stand
8 TDCP Office (below Blue Pines Hotel)
14 Holy Trinity Church
15 Book Gallery
17 TDCP Kiosk
22 Telegraph & Public Call Office
24 General Post Office

2260 metres) looks out beyond the Pir Panjal Range into Kashmir. From Bank Rd, a trail descends for an hour through woods to the Kuldana-Jhikagali road; a branch goes to Kuldana Chowk. Return on the trail or any wagon to Sunny Bank or the general bus stand.

Places to Stay Even the cheapos, eg the *Hotel Al-Nadeem* by the general bus stand and the *Hotel Rahman* and *Grand Hotel* on The Mall, want at least Rs 150 for a double in summer, though few are worth even Rs 50, their approximate off-season price. Decent hotels asking Rs 200 to Rs 300 for a double in summer are the *Gulberg, Tanveer, Chambers* and *Murree International* on Cart Rd. The *Blue Pines Hotel* has clean doubles for Rs 300 and up.

Most of the 50 or more hotels seem to be top-end. The *Dilkusha* wanted Rs 300 for a double in the *off*-season. The centrally located *Marhaba* is in the same range. Doubles at PTDC's *Cecil Hotel* are ridiculous at over Rs 1000 but the grand old building and magnificent views from the garden are worth a look.

Places to Eat A popular cafe opposite the Hotel Murree International has cheap curries, braised chicken, qeema and vegetables. The Mall has fast-food shops and several clean restaurants with identical Pakistani-Chinese-Western menus – *Sam's, Lintott's, Fircos* and *Sizzler's*. The *Marhaba Hotel's* restaurant is good for breakfast.

Getting There & Away TDCP runs coaches between Rawalpindi and Murree for Rs 15, three times a day in peak season. Wagons come from Rawalpindi's Saddar Bazaar, and buses from Pir Wadhai and Faizabad, for Rs 15.

Bhurban

Besides the scenery, Bhurban has a nine-hole golf course and a *Pakistan Youth Hostel*. It's 15 km north-east of Murree, via wagons from the general bus stand and Jhikagali.

Ayubia

Named for Ayub Khan, Pakistan's military ruler from 1958 to 1969, Ayubia is a resort area and national park encompassing the hamlets of Khairagali, Changlagali, Kuzagali, Ghora Dhaka and Khanspur. At Ghora Dhaka, five minutes' drive off the main road, are a few elegant houses, a modest bazaar and a cable car up the mountainside. Three km further on this spur road is Khanspur.

At Ghora Dhaka are the mid-range *Summer Inn*, the old *Ayubia Palace Hotel* and PTDC's *Ayubia Motel*. Khanspur has the small *Kashmir View Hotel* and a *Pakistan Youth Hostel*. There are wagons direct to Ghora Dhaka from Murree's general bus stand.

Nathiagali

At 2500 metres, Nathiagali ('naht-YA-gali') is the prettiest and most popular of the Gali resorts. From the main road it's a 10-minute climb on a link-road to an old wooden church. From there it's three hours up 2980-metre Miranjani Peak, with views across the Pir Panjal Range into Kashmir.

A similar climb is up 2800-metre Mukshpuri Peak behind Dungagali, which is an hour's walk down the road or the ridge from Nathiagali. It's a day's walk from Nathiagali down to Ghora Dhaka.

Places to Stay On the road are some not-so-cheap cheapos with grotty doubles for Rs 50 to Rs 80. Hotels with a view and hot-water doubles for Rs 150 to Rs 300 include the *Skyways* and *Kamran*. Up on the ridge are holiday homes, guesthouses and half a dozen hotels where doubles are Rs 400 and up. In Dungagali is the pricey *Mukshpuri Hotel* (☎ 567).

Getting There & Away Buses between Murree and Abbottabad stop at many of the Galis. Nathiagali is midway between, 1½ to two hours from each, and under Rs 10 either way. A few buses and vans go direct from Nathiagali to Murree early in the morning.

Language

Travelling down the KKH is like passing through half a dozen tiny countries. Every few hundred km you find not just another dialect but a new language. In addition to the two 'national' languages of Urdu and Mandarin Chinese, there are at least six other common tongues, from three different linguistic families. Persian is also understood to some extent throughout the region.

You can get by with some basic Urdu and Chinese, especially in official situations. However, neither is native to Xinjiang or the Northern Areas and they're often used grudgingly. But even the most garbled attempts at local speech can reward you out of all proportion to what you're actually trying to say.

The prominent local languages are Uyghur (Kashgar, Tarim Basin); Wakhi or Tajik (Tashkurghan, Gojal); Burushaski (Hunza); Shina (lower Hunza, Gilgit, Chilas); Kohistani (Indus Kohistan) and Pashto (Besham, Swat and northern Hazara). Included here are common words and phrases in these as well as Urdu and Chinese, plus a few phrases of Balti, the speech of Baltistan.

English is rarely used in western Xinjiang, except by a few educated officials. It's common in larger towns of the Northern Areas and widespread in Rawalpindi and Islamabad. The entire top echelon of the Pakistani civil service speaks English, so if you can't make yourself understood anywhere else, try a government or police official.

Writing

The written characters for numbers and for 'men' and 'women' might come in handy.

	Chinese	Urdu
1	一	۱
2	二	۲
3	三	۳
4	四	۴
5	五	۵
6	六	۷
7	七	۷
8	八	۸
9	九	۹
10	十	۱۰

	Man	Woman
Chinese	男	女
Uyghur	كىشى	ئايال
Urdu	مرد	عورت

Urdu

Urdu is the 'national language' of Pakistan, although fewer than 10% of Pakistanis speak it as a first language. It sounds much like Hindi, the speech of north India, but is written in a modified Arabic script.

Urdu is a scavenger language, swallowing whole phrases verbatim from Persian, Arabic, English, wherever. You'll have no trouble with *plet*, *machiz* and even the word for you, the foreigner, *angrez* (no matter where you're from). It's funny to hear officials on the telephone, popping in and out of English, and TV commercials for things like *kvaliti number vun chai*.

A more detailed guide to grammar, pronunciation and phrases is Lonely Planet's *Hindi/Urdu Phrasebook*. The home-grown *Teach Yourself Urdu in Two Months* (Anjuman Press, Karachi) is available in Pakistani bookshops.

Pronunciation

Most Urdu vowels have more than one sound, which in some English transliterations are distinguished with diacritical marks (eg a bar over long forms of *a*, *i* and *u*). These aren't used here, but you're fairly safe with the following sounds: *a* like 'a' in 'father', *e* like 'e' in 'bet', *i* like 'ee' in 'beet', *o* between 'oh' and 'aw', *u* like 'u' in 'put'. The symbols *ã*, *ẽ*, *õ* and *ŭ* for nasal vowels, spoken with the nose open, are used only in this book.

The combined consonants *th* are pronounced not as in English but separately – 't' with a light exhalation at the end (as in 'fathead'); similarly for *chh* and *dh*. But *sh*, *ch*, *gh*, *kh* and *zh* are not aspirated in this way. Pronounce *g* as in 'go' not 'gin', and *r* with a snap of the tongue.

Questions

Roughly speaking, you can make a phrase into a question with a simple inflexion of your voice, or by adding 'is it?' *(heh?)*.

Postpositions

These are like prepositions except that they go after the word. For example, 'the bus to Passu' is *Passu-ko bas*; 'in the hotel' is *hotel-mẽ*; 'John's wife' is *Jan-ki bivi*.

to	*-ko*
from	*-seh*
in	*-mẽ*
belonging to	*-ka* (m) or *-ki* (f)

Adjectives

The word for 'good' *(achhah)* is Urdu's all-purpose expression. Depending on context

and tone of voice it can also mean 'as you wish', 'I understand', 'I agree', 'right', 'really?' and more.

bad	*kharab*
first-rate	*pakka* ('pukka', eg a *pakka* road is paved)
inferior	*kacha* ('kutcha', eg a *kacha* road is unpaved)
hot/cold	*garam/tanda*
expensive/cheap	*menga/sasta*
left/right	*bayã/dayã*
beautiful	*khubsurut*
delicious	*laziz*
happy	*khush*
hungry	*bukha*
ill	*bimar*
and, more	*or*
one more, another	*ek or*
this/that	*yeh/woh*
here/there	*yahã/wahã*
both	*dono*

Adverbs

The word for 'enough' *(bas)* is another multi-purpose one, for when you've had enough tea, crowds, silly questions, etc. Saying it twice – *bas, bas!* – gives it an edge.

very much, very	*bohut*
a little	*tora*
next, after this	*dusra* or *dusri*
next bus	*dusra bas*

Pronouns

I/we	*mẽ/ham*
you (sg & familiar)	*tum*
you (pl & polite)	*ap*
he, she, they	*yeh*

Possessive pronouns are as follows for masculine objects; for feminine ones they end in *-i* not *-a*.

my/our	*mera/hamara*
yours (sg & familiar)	*tumhara*
yours (pl & polite)	*apka*
his, hers, theirs	*inka*

People

man	*admi* (ahd-MEE)
woman	*orot* (oh-ROHT)
father/mother	*pita/mata*
husband/wife	*shawarh/bivi*
brother/sister	*bhai/behẽ*
friend	*dost*
respected sir	*babu*

Greetings

'Peace be with you.'   *asalaam aleikum*

The nice thing about this general Muslim greeting is that it can pry a response from even the most bloody-minded people, if they are Muslim. The reply to an older or respected person is to repeat the phrase; to anyone else, it's *wa aleikum salaam* ('and with you too').

Sir/Madam	*jenab/begum*
How are you?	*kya hal heh?*
Fine, OK.	*teek heh*
Goodbye (God be with you).	*khuda hafiz* (khu-DA ha-FEEZ)
See you again.	*pir melengeh*

Accommodation

bedding	*bistra*
caretaker	*chowkidar* (CHO-kee-dar)
key	*chabi*
room	*kamra*
rope bed	*charpoi*
toilet	*pakhana* or *latrin*
woman's	*zanana*
man's	*mardana*
travellers' inn	*serai* or *musafir khana*
water heater (geyser)	*gizar*

Food

food	*khana*
bread	*roti*
fried bread	*paratha*
Middle-Eastern rounds	*nan* or *tandoori roti*
sliced bread	*dabl* (double) *roti*
unleavened flat-bread	*chapatti*
butter	*makhan*

cheese	*panir*
chillies	*mirch*
without chillies	*bina mirch keh*
egg	*anda*
boiled egg	*ublahwa anda*
fried egg	*anda frai*
fish	*machli*
fruit	*pal*
banana	*kela*
apple	*seb*
apricot	*khubani*
meat	*gosht*
beef	*gay-ka gosht*
chicken	*murgi*
mutton	*gosht* or *bakri*
rice	*chawal*
fried rice	*pulau*
plain rice	*sadha chawal*
salt	*namak* (NUM-uk)
spices	*masala*
sugar	*chini*
vegetable	*sabzi*
cabbage	*gobhi*
carrot	*gazhar*
lentils	*dhal*
okra	*bhindi*
peas	matar
potato	*alu*
spinach	*palak*
yoghurt	*dãi*

fork	*kanta*
knife	*chhuri*
spoon	*chammach*
small spoon	*chamchi*
I am a vegetarian.	*me shakahari hũ*

Drink

milk	*dudh*
soft drink	*botal*
tea	*chai*
milky tea	*dudh-chai*
green tea	*sabz-chai*
Pathan-style green tea	*khawa*
water	*pani*
boiled water	*ubla pani*

Some Useful Words

candle	*mombatti*

cobbler	*mochi*
hospital	*shafa khana*
hot spring	*garam chashma*
luggage	*saman (sa-MAHN)*
map	*naksha*
mosque	*masjid*
mountain	*pahar*
small mountain	*pahari*
river	*darya*
tributary valley	*nala*
shop	*dukan*
soap	*sabun*
tailor	*darzi*

Karakoram Highway
  Shahrah-l-Kurukoram
Silk Road
  Shahrah-i-Resham

Some Useful Phrases

There's no word for 'please', but adding *-ji* to names or phrases makes them extra polite, eg *shukria-ji, asalaam aleikum-ji.*

Thank you.
  shukria
Special thanks.
  mehrbani
Excuse me (polite).
  mafki-ji
No problem.
  koi bat nãi
Yes./No.
  hã/nãi
Do you speak English?
  ap english bolteh hẽ?
I don't understand.
  mẽ nahin samajta
I can't read Urdu.
  mẽ Urdu nahin parsakta
What's your name?
  apka nam kya heh?
My name is (John).
  mera nam (Jan) heh
What's the name of this place?
  ees jaga-ka nam kya hẽ?
Where are you going?
  ap kahã jateh hẽ?
Is there a (Gilgit) bus today?
  kya (Gilgit)-ko bas aj heh?

What time is it going?
  kitna bajeh jaegi?
Where is (the GPO)?
  (GPO) keddar heh?
Where are you from? (where is your house?)
  apka ghar keddar heh?
I'm from America.
  mera ghar Amrika-mẽ heh
Do you have (food)?
  apka pas (khana) heh?
Is there (hot water)?
  kya (garam pani) heh?
What do you want?
  ap kya chahteh hẽ?
I (don't) want tea.
  muje chai (nãi) chahyeh
How much does this cost?
  kitna rupia? or *kitna paisa?*
too expensive
  bohit menga heh
He is my husband.
  woh mera shawarh heh
She is my wife.
  woh meri bivi heh
God willing.
  inshallah
Stop!
  rukia!

Time

When? (date)	*kab?*
When? (time)	*kitna bajeh?*
What time is it?	*kitna bajeh hẽ?*
How long?	*kitna vakt?*
today	*aj*
tomorrow, yesterday (according to context)	*kal*
day after tomorrow, day before yesterday	*parasõ*
now	*ab*
immediately	*abhi*
(three) o'clock	*(teen) bajeh*
half-past (eight)	*sardeh-(aht) bajeh*
am	*suba*
pm (afternoon/evening)	*dopehar/sham*
hour	*ganta*
day	*din*
month	*mahina*
year	*sal*

Numbers

Urdu number-words don't have the regularity of English, so try to do things in round numbers! Don't confuse 25 and 50, or 7 and 60. To add ½ to a number (except 1 or 2) precede it with *sardeh* (eg 3½ is *sardeh-teen)*; this is common with prices and time.

Lakh (hundred thousand) and *kror* (10 million) are used for big numbers. Once into the thousands, large written numbers have commas every two places, not three.

1	*ek*
1½	*derh*
2	*doh*
2½	*dhai*
3	*teen*
4	*char*
5	*panj*
6	*cheh*
7	*saht*
8	*aht*
9	*nau*
10	*das*
11	*gyara*
12	*bara*
13	*tera*
14	*chuda*
15	*pandra*
16	*sola*
17	*sathara*
18	*athara*
19	*unnis*
20	*bis*
25	*pachis*
30	*tis*
35	*pantis*
40	*chalis*
45	*pantalis*
50	*pachas*
60	*sath*
70	*sattar*
80	*assi*
90	*nabbeh*
100	*sau*
1000	*hazar*
100,000	*lakh*

(Pakistanis write 1,00,000)

10,000,000	*kror*

(Pakistanis write 1,00,00,000)

Mandarin Chinese

Mandarin (or *putonghua*, 'people's speech') is China's official language, the dialect of Beijing and the speech of bureaucrats. Basic spoken Mandarin is surprisingly easy: no conjugations, no declensions, word order like English – just string them together. The hard parts are pronunciation and tones.

Pronunciation

Mainland China's official Romanised 'alphabet' of Chinese sounds is called Pinyin. It's very streamlined, but the sounds aren't always self-evident. The letters that don't sound quite like English are as follows:

Consonants *q* (flat 'ch'); *x* (flat 'sh'); *zh* ('j'); *z* ('dz'); *c* ('ts'); *r* (tongue rolled back, almost 'z').

Vowels *a* ('ah'); *er* ('ar', American pronunciation); *ui* ('oi' or 'wei'); *iu* ('yoh'); *ao* ('ow' as in 'now'); *ou* ('ow' as in 'low'); *e* ('uh' after consonants); *ian* ('yen'); *ong* ('oong'); *u* ('oo', or sometimes like 'ü': say 'ee' with your mouth rounded as if to say 'oo').

Tones

A given sound has many meanings depending on how it's 'sung'. But with common phrases you can get away without tones because the Chinese try hard to figure out what you mean. Syllables aren't stressed strongly.

Negation

Adjectives and present-tense verbs are negated by preceding them with *bu*, or occasionally *mei* (as in the all-too-familiar *mei you*, 'we don't have any').

Questions

A phrase becomes a question if you add *ma* to the end of it (you understand, *ni dong*; do you understand? *ni dong ma?*). Or you can make a question by juxtaposing positive and negative forms (Do you want it?, 'want-not-want?' *yao bu yao?*; Do you have it? *you mei you?*; OK?, 'good-not-good?' *hao bu hao?*).

Books

Be sure your phrasebook or dictionary uses Pinyin, not earlier Romanisations which are even more confusing. It helps if it has Chinese characters too, for showing to Chinese who speak other dialects. Most phrasebooks are full of things you'll never be able to use ('stop or I'll scream') but Lonely Planet's *Mandarin Chinese Phrasebook* has Chinese characters, tones, Pinyin and useful word-lists.

Adjectives

very	*hen* (hun)
good/bad	*hao/huai*
beautiful	*hao-kan*
delicious	*hao-chi* (how-chr)
happy	*gaoxing* (gow-sheeng)
expensive	*gui* (gway)
cheap	*pianyi* (pyen-yee)
left/right	*zuo/you*
open (for travel)	*aifang* (kye-fung)
broken	*huai-le* (hwy-luh)
here/there	*zhe-li/na-li*

Verbs

buy	*mai*
go	*qu* (chü)
live, reside	*shenhuo* (shun-hwoh)

work	*gongzuo* (goong-zwoh)
like	*xihuan* (shee-hwan)

Prepositions

from	*cong* (tsoong)
to	*dao*
in, on, at	*zai*

Pronouns

I/we	*wo/women* (woh-mun)
you (sg/pl)	*ni/nimen*
he, she, it/they	*ta/tamen*

Possessive Form Add *-de* (duh); 'our' is *nimen-de* and so on.

People

person	*ren* (run)
father/mother	*baba/mama* (informal)
husband	*zhangfu* (jahng-fu)
wife	*qizi* (chee-dzih)
son	*erzi* (ar-dzih)
daughter	*nuer* (nu-ar)
friend	*pengyou* (pung-yo)
foreigner	*waiguoren*
student	*xuesheng* (shway-shung)
tourist	*luyouzhe* (lü-yo-dzih)

Countries

Australia	*ao-da-li-ya*
Canada	*jia-na-da*
China	*zhongguo* (joong-gwoh)
England	*yingguo*
Hong Kong	*xiang-gang*
New Zealand	*xing-xi-lan*
Pakistan	*ba-ji-si-tan*
the USA	*meiguo*

Accommodation

dormitory	*sushe* (su-shuh)
double room	*shuang ren fangjian*
guesthouse	*binguan*

hotel, cheaper — *lüguan* (lü-gwahn)
key — *yaoshi* (yow-shr)
shower — *linyu* (leen-yü)
single room — *dan-ren fangjian*
telephone — *dianhua* (dyen-hwa)
toilet — *cesuo* (tsuh-swoh)

Around Town
airmail — *hang-kong*
bank — *yinhang*
hospital — *yiyuan*
post office — *you-ju* (yoh-jü)
Public Security Bureau — *gong-an ju*
stamp — *you-piao*

Getting Around
airport — *feiji chang*
bicycle — *zixingche* (dzih-sheeng-chuh)
bus — *qiche* (chee-chuh)
bus station — *qiche zhan*
ticket to (Ghez) — *dao (Ghez) de piao*
train station — *huoche zhan*
truck — *dakache*

Food
chopsticks — *kuaizi* (kwy-dzih)
menu — *caidan* (tsy-dahn)
restaurant — *fanguar*
beef — *niu rou*
bread — *mianbao*
cake — *dangao*
chicken — *ji rou*
egg — *jidan*
  boiled — *zhu...* (ju)
  fried — *jian...* (jyen)
fried noodles — *chaomian* (chow-myen)
green vegetable — *qingcai* (cheeng-tsy)
hot chillies — *lajiao*
melon — *gua*
MSG — *wei-jin*
mutton — *yang rou (roe)*
rice — *fan*
  steamed rice — *mifan*
  fried rice — *chaofan*
salt — *yan*
soup — *tang* (high tone)
sugar — *tang* (rising tone)

Drink
beer — *pijiu* (pee-joh)
boiling water (for tea) — *kai shui* (ky-shway)
milk — *niu nai*
tea — *cha*
  a pot of tea — *yi-hu cha*
white spirits — *baijiu*
wine — *putaojiu*

Some Useful Words
home-place — *jia*
Silk Road — *Sichou Zhi Lu*
Karakoram Highway — *Zhong-Pa Gong Lu*
Uyghur language — *weizuhua*
money — *qian* (chyen)
RMB — *renminbi*
FEC — *wai hui*
US dollar — *meiyuan*
Hong Kong dollar — *gangbi*
map — *ditu*
toilet paper — *weisheng zhi* (way-shung jr)

Some Useful Phrases
Hello ('are you well?').
  ni hao
Goodbye.
  zaijian
Thank you.
  xiexie
Please.
  qing
Excuse me.
  dui bu qi (dway-bu-chee)
Yes ('you are correct').
  dui (dway)
No.
  bu dui or *bu shi*
Where is (the toilet)?
  (cesuo) zai na li?
Do you have (hot water)?
  (kai shui), you mei you?
I (don't) have rice.
  wo (mei) you fan
I (don't) want tea.
  wo (bu) yao cha
How much does it cost?
  duo-shao qian?
Too expensive!
  tai gui-le!

Too loud!
tai chao le!
Enough!
gou le! (go-luh)
Where are you going?
qu na li? or *qu nar?*
Is it allowed?
ke bu keyi? (kuh bu kuh-yee)
Wait a moment.
deng yi huar (dung yee hwar)
No problem.
mei guanxi (may gwan-shee)
Where are you from?
ni cong nali lai de?
I am from (America).
wo cong (Meiguo) lai de
Do you speak English?
ni shuo Yingyü ma?
a little bit
yi dian-dian (yee dyen-dyen)
I cannot speak Mandarin.
wo bu hui shuo putonghua
Do you understand?
ni dong ma?
I don't understand (your language).
wo ting bu dong
I cannot read that (Chinese characters).
wo kan bu dong

Time

when? (date)	*ji hao?*
when? (time)	*ji dian?*
today	*jintian*
tomorrow	*mingtian*
day after tomorrow	*houtian*
yesterday	*zuotian*
now	*xianzai* (shyen-dzai)
(five) o'clock	*(wu)-dian*
half-past (eight)	*(ba)-dian ban*
(three) hours	*(san)-ge xiaoshi* (...shyow-shr)
half an hour	*ban-ge xiaoshi*

Days of the Week

Use *xingqi* (shing-chee) plus a number (Monday = 1 through Saturday = 6; for example, *xingqi wu* is Friday). Sunday is *xingqi tian*.

Numbers

The simplest way to count is (number)-*ge*-(object); eg, 'two people' is *liang-ge ren*.

½	*ban*
1	*yi*
2	*er* (ar) (simple counting)
	liang
3	*san*
4	*si* (sih)
5	*wu*
6	*liu* (lyoh)
7	*qi* (chee)
8	*ba*
9	*jiu* (jyoh)
10	*shi* (shr)
11	*shi yi*
20	*er shi*
21	*er shi yi*
30	*san shi*
100	*yi bai*
200	*liang bai*
1000	*yi qian* (chyen)

Uyghur

Uyghur (or Turki) is spoken all over Xinjiang and in parts of Kirghizstan and Uzbekistan. It's a Turkic language with words of Mongol, Kirghiz, Uzbek, Wakhi, Russian, Urdu, Arabic and Persian. In China, written Uyghur uses an Arabic script, although for a time children were taught a Romanised alphabet. For more words, a Turkish dictionary will help. This glossary reflects the Kashgar dialect.

The symbol *ü* is pronounced by saying 'ee' with your mouth rounded as if to say 'oo'. Most words are accented on the last syllable.

Pronouns

I/we	*men/biz*
you (sg/pl)	*sen/siz* (*siz* is polite)
he or she/they	*u/ular*

Possessive Form Add -*nung* after the noun.

Adjectives

good/bad	*yakhshe/yaman*
beautiful (place)	*güzel*
beautiful (face)	*cherailekh*
delicious	*mizlik* or *tamlik*
expensive	*khummet*
left/right	*sol/ung*
this/that	*bu/u*
here/there	*buyer/uyer*

People

person	*adem* (AH-dem)
man/woman	*er/ayal*
father	*dada*, *ata*
mother	*mama*, *ana* (old)
	apa (young)
husband	*ireh* (EE-reh)
wife	*ayaleh* (ah-YAH-leh)
elder/younger brother	*akka/hukah*
elder/younger sister	*acha/singil*
friend	*dos*
'brother' (informal, between men)	*burader*
head-man	*mokhtar*, *bashlak*

Accommodation

hotel	*mihman khana*
key	*achkhooch*
toilet	*khala*

Getting Around

bus	*aptus* (ahp-TOOS)
bus station or stop	*aptus biket*
ticket	*bilet*
bicycle	*velspid*

Food

food	*tamakh*
restaurant	*tamakhana*
food stall	*ashkhana*
bread	*nan*
bagel	*gurdah*
flat-bread	*ak nan*
fish	*bilekh*
fried noodles & peppers	*laghman*
fried rice & meat	*pulau* or *pilaf*
meat	*gush*
beef	*kala gush*
chicken	*toha gush*
mutton	*koi gush*

steamed rice	*gampen*
vegetable	*sei*
yoghurt	*kitk* or *airan*
apple	*ulmah*
fig	*enjü*
grapes	*uzum*
melon	*khoghun* or *ko'un*
peach	*shaptul*
pear	*amut*

Drink

beer	*pivo*
tea	*chai*
water	*su*
boiled water	*khainat-kan su*

Some Useful Words

Chinese money:	
yuan or kuai	*koi*
jiao or mao	*mo*
home	*aileh* (AH-ee-leh)
hospital	*doktor khana*
house	*üi*
Sunday Market	*Yekshenba Bazaar*
lake	*kul*, as in Kara Kul
mountain	*tagh*
river	*darya*

Some Useful Phrases

Hello.
  asalaam aleikum or *salaam*
Goodbye.('be happy')
  khayr khosh or just *khosh*
How are you?
  yakhshim siz?
I am well/happy.
  yakhshi/khushal
Thank you.
  rakhmat
Excuse me.
  kechur siz
Yes./No.
  owa/jyok
Where are you going?
  naga barsis?
Where is (the station)?
  (biket) khayerdeh?
What is the name of this place?
  uyarnung ismeh nimeh?

How much does it cost?
neech pul? or *konch pul?*
What's your name?
ismengez nimeh?
My name is (John).
mennung ismim (Jan)
I (don't) understand.
bil (mei) men
Do you have (tea)?
(chai) varma?
We do/don't.
var/yok
Please give me (a beer).
manga (pivo) birsengez
I (don't) like Kashgar.
men Kashgar-neh yakshkur (mei) men

Time

What is the time?
sa'et konche boldeh?
It's (six) o'clock.
sa'et (alteh) boldeh
when? at what time?
sa'et konche deh?
at (five) o'clock
sa'et (besh) deh

today	*bügün*
tomorrow	*atteh*
yesterday	*tünegün*
now	*hazir*
local time	*yerlik vaket*
Beijing time	*Beijing vaket*

Numbers

½	*yerim*
1	*bir*
2	*shkeh* or *iki*
3	*üch*
4	*turt*
5	*besh*
6	*alteh*
7	*yetteh*
8	*saikiz*
9	*tokooz*
10	*un*
20	*yigirmeh*
30	*ottooz*
40	*krk*
50	*ellek*
60	*altmish*
70	*yetmish*
80	*saiksen*
90	*tokhsun*
100	*yüz*
1000	*mung*

(With thanks to Kurt Greussing & Mokimjian)

Wakhi

Wakhi is the speech of the Tajik people in the Tashkurghan region, Gojal, ex-Soviet Tajikistan and Afghanistan's Wakhan Corridor.

Pronouns

I/we	*wooz/saak*
you (sg/pl)	*tu/sasht*
he/they	*yah/yasht*

Adjectives

very	*ghafeh*
good/bad	*baaf/shaak*
beautiful	*khushroi*
delicious	*mazadar*
left/right	*chap/rost*
this/that	*yem/ya*
here/there	*drem/dra*

People

man/woman	*dai/hruinan*
father/mother	*taat/naan*
husband/wife	*shauhar/jamat*
brother/sister	*vrut/hrui*
friend	*doost*
head-man	*arbab*

Accommodation

key	*weshik*
room	*jayi*
toilet	*tarkank*

Food

apple	*mur*
apricot	*chuan*
egg	*tukhmurgeh*
food, bread	*shapik*
meat	*gosht*
rice	*gerangeh*
vegetable	*ghazk*
whole-wheat bread	*kamishdoon,*
	dildungi
yoghurt	*pai*

Drink

buttermilk	*deegh*
milk	*bursh*
tea	*choi*
water	*yupek*

Some Useful Words

hot spring	*theen kook*
house	*khun*
mountain/peak	*kho/sar*
river	*darya*
valley	*zherav*

Some Useful Phrases

Hello.
   asalaam aleikum or *salaam*
Goodbye.
   khudar hafiz
How are you?
   chiz hawleh thei? (chiz HAW-lih tay)

I am	*woozem .... thei*
well	*baaf*
happy	*khush*
hungry	*merz* ('mares')
thirsty	*wesk*

Thank you.
   shukria (shu-KREE-ah)
What's your name?
   ti noongeh chiz thei?
My name is (John).
   zhu noongeh (Jan) thei
I don't understand.
   majeh neh disht
I like (tea).
   woozesh (choiyeh) khush-tsaram
I want (tea).
   woozesh (choiyeh) zokh-tsaram
How much?
   tsumar?
Where is (the hot spring)?
   (theen kook) komar thei?

Time

when?	*tsoghdi?*
today	*wodeg*
tomorrow	*pigah*
yesterday	*yez*
now	*niveh*

Numbers

1	*yew*
2	*bui*
3	*trui*
4	*tsebur*
5	*panz*
6	*shaad*
7	*hoob*
8	*haat*
9	*nau*
10	*das*
20	*wist*
100	*saad*
1000	*hazar*

(With thanks to Haqiqat Ali)

Burushaski

Burushaski is spoken in central Hunza, upper Nagar and the Yasin Valley. Its origins are obscure, but it may be the KKH region's oldest language. Its difficult structure makes it nearly impossible for outsiders to master;

there are said to be 38 plural forms, and words change form at both ends depending on context. But simple ideas are manageable.

The vowel *u* is pronounced 'oo' as in 'moon'. Hunza and Nagar dialects are slightly different, for instance a common form of 'be' is *bila* in Hunza but *dila* in Nagar.

Pronouns

I/mine	*jeh/jah*
you/yours (sing)	*um/umeh*
he/his	*in/ineh*
she/hers	*inegus/inemo*
we/ours	*mi/mi'i*
you/yours (pl)	*ma/ma'a*
they/theirs	*u/ueh*

Adjectives

very	*ghafeh*
good/bad	*baaf/shaak*
beautiful	*khushroi*
delicious	*mazadar*
left/right	*chap/rost*
this/that	*yem/ya*
here/there	*drem/dra*

People

man/woman	*hir/gus*
father/mother	*aya/mama*
husband/wife	*a'uyar/a'us*
brother/sister	*acho/ayas*
head-man	*uyum*
friend	
for men	*shugulo* (shu-GU-lo)
for women	*shuguli*
person from Hunza, Ganesh, etc	
Hunzakut, Ganeshkut, etc	

Accommodation

key	*chei*
room	*kamera*
toilet	*chukang*

Food

apple	*balt*
apricot	*ju*
dried apricot	*batering* (bah-TEHR-ing)
dry cheese	*kurut*
egg	*tigan* (ti-GAHN)
food, bread	*shapik*
meat	*chaap*
noodle soup	*daudo*
rice	*briw* in Nagar, *bras* in Hunza
white cheese	*burus*
whole-wheat bread	*phitti*
vegetable	*hoi*
yoghurt	*dumanu mamu* (du-MA-nu ma-MU)

Drink

buttermilk	*diltar*
grape wine	*mel*
milk	*mamu* (ma-MU)
mulberry spirits	*arak*
tea	*chai*
milk tea	*mamu chai*
green tea	*sabaz chai*
water	*tsil*
drinking water	*minas tsil*

Some Useful Words

channel	*gotsil*
home-place	*watan* (wa-TAAN)
hot spring	*garum bul* (gah-ROOM bool)
house	*ha*
mountain	*chish*
river	*sinda*
valley	*har* or *bar*

Some Useful Phrases

Hello.
  leh or *ajoh*
Goodbye.
  khuda hafiz or *khudayar*
How are you?
  behal bila? (beh-HAL bi-LA)
I am well.
  shuwa ba
Thank you.
  shukria
Yes./No.
  ju/baya
What's your name?
  besan guik bila? (BEH-san gwik bi-LA)
My name is (John).
  ja ayik (Jan) bila

What's the name of this place?
kuteh disheh besan ik bila?
Do you have (tea)?
(chai) bila?
How much does this cost?
besan gash bila?
I don't understand.
o dayalam (o da-YA-lum)

Time

when?	*beshal?*
today	*khultu* or *kulto*
tomorrow	*jimale* (JI-ma-le)
yesterday	*sabur* (sah-BOOR)
now	*mu*

Numbers

1	*han*
2	*alto* (al-TOH)
3	*usko* (oos-KOH)
4	*walto* (WAHL-toh)
5	*tsundo* (tsoon-DOH)
6	*mishindo* (mi-SHIN-doh)
7	*talo* (tah-LOH)
8	*altambo* (ahl-TAHM-boh)
9	*huncho* (hoon-CHOH)
10	*torumo* (TOH-ru-moh)
20	*altar* (ahl-TAAR)
100	*tha* (ta)
1000	*saas*

(With thanks to Latif Anwar)

Shina

Shina is spoken in lower Hunza and Nagar (below the KKH bridge near Minapin); Gilgit and its valleys (Naltar, Bagrot, Haramosh and the Gilgit River watershed); Chilas and north-east Indus Kohistan. Meanings are often expressed by tones, so only the simplest words are given here.

Pronouns

I/we	*ma/beh*
you (sing/pl)	*tu/su*
he/she/they	*roh/reh/rih*

People

man/woman	*manuzho/chei* (ma-nu-ZHO)
father/mother	*maloh/ma*
husband	*musha* (mu-SHA)
wife	*jama* (ja-MA)
brother/sister	*zha/sa*
head-man, representative	*nambardar* (nam-bar-DAR)
friend	*somo*
foreigner, outsider	*darineh* (da-RI-neh)

Food

apricot (common)	*jeroti*
dried apricots	*phator* (fa-TOR)
egg	*haneh* (ha-NEH)
food, bread	*tiki*
meat	*mots*
rice	*briw*
salt	*paju* (pa-JU)
wholewheat bread	*chupatti* (not chapatti)
vegetable	*sha*
yoghurt	*mutu dut* (MU-tu-doot)

Drink

milk	*dut* (rhymes with 'put')
tea	*chai*
water	*wei*

Some Useful Words

home-place	*watan* (wa-TAAN)
hot spring	*tato uts* (TA-to oots)
house	*goht*
mountain	*chish*
river	*sin*
valley	*gah*

Some Useful Phrases

Hello.
asalaam aleikum
Goodbye.
khuda hafiz (khu-DA ha-FEEZ)
How are you?
jek hal hen?
Fine.
shukur (SHOO-kur)

Thank you.
  shukria
Yes./No.
  awah/neh
What is your name?
  tei nom jek han?
My name is (John).
  mei nom (Jan) han
I don't understand.
  mei hir nawato (...NA- wa-toh)
I like (Gilgit).
  mas (Gilgit) pasantamus
  (pa-SAAN- ta-moos)

Time

when?	*kareh?* (ka-REH)
today	*aash*
tomorrow	*loshteh* (losh-TEH)
yesterday	*bala* (ba-LA)
now	*ten*
at once	*dahm*

Numbers

1	*ek*
2	*du*
3	*cheh*
4	*char*
5	*poë* (nasal *e*)
6	*sha*
7	*saat*
8	*ach*
9	*nau*
10	*dai*
20	*bi*
100	*shal*
1000	*hazar*

(With thanks to Latif Anwar & Qurban Ali)

Kohistani

Kohistani is spoken in northern Swat and Indus Kohistan. It's a mish-mash of Shina, Pashto, Urdu, Persian and other languages, and varies from one village to the next. Shina or Pashto may work just as well.

Adjectives

good	*mishto* (meesh-TOH)
bad	*khacho* (KHA-cho)
beautiful	*sudacho* (su-DA-cho)
happy	*khush*
expensive	*keimeti* (kay-meh-TEE)
hot/cold	*tato/shidalo*
left/right	*kabu*/dachinu
this/that	*anu/ro*
here/there	*adayn/al*

People

man/woman	*maash/garyu*
father/mother	*aba* (a-BA)/*ya*
son/daughter	*puch/dhi*
brother/sister	*zha/bhyun*
(my) friend	*(mil) doost*

Food & Drink

bread	*gwel*
egg	*ana* (ah-NA)
meat	*masu* (ma-SU)
milk	*chir*
tea	*chai*
vegetable	*sabzi*
water	*vi* or *wi*
yoghurt	*dudi*

Some Useful Words

high valley, pass	*dara*
home-place	*miwatan* (MI-wa-taan)
mountain	*kor*
name	*na*
river	*seen*

Some Useful Phrases
Hello.
  asalaam aleikum
Goodbye.
  hudar hawala (hu-DAR ha-WA-la)
Good.
  suga (su-GA) or *mihta*
Thank you.
  shukria
Yes./No.
  ah/ni

Time
today	*aaz*
tomorrow	*okot*
now	*uskeh*
(two) o'clock	*(du) masma*

Numbers
1	*ek*
2	*du*
3	*cha*
4	*sawur*
5	*paz*
6	*sho*
7	*saat*
8	*aat*
9	*naan* or *nau*
10	*daash*
20	*bish*
100	*shol*
1000	*zir*

Pashto

Pashto is the speech of the Pathans (Pashtuns) in eastern Afghanistan and Pakistan's North-West Frontier Province. Along the KKH you'll hear it, polluted with other dialects, in Besham, Batagram and Mansehra.

Adjectives
good, very good	*kha, der kha*
beautiful	*khesta*
expensive/cheap	*gran/arazan*

People
man	*sarleh* or *nafar*
woman	*zanana* or *khezeh*
father/mother	*plar/mor*
husband	*khawun* (kha-WOON)
wife	*khazar* (KHAH-zar)
brother/sister	*ror/khor*
friend	*dost*

Food & Drink
egg	*aghai*
food, bread	*dodai* or *ukhra*
meat	*wakha*
tea	*chai*
vegetable	*sabzi*
water	*ubuh*
boiled water	*ishedeli ubuh* (i-SHEH-deh-li...)

Some Useful Words
house	*ghar*
mountain	*kor*
name	*nam*
river	*darya*
valley	*wadi*

Some Useful Phrases
Hello.
  asalaam aleikum
Welcome.
  pakhar raghli
How are you?
  sa hal deh?
Where are you going?
  charta zi?
Goodbye.
  da khudai paman
  (da khu-DEH pa-MAAN) or
  pamakha dekha (pa-MA-kha deh-KHA)
Thank you.
  tashakur or *shukria*
Yes./No.
  ah/na

Time
today	*nun* or *nunroz*
tomorrow, yesterday (according to context)	*balauroz*

day after tomorrow,	
day before yesterday	*dremoroz*
now	*oos*

Numbers

1	*yow* or *yo*
2	*dva*
3	*dreh*
4	*salor*
5	*pinzo*
6	*shpaag*
7	*uwa* or *wo*
8	*atta* or *atto*
9	*naha*
10	*laas* or *loos*
100	*suul*
1000	*zar*

Balti

The Balti people are descended in part from 8th-century Tibetan invaders, and the Balti language is similar to classical Tibetan. Though not actually spoken along the KKH, a few words and phrases are included here for travellers to Skardu.

Food

bread	*kurba* or *chapatti*
tea	*cha*
water	*chu*

Some Useful Words

good	*lyakhmo*
	(lyakh-MO)
bad	*jaangmen*
	(jaang-MEN)
come/go!	*haung/saung!*
eat	*zo*

Some Useful Phrases

Hello. (formal)
   asalaam aleikum
Hello. (casual)
   shokhs or *shakhsa*
Goodbye.
   hudari faghring
Thank you.
   shukria
How much is it?
   khmul cham weh?
Where is...?
   ...po gayutpin?

Numbers

1	*chik*
2	*gis*
3	*sum*
4	*ji*
5	*ga*
6	*trook*
7	*dun*
8	*gyad*
9	*gu*
10	*fchu*
100	*bya*

Index

Keep in touch!

We love hearing from you and think you'd like to hear from us.

The Lonely Planet Newsletter covers the when, where, how and what of travel. (AND it's free!)

When...is the right time to see reindeer in Finland?
Where...can you hear the best palm-wine music in Ghana?
How...do you get from Asunción to Areguá by steam train?
What...should you leave behind to avoid hassles with customs in Iran?

To join our mailing list just contact us at any of our offices. (details below)

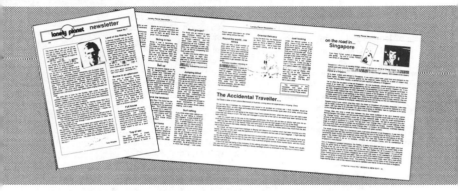

Every issue includes:

- *a letter from Lonely Planet founders Tony and Maureen Wheeler*
- *travel diary from a Lonely Planet author - find out what it's really like out on the road*
- *feature article on an important and topical travel issue*
- *a selection of recent letters from our readers*
- *the latest travel news from all over the world*
- *details on Lonely Planet's new and forthcoming releases*

Also available Lonely Planet T-shirts. 100% heavy weight cotton (S, M, L, XL)

LONELY PLANET PUBLICATIONS
Australia: PO Box 617, Hawthorn, 3122, Victoria (tel: 03-819 1877)
USA: Embarcadero West, 155 Filbert Street, Suite 251, Oakland, CA 94607 (tel: 510-893 8555)
UK: Devonshire House, 12 Barley Mow Passage, Chiswick, London W4 4PH (tel: 081-742 3161)

Guides to the Indian Subcontinent

Bangladesh - a travel survival kit
This practical guide – the only English-language guide to Bangladesh – encourages travellers to take another look at this often-neglected but beautiful land.

India - a travel survival kit
Widely regarded as *the* guide to India, this award-winning book has all the information to help you make the most of the unforgettable experience that is India.

Kashmir, Ladakh & Zanskar - a travel survival kit
Detailed information on three contrasting Himalayan regions in the Indian state of Jammu and Kashmir – the narrow valley of Zanskar, the isolated 'little Tibet' of Ladakh, and the stunningly beautiful Vale of Kashmir.

Nepal - a travel survival kit
Travel information on every road-accessible area in Nepal, including the Terai. This practical guidebook also includes introductions to trekking, white-water rafting and mountain biking.

Pakistan - a travel survival kit
Discover 'the unknown land of the Indus' with this informative guidebook – from bustling Karachi to ancient cities and tranquil mountain valleys.

Sri Lanka - a travel survival kit
Some parts of Sri Lanka are off-limits to visitors, but this guidebook uses the restriction as an incentive to explore other areas more closely – making the most of friendly people, good food and pleasant places to stay – all at reasonable cost.

Tibet - a travel survival kit
The fabled mountain-land of Tibet was one of the last areas of China to become accessible to travellers. This guide has full details on this remote and fascinating region, including the border crossing to Nepal.

Trekking in the Indian Himalaya
All the advice you'll need for planning and equipping a trek, including detailed route descriptions for some of the world's most exciting treks.

Trekking in the Nepal Himalaya
Complete trekking information for Nepal, including day-by-day route descriptions and detailed maps – a wealth of advice for both independent and group trekkers.

Also available:
Hindi/Urdu phrasebook, *Nepal* phrasebook, and *Sri Lanka* phrasebook.

Guides to North-East Asia

North-East Asia on a shoestring
Concise information for independent low-budget travel in China, Hong Kong, Japan, Macau, North Korea, South Korea, Taiwan and Mongolia.

China - a travel survival kit
This book is the recognised authority for independent travellers in the People's Republic. With essential tips for avoiding pitfalls, and comprehensive practical information, it will help you to discover the real China.

Hong Kong, Macau & Canton - a travel survival kit
This practical guide had all the travel facts on these three diverse cities, linked by history, culture and geography.

Japan - a travel survival kit
Japan is a unique contrast of modern cities and remote wilderness areas, of sophisticated technology and ancient tradition. This guide tells you how to find the Japan that many visitors never see.

Korea - a travel survival kit
This comprehensive guide includes an exclusive chapter on North Korea, one of the world's most reclusive countries – finally opening its doors to independent travellers.

Mongolia - a travel survival kit
Truly a destination for the adventurous this guide gives visitors the first real opportunity to explore this remote but newly accessible country.

Taiwan - a travel survival kit
Names of all places, hotels and restaurants are given in Chinese script and Pinyin in this practical guidebook, which also includes useful information for business people visiting Taiwan.

Tibet - a travel survival kit
The fabled mountain-land of Tibet was one of the last areas of China to become accessible to travellers. This guide has full details on this remote and fascinating region, including the border crossing to Nepal.

Tokyo - city guide
Tokyo is a dynamic metropolis and one of the world's leading arbiters of taste and style. This guide will help you to explore the many sides of Tokyo, the modern Japanese miracle rolled into a single fascinating, sometimes startling package.

Also available:
China phrasebook, Korean phrasebook, Tibet phrasebook, and Japanese phrasebook.

Lonely Planet Guidebooks

Lonely Planet guidebooks cover every accessible part of Asia as well as Australia, the Pacific, South America, Africa, the Middle East, Europe and parts of North America. There are five series: *travel survival kits*, covering a country for a range of budgets; *shoestring guides* with compact information for low-budget travel in a major region; *walking guides*; *city guides* and *phrasebooks*.

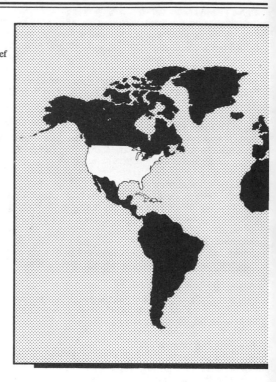

Mail Order

Lonely Planet guidebooks are distributed worldwide. They are also available by mail order from Lonely Planet, so if you have difficulty finding a title please write to us. US and Canadian residents should write to Embarcadero West, 155 Filbert St, Suite 251, Oakland CA 94607, USA; European residents should write to Devonshire House, 12 Barley Mow Passage, Chiswick, London W4 4PH; and residents of other countries to PO Box 617, Hawthorn, Victoria 3122, Australia.

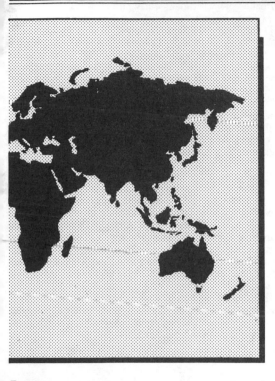

Indian Subcontinent
Bangladesh
India
Hindi/Urdu phrasebook
Trekking in the Indian Himalaya
Karakoram Highway
Kashmir, Ladakh & Zanskar
Nepal
Trekking in the Nepal Himalaya
Nepal phrasebook
Pakistan
Sri Lanka
Sri Lanka phrasebook

Africa
Africa on a shoestring
Central Africa
East Africa
Kenya
Swahili phrasebook
Morocco, Algeria & Tunisia
Moroccan Arabic phrasebook
South Africa, Lesotho & Swaziland
Zimbabwe, Botswana & Namibia
West Africa
Mexico
Baja California
Mexico

Central America
Central America on a shoestring
Costa Rica
La Ruta Maya

North America
Alaska
Canada
Hawaii

South America
Argentina, Uruguay & Paraguay
Bolivia
Brazil
Brazilian phrasebook
Chile & Easter Island
Colombia
Ecuador & the Galápagos Islands
Latin American Spanish phrasebook
Peru
Quechua phrasebook
South America on a shoestring
Trekking in the Patagonian Andes

Europe
Eastern Europe on a shoestring
Eastern Europe phrasebook
Finland
Iceland, Greenland & the Faroe Islands
Mediterranean Europe on a shoestring
Mediterranean Europe phrasebook
Poland
Scandinavian & Baltic Europe on a shoestring
Scandinavian Europe phrasebook
Trekking in Spain
Trekking in Greece
USSR
Russian phrasebook
Western Europe on a shoestring
Western Europe phrasebook

The Lonely Planet Story

Lonely Planet published its first book in 1973 in response to the numerous 'How did you do it?' questions Maureen and Tony Wheeler were asked after driving, bussing, hitching, sailing and railing their way from England to Australia.

Written at a kitchen table and hand collated, trimmed and stapled, *Across Asia on the Cheap* became an instant local bestseller, inspiring thoughts of another book.

Eighteen months in South-East Asia resulted in their second guide, *South-East Asia on a shoestring*, which they put together in a backstreet Chinese hotel in Singapore in 1975. The 'yellow bible' as it quickly became known to backpackers around the world, soon became *the* guide to the region. It has sold well over half a million copies and is now in its 7th edition, still retaining its familiar yellow cover.

Today there are over 100 Lonely Planet titles – books that have that same adventurous approach to travel as those early guides; books that 'assume you know how to get your luggage off the carousel' as one reviewer put it.

Although Lonely Planet initially specialised in guides to Asia, they now cover most regions of the world, including the Pacific, South America, Africa, the Middle East and Europe. The list of *walking guides* and *phrasebooks* (for 'unusual' languages such as Quechua, Swahili, Nepalese and Egyptian Arabic) is also growing rapidly.

The emphasis continues to be on travel for independent travellers. Tony and Maureen still travel for several months of each year and play an active part in the writing, updating and quality control of Lonely Planet' guides.

They have been joined by over 50 auth 48 staff – mainly editors, cartographer designers – at our office in Melbourne, tralia and another 10 at our US offic Oakland, California. In 1991 Lonely Pla opened a London office to handle sales t Britain, Europe and Africa. Travellers themselves also make a valuable contribution to the guides through the feedback we receive in thousands of letters each year.

The people at Lonely Planet strongly believe that travellers can make a positive contribution to the countries they visit, both through their appreciation of the countries' culture, wildlife and natural features, and through the money they spend. In addition, the company makes a direct contribution t the countries and regions it covers. Since 1986 a percentage of the income from each book has been donated to ventures such as famine relief in Africa; aid projects in India; agricultural projects in Central America; Greenpeace's efforts to halt French nuclear testing in the Pacific and Amnesty International. In 1992 $45,000 was donated to these causes.

Lonely Planet's basic travel philosophy is summed up in Tony Wheeler's comment, 'Don't worry about whether your trip will work out. Just go!'

o
e